G. W. Greenwood

Greenwood's Manual of the Practice of Conveyancing

Showing the Present Practice Relating to the Daily Routine of Conveyancing in

Solicitors' Offices. Sixth Edition

G. W. Greenwood

Greenwood's Manual of the Practice of Conveyancing
Showing the Present Practice Relating to the Daily Routine of Conveyancing in Solicitors' Offices. Sixth Edition

ISBN/EAN: 9783337143015

Printed in Europe, USA, Canada, Australia, Japan

Cover: Foto ©Andreas Hilbeck / pixelio.de

More available books at **www.hansebooks.com**

GREENWOOD'S MANUAL

OF THE

PRACTICE OF CONVEYANCING

SHOWING THE

PRESENT PRACTICE RELATING TO THE DAILY ROUTINE
OF CONVEYANCING IN SOLICITORS' OFFICES;

TO WHICH ARE ADDED

Concise Common Forms and Precedents in Conveyancing.

SIXTH EDITION,

THOROUGHLY REVISED.

By HARRY GREENWOOD, M.A.,

OF LINCOLN'S INN, ESQ., BARRISTER-AT-LAW;

AUTHOR OF "RECENT REAL PROPERTY STATUTES," AND JOINT EDITOR OF "NOTANDA."

LONDON:

STEVENS AND SONS, 119, CHANCERY LANE,

Law Publishers and Booksellers.

———

1881.

PREFACE

THE SIXTH EDITION.

In preparing this edition for the press, I have divided Part I. into chapters, and have endeavoured to re-arrange the text in such a manner that the various steps in the transaction which forms the subject of each chapter shall be found as nearly as possible in the order in which they take place in actual practice.

In Part II. I have added considerably to the number of Forms of Agreements—especially those relating to mercantile transactions—Conditions of Sale, and Conveyances, while I have omitted some of the Forms of Mortgages, Settlements, and Clauses in Wills, which found a place in former editions. I have also pruned many of the forms of redundant expressions, and have, throughout Part II., used abbreviations. This course has enabled Part I. to be printed in larger type, without materially adding to the size of the book.

The table of contents is much fuller than in former editions, a new table of cases has been added, and the cumbrous plan of a double index has been discontinued, the references to the forms being given in brackets.

It only remains for me to express my thanks to the members of both branches of the profession, who have rendered me valuable assistance both by the loan of precedents and otherwise. Special acknowledgments are due to my friends Mr. Henry Wright, of Keighley, Mr. Walter L. J. Ellis, of Bedford Row, and to the Committee of the Birmingham Law Society.

H. GREENWOOD.

2, OLD SQUARE, LINCOLN'S INN.
    January 1, 1881.

PREFACE

TO

THE FIRST EDITION.

———•———

In bringing before the profession an experience of many years in the practice of Conveyancing, my principal endeavour has been to produce such a book as may be of service to Articled and other Clerks in the profession, who may sometimes feel the want of a simple guide to enable them to perform, with comparative ease and credit to themselves, such portions of Conveyancing business as may be intrusted to them. I need hardly say, that I have no intention of intruding my experience on those members of the profession who are now in practice, or the numerous gentlemen engaged in the profession, who, instead of requiring help of this description, could afford help and assistance to others, much better than I have done. This book is not intended to be anything more than a manual for those who, from want of experience, feel some difficulty, either at the commencement or during the progress of ordinary Conveyancing business. I have endeavoured to make the book so simple, that a Solicitor may with confidence intrust small matters

of business to Articled and other Clerks to proceed
upon, and submit to him from time to time.
Whether I am deceived in my expectations as to
the utility of my performance, or as to my own
capacity in undertaking it, I must leave others to
judge; in writing it I have not trespassed on the
preserves of others in any one particular, but have
contented myself with a simple statement of the
strictly practical part of Conveyancing as followed
at the present day.

LONDON, *February*, 1856.

CONTENTS.

PART I.

CHAPTER I.

CHAPTER II.

CHAPTER III.

CHAPTER IV.

CHAPTER V.

CHAPTER VI.

CHAPTER VII.

CHAPTER VIII.

PART II.

PRECEDENTS.

CONVEYANCES AND ASSIGNMENTS.

(a.) *Complete Precedents.*

xii CONTENTS.

MEMORIALS.

MORTGAGES.

NOTICES.

PARTNERSHIP DEED.

POWERS OF ATTORNEY.

TABLE OF CASES.

THE

PRACTICE OF CONVEYANCING.

CHAPTER I.

AGREEMENTS.

INTRODUCTORY.—Agreements, on account of their
informal nature, are commonly regarded as instruments of such uniform simplicity that the preparation
of them may safely be ventured on by the most
unskilful, irrespective of the difficulty of their subject
matter.

The best known fact with regard to them is, that
—like wills—they require no set form of words for
their validity. The knowledge of this fact, combined
with an over eager desire to save expense in the first
instance, and an undue estimate of his own legal
knowledge (for almost every one imagines he knows
something about law), often tempts an unwary lay-
man to become his own draftsman, probably to his
future regret; for it may safely be affirmed that, of
all instruments known to the law, none are productive of so vast an amount of needless litigation as
agreements and wills, owing to the careless way in
which they are framed by unlearned persons. This

B

caution cannot appear too early in a treatise like the present.

Because a document is untechnical in form, it must not therefore be assumed that the preparation of it is, by any means, independent of technical knowledge and professional skill. An agreement is the basis of all future operations, and when signed cannot be departed from without the consent of all parties; a consent which can seldom be obtained. If well drawn, it should anticipate the numerous questions which may arise in carrying it into effect, and provide for the various events which may happen. Nothing indicates professional knowledge and ability better than a well drawn agreement.

It must not be too readily inferred from what is before stated, that an agreement, when signed, can be departed from, even with the consent of all parties to it; for it may happen that, after signing it, some of them may die, leaving persons who are not *sui juris*; this therefore should be always borne in mind in the preparation or perusal of an agreement. If the framer of the document perform his task skilfully, none of the parties will be able to withdraw from it without the consent of the others; he will also have the satisfaction of giving effect to his client's intentions; and whatever turn the matter afterwards may take, he can always refer to the agreement as a land mark in enforcing or defending the rights of his client.

INSTRUCTIONS.—On receiving instructions for an agreement, or any other legal document, it is an excellent plan for a solicitor to write out the instructions in the presence of, and get them signed by, his client or clients.

It is better to have a written agreement even when the same solicitor acts for both parties; indeed a written agreement should never be dispensed with, for it saves many difficulties that might otherwise arise during the progress of the business, and experience proves that these difficulties arise even where both parties are desirous of carrying out what they consider the understanding originally come to. Seldom is it that persons having opposite interests, however honestly disposed, will not differ as to the meaning or effect of a prior verbal arrangement. When acting on behalf of both parties, in cases of little magnitude or importance, especially in transactions which will be carried out by means of some subsequent formal instrument—*e.g.*, a conveyance, lease, or partnership deed—the instructions signed by all parties will often constitute a sufficient written agreement. Should any doubt afterwards arise as to what was agreed upon, it will then be set at rest by referring to the instructions, which bear the signatures of the parties.

But in almost all cases where the parties employ separate solicitors, as well as in important cases where the same solicitor acts for all, it is necessary to have a formal and carefully drawn agreement. This is especially the case in transactions where the agreement is the only document which will be required, *e.g.*, agreements for personal service, for the use of a patented invention, or for the compromise of disputed claims.

It may, here, be advisable to mention that with

respect to an equitable interest in property, an agreement alone is sufficient to transfer it from the seller
to the purchaser; for in equity a contract is equivalent to a conveyance, according to the maxim that
equity regards as done that which is agreed to be
done, consequently after a contract for sale and purchase has been signed, the purchaser is in equity the
owner of the estate, and the vendor is entitled to the
purchase-money; and even where the estate which
the vendor has contracted to sell is not equitable
merely but also legal, the High Court of Justice, in
the exercise of its equitable jurisdiction, carries out
the same principle by constituting the vendor a
trustee of the legal estate not yet conveyed for the
purchaser, and the purchaser a trustee of the unpaid
purchase-money for the vendor, and should the purchaser die, his heir or devisee will have the same
equitable interest in the property.

But even if the interest be merely equitable, and
therefore effectually transferred by agreement, it is
not usual to rely on the agreement alone; and the
purchaser of an equitable interest may insist on
having it transferred by the same description of
assurance as is used in the transfer of a legal estate.
And this appears to be the proper course, inasmuch
as the agreement invariably contemplates the doing
of some further act by the parties; and although as
matter of law it may be unnecessary that such act
should be done, yet it is safer to do it, as at some
future time questions and doubts may arise whether
or not it was done, besides leaving the matter in an
unsatisfactory state. It is therefore advisable to
have the agreement carried into effect in the usual

way, by taking a transfer of the equitable interest in the same manner as if it were a legal estate.

PREPARATION OF DRAFT.—In cases where a formal agreement is necessary the first question for a solicitor to decide is whether the matter is of sufficient importance to justify him in laying instructions to prepare the agreement before counsel. If this is not the case, or if his client objects to the expense of such a course, the solicitor will proceed to draft the agreement himself.

In order to prepare an agreement, or any other instrument, properly, the outline or skeleton should be previously arranged in the mind of the draftsman, so that he may have, to borrow a suggestive metaphor, a bird's-eye view of the whole, and a clear and distinct conception of the relation of the various parts to one another. Before commencing the draft he will do well to transfer the mental idea to paper by jotting down in a tabulated form the heads of the draft in the order in which they will occur, so that he may be at liberty to concentrate his whole attention upon each part in succession, without being under the necessity of constantly reviewing the whole scheme to perceive the relation of the clause in hand to the rest of the draft. By adopting this course he will save himself considerable trouble, and be more likely to frame a creditable document. Except in ordinary cases, such as contracts for sale and agreements for tenancy, precedents of agreements are, as a rule, of little service to the draftsman. Other agreements are usually of so special a nature that he must himself frame the necessary clauses, relying upon his precedents only so far as they suggest a style or system of arrangement and conditions which should be provided for.

The forms which are given in the precedents are intended both as a guide to the manner of framing agreements generally and also as precedents for use on any particular occasion, and from these there will be little difficulty in preparing others.

The style of setting out the subject matter in numbered paragraphs will be frequently found a very convenient arrangement to adopt, especially in intricate and involved cases, where clearness and perspicuity are the main objects of the draftsman.

This plan possesses the additional advantage of easy reference to particular clauses of the document —a great facility in the course of correspondence— and saves constant repetition in the commencement of the various clauses of the instrument.

It is quite unnecessary to import into simple agreements the language of covenants or agreements under seal, a form notwithstanding of no unfrequent occurrence, for instance, "An agreement made and entered into this, &c., between, &c., whereby the said A. B. doth hereby for himself, his heirs, executors, and administrators agree, &c.," always was mere verbiage in simple agreements, as the heirs of a person could not be bound by an instrument not under seal, and executors and administrators are bound without being named; but since the 32 & 33 Vict. c. 46, which abolished the priority of payment formerly existing in favour of specialty over simple contract debts, as from the 1st of January, 1870, it has become mere verbiage in covenants or agreements under seal as well.

If A. B. agrees to do an act, and dies before the act is done, his representatives, both real and personal, that is to say, his heirs as well as his executors or administrators, as the case may be, according to whether he died testate or intestate, are bound to do it or pay for it, to the extent of the assets they acquire from the deceased, and that notwithstanding they are not referred to in the instrument creating the obligation; the only exception to this rule is where it is expressly stated that the obligation shall not extend to the representatives of the person bound.

Such a form as that mentioned above does no credit to the framer of it, and it is to be hoped that it may, before long, fall entirely into disuse. Words and phrases that have no meaning should never be introduced into legal documents; for they only tend to encumber the document, conceal the true meaning, and answer no useful purpose. A good draftsman inserts all that should be inserted with clearness and brevity, and leaves nothing to be inferred that ought to be expressed.

Where it is necessary to embrace several distinct matters in the same agreement the most scientific way is to exhaust one subject before commencing another, and this will save much trouble in any subsequent reference to the agreement. A very good illustration of a special agreement is that embodied in Form XII.,[1] and a solicitor will seldom be called upon to prepare one of a more complicated nature. In the agreement alluded to, it will be perceived that three distinct and separate matters, all forming part

[1] *Infra,* p. 205.

of one transaction, have to be carried out. This form is given in order to show at a glance how desirable it is to make every branch of the agreement complete in itself, and so avoid the necessity of continual references from one part to another.

In dealing with the interests of married women in real estate which is not settled to their separate use, provision must be made in the agreement as to the expense of acknowledging the conveyance if it be not intended that the vendor is to do whatever may be necessary at his own expense. It is not an uncommon practice in agreements for sale, for the vendor to stipulate for a certain sum clear, in which case his solicitor must take care to express the intention distinctly, otherwise the vendor may be called upon to pay costs which he had intended to throw upon the purchaser.

COMPLETION.—In cases where the same solicitor is concerned for all parties, he will, after drawing and settling the agreement, have it engrossed, signed by his clients, attested, and properly stamped.

In cases where he is not concerned for all parties, he will, after drawing the agreement according to his client's instructions, make and forward a fair copy to the solicitor on the other side for approval; and, as soon as the draft has been finally settled on behalf of all parties, each solicitor will make one engrossment for signature by his own client. After the engrossments are signed, the solicitors concerned will make an appointment to exchange the parts signed by their respective clients. Strictly, this ought to be done at the office of the solicitor who prepared the draft, but this is seldom insisted on in practice. After this there only remains to carry into effect the terms of the contract according to the circumstances of the case.

STAMPS.—An agreement for a lease requires the same stamp as a lease for the term and at the rent agreed upon. An agreement under hand only (not being an agreement for a lease) requires a 6d. stamp, and not more than 14 days from the date of the agreement are allowed for getting the stamp affixed. If not done within that time it can only be subsequently stamped on payment of a penalty of £10. An adhesive 6d. stamp may be used if it is affixed before signature, and cancelled or obliterated by the party who *first* signs the agreement. Should the agreement be under seal, which must be the case where a company is party to it, it will require a 10s. stamp. In this case the time allowed for stamping is the same as in the case of any ordinary deed, viz., two months; or, if executed abroad within two months from its arrival in England, on a statutory declaration being made to that effect.

CHAPTER II.

SALES OF REAL ESTATE.

INTRODUCTORY.—In sales by private contract it often happens that a vendor enters into a binding contract for sale before consulting his solicitor. But a prudent man will, usually, either consult his solicitor before selling at all, or instruct him to prepare an agreement to carry negotiations or a verbal contract for sale into effect.

With regard to sales by public auction, it can seldom, if ever, happen that the vendor does not consult his solicitor in the first instance.

In each of the above cases the duties of the solicitor will be somewhat different, and it will be convenient to deal with each case separately.

OPEN CONTRACT.—In cases where a client has agreed to sell an estate without having obtained professional assistance, it will generally be found that he has signed what is termed "an open contract," the meaning of which is, that he has made no stipulations with the purchaser as to the title or evidence of title which the latter may require, or in fact inserted any conditions whatever in the contract. Both tact and judgment are required in these cases, and some consideration will be necessary before the abstract of title is furnished to the purchaser's solicitor. In such a case the purchaser is entitled to a forty years' title if the estate be one of ordinary freehold or copyhold tenure;[1] but if it be land held under a grant from the Crown, a reversionary interest, or leasehold property, the abstract must shew the creation of the estate or interest agreed to be sold. In one case[2] it was held that a deed more than twenty years old containing a recital of the seisin in fee of the vendor was a good root of title; but it would not be advisable to act upon this decision. It must be borne in mind that, under an "open contract," the purchaser is not only entitled to have a safe holding title but can require a strictly marketable one; and although to non-professional minds there may not appear any difference between these descriptions of title, yet to a professional man the difference is very great. A person may have a safe holding title from having for twelve years enjoyed property adversely against persons not under disability; but this would not in equity be considered a marketable title: the general rule being, that a vendor must deduce a forty years' title.

Under an open contract the purchaser can also insist, and in most cases does insist, on having every question on the title cleared up and every information furnished at the expense of the vendor; again, he may require possession of the title deeds, or, if they are not in the vendor's possession or relate to an estate part of which the vendor retains, the purchaser is entitled to attested copies, with a covenant for

[1] 37 & 38 Vict. c. 78, s. 1.

[2] *Bolton* v. *London School Board*, 7 Ch. D. 766.

production of the deeds. This covenant is prepared by and at the expense of the purchaser, but the expense of perusal and execution on behalf of and by himself, and all necessary parties other than the purchaser, must be borne by the vendor.[1]

PRIVATE CONTRACT—*Preliminary.*—In cases where a client consults his solicitor with reference to a proposed sale, the first and most necessary step is to examine his title deeds carefully, in order to see whether or not he can sell the estate, and if so, under what conditions it will be safe to do so. It may happen that he has obtained an indefeasible title under the Act to facilitate the Proof of Title to and the Conveyance of Real Estates,[2] or the Land Transfer Act, 1875,[3] or that he has obtained a judicial declaration of title under the Declaration of Title Act, 1862 ;[4] but these Acts having never been popular, have been very little resorted to.

On the other hand, it may turn out that he is only a tenant for life or in tail, without power of sale, or is only entitled to an undivided share in the property jointly with other persons. In such cases the question will arise whether a sale can be obtained under the Settled Estates Act, 1877,[5] whether he can bar the entail under the Fines and Recoveries Act,[6] or whether it is advisable to take proceedings under the Partition Acts, 1868 and 1876.[7]   Every solicitor

[1] 37 & 38 Vict. c. 78, s. 2 (5).
[2] 25 & 26 Vict. c. 53.
[3] 38 & 39 Vict. c. 87.
[4] 25 & 26 Vict. c. 67.
[5] 40 & 41 Vict. c. 18.   See Greenwood's R. P. Stat. 171.
[6] 3 & 4 Will. 4, c. 74.
[7] 31 & 32 Vict. c. 40; 39 & 40 Vict. c. 17.

should know the main provisions of these Acts, as he
may be suddenly requested to advise upon them ; and
should he not previously have read them, or have
only a very superficial knowledge of them, in all
probability he will forget their contents, and it may
be, their existence. At the most, he will have to
turn to the Acts in his client's presence, and fish out
an answer to his question in the best way he can ;
whereas if he had carefully read the Acts previously,
he would be able to turn to the very section required
at almost a moment's notice.

PRIVATE CONTRACT — *Preparation of Draft.* —
Where a vendor has neither signed a binding contract nor previously consulted his solicitor, he usually
instructs the latter to prepare a contract to carry
into effect the sale of property already verbally agreed
upon. Such contract is always drawn by the vendor's
solicitor, he generally having the title deeds in his
possession, and knowing more about the title and the
property than the purchaser's solicitor does; the
latter, in the majority of cases, understands very little
about the matter until after he has received the draft
contract.

In order to prepare the contract properly, it will
be necessary to make a note of the names and ad-
dresses of the vendor and purchaser, the description
of the property, the price to be paid, the time for
completing the purchase, whether any rights or
interests are to be reserved to the vendor, and any
other stipulations upon which the sale is to be made.

Then the deeds must be as carefully examined as
in the last case dealt with ; and, if time permits, an

abstract should be made at once, as it will be useful
in framing the contract, and will afterwards be required for delivery to the purchaser's solicitor. In
case there is not time to prepare an abstract, a careful analysis of the deeds should be made. The principal point here is to decide what shall be made the
root of title. If the abstract commences with a will,
the purchaser may require evidence of seisin by the
testator, unless precluded by special stipulation, or
unless a deed twenty years old contains a recital of
his seisin, and this may be difficult to produce. The
best deed to commence an abstract with is a mortgage,
as it is a safe presumption that the title was investi-
gated and approved on behalf of the mortgagee
before he advanced his money. If the abstract is
commenced with a document less than forty years
old, the contract must contain a stipulation to that
effect; and it is often advisable to stipulate that recitals in deeds less than twenty years old shall be
evidence. But this will entirely depend on the state
of the title. Stipulations throwing certain costs on
the purchaser, and as to the other matters mentioned
in Form X,[1] are usually also inserted.

Having prepared the draft contract, a fair copy
must be sent to the purchaser or his solicitor; and
after he has perused it, and all debateable points
have been disposed of, each solicitor will have one
part fair copied, and get it signed by his client; and
then, having compared both parts, one will be exchanged for the other. It is not necessary that both
parties should sign each part of the contract, it is
quite sufficient if each is signed by the opposite party.

---

[1] *Infra*, p. 200.

PUBLIC AUCTION—*Preliminary.*—On receiving instructions to put property up for sale by public auction the first question for consideration is whether or not the owner can sell, and the second what auctioneer should be employed. In some cases the vendor will name the auctioneer, in others he will leave the matter in his solicitor's hands, in which case it is as well to bear in mind that, with respect to large estates, an auctioneer of repute and standing is likely to realize more than one less known to the public. Having fixed upon the auctioneer he must be seen and instructed upon the matter, and (if a London auctioneer be employed) he will obtain all necessary particulars, and in some cases insert a preliminary advertisement that the property is in the market. He will also prepare and forward to the vendor's solicitor for perusal and settlement the particulars of sale. If, however, the auctioneer is in practice in the country, the solicitor will prepare the particulars of sale, there being a difference in this respect between town and country practice. In some parts of the country the solicitor inserts the advertisement, while in other parts this is done, as in London, by the auctioneer.

PUBLIC AUCTION—*Particulars.*—It is not within the scope of this work to point out what should or should not be stated in the particulars or conditions of sale, as so much depends upon the title. I may, however, say that you cannot state too plainly and distinctly in the particulars the nature and tenure of the property and the burdens thereon, and, in fact, everything that a man intending to purchase ought to be made acquainted with.

In preparing or settling particulars of sale great care should be exercised, as a misdescription may be taken advantage of by an unwilling purchaser to get rid of the contract, or obtain an abatement of his purchase-money by way of compensation. For instance, suppose property is described as being held under a lease, when it is in fact held under a sub-lease, a Court of Equity will not decree specific performance [1] unless it can reasonably be inferred from the particulars and conditions together that an underlease only is intended to be sold.[2] The same rule applies where copyholds are described as freeholds,[3] and generally to cases where misdescription induces a purchaser to enter into a contract he would otherwise have avoided. It is usual to insert a condition to the effect that any misdescription shall not annul the sale; but such a condition does not apply to cases of material misdescription.

The law upon this subject generally is by no means difficult to comprehend, and may be summed up thus: If the particulars of sale fully and accurately describe the property and the tenure, and the vendor's interest therein, so that a person of ordinary intelligence may not fail in discovering precisely what is intended to be sold and conveyed, there will be little fear of any objection being maintained.

PUBLIC AUCTION—*Conditions.*—In the conditions of sale, equal clearness and distinctness are requisite

[1] *Brumfit v. Morton,* 3 Jur. (N. S.) 1198.
[2] *Camberwell Benefit Building Society v. Holloway,* 13 Ch. D. 754.
[3] *Hart v. Swaine,* 7 Ch. D. 42.

in stating upon what terms the property is to be disposed of, and what the purchaser is, and what he is not to be, at liberty to require.

Before attempting to settle either particulars or conditions of sale, it would be advisable to read that part of Dart's 'Vendors and Purchasers' which relates to this branch of the subject.[1] Having carefully settled the particulars, the conditions of sale must be drawn ; and in order to do this it will be necessary to investigate the title carefully. If an abstract has not already been made, it should now be prepared. In simple cases an analysis of the deeds will suffice, but as the abstract must be ready for delivery to the purchaser shortly after the sale, it is just as well to prepare it now. The remarks as to commencement of abstract and other matters in the case of a private contract will equally apply to conditions of sale. The special conditions will give most trouble, for the minor points in the title will usually be covered by the general conditions used on almost every sale.

Should the estate be a large one, or the title complicated, it may be advisable to lay the abstract before counsel, with instructions to prepare the conditions of sale ; as in many cases it will be by far the best, and in the end the least expensive course, to give a fee to counsel to settle the conditions, it being next to impossible for any one in a solicitor's office, even if he felt that he possessed the requisite knowledge, engaged in various matters of business and liable to frequent interruptions, to bestow the amount of care and attention required in settling conditions

---

[1] 5th ed. cap. iv.

for the sale of a large estate, with a complicated and difficult title.

Care should be taken to see that the name, or some unmistakeable description of the vendor, is stated either in the conditions or in the printed form of contract at the end; or he may find it impossible to enforce specific performance.[1]

Having settled the particulars and conditions of sale, the next step is to make a fair copy thereof, and either forward it to the auctioneers to be printed, or send it direct to the printers. When the proof is obtained, it must be carefully examined in order to see that it is correct, and altered where necessary, and then returned to the auctioneer, or the printer. Having obtained a sufficient number of copies, the auctioneer will forward some to the various inns and other places for distribution; he will also prepare and have bills posted in the neighbourhood of the property.

It was formerly not the practice for country solicitors to have the conditions of sale printed and annexed to the particulars; the latter only being printed and distributed, and the conditions written out and read at the sale, as many copies being made as there were lots to be sold. But printing is now so cheap that this old practice is fast dying out, and it is usual, except in the case of a small country property with a very simple title, to have both particulars and conditions printed, in order that an intending purchaser may know not only what is about to be sold, but also the conditions upon which he is

---

[1] *Sale* v. *Lambert*, L. R. 18 Eq. 1 ; *Potter* v. *Duffield*, L. R. 18 Eq. 4 ; *Thomas* v. *Brown*, 1 Q. B. D. 714 ; *Rossiter* v. *Miller*, 3 Ap. Cas. 1124.

to purchase, without hearing such conditions read for the first time among the noise and confusion of the sale room. In some cases a sale is advertised subject to the common form general conditions of the local Law Society, and it is then only necessary to print, or otherwise publish, the special conditions.

Where a large estate, or several fields or closes of land, are intended to be sold, it is advisable to annex a plan to the particulars of sale, in order that the situation of the property and its advantages may be seen at a glance. And if an attractive-looking residence is on the land, it may also be advisable to have a lithographed drawing or photograph of it attached to the particulars. The auctioneer usually prepares the plan and sends it to the solicitor with the draft particulars of sale.

Public Auction—*Sale.*—The day of sale having arrived, the vendor's solicitor will proceed to the place of sale to answer any question that may be put, either as to the property, the conditions, or otherwise. The auctioneer will get through this part of the business, and the solicitor will seldom be called on to interfere, but an intending purchaser will sometimes ask questions about the title, and the solicitor must then be guided by the circumstances of the case as to the course of proceeding; if he gives an answer to any question, it should be given readily and candidly, as it is far better not to give an answer at all than to answer in a manner calculated to shew that the object is to conceal as much as possible; and if lease-holds are being sold, a copy of the lease should be at hand ready for production.

Should the property be purchased, the auctioneer will see that the purchase contract at the end of the conditions is signed by the purchaser; and, if in London, he will also receive the deposit. In country sales the deposit is generally received by the vendor's solicitor, and not by the auctioneer. It may save trouble and delay if the purchaser is now asked for the name of his solicitor, in order that the abstract may be sent to him at once; but as in the hurry of the sale this may be forgotten, it will be found useful to put at the foot of the purchase contract these or similar words—" Abstract to be sent to ——;" in which case the auctioneer or solicitor, as the case may be, in obtaining the purchaser's signature to the contract, will make the necessary inquiry of him.

ABSTRACT OF TITLE.—The sale, whether by public auction or private contract, having progressed thus far, the abstract of title, if not already prepared, must now be prepared, and in any case a fair copy must be forwarded to the solicitor named by the purchaser, or, if he has not named a solicitor, to the purchaser himself, at his address in the purchase contract; and, unless the abstract is delivered by a clerk or messenger, an acknowledgment of its receipt should be requested, in order to know with greater certainty the time within which the purchaser, according to the conditions of sale, will be bound to forward his requisitions on the title. After the receipt of the abstract, the purchaser's solicitor will make an appointment for comparing it with the title deeds; this will be done at the office of the vendor's solicitor if the deeds are there, but if they are not (which will be the case if the vendor is a mortgagor or *cestui que trust*), they must be examined at the place where they may happen to be. Unless, however, bound by the conditions of sale, a purchaser cannot be compelled to incur the expense of his solicitor running about the country from place to place to compare the deeds with the abstract, as he is justified in presuming that the deeds will be found at the office of the vendor's solicitor, or, at all events, within a reasonable distance therefrom, and this should always be borne in mind on preparing conditions of sale in cases where the title deeds are not in the vendor's possession.

On comparing the abstract of title with the deeds, it is the practice, in London, for the purchaser's solicitor to take with him a clerk to read the abstract, while the practice in many parts of the country is for a clerk in the office of the vendor's solicitor to read the abstract, unless the offices of the vendor's and purchaser's solicitors are in the same town, in which case the purchaser's solicitor sometimes takes a clerk with him. As the vendor's solicitor charges a fee of 6s. 8d. per hour, it would not be unreasonable if it were the rule, even in London, for him to find a clerk to read the abstract. The vendor's solicitor will have the deeds ready at the time appointed, and should, if practicable, be at hand himself in case any inquiry should arise on any part of the title.

REPLIES TO REQUISITIONS.—The abstract, having been compared with the deeds, will be perused by the purchaser's solicitor, who will then send the requisitions (if any) on the title, which if forwarded

within the time limited by the conditions, must be
answered ; and in preparing the answers the vendor's
solicitor will be guided by the conditions of sale.   In
some cases it may be necessary to lay the requisitions,
with a copy of the abstract, before counsel; but this
can only arise in cases where the title is complicated.
It may be useful to mention that the usual and most
convenient plan is to copy the requisitions on brief
paper, half margin, and to write the answers opposite to the requisitions, and then to make a copy of
the whole and forward it to the purchaser's solicitor.
A great mistake is often made by the vendor's solicitor in answering requisitions, which puts the purchaser's solicitor to much trouble, *e.g.*, the purchaser's
solicitor asks for particulars of the birth, marriage, or
burial of a certain person.   The vendor's solicitor
turns to the conditions of sale, and discovers that all
certificates are to be obtained by and at the expense
of the purchaser, and then proceeds simply to refer
him to the conditions.   Now this is not such an
answer as the purchaser has a right to demand ; for,
in the first place, the certificate should have been set
out in the abstract, as it is quite as much a matter of
title as any of the proceedings shewn on the abstract,
and in well-drawn abstracts this is done ; and, in the
next place, although the purchaser is to obtain the
certificate and pay for it, he is entitled to call upon
the vendor for information as to where it may be
obtained, in order that he may procure it himself.
This mode of answering requisitions is frequently a
source of much trouble to a purchaser's solicitor, and
is certainly not courteous conduct on the part of the
vendor's solicitor.

In many cases the conveyance will now be prepared, but others may arise in which some difficulties will first have to be surmounted, for instance, the purchaser's solicitor may insist upon being furnished with abstracts of documents referred to in the abstract of title, but not abstracted in chief, or may require the title to be carried further back, or on certain requisitions being answered or more satisfactorily answered ; or he may insist on other covenants being entered into than those he can require, or object to pay any interest on the purchase-money at the time of completing the purchase.

The course of proceeding in any of these cases will be guided by the circumstances of each particular case. The conditions of sale or contract (if any) should be carefully perused in order to see if the purchaser can insist upon his demands; but if the sale has been made by private contract, without any condition as to title, it will be advisable to take the opinion of a conveyancer on the matter. This course, however, will only be necessary where the vendor's solicitor is doubtful as to the purchaser's right ; but in such a case it ought to be resorted to, as the delay and expense that will be occasioned by a long correspondence will be more unpalatable to the vendor than the fee to counsel for his advice.

Sometimes questions are raised through ignorance or forgetfulness of the provisions of Lord Cranworth's Act,[1] the Trustee Act, 1850,[2] and the Vendor and Purchaser Act, 1874.[3] It should be remembered that

---

[1] 23 & 24 Vict. c. 145.
[2] 13 & 14 Vict. c. 60. See also the Extension Act, 15 & 16 Vict. c. 55.
[3] 37 & 38 Vict. c. 78.

§§ 11–16 of Lord Cranworth's Act confer powers of sale with ancillary powers on mortgagees of real estate, although there may be no power in the mortgage ; § 27 gives power in certain cases to appoint new trustees, and s. 29 empowers trustees to give valid receipts.

Under the Trustee Acts, 1850 and 1852,[1] an outstanding legal estate may be vested in a new trustee, or an order made vesting it in the vendor or purchaser at a comparatively small expense, and, what is still better, in a reasonably short space of time. It will be well however to refer to ' Shelford's Real Property Statutes,' ' Morgan's Chancery Acts,' and ' Greenwood's Recent Real Property Statutes.'

DRAFT CONVEYANCE.— The requisitions having been disposed of, the vendor's solicitor will receive from the purchaser's solicitor the draft conveyance for approval. This he will peruse on behalf of the parties for whom he is concerned, and should there be any for whom he is not acting, he will forward the draft to their respective solicitors for approval. After it has been approved on behalf of all parties, he will return it to the purchaser's solicitor ; but, however great the number of solicitors concerned, the vendor's solicitor is the medium of communication between them all.

In perusing the draft on behalf of a vendor it is necessary to see that all recitals of documents and statements of facts are correct, that the vendor is not parting with any more of his property or any greater interest therein than he has contracted for ; that the

---

[1] 13 & 14 Vict. c. 60 ; 15 & 16 Vict. c. 55.

parcels are accurately described, that any reserva-
tions intended to be inserted on his behalf are
correctly inserted ; that any liabilities which the
purchaser is to take upon himself are set out in the
draft, and that the vendor does not enter into
covenants of a more extensive character than he can
be required to do. It will be contrary to professional
usage to alter the form of any recitals or statements
in the draft, provided they are correct in substance,
as the purchaser's solicitor may prepare his draft in
any form he pleases, if the form he uses does not
prejudice the vendor ; and should he think proper to
make the draft unnecessarily long, no other party is
justified in reducing it, in order that it may be in
accordance with the forms generally used by him or
his own notions of conveyancing.

The covenants usually entered into by a vendor
are the following :—

If the beneficial owner of the estate, and having
the legal fee vested in himself, he covenants that
(notwithstanding any act by him, &c.) he has good
right to convey for quiet enjoyment free from incumbrances, and for further assurance, at the cost of
the purchaser.

If the equitable owner of the estate, or beneficially
interested in the purchase-money, his covenants extend to the acts of those in whom the legal estate
is vested.

These covenants are entered into where the vendor
has himself purchased the property (I use the word
purchased in its common acceptation), but should he
take the estate as heir-at-law or under a settlement,
whether voluntary or otherwise, or a will, his

covenants extend to the acts of his ancestor or the person making the will or settlement, as the case may be.

All these covenants are more or less qualified, and therein contra-distinguished from covenants for title given by a mortgagor, which are absolute.

Whatever may be the nature of the contract, the vendor cannot be required, if a trustee or mortgagee, to enter into any covenant other than that he has not done any act to incumber ; but it sometimes happens that a trustee under a will or settlement, with power to sell, enters into a contract to sell the estate, and on examining the will or settlement it is found not to contain the usual clause making the trustee's receipt a good discharge to purchasers, and it may be one of those cases where a Court of Equity would not consider that the testator or settlor must of necessity have intended his trustee to have the power of giving receipts. In such a case, unless it falls within sect. 29 of Lord Cranworth's Act,[1] the person entitled to the produce of the estate is required to join in the conveyance, and enter into covenants for title, which extend not only to the acts of himself, but also to the acts of his testator and trustee. Where trustees sell under conditions of sale, a clause is often inserted providing for this difficulty, by stating that the parties beneficially entitled to the estate shall not be required to join in the conveyance.

COMPLETION.—The draft being finally approved by all the solicitors concerned, and returned to the

[1] 23 & 24 Vict. c. 145.

purchaser's solicitor, will be engrossed by him and forwarded with the engrossment to the vendor's solicitor for examination; and after he has compared it with his own copy of the draft, he will send the draft and engrossment to the other solicitors (if any) who have approved it, in order that it may be examined by them; and this will be a convenient time for getting the deed executed by those (if any) who are merely consenting or nominal parties to it, as the solicitors who have approved the draft on behalf of such parties will readily get the deed executed while in their hands. After the engrossment has been examined, it will be returned to and kept by the vendor's solicitor until an appointment is made for the completion of the business. This appointment is usually made by the purchaser's solicitor, but the completion of a purchase always takes place at the office of the vendor's solicitor, unless the property be in mortgage, in which case the completion will be at the office of the mortgagee's solicitor, the rule being that " the money follows the deeds." On receiving an appointment, the vendor's solicitor must arrange for the attendance of such of the parties interested as have not previously executed the deed. Respecting the completion, the chief points necessary to call attention to are—to have the interest (if any payable) calculated, deducting the income tax in all cases except on a sale under the direction of the High Court of Justice, in which case the income tax is never deducted, but the purchaser may apply for the deduction when the money is paid out of court.[1]

_____

[1] *Bebb* v. *Bunny*, 1 Kay & J. 216.

COMPLETION—*Interest*.— If it should happen that
no time is named for completion, then the purchaser
is in equity entitled to the rents and profits from the
date of the contract, as that is a complete conversion
in equity, and the vendor is entitled to interest on
the purchase-money at the rate specified in the contract or conditions, or if no rate is specified, at 4*l*. per
cent. per annum from the same date until completion. If a time be fixed for completion and the
purchase is not then completed, the purchaser takes
the rents and profits from that time, paying the
vendor interest on the purchase-money, unless the
delay in the completion has arisen on the part of
the vendor, and the purchase-money has been lying
idle with notice to the vendor of that fact.

The most difficult question to deal with is that
relating to interest on the purchase-money; the
solicitors of the vendor and purchaser can seldom
agree as to which of them may have caused the
delay in the completion of the matter. The cases on
the subject are somewhat contradictory and do not
lay down any clear rule by which to act. It appears,
however, that where the conditions of sale state
that interest shall be paid, if " from any cause
whatever" the purchase is not completed by a certain
day, the purchaser must make out a strong case in
order to succeed in his objection to pay interest, and
must shew that considerable delay has been caused
by gross negligence, vexatious conduct, or bad faith
on the part of the vendor or his solicitor.[1] If any

[1] *Bannerman* v. *Clark*, 3 Drew. 362; 26 L. J. Ch. 77; *De Visme* v.
De Visme, 1 Mac. & G. 336; 1 Hall & T. 408; *Williams* v. *Glenton*,
L. R. 1 Ch. 200.

part of the property is in mortgage proper notice must be given to the mortgagee, or, on a delay in completing, the vendor may be liable to a further payment.

COMPLETION — *Generally.*— The deeds, if to be given up to the purchaser, are put in order according to date, so that his solicitor may easily check them with the abstract; and should the sale of the property have been by public auction and a deposit paid to the auctioneer, a written authority will also be taken from the purchaser or his solicitor to the auctioneer, to hand over the deposit to the vendor or his solicitor. Many solicitors require the purchaser or his solicitor to sign a schedule of the deeds handed over to him.

If the property contracted to be sold should be burnt down pending completion (it having been insured by the vendor), the purchaser is not entitled to the benefit of the insurance in the absence of an express stipulation to that effect in the contract.[1]

If the vendor is a lessee or assignee holding under a lease, which contains a covenant not to assign without the lessor's consent, it is incumbent on him and not on the purchaser to obtain the lessor's licence, unless otherwise expressed in the contract.[2]

While on this point attention should be called to the 6th section of Lord St. Leonards' Act, 1860,[3] which enacts, that the waiver of the benefit of any

---

[1] *Poole* v. *Adams,* 12 W. R. 683 ; 33 L. J. (Ch.) 639 ; *Rayner* v. *Preston,* 14 Ch. D. 297.

[2] *Lloyd* v. *Crispe,* 5 Taunt. 249; *Mason* v. *Corder,* 7 Taunt. 9.

[3] 23 & 24 Vict. c. 38.

covenant by a lessor shall be good for that turn
only, and not be considered a general waiver.

Where a railway company takes land under the
compulsory powers of the Lands Clauses Consolidation Act, 1845, the whole of the vendor's costs are
thrown upon the company by § 82 of that Act,
and also the cost of investing the purchase-money
when paid into Court, as in the case of parties
incapacitated to convey. It sometimes happens that
the vendor dies before the conveyance to the company is executed, leaving an infant heir; in this case
the company is not bound to pay the costs of getting
the estate out of the infant.

Before leaving this chapter, it may be well to call
attention to a species of document which is at the
same time a conveyance and mortgage. I allude to
the purchase of a coal-mine, where the consideration
money is payable by instalments, and powers of distress and entry are given to secure payment of the
instalments. This is very common in some parts of
the country.

The practice is, for the vendor's solicitor to prepare
this document, and for his charges to be paid by the
purchaser, except of course such charges as relate to
the abstract and proving the title, which are borne
by the vendor in the usual manner. Many practitioners considered that the powers of distress and
entry given to secure payment of the instalments,
took away from the instalments their character of
unpaid purchase-money, and made them a species of
rent, and therefore, like rent, subject to income tax.
But it has now been decided that income tax cannot
be deducted from the instalments, that, in fact, the

instalments are unpaid purchase-money and not rent.[1] and the same practice appears to prevail with regard to repayments of mortgages to Building Societies.

[1] *Taylor* v. *Evans*, 25 L. J., Exch. 269; *Foley* v. *Fletcher*, 28 L. J., Exch. 100.

CHAPTER III.

PURCHASES OF REAL ESTATE.

INTRODUCTORY.—When a solicitor is professionally concerned for a purchaser, it is usually in one of the following cases :—A client will have bought property at a sale by auction, and will bring the conditions of sale and purchase contract to his solicitor ; or he may bring the conditions of an intended sale and ask for advice on the title to the property or to a particular lot, or he may have entered into " an open contract :" or may inform his solicitor that he has been treating for the purchase of an estate, and instruct him to peruse the draft contract on his behalf; or lastly he may have entered into a contract by letters, or even by telegram.   It may be convenient to mention here that two persons often correspond as to the sale and purchase of an estate, and although the correspondence may apparently be sufficient to form a complete contract, it may happen that either the vendor or purchaser in the last letter has referred to a formal contract to be prepared by his solicitor, or the expressions used by him may point to an intention that a more formal contract shall be entered into.   In such a case there is abundant authority to shew that the letters cannot be considered as forming in themselves a perfect and binding contract, inasmuch as the parties, or at least one of them, contemplated the terms being embodied in a formal manner, and his intention must be carried into effect.

In each of the cases above mentioned the course of proceeding will be different, and it will be convenient, as in the chapter on Sales, to deal with them separately.

OPEN CONTRACT.—If a client has entered into an open contract for the purchase of an estate, his solicitor's duty is to apply to the vendor's solicitor for an abstract of title, and after obtaining it to be careful in seeing that a marketable title is furnished, bearing in mind the distinction that exists between a marketable and a safe holding title.[1] Under an open contract, the expense of everything the purchaser may be entitled to must be borne by the vendor. It is hardly necessary to observe that an open contract is the most advantageous one a purchaser can enter into, and the most disadvantageous to the vendor, the whole expense of proving the title having to be borne by the latter. As to what title should be shewn under such a contract, and as to what evidence is necessary to support it, reference should be made to Dart[2] and to the Vendor and Purchaser Act, 1874.[3]

PRIVATE CONTRACT—*Generally.*—We will now suppose that a client informs his solicitor that he has verbally agreed to purchase an estate, and that he

[1] See p. 11, *supra.*
[2] V. & P. 5th ed. cap. 8.
[3] 37 & 38 Vict. c. 78; Greenwood's Recent R. P. Stat. pp. 109-115.

D

wishes him to do what is needful ; in such a case the solicitor should write to the vendor asking him to instruct his solicitor to send the draft of the proposed contract for perusal on behalf of the purchaser ; as before stated, it is the practice of the vendor's solicitor to prepare the contract, he being of course acquainted with the title and the stipulations necessary to protect his client. When the draft is received the purchaser's solicitor should go through it with his client, in order to see that the amount of purchase-money, the situation and extent of the property, the burdens upon it, and the time of completion are correctly described, as these matters are for the client's consideration. The solicitor's duty is to advise him as to the nature and effect of the clauses in the draft. In many instances these clauses will be similar to those in ordinary conditions of sale, but this is unfair to the purchaser, as there is a material difference between purchasing an estate at an auction and purchasing one by private contract : in the former case a purchaser knows the terms under which he is buying, and is sometimes content to purchase even under stringent conditions, either in the hope that he may make a good bargain, or because he has taken a fancy to the property ; but in the latter case there is no chance of getting a bargain, the terms as to price being agreed upon between the vendor and purchaser with their eyes open, and as generally the latter is compelled to give the full market value of the property he has a perfect right to require a marketable title to be shewn at the vendor's expense ; in other words, as the vendor gets the value of the property, he ought not to be allowed to throw upon the purchaser any part of the expense of deducing a good title. In this case, however, as in many others, some tact is often required : the vendor may be an over-reaching man and the purchaser may not, but, on the contrary, he may be so desirous of becoming the purchaser of the property that he may not feel disposed to pay much attention to what he may consider technical objections to the contract. Under such circumstances the solicitor should lay before his client (in writing if practicable) the consequences of his entering into such a contract, and explain to him fully the meaning of the clauses in it. If he elects, notwithstanding all advice, to become the purchaser on such terms, he is at perfect liberty to do so; he runs the risk and incurs the expense ; the solicitor will have performed his duty, and the matter will proceed.

The two previous chapters contain full information with respect to the preparation and completion of the contract.

It should, however, be mentioned, that until the contract is reduced into writing and signed neither party is bound.[1]

PRIVATE CONTRACT.—*Contract by Letters.*—Should a client inform his solicitor that he has entered into a contract by means of letters, it will be necessary to attentively peruse the correspondence in order to see whether a contract has been entered into, or whether a more formal contract be pointed to.[2]

[1] *Dickinson v. Dodds,* 2 Ch. D. 463.
[2] *Honyman v. Marryatt,* 21 Beav. 14 ; 26 L. J. (Ch.) 619, & 6 H. L. C. 112 ; *Ridgway v. Wharton,* 6 H. L. C. 264 ; *Crossley v. Maycock,* L. R. 18 Eq. 180 ; *Hussey v. Horne Payne,* 4 Ap. Ca 311 ; *Bonnewell v. Jenkins,* 8 Ch. D. 229 ; *Lewis v. Brass,* 3 Q. B. D. 667.

On being satisfied that the letters form a contract they must be carefully read to ascertain what conditions are inserted in the correspondence as to title or evidence of title and completion. It is scarcely necessary to say that a contract by means of letters requires two things; namely, an offer and an acceptance. If an offer is clogged with a particular condition, and an answer is returned accepting the offer but rejecting the condition, that alone will not form a contract; or if an offer be made and an answer is returned accepting the offer, under certain conditions, that alone is not a contract, although in both cases it would be if a third letter was sent simply accepting the last preceding offer.[1]

PUBLIC AUCTION.—*Conditions of Sale.*—It often happens that a client brings to his solicitor the conditions of an intended sale, in order to be advised thereon; that is, he wishes to know whether he may safely purchase under them. In such case, the solicitor's duty will be similar to that above pointed out, with this difference, that in the one case his client will have bound himself by entering into the contract, and in the other he will not. It will be necessary to look carefully over the conditions; and although the client will probably stop while this is being done, it is most important that the solicitor should not "lose his head." It is a very common practice in such cases for young men to glance slightly over the conditions and hand them to the purchaser, saying, "They appear all right," or using some

---

[1] *Hudson* v. *Buck*, 7 Ch. D. 683; see also *Mundy* v. *Asprey*, 13 Ch. D. 855.

similar expression; the fact being that, owing to their client's presence, or their own inability to discover what is really intended to be met by the conditions, they will not have given the matter the consideration it deserves. Another very common practice on the part of a young professional man is to strive to obtain a reputation for superior quickness and penetration, and although these qualities are very excellent, the reputation of possessing them ought not to be obtained at the expense of a client; for, however quick in perception a young solicitor may be, he will find that many conditions of sale used at the present day require all the consideration he can give them before he is able to form a correct opinion as to their meaning. Suppose, for instance, that his client, relying on his representation that he can demand a fair title under the conditions of sale, becomes a purchaser, and a defect afterwards appears which has been successfully guarded against by the conditions, and which a man of fair experience ought to have foreseen. His adviser may be placed in a very awkward position, and at the least lose his client, in addition to which he may have to compensate him for his loss. It is far better, in such a case if, from the general tendency of the conditions, it appears that some defect in the title is attempted to be covered, to inform the client thereof at once, and if, notwithstanding, he still desire to purchase, to offer to accompany him to the place of sale, and when there put such questions to the auctioneer or the vendor's solicitor with respect to the particular objection as may seem advisable. From the answers given (although they, of course, will not vary the terms of the conditions), it will probably be easy to advise the intending purchaser what course he had better adopt; and should he in such case be a trustee, the proper course will be to advise him at once not to purchase, unless the ambiguous condition is struck out or modified.

Should a client have already purchased property at an auction, and bring the conditions of sale and purchase contract to his solicitor, the course to be taken by the latter will be very simple. He will, in the first place, write to the vendor's solicitor for an abstract of the title, and in the meantime diligently peruse the conditions of sale, in order to ascertain what title the purchaser may require, and what restrictions as to title are imposed on him. It may turn out that a serious defect in the title is attempted to be covered by a loose condition, framed in such a manner that a non-professional man on reading it would be thrown off his guard, but yet apparently of sufficient stringency to cover the defect; in this case it is necessary to consider whether the condition is so framed that, by reading it, a man of ordinary intelligence may discover what is intended to be guarded against. If it is so framed, the purchaser will be bound by it, whatever may be its effect; if, on the contrary, it is framed in an obscure manner, and with an evident intention to mislead a purchaser, or is so loosely framed that the meaning of it cannot be easily understood, a Court of Equity would probably refuse to decree specific performance.[1] It may be convenient here to allude to the clause now generally

---

[1] *Gardner* v. *Tate*, Ir. R. 10 C. L. 460; *Best* v. *Hamand*, 12 Ch. D. 1 ; *Re Bannister, Broad* v. *Munton*, 12 Ch. D. 131.

inserted in conditions of sale of leasehold property, namely, that the last receipt for rent shall be conclusive evidence of all the covenants in the lease having been performed up to the completion of the purchase. This condition properly applied is a very useful one in practice for both vendor and purchaser, inasmuch as if such a condition were not inserted, it would be the duty of the purchaser's solicitor to make minute inquiries as to whether all the covenants in the lease had been duly observed and performed, and to take advantage of a breach of covenant, however unimportant it might be; a difficulty that could only be got over by a waiver of the breach by the lessor. On the other hand, the condition is sometimes unfairly extended, and it may sometimes have the effect of compelling a purchaser to take a title that may be worth nothing; in fact, no title at all, owing to a prior continuing breach of covenant, not relievable in equity, having been committed by the vendor.[1]

The covenant to insure is that most frequently found to have been broken, and when this is the case, and the breach must have been known to the vendor at the time of sale, it will be the safer plan, notwithstanding the conditions, to insist on his obtaining a waiver from the lessor. This is now an easy matter, as under § 1 of Lord St. Leonards' Act[2] a lessor may waive such a breach, without prejudice to his right to take advantage of a future breach. § 8 of the same Act protects a purchaser of leaseholds from any liability in respect of any prior breach of which he has no notice, if there be a proper policy

---

[1] See *Lawrie* v. *Lees*, 14 Ch. D. 249.   [2] 22 & 23 Vict. c 35.

in existence at the time of purchase; and under §§ 4–7 of the same Act a Court of Equity will, in some cases, relieve against a forfeiture. Where, however, such relief has already been once granted and a new breach which the lessor refuses to waive has been committed, it is safer to rescind the contract, as it is doubtful if a Court of Equity would, under such circumstances, compel a purchaser to carry it into effect.[1] In many instances a purchaser, whatever may be the state of the title, is so eager to become the owner of the property, that he will pay but slight attention to any caution that may be given him. If such a case arises, his solicitor should take care to have some letter or writing, shewing that he brought the objection to his notice, and that, with a full knowledge of the effect of it, he thought fit to waive it.

Before leaving this branch of the subject, it may be as well to mention that the difficulty experienced by a vendor in selling, after a prior breach of covenant is attempted to be got over by inserting in the conditions the words " notwithstanding a prior breach of covenant may be shewn:" and as words such as these are calculated to put the purchaser on inquiry, no doubt a Court of Equity would decree specific performance, on the principle that if a man will be so blind or wilful as to purchase property under damaging conditions of sale, it is no part of the duty of a Court of Equity to help him.

It will be sufficient here to draw attention to the importance of carefully weighing the effect of the

[1] *Howell v. Kightley*, 21 Beav. 331; *Palmer v. Goren*, 25 L. J. (Ch.) 811.

conditions under which a client has purchased, before proceeding to peruse the abstract of title, as, after some little experience, it will be easy to discover what sort of title may be expected, merely by reading the conditions of sale; and if they are of a stringent character, extra vigilance should be excited when perusing the abstract.

If a client has contracted to purchase property consisting to any material extent of buildings— whether freehold or leasehold—it is advisable either to obtain some memorandum from the vendor with respect to the insurance money, or advise the purchaser to insure immediately, as, if the property be burnt down before completion, the vendor will be entitled to the insurance money, and may compel the purchaser to pay the purchase-money; thus the vendor will be paid twice over, while the unfortunate purchaser gets nothing whatever for his money.[1]

VERIFYING ABSTRACT. —We will now assume that everything has been done respecting the contract, that it is complete, and that the abstract of title has been forwarded to you by the vendor's solicitor. The first point requiring attention will be the time limited (if any) by the contract or conditions of sale for sending in requisitions on the title, for if a short time is limited and time is made of the essence of the contract—as is often the case—it will be necessary to use despatch in verifying and perusing the abstract. Having received the abstract, it is of advantage to cursorily peruse it, in order to obtain

---

[1] *Poole* v. *Adams*, 12 W. R. 683, 33 L. J. (Ch.) 639 ; *Rayner* v. *Preston*, 14 Ch. D. 297.

a general view of the title. This will be of assistance
on afterwards comparing the abstract with the deeds.
The vendor's solicitor should then be written to, to
make an appointment at his office for comparing the
abstract with the deeds, and he will give information
as to where they may be examined. A purchaser,
however, unless bound by the conditions of sale, is
not obliged to incur the expense of his solicitor
taking a long journey to compare the deeds with the
abstract, as, in the absence of any information to the
contrary in the contract or conditions, the deeds are
expected to be in the possession of the vendor or his
solicitor, or, at all events, within a reasonable distance. The appointment having been made, the
purchaser's solicitor will proceed at the time appointed to the place where the deeds are to be found,
and if in London will take a clerk with him, but if
in the country a clerk of the vendor's solicitor will
assist him. The usual course is for the clerk to read
the abstract slowly while the solicitor looks at the
deeds, taking care first to mark the stamps under the
date of the deed in the abstract. It is customary to
mark all the stamps in the abstract, as well followers
as *ad valorem* and other stamps ; but unless the number of folios in the deed are counted (which although
formerly necessary, is no longer so) it is quite useless
to mark the number of followers ; the principal thing
is to see if the *ad valorem* duty is correct, and also
that any other stamps required by the Stamp Act
are affixed. In examining any deed conveying real
estate, dated between the 15th May, 1841, and the
1st October, 1845, care must be taken to observe
that reference is made in the deed to the " Act for

making a Release as effectual as a Lease and Release by the same Parties,"[1] and also that a 35s. stamp in lieu of the old lease for a year stamp, is impressed on the release; but between the latter date and the 14th August, 1850, it will only be necessary to see that an extra stamp of 35s. is impressed on the release, pursuant to § 2 of the Act to Amend the Law of Real Property,[2] which made freeholds lie in grant as well as in livery. Any deed bearing date after the 14th August, 1850, does not require to be stamped with an extra 35s. stamp, as the Stamp Act, 1850,[3] which then came into operation, repealed the lease for a year stamp duty imposed by the Act to amend the Law of Real Property. It is scarcely necessary to mention that the person who compares an abstract of title with the deeds should have a fair knowledge, not only of the theory, but also of the practice of conveyancing, although many consider this a much less important duty than it is. Instances have occurred where, at the end of a very long will, and at a place where few would have expected to find anything of the sort, a most important clause has been put in, materially affecting the interest of the person dealing with the property. This, no doubt, has arisen in the following manner:—After the will had been settled by counsel, the client, on its being read over to him, has thought of some modification of a prior interest or power, and the solicitor, fearing that by inserting it earlier he might interfere with the effect of the preceding clauses, has put it in at the very end; a safe course, certainly,

[1] 4 & 5 Vict. c. 21.   [2] 8 & 9 Vict. c. 103.
[3] 13 & 14 Vict. c. 97, s. 6.

for himself, but likely to be very prejudicial to a
future purchaser who has to rely upon a careless
examination of the abstract with the deeds.   On
arriving at the end of a deed care should be taken to
see that it is executed by all proper parties and duly
attested, and the receipt for the consideration money
indorsed, signed and witnessed; and if a married
woman be a party, that the deed has been duly
acknowledged under the Abolition of Fines and
Recoveries Act,[1] and that the official certificate is
attached.   It is always better to insert in the abstract
the actual number of witnesses, as the deed may
have been made in exercise of a power requiring two
or more witnesses to its execution.   As to powers
exercised by will since the 1st of January, 1838,[2]
and by deed since the 13th of August, 1859, two
witnesses are sufficient.[3]   It should also be observed
whether there is any irregularity as to the position
of the receipt for the consideration money,[4] and in
such a case a note to that effect should be made in
the margin of the abstract.   If the estate be in a
register county, i.e., Middlesex or Yorkshire, the
usual memorandum of the registration of the deed
should be found indorsed on the back of it, and the
reference to such memorandum should be inserted at
the foot of the deed in the abstract, if not already
done; and should the property be subject to the
operation of the Bedford Level Drainage Act,[5] it
should be seen that the requisites of that Act have

[1] 3 & 4 Wm. 4, c. 74.
[2] Wills Act, 7 Wm. 4 & 1 Vict. c. 27, s 10.
[3] Lord St. Leonards' Act, 22 & 23 Vict. c. 35, s. 11.
[4] *Kennedy* v. *Green*, 3 My. & K. 399; *Greenslade* v. *Dare*, 20 Beav.
281.   [5] 15 Car. 2, c. 17.

been complied with.[1] Also, where any succession duty is payable, evidence of its having been paid should be furnished now or in the replies to requisitions. If not produced now a note should be made in the margin of the abstract.

PERUSING ABSTRACT.—Having compared the abstract with the deeds, the next step is to examine the stamps which have been marked in the margin of the abstract, so as to see if they are correct; after which the abstract must be perused and the necessary requisitions prepared. If the purchaser's solicitor does not feel competent to peruse the abstract, or should it be very long and intricate, or any doubtful questions arise on it, or the property be of great value, the best course will be to lay it before counsel with instructions to peruse it and advise on the title. The abstract should be accompanied by the conditions of sale or contract. Counsel's opinion in this case will enable the solicitor to prepare the requisitions on the title, and here it will be perceived how necessary it is to carefully compare the abstract with the deeds, otherwise counsel will, and indeed cannot help, raising a multitude of trifling questions as to whether a particular date or description be correctly stated, or as to the execution of a will or deed, or as to the correctness of a recital, and can only be satisfied on this head by a fresh reference to the deeds, thus incurring additional trouble and expense, besides incurring an obligation to the vendor's solicitor, as, having once produced the deeds, it is hardly fair to put his client to the expense of again

---

[1] But see *Willis* v. *Brown*, 10 Sim. 127.

referring to them for information which might and ought to have been obtained when they were first produced.

The writer has found it a convenient course in perusing an abstract to take a sheet of paper with a double margin and insert the date of the deed in the left hand margin, and on the opposite side put such part of the deed as is necessary to shew the devolution of the title and any special clauses or stipulations, leaving the right hand margin for notes and queries. It may sometimes be convenient to keep the devolution of the legal and equitable estates separate. This will depend on the title; but it is always the best course in perusing an abstract to shew the devolution of the title to any attendant term of years on a separate sheet of paper. All this may be done very briefly; it is only necessary to make a note in the margin opposite any particular clause or matter, in order that attention may be readily called to it afterwards, as perhaps the next or a subsequent deed may have the effect of disposing of the point; and should this be so, it is a good plan to insert a note in the margin of the analysis under the defect previously noted, and thus many of the queries it has been found necessary to raise will be disposed of, and those which are not cleared up will form the material for requisitions on the title. Of course, although only the principal parts of the deed are inserted in the analysis, the whole of the deed as given in the abstract must be carefully read, and in each case the conveyancer must satisfy himself that the deeds are nothing more than what he states them to be.

The following is a specimen of an analysis of part of an abstract, with the notes and queries thereon :—

1852. May 15. (1)	John Williamson . . .	1
	Thomas James Richardson . .	2
	Conson. £1000	
	Convee. by 1 to 2 of	
	Piece of land at Highgate,	
	Mx. 5a. 2r. 25r.	
	called Fallow field.	
	To use of 2 in fee	
	Covts. by 1 for title	
	e. a. r. i. Regd.	

qy.
Identity
qy.
Draws
p. 3.

1856. Oct. 17. (3)	Will of Thomas James Richardson, g. d. & b.	
	All real and personal estate	
	To widow Jane Richardson (sole exix.)	
	e. a.	

Produce
probate
qy. regd.
p. 8.
qy.
certificate.

1860. Jan. 14. 1860. Mch. 26. (3)	Death and Probate of Will of T. J. Richardson.

1861. June 5. (4)	Jane Richardson . . .	1
	William Jackson }	
	James Thornton } . . .	2
	Mtge. by 1 to 2 of	
	Same piece of land.	
	E. R. £750.	
	e. a. r. i. Regd.	

qy. paid off
p. 9.

1875. Oct. 28. (9)	William Jackson }	
	James Thornton } . . .	1
	Jane Richardson . . .	2
	Conson. £750 and interest.	
	Reconveyance of	
	Same piece of land.	
	To use of 2 in fee	
	e. a. r. i.	

qy.
regd.

1878. April 6. (11)	Jane Richardson . . .	1
	William John Phillips . .	2
	Conson. £1500.	
	Convee. by 1 to 2 of	
	Same piece of land.	
	To use of 2 in fee	
	e. a.	

qy.
r. i.
qy. regd.

To face page 47.)

In the annexed analysis it will be seen that the first query is as to the identity of the property described in the abstract with that in the contract for sale. The second is as to whether any widow of T. J. Richardson became entitled to dower. But as, under his will on page 3 of the abstract, his widow takes all his property, the question of dower is set at rest, and therefore the pen is drawn through the query, and " p. 3 " (the reference to the page where the will is abstracted) placed under it.

The letters e. a. r. i. mean "executed, attested, and receipt indorsed."

The query as to whether the will has been registered in the Middlesex Registry is treated in the same way, because it appears that the mortgage by Jane Richardson to Jackson and Thornton was duly registered ; and by § 8 of the Vendor and Purchaser Act, 1874,[1] this renders the non-registration of the will immaterial.

The letters E. R. in the analysis of the mortgage of the 5th of June, 1861, of course mean " Equity of Redemption."

The query as to whether the mortgage has been paid off is answered by the reconveyance of the 28th of October, 1875, at page 9 of the abstract.

There would have been a query as to succession duty on the will of Richardson, had the devise been to anyone but his wife ; but no succession duty is paid by husband or wife.

The usual and most convenient mode of copying requisitions on title is on abstract paper, doubling it in half margin, writing the queries on the left

---

[1] 37 & 38 Vict. c. 78 ; Greenwood's Recent R. P. Stat. p. 118.

hand, and reserving the right hand for the replies, thus :—

Requisitions on the Title to a House and Grounds, known as Fallow Hall, Highgate, in the County of Middlesex :—

1. Evidence must be given of the identity of the piece of land described in the abstract with the property purchased.

2. Probate of the will and certificate of the death of T. J. Richardson must be produced.

And so on until all the requisitions are exhausted.

REQUISITIONS AND REPLIES.—Having obtained the vendor's replies to the requisitions on the title, it will be necessary to consider whether they are satisfactory. This is a duty of equal importance to the perusal of the abstract, and sometimes there may be greater difficulty in deciding whether an answer is sufficient, than in raising the question. If there is any doubt as to the course to be pursued, it is advisable, whether the abstract was or was not in the first place laid before counsel, to place all the papers before him and take his opinion. If, however, there is no serious doubt, then the next step will be either to send further requisitions to the vendor's solicitor, or to prepare the conveyance.

By raising only such questions as are of real importance, much expense will be saved to the purchaser and much trouble to his solicitor. In some cases the solicitor may find it necessary to

consult his client as to whether he will press for a
more satisfactory answer to a particular requisition
(when the vendor's solicitor has declined or expressed
his inability to give any further information), or
whether he will waive it and complete the purchase ;
but this will only arise in cases where the purchaser
is not restricted by the contract from requiring a
more satisfactory answer, and not often in those
cases.

It must be remembered that in case succession duty
is payable, the vendor's solicitor must either produce
the receipt or procure a certificate from Somerset
House, certifying that all duty has been paid.

SEARCHES.—Search must be made for judgments,
crown debts, *lis pendens*, and annuities, at the office
for that purpose of the Royal Court of Justice,
against the vendor and such other persons as may
have any interest in the property dealt with ; except
mortgagees who have been or are about to be paid
off[1]. The search for judgments should be made for
five years prior to the day of sale,[2] but judgments
entered since the 23rd July, 1868, may be disre-
garded unless a writ of execution has been registered.[3] Should the property be in Middlesex or
Yorkshire, the register office for the county in which
the property is situate must be also searched, in order
to discover if any deeds affecting the property have
been executed which do not appear on the abstract.
These searches should be made as near the comple-

[1] 17 & 18 Vict. c. 15, s. 11; *Greaves* v. *Wilson*, 25 Beav. 434.
[2] 2 & 3 Vict. c. 11, s. 4.
[3] See 23 & 24 Vict. c. 38, ss. 1, 2 ; 27 & 28 Vict. c. 112, s. 1.

tion of the matter as possible ; but where the searches
are likely to take up much time they may be made
at an earlier stage of the business, and another
search made from the foot of the prior search immediately before attending to complete the matter. If
a charge or incumbrance of any description not dis-
closed by the abstract should be discovered, a letter
should be written apprising the vendor's solicitor of
the fact, and requiring its removal before the completion. Although a purchaser is not bound to
search for judgments, it is safer for him to do so,
because in the event of a resale a subsequent purchaser might search and find judgments, and put the
vendor to considerable trouble in proving that he
had no notice of them.

PREPARATION OF CONVEYANCE.—If a solicitor has
any doubts as to the proper persons to make parties
to the conveyance, which is very likely to be the case
when dealing with large estates or estates that have
been frequently dealt with, the more prudent course
will be to hand all the papers to counsel and instruct
him to prepare the conveyance.

It may be mentioned that, although the greatest
accuracy should be observed in the description of the
parties to a deed, a misnomer will not be a fatal
objection, if the party can be identified.[1]

With respect to the parties to the conveyance,
should the vendor be seised in fee simple, it will be
necessary only to make him (and his wife if living
and married before 1834) the party of the one part,
and the purchaser of the other part, unless the pur-

---

[1] *James v. Whitbread*, 11 C. B. 406.

chaser was married before 1834, and his wife be
living, in which case the name of a third party should
be inserted, as a trustee to bar the inchoate right of
dower in the wife. It will not be necessary to make
the dower trustee in the conveyance to the vendor a
party to the draft if the property was conveyed to
the vendor and a trustee to the ordinary uses to bar
dower, for in such a case the power of appointment
reserved under that form of conveyance is alone
sufficient to pass the estate, and the granting part
which follows is subsidiary to the appointment.
Should the estate be in mortgage, it will be necessary
to make the mortgagee a party to the draft conveyance, and to recite the mortgage deed. In every case
the draftsman must be guided by the state of the
title, as to whom he will make parties, and the
documents and statements necessary to be recited.
If the whole legal and equitable estates are vested
in the vendor, it is manifest that none but he (and
his wife if entitled to dower) need join in the conveyance. If the estate be mortgaged, then the mortgagee must join; and if any other persons appear by
the abstract to have an interest in the property, then
those persons, whoever they may be, must join in the
conveyance.

It sometimes happens that a judgment creditor is
induced to give up his charge upon part of an estate
contracted to be sold, and in this case he must be
made a party to the deed, and the particulars of the
judgment and his consent to release the estate therefrom should be recited. Before 1859 the judgment
creditor would merely have covenanted not to resort
to the estate conveyed for satisfaction of his judg-

E 2

ment debt, because a release of part of the hereditaments affected by the judgment was at law a release
of the whole, and in equity such a covenant was
considered an effectual release ; but now he will join
in the granting part of the deed, as under § 11
of Lord St. Leonards' Act,[1] the release from a judgment of part of the hereditaments charged therewith
is not to affect the validity of the judgment as to the
hereditaments remaining unreleased, or as to any
other property not specifically released.

Where devisees in trust, with power to sell and
give receipts for purchase-money, are the vendors,
the parties beneficially entitled will, as a rule, not be
necessary parties to the conveyance, inasmuch as in
such cases the trustees can make a title without them ;
and even if the instrument appointing the trustees
does not contain a power to give receipts, that power
is supplied by § 29 of Lord Cranworth's Act[2] in all
cases where trustees have been appointed by any
deed, will, or codicil dated since the 28th of August,
1860.[3]   A similar power is given to mortgagees and
other vendors acting under deeds dated since the
13th of August, 1859, by § 23 of Lord St. Leonards'
Act.[4]

It may happen that the vendor is a married
woman, and as the law respecting a married woman
entitled to real estate is peculiar, it may be better to
state it rather fully.   It appears to be as follows :—

1. A married woman cannot pass the legal estate
in real estate not settled to her separate use, unless

[1] 22 & 23 Vict. c. 35.
[2] 23 & 24 Vict. c. 145.
[3] See 23 & 24 Vict. c. 145, s. 34.
[4] 22 & 23 Vict. c. 35.

the formalities prescribed by Fines and Recoveries Act[1] are complied with; and before the Vendor and Purchaser Act, 1874, came into operation the rule was the same with regard to real estate belonging to her for her separate use.[2]

2. A married woman can dispose of an equitable fee simple estate or estate tail, given to her separate use, without a deed acknowledged.[3] And inasmuch as after a conveyance of her equitable interest she would if seised of the legal estate be a bare trustee for the purchaser, it appears that she could now convey that also by virtue of § 6 of the Vendor and Purchaser Act, 1874.[4]

3. A married woman may dispose of an equitable life interest in real estate given to her for her separate use (and which she is not restrained from anticipating), and also of her absolute interest in personalty (whether in possession or reversion), without a deed acknowledged.[5]

4. A wife, even with the consent of her husband, cannot make an assignment of her reversionary interest in personalty that will be binding on her in the event of her surviving her husband, unless her interest accrued under an instrument dated after the 31st of December, 1857,[6] and in such a case the assignment must be acknowledged pursuant to the Fines and Recoveries Act.[7]

[1] 3 & 4 Wm. 4, c. 74.

[2] But see *Goodchild* v. *Dougal*, 3 Ch. D. 650.

[3] *Taylor* v. *Meads*, 5 N. R. 348, 4 D. J. & S. 597; *Pride* v. *Bubb*, L. R. 7 Ch. 64; *Cooper* v. *Macdonald*, 7 Ch. D. 288.

[4] 37 & 38 Vict. c. 78.

[5] *Lechmere* v. *Brotheridge*, 32 L. J. (Ch.) 577.

[6] 20 & 21 Vict. c. 57.

[7] 3 & 4 Wm. 4, c. 74.

5. In no case can a married woman (during coverture) dispose of property settled on her for her separate use without power of anticipation.

In preparing the conveyance, the draftsman must be guided by the state of the title as appearing on the abstract; for instance, should the last document in the abstract be a conveyance to the vendor in fee, he may either dispense with any recital, or state shortly, in the usual form, that the vendor is seised in fee of the premises intended to be conveyed. Having regard to sub-sect. 2 of § 2 of the Vendor and Purchaser Act, 1874,[1] the latter course is now often adopted, as such a recital will, in any future sale after twenty years have expired, be evidence of the fact recited.[2] In such a case there can be no necessity, neither can it answer any useful purpose, to recite the last or any of the prior deeds in the conveyance to the purchaser. If the last deed on the abstract be a conveyance to the vendor, to uses to bar dower (a form now seldom seen owing to the operation of the Dower Act), it is customary to recite such deed, as the conveyance will, in such a case, be in exercise of the power reserved to the vendor by that deed.

APPROVAL OF DRAFT.—The draft having been prepared, a fair copy of it should be made and forwarded to the vendor's solicitor for approval, and after he has approved it on behalf of his own clients, he will forward it for approval to the solicitors of any of the parties to the draft for whom he may

---

[1] 37 & 38 Vict. c. 78.
[2] See *Bolton* v. *London School Board*, 7 Ch. D. 766.

not be professionally concerned, and return it to the purchaser's solicitor when it has been approved on behalf of all parties. On receiving back the draft he will go carefully through it, in order to see what alterations have been made therein; and should any important alteration have been made, he will consider how it affects the draft, or how far he is obliged to submit to it; and in such a case, if the draft has been prepared by counsel, it should be laid before him to advise on the alterations, the framer of the draft being the most competent person to advise on the effect of any alterations therein. As to how far the vendor's solicitor is justified in insisting on alterations he may have made in the frame of the draft, or in any objection he may make to the mode in which the purchaser thinks fit to have the property conveyed, the authorities should be consulted.[1]

In cases where trustees are parties to the deed, great pertinacity is sometimes evinced by their solicitors in insisting on qualifying words being inserted in the operative part of the deed, such as the following :—" As far as they lawfully can or may, but not further or otherwise, and without warranty of title." Now, these words at the present day have no meaning at all, as trustees cannot convey more than they are authorized to do by the power which they exercise, and as they never enter into any more extensive covenant than that they have not done any act to incumber, it seems clear those qualifying words are not required, and are quite unnecessary.[2]   And with

---

[1] *Clarke* v. *May*, 16 Beav. 273; *Cooper* v. *Cartwright*, Joh. 685; *Earl Egmont* v. *Smith*, 6 Ch. D. 469.

[2] *Calvert* v. *Sebright*, 15 Beav. 156.

respect to the word "grant" creating a warranty, an eminent conveyancer, more than half a century ago, stated his opinion that it would not have that operation; and it was enacted thirty-five years ago[1] that the word "grant" should not imply any covenant. When, however, a solicitor acting for a trustee is disposed to insist on qualifying words being inserted, the better plan is to let them remain, as they are quite harmless, and the point is not worth a long discussion, although it is a pity that men of narrow understandings should have it in their power to incumber a well-drawn draft by useless and unmeaning words.

In case the original draftsman should modify or strike out any of the alterations that have been made in the draft as prepared by him, it should be again forwarded to the vendor's solicitor, as it is not regular to alter a draft after it has been approved by the vendor's solicitor, without submitting the alterations for his approval.

ENGROSSMENT OF CONVEYANCE.—After the draft conveyance has been finally approved, it will be engrossed by the purchaser's solicitor, and the draft and engrossment sent to the vendor's solicitor for examination, and he will also get it examined by any other solicitor concerned in the matter. On sending the draft to the stationer for engrossment, it is better to mark on it the particulars of the stamps on which it is to be engrossed, in order to avoid the possibility, if the deed be engrossed on unstamped parchment, of its being put away and forgotten to be stamped until too late. Never instruct a stationer to engross

the deed " on proper stamps," as it is unfair to him
and may cause the solicitor some annoyance and
expense if he or his clerk forgets on receiving the
engrossment, to examine the correctness of the stamps;
and as he must, or, at all events, ought, to examine
them, it is at least quite as easy to do this before the
draft is sent for engrossment as after. A law stationer is by no means expected to be in a position to
know what stamps should be affixed on any but the
most simple documents. In case of any doubt as to
the correct stamp to be affixed an assessment can be
easily obtained without expense on application at
Somerset House. But in most cases a solicitor can,
himself, ascertain the proper stamps by referring to
the Stamp Act, 1870.[1]

COMPLETION.—On forwarding the draft and engrossment to the vendor's solicitor an appointment
may usually be made for the completion of the business. This appointment will be made with the
vendor's solicitor (unless some other office is named
in the conditions of sale), and he will arrange as to
the place of completion, and inform the purchaser's
solicitor accordingly.

In cases where a married woman is a party to
the deed it must be acknowledged by her, pursuant
to the Fines and Recoveries Act;[2] but the course
necessary to be followed on such occasion will appear
in a subsequent part of this book;[3] and should the
property be in Middlesex or Yorkshire, a memo-

[1] 33 & 34 Vict. c. 97.
[2] 3 & 4 Wm. 4, c. 74.
[3] See Chapter IX. p. 149, infra.

rial of the deed will have to be registered. A memorial can be executed either by grantor or grantee, but care must be taken that one of the witnesses to its execution is also a witness to the execution by the same party of the conveyance. At the time and place appointed for completion, the purchaser's solicitor will attend with his client and pay the money and take the deeds; if the property be leasehold, he will also require the policy of insurance and last receipt for premium to be handed over, and the last receipt for ground rent should be inspected by him. He will also satisfy himself as to the rates and taxes having been paid up to the time appointed for completion, but it is more usual to accept the undertaking of the vendor's solicitor to clear up all rates and taxes to that day. In case the property consists of a house in hand the keys should be handed over on completion, unless possession has previously been given to the purchaser.

CHAPTER IV.

MORTGAGES.

It is scarcely necessary to mention that a mortgage is a security given by one person to another to secure the repayment of a sum of money, or that almost every description of property and all interests therein may be the subject of a mortgage.

ACTING FOR MORTGAGOR.—The observations in Chapter II. as to the duties of a vendor's solicitor, as far as regards the abstract and completion of the matter, will equally apply to the duties of a solicitor acting for a mortgagor.

Also where a client is not absolute owner of the property or the interest therein which he proposes to give as security, the question will arise whether he has power to give a valid mortgage.

Upon this point it should be remembered that under §§ 14 to 18 of Lord St. Leonards' Act,[1] trustees and executors may, respectively, under certain circumstances, raise money by mortgage of their testator's estate for the purpose of paying debts, legacies or specific moneys, notwithstanding the want of an express power in the will. § 16 applies to cases where the testator has not devised the estate in the manner pointed out in § 14.

[1] 22 & 23 Vict. c. 35.

Also, under § 9 of Lord Cranworth's Act,[1] money required for the purposes of equality of exchange authorized by that Act, and for renewal of leases, may be raised by a mortgage of the hereditaments to be received in exchange, or contained in the renewed lease as the case may be.

Attention may also be drawn to the provisions of the Improvement of Land Act, 1864,[2] and the Limited Owners' Reservoirs and Water Supply Further Facilities Act, 1877.[3]

ACTING FOR MORTGAGEE.—On the other hand, if the client is the mortgagee, the course of proceeding on his solicitor's part will be similar to that on a purchase with this important difference, that a mortgagee is never subject to any restrictions as to title or evidence of title, or the time when the matter is to be completed; there is also this further difference, that specific performance cannot be enforced against him. In many cases a willing purchaser will often waive many points on the title through a wish to get what he has purchased: he may require a few extra acres to make his lands lie in a ring fence, or he may want a particular house either for occupation or for removal in order to improve a view; but in the case of a mortgage none of these circumstances can arise, a mortgagee lends his money on a particular security and expects to have it back again, and, therefore, if there is any doubt as to the title, or as to obtaining the evidence necessary to establish it, he should never

[1] 23 & 24 Vict. c. 145.　　　　[2] 27 & 28 Vict. c. 114.
[3] 40 & 41 Vict. c. 31; Greenwood's R. P. Stat. 209.

be advised to advance his money until such doubts are removed. If, however, such doubts resolve themselves merely into a question of expense hereafter in case a sale should have to be resorted to by the mortgagee, the question for consideration will be how far the value of the property will be sufficient to pay for this extra expense; for if the mortgagee gets a marketable title, and is amply covered by the value of the property mortgaged, he will be safe in making the advance. It is also important to see how far the covenant of the mortgagor to repay the money can be relied upon, although this should not be taken into consideration until the mortgagee has been satisfied as to the value of the security and the title to it. The covenant of a responsible man is at all times of some value; if, therefore, a mortgagee or his solicitor is satisfied with the mortgagor's responsibility, he will be justified in abating some of the rigour that he would otherwise exercise; and as the irregularity in payment of interest is often a great source of annoyance to clients it is very desirable to secure a mortgagor who is likely to be punctual. A method now often adopted is to reserve interest at six per cent. reducible to five on punctual payment. There are now such numerous channels for investment that unless clients obtain their interest punctually they call in the money and employ their broker rather than their solicitor; but it should be borne in mind that a good mortgage is still one of the safest securities and at the same time a remunerative one; and that there is generally little difficulty in obtaining a transfer.

In the allusions here to the value of property, "marketable value" is meant; in other words, the amount likely to be realized by a forced sale of the property. It often happens that property in mortgage, consisting of mills, manufactories, furnaces, mines, &c., may be of considerable value, but yet unmarketable in times of commercial depression, and in such a case as this, however anxious the mortgagee may be to realize his security, he cannot do so unless the mortgagor be a man of substance, and can be reached under his covenant for repayment of the money. As there are various descriptions of mortgages, it may be of service if the principal are here stated, and a few remarks made on each. They are as follows:—

1. Freehold land comprising :
   (a.) Broad acres.
   (b.) Ground rents.
   (c.) Houses.
2. Copyhold land or houses.
3. Leasehold houses.
4. Freehold, copyhold, or leasehold mills, manufactories, mines, &c.
5. Life interests.
6. Reversions.
7. Policies of assurance.
8. Furniture, stock in trade, &c.

The following remarks apply principally to the case of a client wishing to invest money of his own —the case of trustees investing trust funds will be dealt with afterwards.

With respect to mortgages of freehold land, a client will be quite safe in advancing to the extent of two-thirds of the value of broad acres or ground rents as certified by a respectable surveyor; for experience proves that commercial depression exercises very little influence on this class of property, unless it be to raise the price, many people at such times being more anxious to invest their money in something secure and tangible than at times when trade is buoyant.

With respect to freehold houses, and indeed house property of any tenure, locality is the principal consideration, and if that is good, the tenant responsible, the property held on lease, and the state of repair satisfactory, then freehold houses form a very good investment, although the advance of much more than one-half the value of the property is not to be recommended.

Copyhold houses or land where the fine on death or alienation is certain, that is, nominal, form an investment of little less value than freehold; but in manors where the fine on admittance is arbitrary, that is, at a rough estimation, two years' annual value, the amount of the fine must be taken into consideration in estimating the value of the property, as every person admitted must pay a fine, and consequently a purchaser would give so much less for the property.

Leasehold houses are never looked upon with so much favour as freehold, unless situated in a first-class position. In advising a client to lend on leasehold security many things require to be taken into consideration, namely, the probability of the property being unlet for a time, the amount of ground rent reserved by the lease, the nature of the covenants in the lease (some of which may be very onerous and may not have been duly performed), and the great depreciation of value experienced by this class of property in a time of commercial depression, unless it happens to be situate in a first-class neighbourhood, or have other corresponding advantages.

Sometimes a solicitor has to advise a client as to his advancing money on leasehold ground rents, or, as they are generally termed, "improved rents." These rents arise in this way: a person holds a house under a lease for, say ninety years, at a rental of 5*l.* per annum; he grants an underlease of this house for the whole of his term, less a few days, at a rent of, say 45*l.* Here the improved rental is 40*l.* per annum. In a case like this, precisely the same questions will arise for consideration, as to covenants, &c., as in the case of a leasehold house offered as a security; but if these questions are decided satisfactorily, and the rents reserved by the underlease should be sufficiently below the rack rent of the property, then improved ground rents will form a better security than any other description of leasehold property.

The next head, freehold or leasehold mills, manufactories, mines, &c., will require very serious consideration before advising a client to advance his money. It is true that in mining and manufacturing districts owners of this class of property do not, in prosperous times, find much difficulty in raising money upon it; but this chiefly arises from the fact of the lender having it constantly before his eyes, and in many cases from the personal knowledge he has of the borrower and the value of the security.

In advising as to a mortgage of this description of property, the value of the building, steam boiler, machinery, gearing, &c., as estimated by a competent person, and also the responsibility of the borrower, must be carefully considered ; and even if everything is satisfactory, not more than one-half of the value should, as a rule, be advanced, because, in the event of a depression of trade, great difficulty might be experienced in realizing such a security. If the mortgage comprises any trade machinery other than fixtures, it must be executed, attested, and registered, as required by § 8 of the Bills of Sale Act, 1878.[1] Trade machinery does not comprise fixed motive power, shafting, drums, steam-pipes, gas-pipes, or water-pipes.[2]

Life interests are seldom taken as securities for money, unless by insurance offices or professed money lenders, and when taken, the mortgagor is always required to effect an insurance on his life to secure the repayment of the mortgage money, a life interest in itself being only of value for securing payment of the interest on the money and the premiums on the policy of assurance. The principal is secured by the policy.

There are many disadvantages in this description of security. The mortgagor may do some act to avoid the policy, or it may be necessary to call in the money during his lifetime, in which case difficulty may be experienced in finding a purchaser. If a client is seeking an investment for his money, and does not make the obtaining of a high rate of interest

---

[1] 41 & 42 Vict. c. 31.
[2] Ibid. s. 5

his primary consideration, he should never be advised to accept this kind of security.

A reversion in any description of property is also a very undesirable security, owing to there being no fund available for payment of the interest until the reversion falls into possession. Of course a vested reversion is here meant, as a contingent reversion is never thought of as a security for money about to be advanced, unless accompanied by a policy of assurance, and even then it is a desperate kind of security. Reversionary interests are always of a certain value, which can easily be ascertained by taking the opinion of an actuary. The character and responsibility of the mortgagor in a security of this nature is the most important consideration, as it enhances its value; but even if that is unexceptionable, the security is not a desirable one, and a prudent man, wishing to secure an investment for which a transfer can speedily be obtained, or in respect of which the property can easily be realized in the market, should hesitate before he accepts a reversion as a security.

A policy of assurance, considered as a security, ranks still lower than a reversion. There is not only no means of paying the interest on the mortgage money, but the annual premiums on the policy (without punctually paying which, the whole security vanishes), must be provided from some source. If these can be guaranteed by the covenant of a third person, the security is thereby improved, but is still undesirable. The value of a policy of assurance may be ascertained at any time by applying to the actuary of the company, who, for a small fee, will certify the office value, which increases every year the policy is kept up. This kind of security is generally taken in cases where the borrower is previously indebted to the mortgagee, in which case he takes an assignment of the policy, as the best or only security he can obtain.

Last of all comes a mortgage of household furniture, stock-in-trade, &c. This can in no case be recommended to an intended mortgagee, as there is very little more than the personal character of a mortgagor to depend upon: for instance, he might sell the property comprised in the security, and put the money in his pocket, and it has been decided that he is not criminally liable for so doing, as he does not come within the Fraudulent Trustee Act. Next, the mortgagee is always under the liability of the goods being distrained upon by the landlord for rent in arrear, and if the mortgagor should become bankrupt while in possession, the chattels would pass to his trustee in bankruptcy as being in his order and disposition. This description of mortgage is generally taken to secure money already due, or which may become due on a trading account between the mortgagor and mortgagee. The security is bad at the best, but it is absolutely worthless as against third parties, unless it complies with the formalities prescribed by the Bills of Sale Act, 1878.[1] It must be attested by a solicitor, who must explain it to the grantor, and state that he has done so;[2] it must be registered within seven days after execution,[3] and it must set forth the consideration for which it is given.[4]

---

[1] 41 & 42 Vict. c. 31, s. 8.
[2] Ibid. s. 10.
[3] Ibid. ss. 8, 10 (2).
[4] Ibid. s. 8

The registration must be renewed every five years.[1] If these formalities are complied with, the chattels comprised in the bill of sale will[2] be taken out of the reputed ownership clause of the Bankruptcy Act, 1869.[3]

LENDING TRUST MONEY.—The foregoing remarks are principally applicable to the case of a mortgagee seeking to advance money belonging to himself; but in advising clients who are trustees, too much caution cannot be exercised. In the first place it must be borne in mind that, until recently, the strict duty of a trustee was to place the trust money in Consols. But trustees are now authorized to invest trust moneys in any securities in which cash under the control of the Court may be invested,[4] namely : Bank stock, East India stock, Exchequer bills, £2 10s. per cent. Annuities, mortgages of freehold and copyhold estates in England and Wales, Consols, and New and Reduced £3 per cent. Annuities.[5] In order, however, that a higher rate of interest may be obtained for the benefit of the *cestui que trust*, settlors and testators almost invariably empower the trustees of the settlement or will to invest the trust funds in any of the parliamentary stocks or public funds, or on mortgage of real or leasehold securities (the latter generally being limited to leasehold property not having less than a sixty years' unexpired term), and sometimes on the deben-

---

[1] 41 & 42 Vict. c. 31, s. 11.
[2] Ibid. s. 20.
[3] 32 & 33 Vict. c. 71, s. 15 (5).
[4] 23 & 24 Vict. c. 38, s. 10.
[5] G. O. Feb. 1, 1861.

tures or stock of any incorporated company, paying a dividend, that the trustees may deem well established and sound. Now, in advising a trustee under such a power as this, it must be remembered that copyhold property is comprised within the words "real securities," but leasehold property is not. If a leasehold security be offered, care must be taken to see that an investment on leaseholds is expressly authorized, and that the term unexpired is sufficient. In case of a security on debentures or stock, it must be seen that the debentures are issued properly, and that the stock is stock and not shares. In all these cases, if a trustee does not exceed his power as to the nature of the security, and does not advance more than a prudent and careful man would advance in dealing with his own money under similar circumstances, he will be protected in what he has done by a Court of Equity; but, as before observed, too much caution cannot be exercised when investing trust money, and in no case should the security be entertained until the valuation of an experienced surveyor has been obtained; and when the mortgage is executed the trustees should retain all the deeds, the *cestui que trust* being only entitled to inspect and take copies.

Under no circumstances should trustees, even though the instrument under which they are empowered to advance money extends to such property (a very rare occurrence), be advised to make advances on mills, manufactories, or mines. Their position is very different from that of an ordinary lender, who, for the sake of obtaining a high rate of interest, will sometimes be content to incur a little risk as to his security; but trustees ought only to look at the value and nature of the security, and the certainty of being able to realize at any time, for, whatever may be the amount of interest obtained, it will not be taken into consideration in favour of the trustees, in the event of the security proving insufficient, and a loss accruing to the trust estate.

The writer has gone thus fully into the question of the value of property submitted to a mortgagee, because a solicitor often has to form and give an opinion on the matter; but it should be borne in mind that it is no part of his duty to look to the value of a proposed security, unless that duty be specially cast upon him.[1]

PREPARATION OF DRAFT.—The title to the property offered as security having been satisfactorily proved, the mortgagee's solicitor will proceed either to prepare the draft mortgage, or send instructions to counsel for that purpose. The draft, when prepared or settled, must be fair copied and sent to the solicitor of the mortgagor for perusal by him. He takes a copy of it in the usual manner, and after approving the draft, returns it for engrossment. The principal differences between a conveyance and a mortgage are these—in the former the agreement for sale or purchase is often recited, and the vendor, after conveying the property, enters into qualified covenants for title only; whereas in a mortgage after reciting the agreement for the advance, a covenant for repayment of the principal money and interest is inserted, then follows the conveyance of the property, then the proviso for redemption on repayment of the money, the power to the mortgagee to sell if not then paid, making his receipts good dis-

[1] *Brumbridge* v. *Massey*, 32 L. T. 108.

charges to the purchaser, lastly, absolute covenants for title by the mortgagor. If house property forms a part of the security, the mortgagor covenants to insure, and if leaseholds are included, the mortgagor, in addition to such a covenant, enters into a covenant to pay the rent reserved by, and to perform the covenants contained in, the lease under which the property is held. If the mortgage is made to trustees it should contain a declaration that the money is advanced on a joint account.

In cases where brevity is desired, the power of sale and the usual clauses ancillary thereto may safely be omitted in reliance upon the statutory powers given to mortgagees by §§ 11 to 16 of Lord Cranworth's Act.[1] But in such cases a short clause to the effect that the power of sale may be exercised at any time after the day named in the deed for payment of the principal money should be inserted.

This part of the Act was evidently intended to operate as a means of shortening mortgages, but for some time it did not have that effect. Now, however, it is often relied upon; and it has certainly been of service in cases where the mortgage deed contained no power of sale. It also gives power to appoint a receiver to collect the rents of mortgaged property.[3]

Although at one time the contrary opinion was entertained, it is now settled that trustees, if raising money under a power to mortgage, are authorized to give the mortgagee a power of sale in case of default in repayment of the money.[4]

---

[1] 23 & 24 Vict. c. 145.   [2] See ss. 17–24.

[3] *Russell* v. *Plaice*, 18 Beav. 21; 18 Jur. 251; *Cruikshank* v. *Duffin*,

It is perhaps scarcely necessary to mention, that,
since the repeal of the Acts of Parliament respecting
usury, any amount of interest may be reserved on
any description of property, and there is now no
restriction whatever on this head, the law leaving it
to the parties interested to make their own contracts.

In some cases where the mortgagor remains in
actual possession, it is usual to insert an attornment
clause ; but it is doubtful whether this does not now
bring the security within § 6 of the Bills of Sale Act,
1878,[1] so as to make the attestation and registration
thereby prescribed necessary.[2]

In case freehold and copyhold property form the
security, it will be necessary to prepare a surrender
of the copyhold property, and recite it in the draft
mortgage ; and the covenants for title in this case
will require some slight alteration in order to comprise both tenures. If copyhold property alone be
mortgaged the surrender and also a further deed
will be necessary. The latter will recite the application for the advance, the surrender and the agreement by the mortgagor to enter into the covenants
thereinafter contained. The witnessing part will
contain the covenant for repayment, then will follow
the proviso for redemption, the power of sale in case
of default, and the covenants for title, and if the
security consists of house property, a covenant to
insure. It will be advisable in all cases to have the
draft surrender perused by the steward of the manor

L. R. 13 Eq. 555, 560; but see *Clarke* v. *The Royal Panopticon Society,*
3 Jur. (N. S.) 178; 5 W. R. 332.

[1] 41 & 42 Vict. c. 31.
[2] See *supra*, p. 67.

before it is engrossed, otherwise he may make such alterations as may necessitate a new engrossment; few stewards will tolerate any surrender but such as complies with their accustomed form. After the surrender has been approved by the steward and the mortgagor's solicitor, an appointment must be made with both for all parties to attend at the steward's office to pass the surrender. There will be no necessity, and it is unusual at that time, for the mortgagee to take admittance. He can at any time procure admittance, if he should have occasion to sell the property; and, if he is paid off by the mortgagor, it is only necessary for the mortgagee to sign a warrant to the steward to enter satisfaction on the mortgage, and the mortgagor becomes in the same position as before the mortgage. Whereas, if the mortgagee were admitted tenant at the time of the surrender, there would be the expense of this admittance, and, on the mortgage being paid off the additional expense of another surrender by the mortgagee and the admittance of the mortgagor. In such a case the hardship on the mortgagor is the greater, because the admittance of the mortgagee, at the time of completing the mortgage, does not give him the smallest additional security, and is generally taken through inadvertence. Should it be inconvenient for the mortgagor to surrender personally, his solicitor will procure a power of attorney from him to a third person, usually his solicitor, empowering him to make the surrender; but he should consult the mortgagee's solicitor before this is done, as a mortgagee is not bound to accept a surrender by attorney, although it is not often objected to.

Having engrossed the deed the mortgagee's solicitor will forward the draft and engrossment to the mortgagor's solicitor for examination, and arrange with him for an appointment to complete the matter (the completion of a mortgage being invariably at the office of the mortgagee's solicitor), and then proceed to make the same searches for judgments, &c., and also at the register office (if the property is in a register county) as in the case of a purchase.

He should also ascertain whether any succession duty is payable, and if so and it is not paid, require the mortgagor's solicitor to prepare and pass an account before completion, so that he may hand over the official receipt for the duty, in order that the mortgagee may put it with the title deeds forming his security.

COMPLETION.—At the time appointed the mortgagor will execute the mortgage deed ; and should his wife have been made a party in order to bar her right to dower, she will also execute and acknowledge the deed in the usual manner. After which the mortgagee's solicitor must take especial care to see that all the deeds are handed over to him, for which, if required, he will sign a schedule and acknowledgment by the mortgagee that he holds them in that character (although this is now seldom required), and obtain the amount of his costs from the mortgagor, or, which is usually the case, deduct them from the mortgage money. If the property is in Middlesex or Yorkshire the deed must be registered (unless registered under the Land Transfer

Act, 1875), and if it comprises chattels of any description (except in the case of fixtures, &c., comprised in a mortgage of the freehold), it must be registered under the Bills of Sale Act.

Costs.—The mortgagor pays the whole of the costs—not only those of his own, but also those of the mortgagee's solicitor. Occasionally the mortgagee's solicitor charges a procuration fee for finding the money, but this is not much adopted at the present day ; and it should be borne in mind that if a procuration fee be charged, the preliminary attendances on obtaining the money, satisfying the mortgagee as to the security, &c., and many other items cannot be charged, as they are all covered by the procuration fee. The fairest way is not to charge a procuration fee, but to include in the costs fair charges for the work done ; or to arrange with the mortgagor at the commencement of the negotiations to conduct the business on the scale of charges approved by the Incorporated Law Society.[1]

In acting on behalf of a person having money to advance on mortgage, a solicitor should take care, in cases where he is not also employed by the mortgagor, to obtain the written undertaking of the mortgagor or his solicitor to pay his charges in case the negotiation goes off on a matter of title, or on any other point except the default of his own client ; as, unless he arms himself with this undertaking, he cannot recover his costs from the intended mortgagor, if the mortgage should go off ; and this is practically losing them altogether, as his own client

[1] See Appendix IV., p. 166, *infra*.

will by no means expect to pay them nor care to enforce his rights against the intended mortgagor.[1]

RECONVEYANCE.—When a mortgagor wishes to pay off his mortgage, his solicitor prepares and forwards to the solicitor of the mortgagee a draft of the reconveyance or reassignment for perusal, it being the practice for the mortgagor's solicitor to prepare this draft. The solicitor for the mortgagee will peruse the draft in the usual manner, keep a copy of it and then return it to the mortgagor's solicitor for engrossment, who will afterwards forward the draft and engrossment to the mortgagee's solicitor for examination, or, if the reconveyance or reassignment be by indorsement on the original mortgage (a very common and convenient practice), he will request the latter to engross the document on the mortgage deed (for which he will be entitled to the usual charge of 8d. per folio). The mortgagor's solicitor will then appoint a time for attending to pay the principal and interest money and costs, and take away the deeds.

COSTS ON RECONVEYANCE.—As to a mortgagee's costs on the mortgagor paying off the mortgage, it may be observed that, if in consequence of the death of the mortgagee any additional expense is occasioned, the mortgagor must pay it; but otherwise if the mortgagee has settled the mortgage money.

The mortgagee may during the continuance of the security become lunatic or die, leaving an infant heir,

[1] *Rigley* v. *Daykin*, 2 Y. & J. 83; *Wilkinson* v. *Grant*, 18 C. B. 319; *Pratt* v. *Vizard*, 5 B. & A. 808; 2 N. & M. 455; *Hollis* v. *Claridge*, 4 Taunt. 807.

in which cases great trouble and expense are incurred
in obtaining a reconveyance. If he becomes lunatic
the costs of obtaining a vesting order are paid out of
his estate, but these do not include the costs of
appearance of the mortgagor;[1] but where a mortgagee dies leaving an infant heir, the mortgagor
must bear the costs of all proceedings necessary to
obtain the reconveyance of the legal estate.

SALE BY MORTGAGEE.—If a mortgagee finds it
necessary to exercise the power of sale in his mortgage his solicitor's course of proceeding will be
similar to that pointed out in the chapter on "Sales
of Real Estate:"[2] and after the purchase-money has
been received he will, in the first place, deduct thereout the costs of and incidental to the sale; in the
next place, pay the mortgagee his principal and
interest, and any moneys he may have properly paid
for insurance or otherwise, and the balance will be
paid to the mortgagor. In arriving at this balance,
it should be borne in mind that the mortgagor must
pay the expense of an abortive sale;[3] and also of an
action of ejectment brought by mortgagee to recover
possession, but not the costs of defending an action
of trespass,[4] nor the costs of an unsuccessful action
for specific performance of a contract for sale by the
mortgagee.[5] Should the mortgagee have been served
with a notice by a second mortgagee of the property

---

[1] *Re Wheeler*, 1 D. M. & G. 134; *Hawkins* v. *Perry*, 25 L. J. (Ch.) 656;
Re Phillips, L. R. 4 Ch. 629; *Re Sparks*, 6 Ch. D. 361.

[2] *Ante*, p. 10.

[3] *Sutton* v. *Rawlings*, 3 Ex. 407.

[4] *Owen* v. *Crouch*, 5 W. R. 545.

[5] *Peers* v. *Ceeley*, 15 Beav. 209.

his security must be inspected by the vendor's solicitor, and if it is correct, the balance of purchase-money, or so much thereof as may be required, will be paid to such second mortgagee, and any residue to the mortgagor. In such a case as this, however, it would be the preferable course before parting with the money to the second mortgagee to inform the mortgagor of the intention to do so, and if he assents, or returns no answer to such notice, the payment may be safely made.

When selling under a power of sale in a mortgage which contains no power of giving receipts, § 23 of Lord St. Leonards' Act[1] will probably meet the case, and will be found of great utility. See also § 12 of Lord Cranworth's Act.[2]

In some cases it may happen, that after the sale of the mortgaged property has been completed the mortgagor cannot be found, or he may be dead, and it may not be known who are his representatives, or several claimants may appear, each one requiring the mortgagee to pay the surplus in his hands to him, or he may be living and may have given notice not to pay the surplus to a subsequent mortgagee. In any of these cases, if no satisfactory arrangement can be come to, the better course will be to pay the surplus into Court under the Trustee Relief Acts,[3] and let the claimants satisfy the Court as to their claims. This course is justifiable,[4] and it will have relieved the mortgagee from all responsibility with respect to the money; and he may

---

[1] 22 & 23 Vict. c. 35.
[2] 23 & 24 Vict. c. 145.
[3] 10 & 11 Vict. c. 96, and 12 & 13 Vict. c. 74.
[4] *Roberts* v. *Ball*, 24 L. J. (Ch.) 471.

deduct his charges in the matter out of the fund before paying it into Court, and the costs of his appearance, on the petition to take the money out of Court, will come out of the fund. No undue haste need be shewn by the mortgagee in paying the money into Court under the above Acts, as it has been decided that a mortgagee, selling under a power of sale and retaining the surplus purchase-money unproductive in consequence of disputes between subsequent incumbrancers, is not chargeable with interest on such surplus.[1]

TRANSFERS.—Transfers of mortgages are very frequent. A mortgagee amply secured, and receiving his interest punctually, may require his principal money for some purpose. The mortgagor may wish to continue the mortgage. The requirements of both are met by a transfer. A third party is sought for, and, when found, comes into the matter as transferee, that is, he consents to pay the mortgagee off, and take a transfer of the mortgage security.

A mortgagee can transfer his mortgage either with or without the concurrence of the mortgagor, but in practice the former course is almost invariably adopted; first, because unless the mortgagor is an assenting party to the transfer the costs of it would have to be borne by the mortgagee,[2] and of course under ordinary circumstances, and where his security is ample, he would rather proceed to a sale or foreclosure of the property than be saddled with the expense of a transfer; and secondly, it is always

[1] *Matthison* v. *Clark*, 4 W. R. 30.
[2] *Re Radcliffe*, 27 L. T. 61.

advisable on the part of the transferee that the mortgagor should join in the deed, by which in effect a new mortgage is made from the mortgagor to the transferee with privity between them, and a new covenant for payment of the principal and interest is given.

Where the same solicitor is concerned for all parties in a transfer the matter is very simple. When instructed he will learn whether a further sum is to be advanced to the mortgagor (as is often the case) or not, and will prepare his deed accordingly, make an appointment for the parties to attend at his office, calculate the amount of principal and interest due to the mortgagee, get the deed executed by him and the mortgagor, pay the mortgagee his money and get the amount of his charges from the mortgagor, who, as the business is done for his accommodation, will pay all the attendant expense.

If he acts for the mortgagee but not for the transferee, the solicitor of the latter will probably apply to him for an abstract of the mortgagee's title which, under ordinary circumstances, will be prepared and sent to him ; for though a solicitor is not bound to do so, nor indeed to do any act which possibly might prejudice the security of his client, the abstract is in most instances, with respectable parties, furnished as a matter of course, because it generally happens that a personal interview has taken place ; or the transferee's solicitor, on applying for the abstract, states that his client is about to pay off the first mortgagee.

If and when the solicitor of the transferee is satisfied about the title, he will send the draft transfer to be perused on behalf of the mortgagee and mortgagor, and their solicitor or respective solicitors will accordingly peruse it, with a view of protecting the rights of whoever he or they may be concerned for, have the usual copy to keep made, and return the draft approved (with such alterations, if any, as may be necessary) to the transferee's solicitor, who, when the draft is finally approved, will have it engrossed, and fix an appointment to settle the business at the office of the solicitor to the mortgagee, which the parties will attend, and the matter will be completed. As in the case of a reconveyance it is desirable whenever practicable to engross the transfer on the original mortgage deed.

CHAPTER V.

INTRODUCTORY.—In preparing a lease a solicitor is often required to act on behalf of both parties, *i.e.*, the lessor and lessee ; and this he may with propriety do in cases where the lessor and lessee themselves fix the terms upon which the lease is to be granted, and in cases where the lessee is willing to accept the terms proposed by or on behalf of the lessor. In such cases a solicitor's duty is not of such a conflicting character as it would be were he concerned for a vendor and purchaser, as the lessor very often fixes the terms on which the lease is to be granted, and declines to grant it upon any other terms.

There are, however, many cases where questions are likely to arise between lessor and lessee, and it is scarcely necessary to say that, in such cases, they should be represented by separate solicitors. It will, therefore, be convenient to consider separately the duties incumbent on a solicitor acting for lessor and lessee respectively.

PART I.—DUTIES OF LESSOR'S SOLICITOR.

POWER TO LEASE.—It will be convenient to deal, first, with the duties of a solicitor when professionally concerned for a person about to grant a lease. If the property is very small, or both parties are content to leave the business in the solicitor's hands, there will be no necessity to prepare any formal agreement; but in all other cases a preliminary agreement should be prepared. This agreement should be prepared with care, as sometimes the lessee repents of his bargain before the lease is granted, and will then use every exertion to get out of his contract. It may be useful to mention here the principal points to be attended to.

The first question to be considered is whether the intending lessor has power to grant the lease proposed. If he or she is an owner in fee of freeholds no difficulty will arise, except in the case of an infant or married woman ; but he or she may be a tenant for life or in tail of a settled estate, or a mortgagor, a mortgagee, a copyholder, or only a lessee In all these cases some care will be necessary, and we will proceed to consider them separately.

Infant.—Where an infant is tenant in fee or in tail of real estate, or absolutely entitled to any leasehold estate, the Chancery Division of the High Court of Justice has power to authorize leases of such estate,[1] although the estate may not be a "settled estate" within the meaning of the Settled Estates Act, 1877.[2]

Married Woman.—Where the proposed lessor is a married woman, not entitled for her separate use, and not under any such further disability as to render an application to the Court necessary, her husband

---

[1] 1 Wm. 4, c. 65, s. 17.
[2] 40 & 41 Vict. c. 18.

should concur in the lease, which should be acknowledged pursuant to § 79 of the Fines and Recoveries Act.[1]

Settled Estates.—In the case of a settled estate, the will or settlement should be carefully examined; and if it contains a power of leasing, the lease must of course be in accordance with the power. If it contains no power, resort must be had to the statutory powers conferred by the Settled Estates Act, 1877.[2] If the will or settlement bears a later date than the 1st of November, 1856, the tenant for life can under § 46 grant leases for various terms according to the nature of the lease. Under wills or settlements dated prior to the 1st of November, 1856, a petition to the High Court of Justice will be necessary. § 4 enables the Court to authorize leases of property in settlement upon certain conditions mentioned in that section; and the Court[3] may either approve of particular leases, or make an order vesting powers of leasing either in the existing trustees of the settlement or in any other persons. All applications to the Court under this Act are to be by petition to the Chancery Division.[4] §§ 5 to 15 inclusive of the same Act also contain other provisions as to leases authorized by the Court.[5]

Mortgagor.—Should the property be in mortgage, it must be borne in mind that the mortgagor alone cannot make a lease binding on the mortgagee,[6]

[1] 3 & 4 Wm. 4, c. 74.
[2] 40 & 41 Vict. c. 18.
[3] Sect. 13.
[4] Sect. 23.
[5] See Greenwood's R. P. Stat. pp 162–171.
[6] See *Lows v. Telford*, 1 Ap. Ca. 415.

although in such a case the lease would be binding upon the mortgagor by estoppel; but a lessee claiming under a lease granted by a mortgagor, after the execution of the mortgage, will be protected in paying rent to the mortgagor until he receives notice from the mortgagee to pay the rent to him; and even if he has received such notice, but has not actually paid the rent to the mortgagee, the receipt of such notice will be no answer to an action by the mortgagor for the rent.[1]

Mortgagee.—On the other hand a mortgagee has properly speaking, no power to grant a lease, unless, the mortgage contains a power enabling him to do so; but if the lease granted by him be a beneficial one to the estate and for an ordinary term, and such as a prudent man would grant if the property were his own, it would probably be supported in equity; and one should not hesitate in advising a mortgagee to adopt this course if it were the only one by which he could make the property productive. If the mortgage contains an express power enabling the mortgagee to grant leases, it will only be necessary to see whether the lease proposed to be granted is within the terms of the power. It is very seldom this power is found in mortgages of small properties; but in a mortgage of a large property it should never be omitted.

The proper course, in the absence of an express power, is to make both the mortgagor and mortgagee parties to the lease. The mortgagee by direction of the mortgagor will demise, and the mortgagor will demise and confirm the property to the lessee. The

---

[1] *Wilton* v. *Dunn*, 17 Q. B. 294.

rent will be reserved generally in this form : " Yielding and paying therefor yearly during the said term the rent of £——," as the law will carry the rent to the party for the time being entitled to the property, it being unnecessary to mention in the reddendum the name of the person to whom the rent is to be paid. Sometimes a proviso is inserted that the rent may be paid to the mortgagor until the lessee shall receive notice requiring him to pay it to the mortgagee.

Copyholds.—With respect to copyhold property it will, as a rule, be necessary to obtain a licence from the lord of the manor before the lease is executed, as the grant of a lease by a copyhold tenant, without previously obtaining a licence from the lord of the manor, may be a forfeiture of the copyhold. In this case, it will only be necessary to write to the steward of the manor for a licence, informing him of the names of the parties, the property to be demised, and the term to be granted, and he will forward a licence to grant the lease, for which he will charge a fee, and a small fine will also generally become payable to the lord. These fines and fees, if not otherwise provided for by the agreement, must be paid by the lessor.

A licence to demise for more than a year is necessary in most cases ; but there are a few exceptions : for instance, in the manor of Highbury, in the county of Middlesex, a copyholder may grant a lease for twenty-one years without licence ;[1] and in the manors of Stepney and Hackney a copyholder may grant a lease for thirty-one years and four months in pos-

---

[1] *Rawstone v. Bentley*, 4 Bro C. C. 415.

session without a licence, so that the lease be presented to the homage, and entered on the court rolls at the first or second court after making it.[1]

Leaseholds.—A lessee can, of course, only grant an underlease; and, for his own protection, it must be granted upon terms similar to those upon which he holds the property.

PREPARATION OF AGREEMENT.—In cases where an agreement is necessary it must contain the terms on which the lease is to be granted, and in preparing an agreement of this nature, general words or expressions should not be used. The agreement is prepared by the lessor's solicitor, who must, if acting for a limited owner, take care to insert all necessary restrictions, and if not, make particular inquiry of his client whether the lessee is to be restricted from carrying on any particular trades or businesses, or any trade or business at all on the premises, whether he is to be restricted from having any sale of household furniture or other things thereon, whether he is to be restricted from assigning or parting with the lease or the possession of the premises for the whole or any part of the term, without the licence of the lessor, and also as to any other special covenants it may be necessary to insert, as all these should be concisely mentioned in the agreement. All this may be done, and the agreement still comprised within reasonable limits.

Where the agreement is for an underlease, the best course will be to read the covenants in the original lease to the person intending to take such

---

[1] Scriven on Copyholds, 5th ed., p. 330.

underlease, and then express in the agreement that
the underlease is to contain similar covenants to those
in the lease under which the lessor holds the property; and it may be advisable to state in the agreement that such lease has been previously read over
to the lessee, after which it will only be necessary to
state shortly what other covenants (if any) are to be
inserted.

With respect to the production of the lessor's
title, where the agreement is silent as to it, the lessor
need not now, if a freeholder, produce his title.[1] But
where the lessor is not a freeholder the result of the
decisions appears to be that, though the lessee could
not compel its production, he could recover damages
for breach of contract;[2] and the lessor could not, if
he refused to furnish his title, enforce specific performance of the contract to take the lease. In such
cases, therefore, the right to production or investigation of the lessor's title should be expressly ne-
gatived.

Should the intended lease be for building purposes,
it will be necessary to insert stipulations as to making
roads, sewers, pavements, &c., and for the lessee's
fencing off the demised land from the other land of
the lessor within a given time. If, on the other
hand, it is an agricultural lease, or a lease of a house
with farming land attached, it will be necessary to
state in the agreement the manner in which the
lessee is to use the land, and also as to the state of
of cultivation, &c. ; but whatever may be the nature
of the property, care should be taken, unless the

---

[1] Vendor and Purchaser Act, 1874 (37 & 38 Vict. c. 78, s. 2).
[2] *Stranks* v. *St. John*, L. R. 2 C. P. 376.

parties agree to the contrary, to stipulate in the agreement that the lessee shall pay the land tax, sewers rate, tithes, or rent-charges in lieu of tithes, and all other rates, taxes, charges, and assessments whatsoever, as, if this be omitted, the lessee may possibly, and in some cases successfully, resist being made liable to the payment of the three first-mentioned charges. As to whether he is bound to pay land-tax and sewers rate without express mention will depend altogether on the wording of the agreement. The cases on this point are collected and commented on in Woodfall's 'Landlord and Tenant';[1] Unless the lessee binds himself expressly to pay tithes, or the rent-charge in lieu thereof, the lessor probably could not compel him to pay it, but the safest course is to express concisely in the agreement what the lessee is and what he is not to do, and to leave as little as possible to be gathered from inference or implication. A clause should also be inserted that the lease and a counterpart thereof shall be prepared and engrossed by the lessor's solicitor, and that the expenses thereof and also of the agreement shall be paid by the lessee. This will prevent the lessee's solicitor from claiming to engross the counterpart.

The agreement being prepared, the lessor's solicitor will make a fair copy thereof and forward it to the solicitor of the lessee for perusal, he will return it approved, and either with or without having altered it. When it has been finally settled, it will be engrossed, executed in duplicate, and exchanged, as pointed out in the chapter on " Agreements."[2]

[1] Pages 529–534.   [2] Ante, p. 8.

PREPARATION OF LEASE. —The agreement having
been exchanged, the lessor's solicitor will proceed to
prepare the draft lease, the stipulations to be inserted
in which will be regulated by the agreement previously entered into. These stipulations, however,
will have to be clothed in appropriate and legal
language as concisely but as clearly as practicable.
Should the lease be of a house, there will be little
difficulty in preparing the draft, as the covenants
generally entered into by the lessee are to pay rent,
rates, and taxes (specifying land tax, sewers rates,
and tithes, or rent-charges in lieu thereof, if any), to
repair and keep in repair during, and to yield up in
good repair at the end of the term, to insure, not to
carry on certain particular trades, or any trade or
business of any description on the premises; not to
assign or part with the possession of the premises
without the license of the lessor, and any other special
stipulations that it may be considered necessary or
advisable to insert. If the lease is of agricultural or
mining property or of manufacturing premises, the
covenants will be of an entirely different nature.
The forms given in this volume will furnish a guide
for leases of this description of property, but it will
not be safe to rely entirely on them in every case, as
both in agricultural and mining districts the customs
vary considerably, and that which in one county
would be a very appropriate form of lease, would in
another be quite the contrary; and although the
agreement (if any) may be decisive as to the nature
of the covenants and stipulations to be inserted, it
will afford no information as to carrying it into effect
in a business-like and creditable manner.

A lease is sometimes granted under a power, in which case the power may be recited or the lease prepared in the common form. It is of little importance which course is adopted, although, if the lease is a valuable one or of extensive property, it is usual to shortly recite the power and make the lessor demise, &c. (following the words of the power), in pursuance thereof; but, in any case, the conditions under which the person empowered to grant the lease is enabled to do so, must be strictly complied with.

COVENANTS.—Should the agreement express that the lease is to contain ordinary covenants, or, which is much the same thing, be silent as to the covenants to be inserted, then it is advisable only to insert the ordinary covenants, as the lessee's solicitor will be sure to object to any others being inserted. The usual covenants are to pay rent, rates and taxes (except land tax, sewers rate, and tithes or rent-charge in lieu of tithes), to repair during the term, and to yield up the premises in good repair at the end of the term, that the lessor may from time to time during the term enter on the premises to view the state of repairs thereof, and that the lessee will repair within a given time (usually three months after notice). Also a covenant by the lessor for quiet enjoyment.[1] Whether the agreement be to grant a lease to contain "ordinary" covenants or "usual" covenants, or contains no mention of covenants, or the agreement be only verbal, the above are the covenants that the lessor could insist upon. In a

---

[1] See Davidson, vol. v. part i. p. 53.

lease of agricultural property, granted under such an agreement, the covenants would be those usually inserted in leases of similar property in the neighbourhood, and probably even with respect to the lease of a house, to be granted under such circumstances, the locality would to a certain extent be taken into consideration, and a covenant not to use the premises as a shop, or to carry on any trade or business, would be considered a usual covenant in a lease of a house in one of the principal residential streets at the west end of London, though not in a trading street. But it is clear the lessor could not require the lessee to enter into a covenant to insure the premises or not to assign or underlet without license, or to contribute towards planting and keeping in condition any inclosed piece of ground, or covenants of a similar nature.

COMPLETION.—Having prepared the draft lease, the lessor's solicitor will make a fair copy of it; and send it to the solicitor of the lessee for perusal. He will return it, and if no alterations are made, or none that can fairly be objected to, the next step will be to engross the lease. Sometimes a long correspondence and several interviews take place before the draft lease is finally settled.

The draft lease having been engrossed, together with a counterpart thereof, the draft and engrossments must be forwarded to the lessee's solicitor; but if there is no agreement, or if it is silent as to who is to engross the counterpart, the lessee's solicitor may claim to do this, although it is not usually done.

After comparing the engrossment with the draft

lease, the lessee's solicitor will return it for execution by the lessor; and if he has engrossed the counterpart, he will forward such engrossment at the same time, in which case it must be compared with the draft, and returned to him for execution by the lessee. The lessor's solicitor's costs relating to the transaction should be forwarded to the lessee's solicitor about this time, in order that he may have an opportunity of examining them, and, if necessary, obtain the amount of his client. After the execution of the lease by the lessor, his solicitor will make an appointment with the lessee's solicitor for the completion of the matter at the office of the former. At this meeting, the lease will be exchanged for the counterpart, after having seen that it is duly executed and attested. The lessee's solicitor will pay the costs, and the matter will be completed.

Costs.—The costs of the lease, as well on the part of the lessor as the lessee, must be paid by the latter, unless there is an agreement to the contrary; but the costs of the lessor's solicitor, respecting the negotiations for granting the lease, or, in the case of copyhold property, the steward's fees for granting a licence to demise, do not form any part of these costs. As against the lessee, the costs of the lessor's solicitor should, in the absence of any agreement to the contrary, commence with "instructions for lease," and include all the costs incurred by the lessor in respect of the lease, up to the completion of the matter. If a plan is made and referred to in the lease, the lessee must pay the costs of it. In some cases a special agreement is made for the lessor and lessee to pay the costs in equal shares : and this is by no means an unfair arrangement.

PART II.—DUTIES OF LESSEE'S SOLICITOR.

PERUSING DRAFT LEASE.—We will now consider the duties of a solicitor who has received instructions to peruse a draft lease on behalf of an intended lessee. The draft lease is always prepared by the solicitor of the lessor, and he forwards it to the solicitor of the lessee for perusal. On receiving the draft, the latter should, as acting for the lessee (unless already satisfied that the premises, the rent, the duration of the lease, and the covenants are according to the instructions received from his client), make an appointment with him for reading through the draft; or, if he lives at a distance, send it to him for perusal. In either case his solicitor should call his attention to any covenants or stipulations he may think objectionable, and inform him whether they can be insisted on by the lessor, and take his instructions accordingly. The first thing his attention will be directed to is to see that the premises are correctly described and that the covenants are not of a nature calculated to interfere with the full enjoyment of the property by the lessee, although in the majority of cases he will not be able to do more than obtain some slight modification of any objectionable covenants, and in others he will not be able to obtain any modification at all : it may happen that the person granting the lease is himself a lessee, in which case, as a matter of course, all the covenants and stipulations under which he holds the property will be repeated in the lease he is granting. In other cases the only course will be to turn to the written agreement, if there is any between the parties ; and should no agreement have been entered into, it will be for the lessee, if his solicitor is unsuccessful in obtaining a modification of the objectionable covenants, to elect whether or not he will take the lease ; and in assisting him to make his election the nature and probable operation of the covenants in question should be fully explained to him. If, however, the parties have entered into a prior binding agreement, then the terms of such agreement must be carried out, as the lessor will be able to enforce specific performance of it.

COVENANTS.—The covenant frequently inserted in leases prohibiting the lessee from assigning or underletting or parting with the possession of the premises for the whole or any part of the term, without the written consent of the lessor, is very objectionable, and seriously affects the marketable value of the property. This covenant is unreasonable, inasmuch as its tendency is to restrain the lessee in the enjoyment of the property and the free alienation thereof, and ought never to be consented to in a lease of ground intended to be built upon. Take the case of a man having a field which other persons wish to erect buildings upon ; this is neither more nor less than a sale of the property for so many years under certain conditions ; but, instead of receiving the consideration money at once, the lessor prefers to reserve a yearly payment, and the understanding implied between the parties always is, that the one shall give

up possession of the land to the other for a certain
term at a ground rent in consideration of such other
erecting buildings on the land and consenting to
certain stipulations, the breach of any one of which
will enable the lessor to recover possession of the
property. The lessee ought to be unfettered as to
his enjoyment of the property and the free disposal
of it, and it is unfair on the part of the lessor to
insist on the lessee obtaining his sanction before he
can deal with it. It is clear that, by the erection of
a house or other building on the land, the lessor is
always sure of his ground rent, which bears but
a small proportion to the annual value of the property; and the covenants in the lease will always
enable the lessor to insist on the premises being kept
in good repair and free from damage by fire, in
order that at the end of the term he may enjoy the
benefit of the outlay of the lessee : and the original
lessee remains liable on the covenants, even after he
has assigned.

That is all that a lessor ought to ask for : but even
should he wish to go a step further, the extent should
be to require the lessee or assignee to furnish him
with a copy of every assignment, within a given
time after its execution, or, which is better still,
to furnish the lessor with the date of the assignment
and the name and address of the assignee, so that he
may know from time to time who is the tenant of the
property. This is not an unreasonable request, and
it leaves the lessee in the full, unrestrained enjoyment of the property.

If, however, the covenant not to assign be inserted,
a proviso should be added at the end of it that the

consent of the lessor to any assignment or underlease shall not be capriciously or unreasonably withheld, nor withheld at all to a responsible assignee, and this is the next best step to obtaining the total omission of the covenant.

In some cases the solicitor to the lessor will insert a covenant that all assignments and underleases shall be prepared by him. This is a most unfair and unjust covenant, inasmuch as it does not in any way add to the security of the lessor, and the only effect of its insertion is to put costs in the solicitor's pocket. It is not very often, however, at the present day, that such a covenant as this is inserted; but where it is inserted it is binding, and a breach of it would cause a forfeiture of the lease. It is, however, generally found that the lessor's solicitor waives his right to the preparation of the deed on receiving a fee of two or three guineas. A more reasonable covenant in the case of a large estate is that every assignment and underlease shall be registered or docketed at the office of the lessor's solicitor, so that he may always know who is the occupier of every house.

Where the lessor is a copyholder it will be advisable for the lessee's solicitor to inquire what interest the lord has in the manor, because should he only have a partial interest, *i.e.*, be tenant for life without express power to grant licences to demise, the licence by him will only exist so long as his interest exists; for instance, if the lord be a tenant for life without power to grant licences to demise, and he should grant a licence to demise for twenty-one years, and live only seven years after the date of the lease, it will be necessary to obtain a new licence from the remainderman on his coming into possession. As to this see § 9 of the Settled Estates Act, 1877.[1]

If the lease in question is of coal or iron mines, the lessee's solicitor will, unless there is an express stipulation to the contrary, be careful in inserting a provision for cesser of rent, in case the mine is exhausted, or becomes unworkable during the term. This is not an unfrequent case. The lessee may have formed an erroneous opinion as to the quantity of coal or ironstone or other mineral to be obtained, or the mine may become filled with water, and this may arise from various causes, or become otherwise unworkable. Now, in leases of this description of property, there is invariably a minimum rent reserved, and the ordinary reddendum clause would bind the lessee to pay such rent, notwithstanding the mines had become exhausted or unworkable until the expiration of the term granted by the lease; and this would be so, although the lessee could establish his inability to reap one farthing's benefit from the mine. A case has come under the writer's notice, where a person who took a lease of a colliery as trustee for persons who afterwards abandoned it, was compelled to pay a minimum rent of more than £1000 a year. This is a matter of such a serious nature in mining leases, that it excites one's surprise how professional men residing in the neighbourhood and advising the lessee, can omit to provide for it; but that such omission very frequently takes place, is proved by many cases, both reported and unreported.[2]

[1] 40 & 41 Vict. c. 57.
[2] *Clifford* v. *Watts*, L. R. 5 C. P. 577, 587; *Rex* v. *Bedworth*, 8 East, 387; *Mellers* v. *Devonshire*, 16 Beav. 252; *Ridgway* v. *Sneyd*, K. 627.

The proviso to be inserted on the part of the lessee should be to the effect, that in case the mine should become exhausted or unworkable at a profit to the lessee, at any time during the term, he should have power to determine the lease on giving six months' notice to the lessor of his desire to do so.

COUNTERPART—*Engrossment.*— Having perused the lease and made such alterations as are necessary or advisable, it must be returned to the lessor's solicitor, and after the draft is finally approved of, he will engross it and forward it to the lessee's solicitor for examination ; but, unless so expressed in the agreement (if any), the lessor cannot require a counterpart of the lease to be executed at the expense of the lessee : he may require the lessee to execute a counterpart, but it must be at his own expense, and if the agreement states that the lease is to be prepared by the lessor's solicitor, and that the lessee shall execute a counterpart thereof, and pay the costs of the lease and counterpart, then, although it is not always the practice to do so, the lessee's solicitor is entitled to engross the counterpart of the lease, and forward it to the lessor's solicitor for examination ; as although the latter prepares the lease as a matter of right, yet, so long as the counterpart is executed by the lessee and handed to the lessor, he gets what the agreement binds the lessee to give him. If this course is adopted the counterpart can be engrossed from the lessee's copy of the draft lease, but notice ought in fairness to be given to the lessor's solicitor of the intention of the lessee's solicitor to engross the counterpart, on returning to him the draft lease.

COMPLETION.—With respect to the completion of the matter, a meeting may be arranged with the lessor and lessee at the office of the solicitor for the former, or the lease and counterpart may be previously executed, and an appointment made by the solicitors for exchanging the counterpart for the lease. The latter is the more usual course.

On exchanging the lease and counterpart it should be seen that the lease is properly executed and attested, and, in the case of a house or other buildings, the keys should be handed to the lessee unless possession has been previously given. It is also usual to pay to the lessor's solicitor the amount of his charges, a bill of which should have been previously delivered. The better plan is to request him to send his costs at the same time that he forwards the engrossment of the lease, in order to enable them to be examined before the appointment for completing the matter, as, in case the lessor and lessee are present at the completion, it is unpleasant to have any dispute about the charges, notwithstanding the lessee's solicitor may feel it necessary to perform his duty in objecting to some of the items in the bill of costs.

REGISTRATION.—If the lease comprises property in Middlesex or Yorkshire, but does not exceed twenty-one years, the lessee being the actual occupier, or reserves a rackrent (*i.e.*, the full annual value of the premises), it will not require registering; but if for more than twenty-one years, in cases where the occupation does not go with the lease, or when the rent is less than the full annual value, as in the case of building leases, it must be registered. A lease, con-

veyance, or assignment of property situate in the
city of London or any of the Inns of Court does
not require to be registered, these places not being
within the scope of the Act establishing the registry
for the county of Middlesex. By the Land Transfer
Act, 1875, no document relating to any land in
Middlesex or Yorkshire which is registered under
that Act need be registered in the local registries.

It is no part of the duty of the lessor's solicitor to
register the lease; the registration or putting it on
record is for the lessee's security, and it cannot by
any means benefit or injure the lessor, whether registered or not. In this case, therefore, the lessee's solicitor will prepare a memorial of the lease, and get it
signed by his client, at the same time putting an
extra seal on and obtaining the execution of the lease
by him. But if an intimation has been given that
the lessor will be present at the time of completing
the matter, a memorial of the lease can be executed
by him, and this will avoid the necessity of the lease
being executed by the lessee. The memorial must
be attested by two witnesses, one of whom must be an
attesting witness to the execution of the lease.

STAMPS.—Where there has been an agreement
in writing for a lease such agreement should be
stamped as a lease; and the lease will, then, only require a 6d. stamp. See § 96 of the Stamp Act, 1870.[1]
In other cases, the lease must bear an *ad valorem*
stamp which varies according to the term and the
rent. On leases for less than thirty-five years, the
stamp duty is 6d. for every £5 of rent up to £100,

[1] 33 & 34 Vict. c. 97.

and afterwards 5*s.* for every additional £50. For terms between thirty-five and one hundred years the duty is 3*s.* for every £5 up to £100, and then 30*s.* for every additional £50; while for terms exceeding 100 years, the duty is doubled, being 6*s.* for every £5 up to £100 and £3 for every £50 beyond.

With regard to leases for less than a year it should be borne in mind that on leases of houses at a rent not exceeding £10 the stamp duty is only 1*d.*, while on leases of furnished houses at a rent exceeding £25 the duty is 2*s.* 6*d.* For this, adhesive stamps may be used if cancelled by the person who first signs.[1]

---

[1] 33 & 34 Vict. c. 97.

CHAPTER VI.

COPYHOLD TENURE.—It appears somewhat like an anomaly in the latter half of the nineteenth century to find that there is property in this country which is neither freehold nor leasehold, nor transferable direct from one party to another, but by the medium of a gentleman called a steward (usually the family solicitor of the lord of the manor), that such property is held by the purchaser by the tenure of a rod at the will of the lord according to the custom of the manor, and that the usual mode of transfer is by means of a surrender to the steward in this wise :— The vendor and purchaser and their respective solicitors meet together at the office of the steward of the manor, when the following ludicrous scene takes place :—The vendor takes in his hand a ruler, or a walking-stick, or an umbrella, and repeats after the steward, " I, A. B., in consideration of, &c., surrender such and such property (naming it) to the lord of the manor to the use of C. D., in token whereof I deliver you this rod," whereupon he gravely hands to the steward the walking-stick or umbrella. It is now the steward's duty to take the active part, and accordingly he says to the purchaser (holding out, as he speaks, the walking-stick or umbrella), " I, E. F., in the name of the lord of the manor, do admit you, C. D., tenant of such and such property, this day surrendered to your use by A. B., in token whereof I deliver you this rod," and accordingly he hands the umbrella or walking-stick to the purchaser, who *ipso facto* becomes seised in fee, according to the custom of the manor, of the property he has bought. The purchaser thinks all this uncommonly droll, and rather likes it than otherwise; but his eyes presently become very considerably opened—he wants to grant a lease of the whole or a portion of the property, or to cut timber growing upon, or dig valuable mines which may lie under his property; but if he were rash enough to do this without first obtaining the consent of the lord of the manor and paying certain fines and fees, his property would in most cases be absolutely forfeited to the lord, who could eject him therefrom as easily as a lessor could eject a lessee for breach of covenant. Or, supposing the purchaser does not think fit to lay out his money in keeping his property in repair, but prefers to let it remain out of repair, it is also a cause of forfeiture, and the lord of the manor may seize it. The more the copyholder expends upon his property the greater the benefit to the lord; for instance, a piece of land in a manor where the fine is arbitrary may be worth 20s. per annum; in this case, on admittance, the lord of the manor at the utmost could demand as a fine the sum of 2l. Upon this land, the copyholder may erect buildings worth 100l. per annum. Immediately after he finds that if he sells the property the purchaser must pay on admittance, or, if he dies without having sold the property, his heir or devisee must pay on admittance, to the lord of the manor 200*l.* instead of 2*l.* as before, and that, not because of any exertions or outlay on the part of the lord, but solely because of the exertions and expense of the owner of the property. Such a tenure, to say the least of it, savours greatly of absurdity, and it is astonishing, in these days of general progress to find its existence; it should, so far as this country is concerned, have disappeared with the mammoth and the elk.

Although many Acts have been passed of late years to facilitate the extinction of copyhold tenure, there is still much copyhold property in this country, the practice respecting which, although by no means difficult to master, is less understood than that relating to any other branch of conveyancing. As there can be no doubt that for some years to come a knowledge of this practice will be necessary, the following remarks may prove useful :—

PURCHASE.—Suppose that a client has purchased an estate of copyhold tenure, it is of no consequence for the present purpose whether he has purchased by public auction or private contract: on receiving the abstract, his solicitor will perceive what manor the property is part of; and on afterwards examining the abstract of title with the copies of court roll, at the office of the vendor's solicitor, in the usual manner, he will learn from those copies the name of the steward of the manor.

Searches.—It will be necessary to make an appointment with the steward, to compare the abstract with the court rolls, *i.e.,* to search the court rolls, in order to discover whether the abstract contains particulars of every act that has been done respecting the title since the period of its commencement on the abstract. This is of equal importance to that of searching at the register office, on the purchase of an estate situate in a register county, as the court rolls are the only means of discovering what dealings have taken place respecting the property in question. If on searching the rolls it appears that the property has been dealt with in any manner inconsistent with the abstract of title, such inconsistency must be pointed out to the vendor's solicitor, and he should be required to amend the abstract accordingly.

PURCHASE—*Inquiries.*—Having finished the examination of the court rolls, it will probably be found necessary to make inquiries of the steward respecting the customs of the manor. For instance, the abstract may shew that A. B. was admitted tenant as heir of C. D., or that a recovery has been suffered, or a surrender made and admission taken thereon, in order to bar a recovery. Now, in any of these cases, it will depend on the custom of the manor whether or not a good title be shewn. In the first-mentioned case inquiry must be made of the steward as to the usual course of descent in the manor, whether according to the common law or otherwise, for in some manors the eldest son is heir, in others the youngest, following the custom of lands of borough English tenure. Sometimes the custom carries the property to the second son, and sometimes to all the sons according to the custom of gavelkind. It is manifestly, therefore, of great importance to make these inquiries of the steward, as the title may depend upon a particular person being properly admitted: for, although the eldest son may have been admitted as heir-at-law, yet if, according to the custom of the manor, the youngest or second son is the heir, such admittance gives no title to the eldest son; it is simply of no force whatever. In the cases secondly mentioned, *viz.*, the barring of an entail, it will be necessary to inquire of the steward whether it has been perfected according to the custom of the manor. In some manors a recovery was formerly suffered at the copyhold court in precisely the same manner as in the superior courts, while in others an entail was barred by forfeiture and re-grant, or by a new surrender and admittance; and in any dealing with copyhold property, and any question arising on the title to it, before the Fines and Recoveries Act[1] came into operation, it will still be necessary to make these inquiries.

Since the above Act, legal estates tail in copyholds can be barred only by surrender, but equitable estates tail may be barred either by surrender or deed.[2] The provisions with respect to the protector apply to copyholds, and the consent of the protector may be given by deed entered on the court rolls of the manor, or personally to the person taking the surrender of the tenant in tail.[3]

Should an equitable tenant in tail bar the entail by deed, such deed must be entered on the court rolls of the manor, but need not be enrolled in Chancery.[4]

It is not uncommon for a purchaser's solicitor to

[1] 3 & 4 Wm. 4, c. 74.
[2] Sect. 50.
[3] Sects. 51, 52.
[4] Sects. 53, 54.

refrain from making these inquiries, under the impression that the steward would always have taken care to see that the right person was admitted; but this is by no means the case, as it must be remembered that the steward is bound to admit any person shewing a colourable title; and in some few manors it is the custom to admit any person who will pay the fine and fees, the steward knowing that the mere fact of admission gives no title whatever. The proper and safer course is to make these inquiries of the steward. There is yet a further inquiry to be made, and that is as to freebench, which corresponds in copyhold tenure to dower in freehold tenure. This only arises by special custom, and varies in different manors. You should learn whether the widow of a copyholder can claim dower out of land of which the husband was seised at any time during the coverture, or only out of land of which he died seised. This freebench is a serious matter, as in most manors it entitles the wife to one-half, and in others to the whole estate during her life.

PURCHASE—*Requisitions.*—These preliminary inquiries having been satisfactorily disposed of, the requisitions on the title (if any) should be forwarded to the vendor's solicitor, and the proceedings thereon will be much the same as on a purchase of any other description of property.

The inaccuracy of the description of property on the court rolls is so well known, that, even in the absence of any stipulation as to identity, a vendor cannot be required to identify the property contracted to be sold with the description of it on the court rolls, but he must shew that the property has been actually held under such a description.[1] But where freehold and copyhold property are sold together, the purchaser can require the vendor to distinguish the boundaries of the copyhold land, and to state which part is freehold and which copyhold, unless there is a stipulation to the contrary.[2] If, therefore, a solicitor is intrusted by a client to sell freehold and copyhold property, which have been held together for a long period, he should insert a stipulation restricting the purchaser's right to have the boundaries of each distinguished.

While on this subject it may be useful to call attention to the importance of having all the copies of court rolls (which are, in fact, the copyholder's title deeds) satisfactorily accounted for. It sometimes happens that the vendor has not all the copies of court rolls in his possession, and can give no account of their absence; in such a case it will be prudent to decline completing the matter until a satisfactory explanation has been given of the missing copies; for, should they have been deposited as security for an advance of money, it would make a good equitable mortgage.[3] If the vendor cannot account for the copies of court rolls not being in his possession, and the purchaser has no notice of their having been deposited, and nothing appears on the court rolls in the nature of a charge on the property, and after making every inquiry a prudent man ought to make, nothing is discovered to lead to the

[1] *Long* v. *Collier*, 4 Russ. 267.

[2] *Cross* v. *Lawrence*, 9 Hare, 462; *Dawson* v. *Brinkman*, 3 Mac. & G. 53; 3 De G. & S. 385.

[3] *Whitbread* v. *Jordan*, 1 Y. & C. 301.

supposition that they have been deposited by way of
security, the purchaser would probably be safe in
completing the matter. The circumstances of every
case of this nature must influence the advice given
to the purchaser and his course of action. Should
the vendor have been in possession for some years,
and be a responsible man, or if the earlier part only
of the copies of court rolls are missing, there cannot
be much risk in completing. It may sometimes
happen that the missing copies are with the steward,
for there are few stewards who have not in their
possession many copies of court rolls which have
never been asked for, and doubtless many purchases
have been completed without any inquiry, or, if any
inquiry has been made, without any satisfactory
explanation as to the custody of the missing copies.
This is, however, a matter of much more importance
than it is sometimes thought, and it is wise always
to keep on the safe side with respect to these copies
of court rolls.

PURCHASE—*Conveyance.*—The purchase will proceed in much the same manner as a purchase of any
other description of property ; but as soon as the
time arrives for the preparation of the necessary
assurances for carrying the contract into effect, a
widely different course of practice becomes necessary.
Instead of preparing a draft conveyance or assignment, a draft surrender will be necessary—a surrender being the only instrument that has any
operation on copyhold property—and as a surrender
cannot contain any covenants or other stipulations in
the nature of covenants, it is usual to prepare a deed
to bear even date with the surrender, containing, in

the case of a sale, the usual recitals and vendor's covenants for title, and in the case of a mortgage the recitals, mortgagor's covenants for title, &c., and power of sale; and this is the most proper course, the surrender being nothing more than an instrument whereby the vendor or mortgagor divests himself of the legal estate in the property, and the use limited by the surrender is the direction to the lord of the manor to admit the person in whose favour the surrender is made.

With respect to copyhold property settled on a marriage or otherwise, the court rolls seldom shew anything more than a surrender, by A. to B., and B.'s admittance. The trusts on which the property are to be held, and the numerous provisions usually contained in settlements, are generally declared by a separate document. Many stewards of manors will not allow any trusts whatever to appear in the surrender; others are not so strict. It is, however, not usual to declare the trusts in the surrender, but by means of a separate document.

The customs in many manors authorize the steward to charge for preparing the surrender, notwithstanding the purchaser's solicitor may have prepared it himself, and this has been decided to be a reasonable custom. Knowing this, some practitioners send instructions to the steward to prepare the surrender, instead of preparing it themselves; but the better plan is for the purchaser's solicitor to prepare it himself as, having the abstract before him, he knows more about the parties necessary to concur in the surrender than the steward. He may also think it advisable to have a new description of the property;

but in this case the steward will invariably insist on the old description appearing on the surrender as well as the new one, and considering the loose description of property found on the court rolls, there can be no doubt that, unless the old description appears as well as the new one, it would be almost impossible on a subsequent sale to identify the one with the other.

Where freehold and copyhold property are purchased together, the freehold portion will be conveyed in the same manner as in an ordinary case, and the only difference in the form of the draft will be that the surrender must be recited and the covenants made to extend to both descriptions of property, and in this case the Stamp Act requires the apportionment of the *ad valorem* duty on the purchase-money : for instance, if freehold and copyhold property are purchased for £1000, so much must be apportioned for the freehold and so much for the copyhold, and the conveyance and surrender stamped accordingly. This apportionment may be made in any manner the purchaser thinks fit.

It was formerly the practice to execute the deed of covenant, as it is generally called, first, whereby the vendor or mortgagor covenanted to surrender the property at the next copyhold court or out of court; but as surrenders are now much more frequently passed out of court than in court, the usual and more correct course is to pass the surrender first, and to recite it in the deed bearing even date, as in this latter case the covenants run with the land; but it is doubtful if they would do so in the former case, in consequence of the legal estate not being vested in the covenantee at the time the deed of covenant was executed.

When the drafts of the surrender and deed of covenant are prepared, they must be fair copied and forwarded to the vendor's or mortgagor's solicitor in the usual manner; but after he has returned the draft surrender approved, it will be advisable, unless it has been prepared by the steward of the manor, to forward it to him for his approval, as some stewards are very particular with respect to the form of surrender they adopt; and as a steward is not compelled to take a surrender in a form materially different from the one usually followed in the manor, some delay may be occasioned. The form of surrender, however, is similar in most manors.

Should the steward approve of the draft surrender, he will return it to the purchaser's solicitor for engrossment, and he will engross it and the deed of covenants, and forward them to the vendor's solicitor for examination, and the latter will then make an appointment with the steward to take the surrender. This appointment should be at the steward's office, but, if more convenient to be taken elsewhere, he will seldom insist on its being taken at his office, as the extra fee charged by him for the attendance elsewhere will compensate him for his trouble.

PURCHASE—*Completion.*—An appointment having been made with the steward for taking the surrender, either at his office or elsewhere, the purchaser's solicitor will make the usual searches as to judgments, &c., and inquire as to succession duty (if any) payable, and if all be satisfactory, will, either with or without his

I

client according to circumstances, attend the place of completion. The vendor will either personally or by attorney (although a purchaser is not obliged to accept a surrender by attorney) surrender the property into the hands of the lord of the manor, by the acceptance of his steward, and pay all arrears of quit rent up to the time of passing the surrender, or such other time (if any) as may be named in the contract or conditions of sale; also all rates, taxes, and other outgoings, in the same manner as on the completion of a conveyance. This completes the business on the vendor's part, and it now only remains for the purchaser to take admittance to the property surrendered to his use.

It may be useful to mention here, that in cases where the steward lives at a distance from the place where the matter is to be completed, it is usual to write to him for a deputation to take the surrender. On giving him short particulars of the property, with the names of the vendor and purchaser, he will forward to the purchaser's or vendor's solicitor the deputation, which merely consists of a letter authorizing one of them to take the surrender. It does not require any stamp or other formality. For this deputation the vendor must pay, as it is usually obtained for his convenience. The usual fee is one guinea.

After the surrender has been perfected, the steward will take it with him; or, should it have been taken by deputation, it must be forwarded to him, in order that he may enter it on the court rolls. It is the best plan on all these occasions to ask the steward whether it is his practice to keep the surrender. It is the practice to do so in nineteen manors out of twenty, but there are stewards who do not. It is not of much practical importance whether he does so or not, as he will forward to the purchaser's solicitor a copy of the entry on the court roll, which is sufficient evidence of the transaction. If an admittance has taken place on the surrender, the copy of court roll will comprise both the surrender and admittance. It is the practice to pay the steward's fees at the time of passing the surrender, and, unless there is an express agreement to the contrary, the purchaser always pays for both the surrender and admittance, as the two together form the conveyance of the property.

PURCHASE—*Admittance.*—The admittance may be taken either at the time of passing the surrender (if the surrender is taken by the steward) or at any time afterwards, and either at a copyhold court or anywhere else. If the purchaser is not present at the completion, his solicitor can take admittance as his attorney without any power of attorney or authority from him. After the admittance, which simply consists in the steward handing a rule or stick, or some other symbol, accompanied by these or similar words—" The lord of this manor, by me his steward, admits you tenant to the premises this day surrendered to your use by A. B., in token whereof I deliver you this rod ;" the whole ceremony is concluded. It is not usual in the case of a mortgage of copyhold property for the mortgagee to take admittance immediately after the surrender. He can take admittance at any time, and generally does when he finds it necessary to take possession of the property, receive the rents and profits, or to sell it under his power of sale. It is quite optional with the mortgagee whether he takes admittance immediately or not. Should he wish to do so, or should you think it necessary that he should do so, he is quite at liberty to be admitted ; but it is seldom done, as in case the mortgagee is admitted, he must re-surrender to the mortgagor on being repaid his mortgage money, and this saddles the mortgagor with the fines and fees on two admittances and a surrender, which in some manors will amount to a large sum ; whereas if the mortgagee had not taken admittance, it would only have been necessary for him, on receiving his mortgage money, to give a written authority to the steward of the manor to enter satisfaction on the court rolls of all moneys due under the conditional surrender having been paid, on receiving which the steward enters the satisfaction on the court roll, and the matter is at an end.

The fine payable to the lord on admission varies in different manors ; in some it is certain, that is, a nominal sum, seldom or never varying ; in others it is arbitrary, and the fine is generally payable both on death and alienation.

In the case of an arbitrary fine, the law allows no more to be demanded by the lord than two years' improved annual value of the property, that is, where the custom has fixed it at that amount. In some manors the custom has fixed the fine at two years on death and one year and a half on alienation. The steward will always give any information on this head. Where more than one person is admitted in joint tenancy, the fine is increased : thus, suppose

four persons to be admitted as joint tenants, the first
would pay a full fine, *i.e.*, either two years improved
annual value or one year and a half, as the case may
be; the second would pay half that amount; the
third, one-fourth; and the fourth, one-eighth; all
these added together would make the fine, but in the
case of coparceners, however many, only one fine is
payable.

Tenants in common are admitted severally, and
pay one fine between them, and on the death of
either, his heir or devisee pays another fine, and the
same on the admittance of a purchaser from one of
the tenants in common; but immediately on the
whole property becoming vested again in one person,
only one fine is payable.[1]

In some manors heriots become due on the death
of a copyhold tenant. The custom here again varies :
sometimes it is one thing and sometimes another, but
generally it is the best live beast. The heriot is
usually compounded for, and a sum of money paid to
the lord in lieu thereof.

In the case of tenants in common, a heriot is due
on the death of each; but when all the property becomes again vested in one individual, only one heriot
can be demanded.

The steward may demand payment of his fees
before admittance, but seldom refuses to admit until
they are paid. The lord, however, has not the same
right, as the fine is not due until after admittance.

Should the steward refuse to admit a claimant,
either on the ground of the fine not being first paid
or on any other insufficient ground, the purchaser's

[1] *Garland* v. *Jekyll,* 2 Bing. 273; *Holloway* v. *Berkeley,* 6 B. & C. 11.

remedy is by application to the High Court of Justice for a mandamus to compel admittance.

The above remarks will shew that the principal difference between copyhold and freehold property consists in the intervention of the steward and the court rolls; the former is the instrument through which any dealings with the copyhold property must be made, and the latter the record of all proceedings respecting transactions relating to property in the manor.

PURCHASES BY CORPORATIONS.—Where copyhold property is taken by a railway company, or any municipal or other public body under the Public Health Act, it is not necessary or usual to have any surrender. The property is conveyed by deed pursuant to § 95 of the Lands Clauses Consolidation Act, 1845,[1] as in the case of freehold; and, on payment of the steward's fees, he is to enter it on the court rolls, when it is to have the same effect as if the land had been of freehold tenure ; but, until enfranchisement, the lands will continue subject to the same fines, rents, heriots, and services, as before. § 96 compels the company or corporation to enfranchise the copyhold land so conveyed within a certain time. § 97 applies to refractory lords of manors and to those who cannot shew a good title; and § 98 applies to an apportionment of the customary rents where all the copyholder's land is not taken by the company.

ENFRANCHISEMENT.—Under § 1 of the Copyhold

[1] 8 & 9 Vict. c. 18.

Act, 1852,[1] and § 6 of the Copyhold Act, 1858,[2] either the lord of the manor or his tenant may compel enfranchisement of the copyhold land held by such tenant; and after such enfranchisement it will be held by the tenant in free and common socage, *i.e.* as ordinary freehold land.

In the case of an enfranchisement of copyhold property, the title of the lord of the manor should (unless there is some stipulation to the contrary) be called for by the copyholder's solicitor, and inspected in the usual manner, in order to see if he has power to enfranchise. He may be tenant for life of the manor, with power to enfranchise; or the manor may be in settlement, and the trustees under the settlement have power to enfranchise ; and in carrying out the enfranchisement, the terms of the power must be strictly followed. Should the lord be tenant for life, without power to enfranchise, he can, under the authority of the unrepealed provisions of the Copyhold Acts prior to and incorporated with the Copyhold Act, 1852, with the consent of the Copyhold Commissioners, enfranchise the property: however, in this case they must be parties to the deed.[3]

In the case of an enfranchisement, where the title is clear, and the aid of the Copyhold Commissioners is not required, it is the practice for the steward to prepare the necessary deed, and to forward it to the copyholder's solicitor, for perusal. The duty of the latter will be to see that the lord has power

[1] 15 & 16 Vict. c. 57.
[2] 21 & 22 Vict. c. 94.
[3] See 4 & 5 Vict. c. 35; 6 & 7 Vict. c. 23 ; 7 & 8 Vict. c. 55.

to enfranchise, that the property is correctly described, and that proper covenants for title and a covenant for production of the title deeds are inserted, an enfranchisement being, in fact, a purchase of the freehold.

The Copyhold Act, 1852, has an express provision to the effect that, notwithstanding the enfranchisement, the copyholder shall have the same right of common as he had before.[1]

It will be necessary to search for judgments, &c., against the lord of the manor, and if the manor is situate in a register county, to search the register for incumbrances, for a manor is within the Registry Acts, although copyhold property held of such manor is not.

In case a solicitor is concerned for a copyholder seeking to enfranchise, and a difficulty should arise between him and the steward as to the proper amount of compensation for fines and fees, the better course will be to carry it into effect through the Copyhold Commissioners. Or, if preferred, the enfranchisement can be carried out altogether through the commissioners. It is only necessary to send or write to the Copyhold Commission in St. James's Square, for their printed instructions and a list of forms, and these will be immediately supplied. After reading the printed instructions, no difficulty will be found in doing what is necessary to carry out the enfranchisement. It is generally cheaper for the copyholder to enfranchise through the medium of the Copyhold Commissioners, and for his solicitor to begin with them in the first place, than to open a

---

[1] Sect. 45.

communication with the steward of the manor, who often wishes to procure as much as possible for his lord in the shape of compensation for fines, and as much as possible for himself in the shape of compensation for fees.

CHAPTER VII.

PART I.—PARTNERSHIP DEEDS.

IN some few cases persons join together for the purpose of carrying on a trade or business without any written document being previously executed : but as this invariably leads to much difficulty and confusion at or before the termination of the partnership, it is always the safest course to have a proper document prepared, in order that the position of the partners and their interests in the concern may be defined.

ACTING FOR ALL PARTIES.—When concerned for all the parties intending to enter into partnership, a solicitor should take down the names and descriptions of the parties, the time at which the partnership is to commence, the duration thereof, the mode of winding up on dissolution either by the death of a partner or otherwise, the amount of capital, and the manner in which it is to be brought in, and whether any partner is to bring in any goods or stock as part of his capital : whether all or which of the partners are to give their whole time and attention to the business, and any other matters which the parties may wish to have inserted beyond what are to be

found in the usual and common clauses of a partnership deed. If some little care is taken in obtaining
accurate and full instructions, there will not be much
difficulty in preparing the draft of an ordinary deed
of partnership, or an agreement under hand which
is quite as effectual. In some cases, however, the
intending partners have such unbounded confidence
in each other that it is only with great difficulty that
they are induced to consent to the insertion of the
usual and necessary clauses for their mutual protection.   Afterwards disputes may arise, confidence
vanishes, and if their solicitor has not insisted upon
the insertion of such clauses, both he and his clients
find themselves in a most unpleasant position. When
the draft has been prepared, and fair copied, it
should be sent to one of the partners with instructions for him to read it over and afterwards to hand
it to the others, or they should all meet at the
solicitor's office for the purpose of having the draft
read over and settled. A solicitor ought never to
take the responsibility of engrossing the draft until
it has been approved by all the partners.

After the draft has been finally agreed upon, the
solicitor will have it engrossed (and he will find
it much the more convenient practice to have
partnership deeds engrossed on parchment folded
bookwise), and then make an appointment for the
parties to execute the deed. This can be a matter of
previous arrangement. Sometimes the deed is executed at the solicitor's office, and sometimes at the
counting-house or place of business of the firm. It
is usual to consult the convenience and wishes of
the clients in the matter.

After the deed has been executed the partners will either keep it at their place of business or request their solicitor to keep it for them for the purpose of general reference : if the latter, a plain copy should be made for the use of the partners, to be kept by them at their place of business.

ACTING FOR ONE PARTNER.—The above remarks apply to an ordinary matter where the same solicitor acts for all parties; but in some cases he may be concerned for a person about to join another in partnership, or for a firm about to admit a new partner, or for such new partner. In the case first put it will be a matter of prior arrangement between the solicitor on each side as to which shall prepare the deed ; the most usual and most equitable arrangement is for both their bills of costs to be added together and paid by the clients equally, and for them afterwards to divide the profit on the whole business; in this case it becomes quite a matter of indifference which prepares the deed, but it will be a graceful act for the youngest to offer to prepare it, besides being good practice. These deeds are awkward matters to handle unless the draftsman has had some previous experience, and one cannot begin too soon to obtain all the experience he can ; as no amount of theory can compensate for a deficiency in practical knowledge, and in partnership deeds a good deal of practical knowledge is necessary.

The solicitor who prepares the draft will forward a copy of it to the other solicitor concerned for his perusal, and afterwards the engrossment for examination in the usual manner; and when this has been done an appointment will be made at one of their offices (the convenience of their clients being considered), for all parties to meet for the purpose of executing the deed. A partnership deed is generally executed by all the parties together, although, of course, this is not necessary.

ACTING FOR FIRM.—A solicitor concerned for a firm about to admit a new partner, will probably find that the latter wishes his own solicitor to look after his interests in the transaction. In this case the firm's solicitor will, as a matter of right, prepare the deed, and forward a copy thereof to the incoming partner's solicitor for his perusal, and when all points have been settled and the former has engrossed the draft, both draft and engrossment will be sent to the latter for examination.

The appointment to execute the deed will be at either office or at the firm's place of business. In a case of this description the general rule is, that each party pays his own costs.

ACTING FOR NEW PARTNER.—If, on the other hand, a solicitor is acting for the new partner instead of the firm, his position will be reversed, and he will on receiving the draft either forward it to his client or get him to call for the purpose of going through it with him. After perusing the draft it will be returned to the solicitor who prepared it, and when all points in dispute have been settled, he will forward the draft and engrossment for execution, and either at the same time or afterwards make an appointment for the new partner and his solicitor to attend and complete the business.

These matters generally proceed without much difficulty after the preliminaries are arranged, if sufficient care is taken in obtaining full instructions in the first place.

STAMPS.—A deed of partnership requires to be stamped with a 10s. stamp, but *ad valorem* duties are necessary if a premium is paid.

PART II.—DEEDS OF DISSOLUTION.

DISSOLUTION INTER VIVOS.—A dissolution of partnership may take place either on a total giving up of the business by the partners, or on the death of one partner, or on one partner retiring from the firm. In the case first mentioned, whether a solicitor acts for one or both partners, the course before suggested as to the preparation of the partnership deed will equally apply. If, on the other hand, the dissolution is only a partial one, and is confined to a partner retiring from the firm, and a solicitor is concerned for the firm, he will prepare the deed of dissolution, and send it to the solicitor of the retiring partner for his perusal, and afterwards the engrossment for examination and execution, as in such a case it is seldom that the parties meet on the completion of the business. After execution the two solicitors will meet together and complete the matter. In this case the solicitor of each party looks to his own client for his charges.

Should a solicitor be concerned for a partner retiring from the concern, then the solicitor of the continuing partners will prepare the deed of dissolution and assignment of the retiring partner's share. This dissolution is, of course, confined to the retiring partner. The solicitor for the retiring partner will refer to the deed of partnership, for the purpose of ascertaining what his client becomes entitled to on his retirement, unless it be a matter of arrangement between the parties; and it will then be his duty to peruse the draft and examine the engrossment, and perform the duties above pointed out, as being done by the retiring partner's solicitor, and he will charge his client with his costs in the matter.

After a dissolution of the partnership by effluxion of time, or consent, notice should be inserted in the *London Gazette* and other newspapers, in order that any person who had been in the habit of dealing with the firm may not be in a position, after the dissolution, to say that any subsequent dealings were entered into and credit given on the faith of the retiring member continuing to belong to the partnership. This is very important, and, when acting for a retiring partner, a solicitor should always take care that it is done.

DISSOLUTION BY DEATH.—If the dissolution of the partnership is by death, then for whichever party a solicitor may be concerned, he must turn to the deed of partnership (and if he is advising the representatives of a deceased partner, and does not happen to have a copy of the deed, he will obtain one from the solicitor of the surviving partner), in order to see its provisions in the event of the death of one of the partners. In some cases the deed provides that, in the event of one partner dying during the continu-

ance of the partnership, his representatives shall
assign all their interest in the concern to the surviving partner, and that he shall give a bond to such
representatives for the deceased partner's share of
capital in the concern, and in a proportionate share
of profits, or a given sum in lieu of profits, for the
current year. In other cases it goes further, and
provides, in addition, that the surviving partner
shall pay an annuity to the representatives of the
deceased partner for a given period. The usual course
is for the solicitor of the surviving partner to prepare the assignment from the representatives of the
deceased partner, and for their solicitor to prepare
all bonds or other securities which may be provided
for by the partnership deed for securing the share of
capital or the annuity, or both, as the case may be.
If both the share of capital and an annuity are to be
paid, it will be better to have separate bonds. The
share of capital is generally provided to be paid by
instalments, but the current year's share of profits, or
the given sum to be paid in lieu of profits, is usually
provided to be paid on the execution of the necessary
assignment and bonds. With respect to the costs of
these documents, the partnership deed generally provides for them; but if it should contain no provision
in this respect, the practice is for the surviving partner to pay his own solicitor's charges for preparing
the deed of assignment, and the costs on both sides
of the preparation and execution of the necessary
bonds; but the charges of the solicitor of the representatives of the deceased partner for perusing and
completing the assignment by his clients are generally
paid by them.

In any case the previous observations as to preparing, perusing, engrossing, and completing the matter, will apply.

This chapter would be incomplete without some reference to Bovill's Act,[1] under which persons who do not wish to incur the liabilities of partners, but are willing to risk a certain amount of capital, often lend money to traders on the terms of receiving a share of the profits instead of interest. In cases of this kind it must be remembered that a contract in writing[2] is necessary, and that in the event of the failure of the trader, the lender can recover no portion of his loan, unless it is secured by mortgage,[3] until all other creditors have received twenty shillings in the pound. This Act has not given so much protection to lenders as many practitioners anticipated, and further legislation on the subject is imminent. Meanwhile it is important to bear in mind that, however clearly an agreement may express the intention of the parties to enter into the relation of lender and borrower, they will be held to have entered into that of partners, with all its attendant liabilities, if the practical effect of the agreement is to confer upon the lender the rights and privileges of of a partner.[4]

---

[1] 28 & 29 Vict. c. 86.

[2] Sect. 1.

[3] *Ex parte Sheil*, 4 Ch. D. 789.

[4] *Pooley* v. *Driver*, 5 Ch. D. 458; *Syers* v. *Syers*, 1 Ap. Cas. 174; *Ex parte Delhasse*, 7 Ch. D. 511.

CHAPTER VIII.

PART I.—MARRIAGE SETTLEMENTS.

INTRODUCTORY.—There are various descriptions of settlements; *e.g.*, those executed before marriage and those executed after, those *bonâ fide*, and those for fraudulent purposes. Marriage is a good consideration for a settlement executed prior to the marriage, or even subsequently in pursuance of an ante-nuptial agreement.

REAL ESTATE—*Strict Settlement.*—Settlements executed in contemplation of marriage may be divided into two parts, viz., settlements of real estate and settlements of personal estate. With respect to the first, it is always desirable, after receiving instructions to prepare a marriage settlement, to look into the title, in order to see what is necessary to be done before the estate can be settled in the manner required. Take, for example, the case of an intended marriage of the heir of a family estate. In most cases the title was examined on the marriage of the parent, and if that be so, the settlement then executed will be the only document requiring attention, and it will probably be much in the following form :—Habendum to trustees : To the use of the trustees for a term of 500 or some other number of years, upon trust to secure pin-money to the wife, and subject thereto to the use of the husband for life, remainder to trustees to secure the wife's jointure, remainder to trustees to secure the portions of younger children, remainder to the use of the first and other sons of the marriage in tail male, remainder to the first and other sons of the marriage in tail general, remainder to the first and other daughters in the same manner, with remainders over. There may be other terms created for various purposes, or the uses may be somewhat varied, but the above will be the main provisions and are sufficient for our present purpose.

Now on receiving instructions to prepare a settlement, to be executed on the marriage of the eldest son of the settlor who has attained his majority, and the father and mother both living, the first thing to be done will be to bar the entail created by the existing settlement, and this may be done by the father and eldest son executing a disentailing deed. This deed will be between the father of the first part, the son of the second part, and a nominee of the third part: it will recite the settlement, and that the eldest son has attained his majority; and then the father and son, in order to bar and destroy the estate tail created by the settlement and all other estates tail and vest the estate in manner thereinafter mentioned, will convey the estate to the party of the third part to such uses as the father and son may jointly appoint.[1] The new settlement will be by another deed, by which the father and son will appoint the estate to A. B. to the use of trustees for

---

[1] See Chapter IX. p. 119, *infra*.

a term of, say, 1000 years, remainder to the use that the son shall during the joint lives of his father and himself receive a certain annual sum, with powers of distress and entry for securing the same, remainder to the use that after the death of the father his widow, if living, may receive an annuity by way of jointure, with powers of distress and entry, remainder to the use of the father for life, remainder to the use of the son for life, remainder to the use of the trustees for, say, 500 years, remainder to the use of the first and other sons in tail male, and so on, as in the former settlement, with an ultimate remainder to the use of the son in fee. Then the trusts of the terms which have been limited are declared. The first term (1000 years) is declared to be for securing the portions of the younger children of the father, the second (500 years) for securing the portions of the younger children of the son, and if any other terms are limited, the trusts will be declared in a similar manner. Should, however, there have only been one son of the marriage, or the mother be dead, of course in the first case no term will be necessary for securing the portions of younger children by the father's marriage, and in the second case no provision will be necessary for securing the mother's jointure. The above illustration is given simply to draw attention to what will be required in instructing counsel to prepare the settlement, as it is very seldom that such a settlement as the foregoing is prepared in a solicitor's office; neither is it expected of the solicitor that he should prepare it, although there is no reason why he should not do so if he feels himself competent, and likes to undertake the trouble and responsibility.

Having formed a mental outline of the intended settlement, there will not be much difficulty in preparing proper instructions to counsel. On receiving the draft from counsel, it will be necessary to go carefully through it, in order to see if it is prepared in accordance with the intentions of the parties. This should never be omitted, more especially as the instructions to counsel often consist only of a copy of the existing settlement, and a statement of the particulars of the family and of the intended marriage.

REAL ESTATE—*Conversion and Division.*—If the property intended to be settled be a small freehold, leasehold, or copyhold estate, the object of the parties is often to benefit the issue equally, and not, as in the case of a family estate, to entail it. The better course, in a case of this nature, will be to convey the property to trustees upon trust, that the husband may receive the rents for life. This will give him ample power, and make him quite independent of the trustees as to the receipt of the rents and management of the property, as the difference between a trust to pay the rents and profits to a person for life, and a trust that such person shall receive and take the rents and profits during his life is, that the first-mentioned trust gives the beneficiary no power over the property, while the second gives him every necessary power over the management of it. The settlement will then proceed as follows :—Upon trust after the death of the husband that the wife may receive the rents during her life, or if the other course is preferred, then that the trustees may pay the rents to the wife during her life; and after the death of the survivor of the husband and wife, upon such trusts in favour of the children, or other issue of the marriage to be born during the lives of husband, wife, or life of survivor, or within twenty-one years after the death of the survivor as the husband and wife may jointly by deed appoint; and in default of a joint appointment as the survivor may by deed or will appoint, and in default of appointment by the survivor, and subject to any partial or incomplete appointment upon trust for the children in equal shares as tenants in common, the issue of deceased children to take their parents' shares, and in default of issue, upon any other trusts the parties may wish to have inserted. Care must be taken to give either the husband or the trustees, and if the latter (then with the consent of the husband and wife during their joint lives, or of the survivor during his or her life) a power to grant leases and also a power to sell the property; and whenever a power to appoint among a class is given by any document, the hotchpot clause should be inserted. This clause is inserted for equalizing as much as possible the shares of the children; otherwise a child who claimed, say, one-third of the property under an appointment, would, if the other two-thirds remained unappointed, share with his brothers and sisters in such other two-thirds under the gift over in default of appointment, unless there were some special stipulation excluding him in the appointment under which he claimed. In the case of a settlement such as we are now considering, if the property brought into the settlement belongs to the lady, the first life estate will generally be given to her and the ultimate remainder will be to her or her family.

If the lady is represented by a separate solicitor, a fair copy of the draft must be made, forwarded to him for perusal, and afterwards to the solicitor of the trustees, if they are separately represented, and the same with respect to any other parties to the deed for whom the settlor's solicitor may not be concerned. It will be the province of the solicitor to the intended husband to prepare the settlement (though in most cases the lady's solicitor has the right to do so at the expense of the intended husband); and if there be a settlement on the lady's part, which is often the case, it will be by a separate deed, which her solicitor will prepare and forward for perusal, and afterwards engross it and get it executed in the usual manner. The real estate draft, having been finally approved, will be engrossed by the settlor's solicitor, and the engrossment and draft forwarded to the other solicitors concerned for examination, after which he will get it executed by the necessary parties.

REGISTRATION.—Should settled real estate or any part of it be in a register county, the settlement must be registered in the same manner as any other deed.

It may be well again to remind the reader [1] that, although a settlement of real estate may contain no powers of sale or leasing, settled land may be sold or leased under the powers of the Settled Estate Act, 1877.[2] A sale can only be authorized on petition to the Chancery Division of the High Court of Justice,

---

[1] See pp. 12-83, *ante*.   [2] 40 & 41 Vict. c. 18.

while leases can, in some, but not all, cases, be granted without any application to the Court.

Personal Estate.—The process of settling personal property is generally very simple, and after some little experience a young solicitor will not have much difficulty in preparing such a settlement, although at all times he would be justified in resorting to counsel for assistance.

The recitals and *testatum* in a personalty settlement vary according to the nature of the property.

Cash.—In a settlement of a sum of money possessed by one of the parties, it will only be necessary to recite that the marriage is contemplated, and that in pursuance of an agreement made on the treaty for such marriage such sum of money has been handed over to the trustees upon the trusts thereinafter declared. The settlement will then proceed to declare that the trustees shall invest the money and stand possessed thereof and of the interest thereof upon the trusts thereinafter declared. These trusts will be referred to presently.

Stock.—Stock or money invested in public securities may be transferred to the trustees, either by power of attorney or personally. If by power of attorney the power must be bespoken at the Bank of England one clear day before the day appointed for executing the settlement; and in this case the settlement and the power of attorney for transferring the stock will be executed together, and the transfer made immediately after. If, on the other hand, the transfer is made personally, it should be done immediately before the settlement is executed.

In the first case the recital will be that on the treaty, &c., it was agreed that £—, stock then standing in the name of the settlor, should be transferred into the names of the trustees upon the trusts, &c. In the other case it will be that, in pursuance of an agreement made on the treaty for the marriage, £— stock lately standing in the settlor's name in the books of the Governors and Company of the Bank of England, has been transferred into the names of the trustees upon the trusts, &c., as before. The declaration of trust in this case will authorize the trustees either to allow the stock to remain in its then state of investment or to sell it and invest the produce either in similar or other stocks or otherwise, as may be desired, and the trusts will follow in the same manner as before.

Shares.—Shares in railways, canals, or other companies are transferred by the ordinary and usual transfer, and the recitals in a settlement of such property will be similar to those in a settlement of stock ; and the trusts upon which they are to be held are declared by the settlement in a similar manner.

Bonds.—In cases where bonds are settled they will be assigned to the trustees by the settlement, in which case full power must formerly have been given to the trustees to use the name of the obligee to the bond to sue for and recover the moneys secured thereby, a bond being what is called a *chose in action*, in other words, something that is not in possession, and the recovery whereof can only be enforced by an action. But now, under the Judicature Act, 1873,[1] an absolute assignment of a *chose in action*

---

[1] 36 & 37 Vict. c. 66, s. 25 (6).

passes the legal estate and enables the assignee to give a good discharge, if notice of such assignment be given to the person liable, *e.g.*, in this case the obligor of the bond. So that trustees of a *chose in action* should always give immediate notice of the settlement to the person liable to make a payment in respect of the *chose in action*. The trusts are declared in the usual way.

Promissory Notes.— But where promissory notes are settled they will simply be indorsed to the trustees, and the fact of their having been so indorsed will be recited in the settlement, a promissory note being, by the law of commerce, capable of transfer by indorsement. In this case the settlement proceeds to declare the trusts upon which the money secured by the promissory note is to be held; and, unless it is intended to call in the money immediately it is due, or the promissory note be payable upon demand, power must be given to the trustees to allow the money to remain on the promissory note, without being liable for any loss occasioned thereby, as it would be a breach of trust to allow the money to remain on such security, even in a case where money so secured is part of the settled property.

Life Policy.—In some cases the subject of the settlement is a policy of assurance on the life of the husband. This should be assigned to the trustees upon trust, after the money has been received, to invest it and pay the interest to the wife for life, with remainder to the children in equal shares. The husband must covenant to keep the policy on foot, and not to do anything to invalidate it, and if it is not easy to find trustees, there are offices which will constitute themselves trustees of the policies they issue for such a purpose.

It would be useful in such a settlement as this to insert a clause that, in case of the death of the wife in the lifetime of the husband, without leaving issue who have attained a vested interest in the money secured by the policy, it should be lawful for the husband, if he should think fit, to permit the policy to drop or to sell or assign it to the company.

Under the Married Women's Property Act, 1870,[1] a man can effect a policy for the expressed benefit of his wife and children, and if no settlement is executed the Court will, on petition, give directions for the application of the money on the husband's death.[2]

Furniture.—In the case of household furniture, it is assigned to the trustees and the trusts afterwards declared. The only way of securing this description of property against the liabilities of the husband, is to settle it upon trust for the separate use of the wife, free from the control, interference, debts, or engagements of the husband, and the settlement should give power to the trustees to insure the furniture from loss or damage by fire, or to sell it if the wife should so direct, or if she is not living, then if the trustees shall think fit to do so.

A settlement of chattels executed on marriage does not require to be registered as a bill of sale.[3]

Mortgage Debt.—If the property intended to be

---

[1] 33 & 34 Vict. c. 93, s. 10.

[2] *Re Mellor's Policy,* 6 Ch. D. 627; 7 Ch. D. 200; *Re Edwards' Policy,* 28 W. R. 72.

[3] 11 & 12 Vict. c. 31, s. 4.

settled consists of money secured on mortgage, two deeds will be necessary, viz., an ordinary transfer of the mortgage to the trustees upon the trusts of the settlement, in which transfer will be inserted power to give receipts for the mortgage money, in order to avoid the necessity of making the settlement part of the title to the property comprised in the mortgage. The settlement will recite the transfer of the mortgage by deed of even date, and declare the trusts upon which the mortgage money is to be held by the trustees.

Investment.—The first trust in a personalty settlement is that for investment, and it is a convenient plan to specify the modes of investment in a schedule. In the case of money on mortgage, stock, or money otherwise already invested, the trust is often either to retain existing investments or to convert and invest according to the schedule; in the case of a sum of money the trust will be simply for investment, while in the case of a policy of assurance or furniture the trust for investment will not arise until the death of the husband, or the sale of the furniture. In the absence of a trust for investment, it is the duty of trustees to invest in the securities authorized by Lord St. Leonards' Act, 1860.[1]

Beneficial Trusts.—The beneficial trusts are generally as follows:—If the property is the husband's, the first life estate is given to him, unless he is in business, and it is wished to preserve the income for the maintenance of the family in case of bankruptcy; but even this may be done and the life interest given to the husband, provided such life interest is made

[1] 23 & 24 Vict. c. 38, ss. 10, 11.

determinable on the bankruptcy or insolvency of the
husband, and given over to the wife or to the trustees
for the maintenance of the family on either of those
events happening. If, on the other hand, the
property is the wife's, the first life interest is given
to her, unless the contrary is wished, which is
seldom the case ; and after the death of one the
life interest is given to the other. Whenever a
life interest is given to the wife, it should be for
her separate use, and without power of anticipation.
With respect to the separate use of the wife, and
restraining her alienation of the income, and under
what circumstances such restraint is binding on
her, see *Tullett* v. *Armstrong*.[1] After the death
of the survivor of the husband and wife, the fund
will be held by the trustees upon trust for such
one or more of the children of the marriage as the
husband and wife shall jointly by deed appoint, and
in default of any joint appointment as the survivor
shall by deed or will appoint, and in default of such
appointment upon trust for such of the children of
the marriage as being sons shall attain twenty-one, or
being daughters shall attain that age or marry, equally,
the issue of a deceased child taking the share their,
his, or her parent would have been entitled to if
living. Then follows the hotchpot clause, the effect
of which has been already mentioned ; and in default
of any of the children taking a vested interest, then,
if the property is the husband's, upon trust for him,
his executors, administrators and assigns. If the

[1] 1 Beav. 1; affirmed on appeal, 4 My. & Cr. 377; see also *Cooper* v. *Macdonald*, 7 Ch. D. 288.

property be the wife's and she predecease her husband, then upon trust as she shall by deed or will notwithstanding coverture appoint; and, in default of appointment, to such persons as would have been her next of kin if she had died a spinster, and if she is the survivor, for her, her executors, administrators, and assigns. In either case, on the death of one without leaving issue of the marriage living to attain a vested interest, the husband or wife, as the case may be, may, by appointing the property to himself or herself by deed, obtain the absolute control over it.

Maintenance and Advancement.—There formerly followed a provision authorizing the trustees to apply the annual income, or any part thereof, arising from the trust property, for the maintenance of any infant taking a vested or presumptive share of the capital; but now § 26 of Lord Cranworth's Act[1] renders it unnecessary to insert such a clause; but a clause enabling the trustees to apply a portion of the capital of the share of any such infant for his or her advancement or preferment in the world should still be inserted. This portion may either be limited (usually to one half), or, which is the preferable plan, if the trust fund is of small amount, may be left to the discretion of the trustees. The clause for advancement should apply to all infants, whether male or female, as in settlements of small property it is a provision very likely to be needed by females.

Miscellaneous Provisions. — If the property be brought into the settlement by the wife a provision should be inserted enabling her to settle some part

[1] 23 & 24 Vict. c. 145.

of it on the children of any future marriage, or, which is by far the better plan, instead of settling the property on the children of the present marriage, settle it generally on the children of the wife ; this will embrace all her children, and the justice of such a course is obvious ; for, supposing there be only one child of the marriage, and the husband die, and the wife marry again and have a large family, if the property be settled on the children of the first marriage, the one child will take all, to the total exclusion of the others, although his claim to it would be no better than that of the other children.

In some cases a clause is inserted authorizing the trustees to lend a portion of the trust money to the husband, on his giving to the trustees his bond or other security for the repayment thereof. If instructions are given to insert such a clause (and it should not be inserted without authority), the deed should declare in express terms that the trustees shall not be answerable or responsible for the loss of the whole or any part of the money so lent.

It will not be necessary to insert a clause declaring the receipts of the trustees good discharges for the trust money or any part thereof, for that power is given by § 29 of Lord Cranworth's Act.[1]

For the same reason it will be unnecessary to insert a power to appoint new trustees, inasmuch as § 27 of the same Act gives a general clause framed to meet almost every case that may arise, and it will apply to every future deed, will, or other instrument. A short clause nominating the persons who are to exercise this statutory power, and providing for an

[1] 23 & 24 Vict. c. 145.

increase or decrease in the number of trustees may, however, be inserted.[1]

In preparing a personalty settlement it is necessary to bear in mind that there exists a rule respecting personal estate somewhat analogous to the well-known rule in *Shelley's case*, namely, that a gift to A., followed by a gift to the executors or administrators of A., is an absolute gift to A. This is well illustrated by a case[2] where funded property settled upon A. for life for her separate use, and after her decease to such persons as she should by will appoint, and in default of appointment, for her executors or administrators, was declared to belong to A. absolutely. A serious mistake might easily be made through ignorance of the above rule.

NOTICE OF SETTLEMENT.—After executing a settlement of a policy of assurance or reversionary interest, notice of the settlement should be given by the trustees to the assurance office, or to the trustees of the deed or will under which the reversionary interest was created, as the case may be, and as to notice of a *chose in action*, see p. 138, *ante*. The neglect to do this is in itself a breach of trust; and should the settlor, owing to such neglect, effect a charge on the policy or reversionary interest, and the person in whose favour such charge was made should give notice to the assurance office or the trustees of the deed or will as before mentioned, before any notice is given by the trustees of the settlement, such trustees would be liable in equity to make good any loss

---

[1] See Form No. CXXII., p. 426, *infra*.
[2] *Page v. Soper*, 17 Jur. 851; S. C., 22 L. J. (Ch.) 1044.

occasioned by their neglect; but if the settlor were living and a party to an action, by some of the objects of the settlement for the purpose of charging the trustees, the judgment charging them would probably order the settlor to recoup the trustees. As, however, the settlor is seldom able to do this, or, which is the most frequent occurrence, no proceedings are taken against the trustees until after his death, the solicitor to trustees always makes it a point, in the case of a settlement of property of this description, to give immediate notice of the settlement to the necessary parties; and likewise, if money secured by a bond or covenant is settled, notice of the settlement should immediately be given to the obligor or covenantor.

It is advisable in every case where stock or shares form part of the settled property to serve a notice under R. S. C. Ord. XLVI. r. 4, immediately after the settlement is executed. This may be done either on the affidavit of the trustees or of any person taking a beneficial interest under the settlement, or on the affidavit of the solicitor, and is a very simple process.

Among the precedents will be found the forms of affidavit and notice required; and on taking the affidavit and the notice to the central office of the High Court of Justice they will be filed, and an office copy and an authenticated duplicate of the notice can be obtained. Then the office copy affidavit, and duplicate notice must be served on the company, or in case of money in the funds, at the Chief Accountant's office at the Bank of England. If the names of the persons holding the stock or shares

L

and the amount and description of the stock or shares are correctly described, this notice effectually prevents any dealing with the stock or shares without notice; and in case it should become necessary to deal with the stock or shares for the purposes of the settlement, the notice can be speedily withdrawn. For the purpose of withdrawing such notice it is only necessary for the person on whose behalf it has been given to sign and serve a written request to that effect. Any other person claiming to be interested in the stock or shares may apply to the Court by motion or petition to discharge the notice.

These proceedings are substituted for the writ of *distringas* under 5 Vict. c. 5, s. 5, and their cost is of trifling amount, but the security to the fund and to all parties concerned is incalculable.

CUSTODY OF DEEDS.—With respect to the custody of the deeds, the following appears to be the rule and practice.

If the property settled be real estate, the tenant for life having the legal estate is entitled to the custody of the deeds, as it devolves upon him to defend the inheritance. If the legal estate be in trustees they hold the deeds. If the property is leasehold the trustee holds the deeds, and where there are more trustees than one they usually arrange among themselves which of them shall hold them, or agree to deposit them with some solicitor or banker. There is seldom any difficulty on the point.

PART II.—VOLUNTARY SETTLEMENTS.

A settlement executed after marriage, where no marriage articles have been executed previously to the marriage, will be void if the settlor is a trader and becomes bankrupt within two years. In other cases the principal question will be whether the husband is or is not solvent at the time of making the settlement. A man owing as much or nearly as much as he is worth cannot make a voluntary settlement binding on his creditors; but if a man owes to his creditors, say £500, and has property worth, say £2000, then he may make a settlement after marriage binding on his creditors, provided he leaves sufficient in his hands to pay off his debts. The case of *Crabbe* v. *Moxey* [1] is worthy of an attentive perusal as illustrating the principle by which the present law on this point [2] would be construed. In deciding that case the Vice-Chancellor said: "It is not sufficient, in order to set aside a voluntary settlement, to shew that the settlor had at the time of executing the deed some debts; neither, on the other hand, is it necessary to prove that he was absolutely solvent. The question must always be whether the effect is such as to be injurious to the creditors." In that case an inquiry was granted as to the state of the settlor's property, and the amount of his debts at the date of the settlement. [3]

A voluntary settlement is binding on the settlor and all volunteers claiming under him; and the

---

[1] 21 L. T. 99.
[2] 32 & 33 Vict. c. 71, s. 91.
[3] See also 13 Eliz. c. 5; 3 Dav. 675 *et seq.*

L 2

settlor cannot revoke the trusts of such settlement unless express power is therein reserved to him to do so ; but if the property settled be freehold, copyhold, or leasehold, he can in effect revoke them by conveying the property to a purchaser for valuable consideration ; and even if the purchaser had notice of the settlement before entering into the contract, he could hold the property without being affected by the trusts of the settlement.[1]

STAMPS.—The stamp duty on a settlement of real estate is the same as that on a conveyance. On settlements of money and stock the duty is 5s. for every £100 or fractional part thereof. Stock is to be valued at the average price of the day.[2] As to policies of assurance, see § 124 of the Stamp Act, 1870.[3]

[1] See *Hall* v. *Hall*, L. R. 8 Ch. 430, 438.
[2] 33 & 34 Vict. c. 97, ss. 11, 12, 13.
[3] 33 & 34 Vict. c. 97.

CHAPTER IX.

DEEDS UNDER THE FINES AND RECOVERIES ACT.

PART I.—DISENTAILING DEEDS.

FIFTY years ago the only mode of barring an entail was by fine or recovery. The latter was the more frequent mode of assurance, as it not only barred the entail, but all remainders over. But in 1833 the Fines and Recoveries Act[1] abolished fines and recoveries,[2] and substituted new modes of assurance much better adapted to the modern and more simple system of conveyancing. Under the provisions of this Act, an entail can be barred by a deed,[3] which must be enrolled in Chancery, within six months after its execution.[4] There is no particular name attached to this deed, and for want of a better it is known as a disentailing deed.

If a tenant in tail in possession wishes to bar the entail, he can do so without the necessity of any other person concurring in the deed. He has merely to execute a deed between himself of the one part, and A. B. of the other part, and declare that, in order

[1] 3 & 4 Will. 4, c. 74.
[2] Sects. 2, 3.
[3] Sect. 40.
[4] Sect. 41.

to bar all estates, he grants the estate to A. B., to the use of himself in fee; if this deed be enrolled in Chancery within six months from its execution, the entail is at an end, and the former tenant in tail becomes as much tenant in fee simple as if the estate had been so vested in him in the first place.

Now, take the case of a tenant in tail not in possession, *i.e.*, the tenant for life may be living, or the trustee of an estate prior to that of the tenant in tail may be in possession. In this case the tenant for life or the trustee will be called the "protector" of the settlement,[1] unless a protector has been appointed under § 32 of the Act. In all cases where there is a protector the tenant in tail must procure the consent of such protector,[2] and this consent may be given either by the disentailing deed, or by a separate instrument,[3] which must also be enrolled in Chancery within six months;[4] but even if the protector will not give his consent, the tenant in tail is not prevented from barring the entail, although his power is limited, the effect being that his issue only is barred, and not the remainders over, and he has therefore what is called a base fee in the property; the deed in such a case having the same operation as a fine had before the passing of the Act abolishing fines and recoveries.

We will now suppose that the tenant for life, or protector, concurs in the deed; in this case it is made between three parties, viz., tenant for life, or pro-

---

[1] Sects. 22–31.
[2] Sect. 34.
[3] Sect. 42.
[4] Sect. 46.

tector, of the first part, tenant in tail of the second part, and A. B. (a nominee) of the third part. It usually recites the instrument creating the entail, and any facts necessary to shew the title of the tenant in tail, his desire to bar the entail, and that the tenant for life or protector had agreed to concur. The tenant in tail, with the consent of the tenant for life, or protector, (testified, &c), and in order to bar and extinguish the entail created by the recited assurance and all other entails in the property, and to limit the property in manner thereinafter mentioned, conveys the property to the party of the third part. Habendum to him and his heirs to such uses as may be necessary to carry into effect the intentions of the parties.

This deed must be enrolled in Chancery within six calendar months after its execution, and the entail and all remainders over will then be effectually barred. If a solicitor is concerned only for the tenant in tail, and a separate solicitor is concerned for the tenant for life, or protector, the former will forward to the other solicitor the draft of this deed for perusal, and afterwards the engrossment for examination in the usual manner.

No acknowledgment of a disentailing deed is necessary before enrolling it,[1] but if the tenant in tail is a married woman she must acknowledge it either before or after enrolment.[2] After the deed has been duly executed, it must be taken to the central office of the Royal Courts of Justice, where it will be enrolled, and handed back a few days after

[1] Sect. 73.
[2] Sect. 40. *Ex parte Taverner*, 7 D. M. & G. 627.

leaving it. Thus an entail may now be barred at a
small expense and less difficulty, although before the
passing of the Act above referred to it was an expensive and troublesome process, and one requiring
great experience to do effectually.

STAMPS.—The stamp duty will, of course, be the
same as on a conveyance of the same property.

PART II.—DEEDS BY MARRIED WOMEN.

The Fines and Recoveries Act also provides a new
mode by which a married woman, whether the owner
of, or having only an inchoate right of dower in,
freehold property, can part with her interest therein.
The practice formerly was for the husband and wife
to levy a fine; but under the above Act the husband
and wife join in the conveyance,[1] and after they have
both executed it, the latter acknowledges the deed[2]
before a Judge or before two Commissioners appointed
under § 81 or § 83 of the Act to take acknowledgments of deeds by married women Commissioners are
now appointed by the President of the Common
Pleas Division of the High Court of Justice. The
forms of certificates and affidavit used on this occasion
may be obtained at any law stationer's.

The Act requires the deed to be executed by the
husband before it can be acknowledged by the wife;
but where it is the wife's estate, and the interest of
the husband is only such as he takes by virtue of his
marital right, and he is either a lunatic or abroad,
not having been heard of for some time, and in some

[1] Sect. 77.
[2] Sect. 79.

other cases enumerated in the Act, the Court will, on application being made for that purpose, dispense with the concurrence of the husband in the deed.[1]

This application is made by motion, supported by an affidavit of the facts.

The Act gives the option of taking the married woman either before a Judge at chambers, or County Court Judge, or two Commissioners authorized to take acknowledgments of deeds by married women for the county in which the property is situate; in London where the property is small the acknowledgment is generally taken before a Judge, on account of the fees being less than those paid to two Commissioners; but in larger matters a client would rather pay the extra fees than undergo the inconvenience of attending at chambers.

Before the day appointed for the completion of the business the solicitor should call at the Judge's chambers, and inquire which Judge will be at chambers on that day. Having obtained the name of the Judge fill up the certificate of acknowledgment accordingly. The lady, accompanied by her solicitor, proceeds to the Judge's chambers, where the solicitor first attends the Judge alone, and answers any questions he may put respecting the deed; next the lady is examined in private by the Judge, and acknowledges the deed, after which the Judge signs the certificate, and also the memorandum indorsed on the deed. The solicitor then makes the affidavit as to the identity of the lady, and as to her being of full age, &c., and this is usually sworn before the Judge's clerk. The certificate and affidavit are afterwards

___

[1] Sect. 91.

left at the central office of the Royal Courts of Justice, and five shillings paid, and, on inquiring a fortnight after, a certified copy can be obtained.

In the country the acknowledgment is taken by two Commissioners, one of whom only may be a solicitor engaged in the transaction. The appointment with the Commissioners having been made, they will attend at the time appointed to take the acknowledgment, sign the memorandum on the back of the deed and the certificate, and one of them will make the affidavit. The certificate and affidavit are then sent to and left by the London agent, and a certified copy obtained as before pointed out.

The provisions of the Fines and Recoveries Act are extended by the Act to amend the Law of Real Property[1] to contingent and executory interests.

Until the passing of Malins' Act,[2] a married woman could not by any process dispose of a reversionary interest in personal property, unless settled upon her for her separate use. As no reason could be discovered why any difference should exist in this respect between real and personal property, the above Act was passed, in order that both those descriptions of property might be placed on the same footing. It must, however, be borne in mind that the old law still continues in force as to all instruments made before the 31st of December, 1857,[3] and that even the new law does not extend to settlements made on the marriage of the *feme covert*.[4] All deeds executed under this Act must be executed by

[1] 8 & 9 Vict. c. 106, s. 6.
[2] 20 & 21 Vict. c. 57.
[3] Sect. 1.
[4] Sect. 4.

the husband and acknowledged by the wife, in the same manner as required by the Fines and Recoveries Act.

SEPARATE USE.—Where a married woman is seised of, or entitled to freehold property for her separate use, whether for life only or in fee, and of which she is not restrained from alienation, she can dispose of such property without the concurrence of her husband ; and whether the husband does or does not join in the conveyance of such property, the deed does not require to be acknowledged by the wife, inasmuch as, with respect to that property, she has the same right of disposition as a *feme sole* would have of it,[1] and even though she may be restrained from anticipation during her life she may dispose of the reversion expectant on her death.[2] And under § 6 of the Vendor and Purchaser Act, 1874,[3] where any freehold or copyhold hereditament shall be vested in a married woman as a bare trustee, she may convey or surrender as if a *feme sole*.

[1] *Taylor* v. *Meads*, 11 Jur. (N.S.) 166.
[2] *Cooper* v. *Macdonald*, 7 Ch. D. 288.
[3] 37 & 38 Vict. c. 78.

CHAPTER X.

WILLS.

INTRODUCTORY.—A prevalent, but most erroneous, impression prevails among non-professional persons that a will is a very simple document and easily prepared by almost anyone, and the consequence is that agents, schoolmasters, and others quite incompetent, are frequently entrusted to prepare an instrument that above all others requires the greatest skill and legal knowledge. The reports shew that by far the greater number of cases have arisen in consequence of ill-drawn and obscure wills. Although the Wills Act [1] has set at rest a great many questions that previously were continually arising on wills, and which could only be decided by resorting to the aid of a Court of Equity, yet the cases arising upon ill-drawn wills are still very numerous, and can only be determined after much delay and expense, which, to a great extent, would be avoided, if they were prepared only by skilful and experienced persons.

INSTRUCTIONS.—On being instructed to make a will a solicitor should take down in writing full particulars respecting the testator's property, whether

[1] 7 Will. 4 & 1 Vict. c. 26.

in possession, reversion, remainder, or expectancy, and also the particulars of his family. After doing this he should insert opposite each description of property the name and any necessary identification of the person to whom the testator intends to devise or bequeath it; and this should be continued until the whole property is disposed of. The following is an outline that may prove of assistance :—

Testator.	James Thompson, of 1, Cheapside, hatter.
Freehold messuage, 1 Cheapside, in occupation of Testator.	To son William Thompson, in fee and £500.
Stock in Trade.	To be valued and taken by son William at his option (if taken, to be paid for with interest by quarterly instalments in three years) : if not taken, to be sold by executors.
Freehold farm containing about 100 acres, at Twyford, Berks, let to John Jones as yearly tenant.	To son James Thompson for life, remainder to his issue as he may appoint, in default to his children equally : in default of issue, to testator's other children.
£100 cash, and an annuity of £50 per annum out of farm, and another annuity of £50 per annum out of messuage at Cheapside.	To his wife, she giving up her right of dower in freeholds.
£1,000.	To daughter Sarah, to be settled on her and her issue.

£50. To shopman James Tom-
kins, if in testator's service at time of death.

And so until all the specific devises and bequests the
testator wishes to make are disposed of, and then
wind up as follows :—

Residue. To sons William and
James and daughter ab-
solutely, as tenants in
common.

Executors. Son William and Simon
Jackson, of 100, Watling
Street, to each of whom
a legacy of £100 to be
given.

PREPARATION OF DRAFT.—With particulars like
the above there will not be much difficulty in the
preparation of the will. Should the testator's property be very large, and the devises and bequests
intricate and complicated, the safest course will be to
lay instructions before counsel to prepare the will ;
and such memoranda as the above will be of great
assistance in giving him every information he may
require. When the will has been prepared, the
solicitor must make a fair copy of it, and either send
it to the testator to read over, or make an appointment and read it over to him himself. The first
course is preferable, as the testator will more readily
remember any omission that may have been made, or
any alteration he may wish to make, if he reads
over the draft in his own way, than he would be
able to do if it were read to him.

Locke King's Act.—If the testator has any property in mortgage, and intends the person to whom such property is devised or bequeathed to take it subject to the mortgage, the best course will be to make the devise or bequest as if the property were not subject to the mortgage, as Locke King's Act[1] and the Amendment Acts[2] have taken it out of the power of the devisee or legatee to require the mortgage to be paid off out of the testator's personal estate, unless a contrary intention appears in the will. If, therefore, the property is devised or bequeathed in the same manner as it would be were there no mortgage on it, the testator's wishes will be carried into effect, and the devisee or legatee, if he takes the property at all, must take it subject to the mortgage, as no contrary intention will appear in the will. But if the testator intends the property to be taken by the devisee or legatee free from the mortgage, then it must be so expressed in the will; and precisely the same care will be required in this case as was formerly required, where it was intended that a devisee or legatee should take property subject to the mortgage upon it.

Devise of Trust Estates.—A devise of trust estates was formerly of great importance, but now § 48 of the Land Transfer Act, 1875,[3] provides that where a person dies intestate as to trust estates they shall vest in his executors. The clause is very short, and, if not required, can do no harm;

---

[1] 17 & 18 Vict. c. 113.
[2] 30 & 31 Vict. c. 69; 40 & 41 Vict. c. 31.
[3] 38 & 39 Vict. c. 87.

while, on the contrary, it may save great trouble and expense if questions arise as to whether trust estates are included in any general devise in the will. Of course, some discretion must be exercised as to the insertion of this clause, as in the will of a person possessed of very little property, and who never remembers having been made trustee or advancing money on mortgage, it can scarcely be necessary.

NUMBER OF TRUSTEES.—Sometimes a testator is desirous of appointing a great many trustees or executors. This should be discouraged, as it is seldom that more than two or three will act, and the others must at some time execute a disclaimer of the trusts and a renunciation of the will—a proceeding that causes expense for no useful purpose. Two, or at the outside three, trustees or executors are sufficient for almost any case, and it will usually be found desirable to make the same persons both trustees and executors.

Sometimes it is advisable to have two or more sets of trustees, each set taking a particular property, with trusts attached to it, as in the case of a successful colonist who has property both abroad and in this country. The necessity for this, however, only arises where an extensive property is intended to be dealt with, and the trusts of one part of it may be inconsistent with the trusts of another part. It certainly should not be recommended, unless absolutely unavoidable. A case recently came before the present writer where a testator appointed nine persons trustees and executors; but only two proved his will.

COPYHOLDS.—Should the testator be seised of copy-hold property, which he intends to have sold by his trustees, care must be taken to give to the trustees a power only to sell the property, and by no means to devise it to them, as, if devised, they must take admittance to it, and pay the fine, which, if arbitrary, will amount to two years' improved annual value, and if there is more than one trustee admitted, the fine would be greatly increased. Take the case of property worth £50 a year. Then if three trustees were acting, the fine would be two years' annual value for the first, say £100; one-half of this amount for the second, and one-fourth for the third; this would amount to £175, besides the steward's fees: whereas, if the will merely directed the trustees to sell the copyhold property, the whole of this expense would be saved, as the persons taking the power would exercise it by deed in favour of the purchaser of the property, who thus would come in as a person claiming under the will, and take admittance accordingly, and pay the fine and fees due thereon.[1]

CHARITABLE DEVISES.—The statute of Charitable Uses,[2] the full title of which is, "An Act to restrain the Disposition of Land, whereby the same becomes Inalienable," (commonly called "The Mortmain Act,") is of great importance where a testator wishes to make charitable gifts. It has been amended and improved by several subsequent Acts,[3] all of which

---

[1] See Form LXXIX., p. 361, infra.

[2] 9 Geo. 2, c. 36.

[3] 21 Vict. c. 9; 25 Vict. c. 17; 26 & 27 Vict. c. 106; 27 Vict. c. 13; 35 & 36 Vict. c. 31.

M

should be read, and the effect of the alterations carefully noted up.

EXECUTION.—The draft, having been approved by the testator, will be fair copied on brief paper, and signed by him in the presence of two witnesses, who will sign their names in the presence of each other and in the presence of the testator, neither sealing nor publication being necessary. Care must be taken that neither of the witnesses nor their wives take any benefit under the will, otherwise such witness, although competent to prove the due execution of the will, will lose any benefit intended to be given to him or his wife by it.

After the will has been signed and witnessed, the solicitor should seal it up and hand it to the testator, as most people like to keep their own wills; some, however, prefer leaving it with their solicitors. The best course, when the testator is a man of property, is to engross two parts of the will, and let him sign them both, the solicitor keeping one part and the testator the other.

CHAPTER XI.

INTRODUCTORY.—A disclaimer is a deed executed for the purpose of proving at all future times that a person to whom property has been devised as a trustee declines to accept the trust, or take any interest under the will; in other words, he disclaims the estate devised to him by the will. Disclaimers are principally used in cases where trustees appointed by a will refuse to act in the trusts thereof. A verbal refusal to act is a sufficient disclaimer, and where a trustee has never acted or interfered in any way, it will be considered that, by his conduct, he has disclaimed any intention of ever interfering; but, notwithstanding this, a deed is generally executed, as it is the best evidence that can possibly be obtained of the refusal to act on the part of the trustee.

FORM OF DEED.—This deed is very simple; it usually recites so much of the will as is necessary to shew the devise to the trustee, and what property the deed is intended to act upon. and then the trustee proceeds to disclaim the estate devised, and all trusts and powers created by the will. The forms in the

M 2

precedents[1] will give an idea of the manner in which this document is generally prepared.

TRUSTEES OF COPYHOLDS.—A disclaimer is often resorted to, and very usefully, in the case of copyhold property held of a manor in which the fines are arbitrary. If there are several trustees of a will, and all the trustees take admittance, the fine, as previously stated, is considerably increased; whereas, if all the trustees except one disclaim, then, on the admittance of that one, a single fine is payable; and it does not follow that the other trustees by executing the disclaimer are shut out from interfering in the trusts of the will, inasmuch as they merely disclaim the copyholds in order that the one trustee may take admittance to the property : it is true that he alone has the legal estate, but the other trustees are still necessary parties to any act done under the will, as in the execution of a power, for instance; and the steward of a manor is bound to admit one trustee, where such a disclaimer has been executed, even although he knows that the others disclaimed their right to be admitted, merely to save the fine.[2] He can, however, require the disclaimer to be entered on the court rolls, and, in practice, it is generally sent to him for that purpose with instructions for the admittance.

COSTS.—The disclaimer is prepared by the solicitor of the acting trustee, and paid for out of the testator's estate. It is very unusual for the disclaiming trustee

[1] Page 360, infra.
[2] Wellesley v. Withers, 4 E. & B. 750.

to wish the draft to be sent to his own solicitor, and if he does he ought to pay the costs of perusing the deed; but as there is no mode of compelling a trustee to execute a disclaimer without litigation, it sometimes is necessary to exercise some discretion as to insisting on the disclaiming trustee paying his own solicitor's costs. The writer knows of no rule of practice on the point, and considers that the acting trustee would be justified in paying the costs.

REGISTRATION.—Where a disclaimer relates to freehold property situate in Middlesex or Yorkshire, it should be registered.

STAMP.—A deed of disclaimer requires a ten shilling stamp to be impressed on it.

CHAPTER XII.

PROBATES AND LETTERS OF ADMINISTRATION.

INSTRUCTIONS.—On receiving instructions to prove a will, a solicitor should obtain from the executor the particulars of all the personal property the testator died possessed of, and for this purpose he will find it useful to have the form of a residuary account before him, as it will assist his memory, and also the memory of the executor, as to the particulars of the estate of the deceased.

PROBATE DUTY.—In estimating the amount under which the property is to be sworn for probate, no deduction must be made for any debts or payments of any description, except mortgage debts. For instance, suppose the personal estate of the testator to consist of £10,000 in the funds, and nothing more, and his liabilities (there being no mortgages) to amount to £9,900, the probate must be sworn under £10,000, and probate duty paid on that amount; but after passing the residuary account a return of duty may be obtained on the ground of debts, and the account will shew that the proper stamp on the probate should be £2, the property being under the value of £200. In proceeding for a return of duty, some trouble may be saved by bearing in mind that every receipt produced in proof of debts must be stamped and signed by the proper person, otherwise no deduction will be allowed on account of the money mentioned in such receipt.

It should be mentioned that the Bank of England never, under any circumstances, takes notice of trusts affecting stock; it frequently happens, therefore, that stock standing in the name of a testator does not belong to him beneficially, but as trustee, and in such case, if the stock is of large amount, it becomes a matter of considerable importance to save the probate duty which would be payable thereon, and there is a statutory provision [1] enabling executors or administrators of a deceased trustee of government stock to exempt such stock from probate duty. The Bank requires the provisions of that Act to be strictly followed, and will furnish, on application, a form of affidavit which will be found applicable in most cases.

If the deceased had any beneficial interest in the stock, the particulars and the value of such interest must be stated, together with the fact that the duty paid on the probate or letters of administration is sufficient to cover such value, as well as the residue of the personal estate of the deceased, in respect of which such probate or letters of administration have been granted.

Should the facts not be within the personal knowledge of the executor or administrator any other competent person may depose to them, in which case the executor or administrator must join and state

[1] 48 Geo. 3, c. 149, ss. 36, 37.

that such deposition is true to the best of his knowledge, and also that he intends to apply the funds accordingly.

Having estimated, as nearly as possible, the value of the personal estate of the testator at the time of his decease, the amount under which the probate is to be sworn must be decided upon; and, in some cases, there will be a margin of one or two thousand pounds between the different amounts under which the probate may be sworn; in others, the value of the property will, within a few pounds, amount to the nearest sum in the scale; and should this be the case, the better course will be to take the next higher sum in the scale, and swear the probate under that, for it is frequently found afterwards that something was forgotten in estimating the value of the personalty; and although it may appear somewhat strange, there is less difficulty in getting a return of overpaid duty than in obtaining permission from the Board of Inland Revenue to pay additional duty.

PROVING A WILL.—Having arrived at this point, the solicitor's course will be very different from what it was formerly; for, instead of handing the business over to a proctor, he will now proceed himself to prove the will, and perform the duties formerly as a matter of right done by a proctor. This can be done either at the principal registry at Somerset House in London, or in the country at the district registry in which the deceased at the time of his death had a fixed place of abode.

The present practice is shortly as follows: It is necessary, in order to obtain either probate or letters of administration, to fill up the printed forms of affidavits, No. 1 being called "Oath of Executors (*or* Administrators)," which is filed in the principal registry in London, or in a district registry in the country, according to where the application is made; and No. 2 being called "Affidavit for Commissioners of Inland Revenue." For probate a *fac simile* copy of the will, which may be in ordinary round-hand, must be engrossed on parchment. Both affidavits must then be sworn by the executors who intend to prove, or by the administrator, as the case may be. The administrator must execute a bond with two sureties. These affidavits may be sworn in London at the Principal Registry, or before a commissioner properly appointed, and in the country before a country commissioner, who must attest the execution of the bond. The most convenient plan in either case is to get the affidavits sworn and bond attested before a commissioner, and save the executors or administrators the time and trouble of attending at the registry. When the affidavits are sworn a parchment form duly stamped with *ad valorem* duty, called the act, and a printed schedule to which the adhesive stamps for court fees are to be affixed, must be obtained from the stationers or from Somerset House; these with the affidavits must be taken in cases where a grant of administration is required, direct to the clerk of the seat to whose division, according to the surname of the deceased, the matter will belong; and in cases where probate is required, the affidavits and schedule, together with the original will and the engrossment, must be first taken to the Examiner of Wills, from whom they will be forwarded to the seat, if the engrossment is correct ; but if it is not, a notice will be sent to the solicitor requiring him to attend and rectify the errors. It is also essential to have the folios[1] counted and marked on the engrossment. Within a few days (if there is nothing to raise any impediment) the probate or letters of administration will be ready for delivery at the sealer's room. In the country the most convenient way is to send the documents by post, registered, to the district registrar, with a request for probate or letters of administration as the case may require, and he will, by return of post, send a receipt for the documents, and either then, or a few days afterwards, an account of fees, saying that on payment of them the probate or letters of administration are ready, and on receipt of the amount will be forwarded by post. The previous remarks apply to what is termed non-contentious business, that is, when no opposition or impediment is raised against the grant of probate or administration by any third parties ; but when such is the case, the business is properly termed contentious, and commences with the entry of a caveat at the registry. In both contentious and non-contentious business, numerous peculiar and difficult points constantly arise, both as to practice and forms ; and it always becomes necessary to refer to some standard work on probate practice.[2]

[1] Ninety words make a folio in probate matters.
[2] See Coote, Brown, or Dixon.

CHAPTER XIII.

LEGACY AND SUCCESSION DUTIES.

INTRODUCTORY.—In addition to the payment of probate duty, part of the duty cast upon executors and trustees under wills, and administrators of the estates of intestates, is to pay all legacy duties, duty on residue and succession duty (if any) in respect of the property of their testator or intestate.[1] A similar duty has also to be performed by either beneficiaries or trustees under deeds or other instruments, upon any succession arising to property under the Succession Duty Act.[2]

With respect to all these matters, the proper forms of legacy and annuity receipts, residuary accounts and succession accounts, can be obtained in London at the office of the Commissioners of Inland Revenue, Somerset House, and in the country from the stamp distributor of the district. The following instructions as to these matters may prove useful :—

LEGACY DUTY.—Fill up separate receipts on the printed forms, according to the instructions on them, for each legatee and annuitant, specifying whether the legacy is pecuniary or specific ; if the latter, it is

---

[1] 36 Geo. 3, c. 52 ; 55 Geo. 3, c. 184 ; 8 & 9 Vict. c. 76, s. 4.
[2] 16 & 17 Vict. c. 51.

often necessary to get the value assessed by an appraiser; calculate and fill in the amount of duty. Do the same with the annuity receipts. If the legacy consists of stock in the government funds, its value in money must be calculated at the price at which the stock may be officially quoted, at or about the day on which you pass the accounts and pay the duty. In London take the accounts and duty to the Legacy Duty Office at Somerset House, where the clerk in the department will examine the former, and, if correct, will pass them, and you can then pay the duty, and get the proper stamps affixed. Should the account or receipts require any material alteration or amendment, you may have to take them away, and attend another day to pass them and pay the duty. In the country take the account and receipts with the total duty in cash as you have calculated it to the stamp distributor of the district, and take his official receipt for them. He will forward them to Somerset House, and in about a fortnight you will have the account and receipts back through him, either passed and completed, or with written queries and requirements by the clerk in London, which you must answer, and return the accounts to London through the distributor, until the matter is completed.

The previous remarks apply to residuary accounts of personal property of testators and intestates, and legacy and annuity receipts to be prepared and passed, and the duties in respect of them paid, by executors or administrators pursuant to the provisions of the Legacy Duty Acts. The preparing and passing these accounts, although not strictly forming any part of conveyancing business, is generally performed, as a

matter of course, by the solicitor who acts for the
executors or administrators in proving the will, or
procuring a grant of letters of administration of the
personal estate of the testator or intestate, as the case
may be. The legacy and residuary accounts affect
only personalty, and a purchaser of real property is
not in any way concerned with, or affected by, them,
but the case is different with regard to succession
duty.

SUCCESSION DUTY.—The passing of the Succession Duty Act[1] has cast an additional and important
onus upon solicitors in numerous conveyancing
matters, and affecting both real and personal property. By that Act it is declared, that as regards
the sale of any property within the scope of the Act,
both freehold and leasehold (the latter being declared
real estate for the purposes of the Act), if the vendor,
either beneficially or in a fiduciary character, derives
the property as successor under a deed, will, or other
instrument upon the death of any person after the
Act came into operation,[2] such property in the hands
of the purchaser is liable to the succession duty,
which will have accrued on such death, and he is
entitled, before completing, to have official evidence
that such duty has been paid, and a proper receipt
given for it by the Board of Inland Revenue.

It is therefore necessary as well when acting for a
vendor on the sale of freehold or leasehold property
as for beneficiaries, trustees, executors, or administrators, that a solicitor should take care to ascertain

[1] 16 & 17 Vict. c. 51.
[2] 19th May, 1853.

whether any and what succession duty is payable in respect of real or personal estate, which may have in any manner devolved upon them, and proceed to prepare and pass the proper accounts and pay the duties. After the accounts are prepared in duplicate in London, they are taken to the Succession Duty Office at Somerset House, and settled with the clerk there. The duties are paid in another part of the building. In the country the business is transacted through the stamp distributor, but there is this difference between legacy and succession accounts, that the country distributor will not take any money on account of succession duty until after the account has been examined and approved, and the duty assessed at Somerset House.

There are various forms of succession accounts issued by the Commissioners of Inland Revenue, all of which can be readily obtained on application, except that which is used when for any particular reason it is wished to anticipate the time when duty would accrue, and have such duty commuted and paid forthwith. With respect to this the commissioners have a discretion, which they only exercise upon a written statement of the circumstances, and the reason for anticipating the time of payment. The legacy and succession duties are important matters, and numerous difficult and special questions constantly arise regarding them, and reference is often necessary to some treatise on the subject.[1]

---

[1] See Hanson's Probate, Legacy, and Succession Duties Acts.

CHAPTER XIV.

ADMINISTRATION.

ACTING BEFORE PROBATE. — When professionally concerned for an executor, a solicitor should remember that there are many acts he may do before proving the will; but as this is a very wide field, and not within the scope of this book, reference should be made to some text-book on the subject.[1]

ADMINISTRATION ACTION.—Sometimes when consulted by executors or trustees, as to whether they can safely proceed to administer the estate, a solicitor may feel it to be his duty to inform them that it is doubtful whether they ought to proceed to do so without the assistance and protection of a Court of Equity. Questions of this nature will only arise when the will is of a complicated nature, or where the testator has been engaged in various mercantile or other complicated transactions, or where great trouble and difficulty or responsibility is anticipated in the performance of the trusts of the will. Every case must rest on its own peculiar circumstances. It will be the solicitor's duty to consider the matter carefully, and, if he deems proper, to advise his

[1] Williams on Executors.

client to have the estate administered under the
direction of a Court of Equity, which never refuses
to assist a trustee seeking its aid; but notwithstanding this, it is the paramount duty of a trustee or
executor, after having accepted the trust, to perform
it, if he can do so without involving himself in responsibility, or the estate in needless expense. A
testator on making his will expects his trustees and
executors to administer his estate in the best and
least expensive manner they can, and by no means
considers that, in order to escape trouble or imaginary
responsibility, they would involve the estate in expensive litigation. Before, however, advising a client
to seek the aid of a Court of Equity, his solicitor
should as a matter of precaution take the opinion of
counsel, although counsel will almost invariably re-
commend the estate being administered in Chancery;
and indeed he cannot well do otherwise, for the
question generally put to him is, "What is the safest
course the trustees can take in administering the
estate?" To this there can only be one answer, and
that is, "by administering under the direction of the
Court." But, notwithstanding this, the solicitor will
be placed in a much better position if he is fortified
with the opinion of counsel on the propriety of such
a step before commencing proceedings.

ADVERTISEMENTS FOR CREDITORS.—It should, however, be borne in mind that the modern practice of
advertising for creditors under s. 29 of Lord St.
Leonards' Act[1] is a great protection to an executor

---

[1] 22 & 23 Vict. c. 35.

or administrator.[1] A form of advertisement will be found in this volume.[2]

PETITION FOR ADVICE.—If a trustee, executor, or administrator merely wants to obtain advice or direction as to some particular clause in the will, it may be obtained by petition to any equity judge, or by summons at chambers under Lord St. Leonards' Acts,[3] but it should be taken by petition, with the assistance of counsel, rather than upon summons.[4]

QUESTIONS OF CONSTRUCTION.—Trustees cannot, under this Act, obtain the opinion of the Court on questions of construction.[5]

Where it becomes necessary to obtain the decision of the Court on a simple question of construction, the proper and least expensive course is to issue a writ for administration, to waive accounts and inquiries, and to take out a summons which will raise the question. The summons can then be at once adjourned into Court and the matter decided.[6]

Questions of construction can also be decided on a special case under Sir G. Turner's Act[7] and the Rules of Court.[8]

---

[1] See *Clegg* v. *Rowland*, L. R. 3 Eq. 368; *Newton* v. *Sherry*, 1 C. P. D. 246.

[2] Page 194, *infra*.

[3] 22 & 23 Vict. c. 35, s. 30; 23 & 24 Vict. c. 38, s. 9. See also R. S. C. Ord. XIX. r. 4.

[4] *Re Dennis*, 5 Jur. (N.S.) 1388; *Re Miles*, 27 Beav. 579; *Re Pell*, 27 Beav. 576.

[5] *Re Hooper*, 9 W. R. 729.

[6] *Re Birkett*, 9 Ch. D. 576.

[7] 13 & 14 Vict. c. 35.

[8] R. S. C. Ord. XXXIV. r. 9.

LEGACY RECEIPTS AND RELEASES.—In paying legacies bequeathed by a will an executor should see that the legatee signs the proper form of legacy receipt, which can be obtained at Somerset House; and in distributing the residue the safer course always is to take a release from the residuary legatees. Releases, however, are more generally prepared than is necessary. It is only under certain circumstances that a release may strictly be demanded.[1]

BEQUESTS OF LEASEHOLDS.—Before advising executors to give up possession of leasehold property of their testator to a legatee under the will their solicitor should refer carefully to §§ 27 and 28 of Lord St. Leonards' Act,[2] which define the liability of executors or administrators in respect of rents, covenants and agreements, and also in respect of rents, &c., in conveyances or rent-charges.

REGISTRATION.—A will of real estate, situate in a register county, must be registered, but a will relating only to leasehold estate, wherever situate, need not be registered; it is often done, although quite unnecessary. The primary object of registration is notice, and as neither an executor nor a legatee can dispose of leaseholds without producing the probate or referring to the will, which would, of course, be inspected by the purchaser's solicitor, it seems difficult to comprehend what further publicity can be gained by registering the probate.

---

[1] *King* v. *Mullins*, 1 Drew. 308; *Warter* v. *Anderson*, 11 H. 301; Godefroi on Trusts, 236.
[2] 22 & 23 Vict. c. 35

APPENDIX I.

PREPARATION AND EXPENSE OF DOCUMENTS.

THE following table shews by whom, and at whose expense, it is customary for various documents to be prepared, in the absence of any stipulation to the contrary.

Documents.	By whom prepared.	At whose expense.
Abstract of title . . .	Vendor's solicitor . .	Vendor.
Agreement for purchase .	Vendor's solicitor . .	Vendor.
Assignment	Assignee's solicitor . .	Assignee.
Conditions of sale . . .	Vendor's solicitor . .	Vendor.
Conditional surrender . .	Mortgagee's solicitor. .	Mortgagor.
Conveyance . . .	Purchaser's solicitor . .	Purchaser.
Counterpart of lease . .	Lessor's or lessee's solicitor.	Lessor.
Disentailing deed . .	Tenant in tail's solicitor	Tenant in tail.
Lease	Lessor's solicitor . . .	Lessee.
Marriage settlement of lady's property.	Wife's solicitor . . .	Husband.
Marriage settlement of gentleman's property.	Husband's solicitor . .	Husband.
Mortgage	Mortgagee's solicitor .	Mortgagor.
Reconveyance, on mortgage being paid off.	Mortgagor's solicitor. .	Mortgagor.
Surrender . . .	Purchaser's solicitor, or steward of the manor	Purchaser.
Deed of covenants to accompany same.	Purchaser's solicitor . .	Purchaser.

APPENDIX II.

Usual Conveyancing Charges.

	£	s.	d.
Instructions	0	6	8

This charge is always allowed for any document, whatever its nature.

| Drawing, 1s. per folio . . . . . | | | |

This charge of 1s. per folio is allowed for all documents.

| Fair copy, 4d. per folio . . . . . | | | |

This charge is always made, but will not be allowed by a taxing master unless the copy is made.

| Engrossing, 8d. per folio . . . . . | | | |

This charge includes the examination of the draft with the engrossment.

| Stamps (as paid) . . . . . . | | | |
| Attending to stamp . . . . . . | 0 | 6 | 8 |

This charge is always made, but is not allowed by a taxing master unless *ad valorem* duty is paid.

Parchment, per skin	0	5	0
Letters, each	0	3	6
Ditto, if special	0	5	0
Perusing document, when drawn by another solicitor, per skin of 15 folios	0	5	0

No charge is allowed for perusing any alterations made by another solicitor in a draft prepared by yourself, but all correspondence and attendances respecting such alterations are allowed.

	£	s.	d.
Examining engrossment with draft, per skin of 15 folios	0	3	4
This is only allowed when the draft is prepared by another solicitor.			
Attendances, of whatever description, per hour or fractional part	0	6	8
Journeys, per day (exclusive of expenses)	3	3	0
£2 2s. only is allowed by some of the taxing masters.			
Making attested copies of documents, per folio	0	0	6
Stamps and paper for same (as paid)			
Examining and attesting same, 3s. 4d., or 6s. 8d., according to length			
Attending searching for judgments	0	13	4
The like, crown debts	0	13	4
The like, annuities	0	13	4
Paid	0	1	0
Attending making search at the Middlesex Registry for incumbrances	0	13	4
Or according to the time engaged, besides the fee paid on the search and for references.			
Attending reading over and attesting execution of deed	0	6	8
This charge is allowed, irrespective of the number of persons executing the deed, if done at the same time; but for each separate attendance the same fee is allowed.			

		£	s.	d.
Attending completion	⎰	0	6	8
	⎱	0	13	4
		1	1	0

Or according to circumstances.

	£	s.	d.
Instructions for case for the opinion of counsel	0	6	8
Drawing same, per sheet	0	6	8
Fair copy per sheet	0	3	4
Fee to Mr. X. and clerk, with same (as paid)			
Attending him	0	6	8
Instructions for abstract	0	6	8
Drawing same, per sheet	0	6	8

	£	s.	d.
Fair copy, per sheet	0	3	4
Attending examining same with deeds, per hour .	0	6	8

This charge does not include the clerk taken with you, for whose attendance 3s. 4d. per hour is allowed, but if a journey is undertaken, then the charge is made by the day, and the expenses of the journey must be added.

Perusing abstract . . . .

The charge usually made is 6s. 8d. for every three sheets.

Fee to Mr. X. and clerk, to advise on same (as paid)

Attending him	0	6	8
Instructions for requisitions on title . .	0	6	8
Drawing same, per brief sheet . . .	0	6	8
Fair copy	0	3	4
Perusing answers to requisitions on title, if short .	0	6	8

Or according to length.

Instructions for further requisitions . .	0	6	8

Drawing same (as before) . . . . .

Perusing requisitions on title . . .	0	6	8

Or according to length and the difficulty of the matter.

Drawing answers thereto . . . . .

This is regulated by the difficulty of the matter.

Fair copy of the whole, for purchaser's solicitor, per brief sheet	0	3	4

APPENDIX III.

Proposed by the Council of the Incorporated Law Society for the remuneration of solicitors for their skill, labour and responsibility in respect of loans and sales.

The commission is intended to include all charges for negotiation, but to be exclusive of all disbursements and of charges for searching and registering in register counties, also of journeys out of England, and any extra work occasioned by changes occurring in the course of the business such as the death or insolvency of a party to the transaction. It is not to include any business of a contentious character nor any proceedings in any Court, such as an application for a vesting order, or payment of money into Court on a Chancery sale.

AS TO FREEHOLDS AND COPYHOLDS.

SALES AND PURCHASES.

	Vendor's Solicitor.	Purchaser's Solicitor.
For every £100 up to £1000	A sum equal to three-fourths of the purchaser's solicitor's allowance.	£3 per cent.
And in addition After the first £1,000, for every £100 up to £5,000	Ditto ditto	£2 per cent.
And in addition After the first £5,000, for every £100 up to £50,000	Ditto ditto	£1 per cent.
And in addition After the first £50,000, for every £100	Ditto ditto	½ per cent.

LOANS.

	Mortgagor's Solicitor.	Mortgagee's Solicitor.
For every £100 up to £2,000	A sum equal to three-fourths of the mortgagee's solicitor's allowance.	£2 per cent.
And in addition After the first £2,000, for every £100 up to £15,000	Ditto ditto	£1 per cent.
And in addition After the first £15,000	Ditto ditto	½ per cent.
Loans under the Drainage Acts—on County and Borough Rates—Dock Dues—and for other purposes under statutory powers, and securities of a like nature.	The Council is not prepared to suggest a scale for the remuneration of the mortgagor's solicitor on this class of securities.	At the rate of one-half of the allowance of the mortgagee's solicitor in respect of freeholds and copyholds.

The commission on sale or mortgage of leaseholds for terms not exceeding originally 100 years, shall be one-fourth less than the scale on sale or mortgage of freeholds and copyholds.

Fractional parts of £100 to be reckoned as £100.

Where the same solicitor acts for both mortgagor and mortgagee, he should have the mortgagee's solicitor's allowance, and one-fourth of the allowance of the mortgagor's solicitor.

Where a loan on mortgage forms part of a sale and purchase transaction, and the same solicitor acts, the solicitor should be entitled to one-half the allowance for a mortgage in addition to the allowance for a sale and purchase.

Where the same solicitor acts for both vendor and purchaser, he should have the purchaser's solicitor's allowance, and one-fourth of the allowance of the vendor's solicitor, of the aggregate of which, in the absence of a special agreement, the vendor should bear two-fifths and the purchaser three-fifths.

Sales in lots to be treated as separate transactions if lots are sold to separate purchasers.

On sales by auction, if a contract is not entered into for the sale of the property, or (if there be more than one lot), for the sale of all the lots, then the vendor's solicitor shall have only one-third of the allowance calculated on the reserved price of the property, or of the several lots unsold.

APPENDIX IV.

NEW SCALES OF FEES

Suggested by the Council of the Incorporated Law Society for the remuneration of Solicitors in Conveyancing Transactions—June, 1880.

These Scales are intended to include all charges for procuration and negotiation, but not counsel's fees, stamps, plans, travelling expenses, or other disbursements, or time expended on journeys beyond 200 miles, or out of England; nor any business of a contentious character, such as proceedings to enforce performance of a contract, nor any proceedings in any Court, such as a vesting order or payment of money into or out of Court on a Chancery Sale; nor charges for searching and registering in register counties, nor acknowledgments by married women, nor extra work occasioned by changes occurring in the course of the business, such as the death or insolvency of a party to the transaction.

Fractions of £100 are, throughout, to be reckoned as £100 in the case of sales, purchases, and mortgages. As to leases at rack rent, fractions of £10 are to be reckoned as £10, and as to conveyances reserving rent, and building or repairing leases, fractions of £5 as £5.

SALES AND PURCHASES.

AMOUNT OF PURCHASE-MONEY.	VENDOR'S SOLICITOR ¾ of Purchaser's Solicitor	PURCHASER'S SOLICITOR 3 per cent to £500 1½ „ £5,000 ¾ „ £50,000 ⅜ „ afterwards
£	£ s. d.	£ s.
300	6 15 0	9 0
500	11 5 0	15 0
1,000	16 17 6	22 10
2,000	28 2 6	37 10
3,000	39 7 6	52 10
4,000	50 12 6	67 10
5,000	61 17 6	82 10
6,000	67 10 0	90 0
7,000	73 2 6	97 10
8,000	78 15 0	105 0
9,000	84 7 6	112 10
10,000	90 0 0	120 0
15,000	118 2 6	157 10
20,000	146 5 0	195 0
30,000	202 10 0	270 0
40,000	258 15 0	345 0
50,000	315 0 0	420 0
60,000	343 2 6	457 10
70,000	371 5 0	495 0
80.000	399 7 6	532 10
90,000	432 0 0	576 0
100,000	455 12 6	607 10
200,000	736 17 6	982 10

Sales in lots to be treated as separate transactions, if lots are sold to separate purchasers.

In sales and purchases of equities of redemption, the Scale to be calculated on the money paid, and the principal of the mortgage debt.

LOANS.

AMOUNT OF LOAN.	PROPOSED SCALE.	
	MORTGAGOR'S SOLICITOR	MORTGAGEE'S SOLICITOR
	⅔ of Mortgagee's Solicitor.	2 per cent. to £2,000 1 „ £15,000 ½ „ afterwards
£	£ s.	£
300	4 10	6
500	7 10	10
1,000	15 0	20
2,000	30 0	40
3,000	37 10	50
4,000	45 0	60
5,000	52 10	70
6,000	60 0	80
7,000	67 10	90
8,000	75 0	100
9,000	82 10	110
10,000	90 0	120
15,000	127 10	170
20,000	146 5	195
30,000	183 15	245
40,000	221 5	295
50,000	258 15	345
60,000	296 5	395
70,000	333 15	445
80,000	371 5	495
90,000	408 15	545
100,000	446 5	595
200,000	821 5	1,095

LEASES AND CONVEYANCES IN FEE, OR FOR LONG TERMS ON RENTS (which are usually called chief or fee farm rents).

(*a*) FOR LEASES AT RACK RENT (EXCEPT MINING LEASES).

LESSOR'S SOLICITOR, for preparing and completing lease.

Up to £40 rent ... ... £4.

For every £10 beyond £40 to £100 ... ... 15s.

For every £10 beyond £100 to £200 ... ... 5s.

For every subsequent £10 { 2s. 6d., but the total not to exceed £20.

LESSEE'S SOLICITOR for perusing draft and completing ... ... { One-third of the amount payable to the Lessor's Solicitor, but never to be less than £2.

The Lessor's Solicitor to have £2 in addition in all cases where there is a counterpart.

(*b*) FOR CONVEYANCES IN FEE, OR FOR ANY OTHER FREEHOLD ESTATE RESERVING RENT, OR BUILDING LEASES RESERVING RENT.

VENDOR'S or LESSOR'S SOLICITOR, for preparing and completing conveyance or lease (exclusive of abstract of title, if furnished) :—

Up to £5 rent ... ... £5.

For every £5 beyond £5 to £50 ... ... 20s.

For every £5 beyond £50 to £150 ... ... 10s.

For every £5 beyond £150 { 5s., but the total not to exceed £50.

PURCHASER'S OR LESSEE'S SOLICITOR, for perusing draft and completing ... { One-third of the amount payable to the Vendor's or Lessor's Solicitor, but never to be less than £3.

The Vendor's or Lessor's Solicitor to have £2 in addition in all cases where there is a counterpart or duplicate.

MARRIAGE SETTLEMENTS.

FOR THE LADY'S SOLICITOR.

For the first £2000, one per cent.

After the first £2000, and up to the first £10,000, ten shillings per cent.

After the first £10,000, 2s. 6d. per cent.

FOR THE GENTLEMAN'S SOLICITOR.

One-half of the charge of the Lady's Solicitor.

In capitalising, land is to be taken at thirty years' and houses at twenty years' purchase; Policies of Life Insurance where the annual premiums are secured by income arising from property, are to be taken at the amount insured; in other cases at half the amount insured. Where an estate is settled subject to prior charges, one-half of such charges to be deducted.

APPENDIX V.

INSTRUCTIONS

To be sent to a Non-professional Person with a DEED FOR EXECUTION.

Instructions for Execution of the accompanying Deed.

SIGN the deed at the foot, in front, opposite the seal [and also under the receipt indorsed at the back] in the place where your name is written in pencil : place a finger on the seal and say, "I deliver this as my act and deed." A witness should see you sign the deed [and receipt] and should write his or her name, place of abode and profession or calling, under the attestation at the back where " Witness's name, &c.," is written in pencil, [and should write his or her name only under the receipt where " Witness's name only " is written in pencil.]

PART II.

——◦——

PRECEDENTS.

PRECEDENTS.

ADVERTISEMENTS.

I.

ADVERTISEMENT *for Creditors by* EXECUTOR *under Lord St. Leonards' Act.*

A. B., deceased.

NOTICE is hereby given, that all creditors and other persons[1] having any debt or claim upon or affecting the estate of A. B., late of &c., who died on [*date*], and whose will was proved in the Principal Registry of the Probate Division of the High Court of Justice on [*date*], by C. D., of &c. [the relict of the deceased], and　　　, the executors thereof, are hereby required to send in the particulars of their claims to the said executors, at [*specify residence or office of exors or solrs*], or to us the undersigned, their solicitors, on or before [*date*], at the expiration of which time the said executors will proceed to distribute the assets of the said A. B., the testator, among the persons entitled thereto, having regard to the debts and claims only of which the said executors shall then have had notice; and the said executors will not be liable for the assets so distributed to any person of whose debt or claim they shall not have had notice at the time of such distribution.

Dated the　　　day of　　　, 18 .

[*Signature*], London, solicitors to the executors
of the said A. B.

---

[1] See *Newton* v. *Sherry*, 1 C. P. D. 246.

O

II.

ADVERTISEMENT *for Creditors by* ADMINISTRATOR *under Lord St. Leonards' Act.*

A. B., deceased.

Pursuant to the statute 22 & 23 Vict. c. 35, intituled "An Act to Amend the Law of Property and to Relieve Trustees," notice is hereby given, that all persons having any claims against the estate of A. B., late of &c., in the county of Y., Draper, deceased (who died intestate on the [*date*], and of whose personal estate and effects letters of administration were granted by the W. District Registry of the Probate Division of Her Majesty's High Court of Justice, on the [*date*], to C. B., [the natural and lawful brother, and] one of the next of kin of the deceased), are required to send particulars thereof in writing to the administrator, at my office, R. Street, X., in the said county, on or before the [*date*], after which day the administrator will proceed to distribute the assets of the said deceased, having regard only to the claims of which he shall have had notice.— Dated this &c.

T. W., Solicitor for the administrator, R. Street, X., in the county of Y.

AFFIDAVITS.

III.

AFFIDAVIT *verifying* NOTICE OF DISSOLUTION *of Partnership.*

I, G. H., of &c., make oath and say, that I was present on the [*date*], and saw A. B., of &c., C. D., of &c., and E. F., of &c., severally sign the notice of dissolution of partnership hereto annexed, and that the names "A. B.," "C. D.," and "E. F.," severally subscribed, at the foot of the sd notice of dissolution, are the several handswriting of the said A. B., C. D., and E. F., respectively, and that the name "G. H." appearing as that of the attesting witness of the said notice, is my own handwriting.

G. H.

Sworn at X., in the county
of Y., this   day of
        1880, before me
K. L., a commissioner to
administer oaths in the
Supreme Court of Judica-
cature in England.

IV.

AFFIDAVIT *to obtain* DISTRINGAS *on Stock.*

In the matter of [*state will or settlement*]
and
In the matter of the Act of Parliament,
5 Vict. c. 5.

I, A. B., of &c. [*or*, X. Y., &c.],[1] make oath and say that, according to the best of my knowledge, information and

---

[1] The affidavit may be made by the party himself or his solicitor. For Form of Notice to Company, see Form CV, p. 404, *infra.*

belief, 1 am [*or, if the affidavit is made by A. B.'s solicitor,
A. B. of &c.,*   *is*] beneficially interested in the stock
comprised in the [*settlement or will*] above mentd, which stock,
according to the best of my knowledge and belief, now con-
tists of the stock specified in the notice hrto annexed.

Sworn, &c. [*as in Form III.*]

This afdt is filed on behalf of A. B., whose address is &c.

V.

AFFIDAVIT *of due Execution of* BILL OF SALE.

In the High Court of Justice,
    Queen's Bench Division.

I, A. B., of &c., a solicitor of the Supreme Court, make
oath and say as follows :—

1. The document hereto annexed and marked A is a true
copy of a bill of sale and of every schedule or inventory
thereto annexed or therein referred to, and of every attestation of the execution thereof, as made and given and executed
by C. D.

2. The sd bill of sale was made and given by the sd C. D.
on [*date*].

3. I was present and saw the sd C. D. duly execute the
same on the [*date*].

4. The sd C. D. resides at &c., and is a [*occupation*].

5. The name, A. B., subscribed as the attesting witness
thereto is in my own handwriting.

6. I am a solicitor of the Supreme Court.

7. Before the execution of the said bill of sale by the sd
C. D. I fully explained to him the nature and effect thereof.

Sworn at &c., on [*date*].

VI.

AFFIDAVIT *of due Execution of* BILL OF SALE *given by* SHERIFF.

I, A. B., of &c., a solicitor of the Supreme Court, make oath and say as follows:—

The document hereto annexed is a true copy of a bill of sale and of every schedule or inventory thereto annexed or therein referred to and of every attestation of the execution thereof.

The said bill of sale was given on [*date*] by C. D., the sheriff of the county of X. therein named [*or* by E. F. who was then one of the deputies of the said C. D. the sheriff of the county of X.], under and in execution of a writ of *fi. fa.* issued out of the Chancery Division of the High Court of Justice against E. F., the person named in such bill of sale.

The said bill of sale was duly executed in my presence and was duly attested by me.

The said G. H. resides at &c., and is a &c.

The signature A. B. subscribed as the attesting witness to the said bill of sale is in my own handwriting, and I reside at &c., and am a solicitor of the Supreme Court.

Sworn, &c.

VII.

AFFIDAVIT *for the* RE-REGISTRATION *of a Bill of Sale.*

I, A. B., of &c., do swear that a bill of sale dated, &c., and made between [*insert the names, &c., of the parties of the bill of sale as in the original bill of sale*] and which said bill of sale [*or,* and a copy of which said bill of sale] was registered on the [*date*] and is still a subsisting security.

Sworn, &c.

VIII.

AFFIDAVIT *verifying Consent to Order for entering*
SATISFACTION *of Bill of Sale.*

I, A. B., of &c., a solicitor of the Supreme Court, make
oath and say as follows :—

I was present on the [*date*] and saw E. F., of &c., who at
the time the bill of sale hereinafter mentioned was given
resided at, &c., and was, &c., sign the consent hereto annexed
to an order that a memorandum of satisfaction be written
upon the registered copy of a bill of sale dated, &c., and
made between C. D. of the one part and E. F. of the other
part, and registered on the [*date*], the debt for which such
bill of sale was given having been satisfied or discharged.

Sworn, &c.

AGREEMENTS.[1]

IX.

AGREEMENT *for* SALE *of* FREEHOLD *House—Short Form.*[2]

An Agreet, made the   day of, &c., between A. B., of &c., of the one part, and C. D., of &c., of the other part :—

1. The sd A. B. agrees to sell and the said C. D. to buy for £   the inheritance in fee in possession of and in ALL that messe known as North Villa, situate in X. Road at Y., in the county of Z., with the garden, outbuildings and appurts as now in the occupation of the sd A. B.

2. The pche shall be completed on the [*date*], when the sd C. D. shall be let into possession of the prems, all outgoings up to that time being cleared by the sd A. B.; and if from any cause (not being the fault of the sd A. B.) the pche shall not be then completed, the sd C. D. shall pay interest on the balance of pche-moy from that day until the actual payment thereof at the rate of £5 per cent. per annum.

3. The title to the prems shall commence with a convce dated &c., and no earlier title shall be called for or objected to, and all certificates from registers and declons which the said C. D. may require, whether for the purpose of title, identity or otherwise, shall be paid for by him; all recitals and statements in the said conveyance shall be deemed conclusive evidence of the matters, facts, and conclusions of law therein recited, stated, or implied.

4. The sd C. D. shall pay a deposit of £   on the signing hereof, and in case the sd C. D. shall make a valid

[1] Precedents of documents which, although in form Agreements, take effect as Leases, will be found under the head of " Leases and Tenancy Agreements," *infra*, p. 365.

[2] This is a form which does not unduly curtail the ordinary rights of a purchaser.

objection to the title which the A. B. shall be unable to remove, the sd A. B. may put an end to this agreement by notice in writing to the sd C. D. to that effect, in which case the sd A. B. shall repay the said sum of £   which shall be accepted by the sd C. D. in full satisfaction of all claims in respect of this agreement.

As WITNESS the hands of the parties.

X.

AGREEMENT *for* SALE *of a* FREEHOLD *Farm by* TRUSTEES *of a* *Will*.[1]

AN AGREET made the   day of &c., between A. B. of &c., and C. D. of &c. (hrnftr called the vendors) of the one part, and E. F., of &c. (hrnftr called "the purchaser") of the other part.

1. The vendors will sell and the purchaser will buy for £——, the inheritance in fee simple in possession of and in ALL THAT farm known as X. farm, in the parish of Y., in the county of Z., with the messe and farm buildings thereon, and the appurts, which sd farm comprises the closes of land specified (with the approximate dimensions thof resply) in the schedule hereto.

2. The vendors will deliver to the purchaser an abstract of title to the prems, to commence with an [award dated in April, 1804, under the Y. Inclosure Act, and the regularity of such award, and its validity in all respects, shall be admitted by the purchaser, and he shall not be entitled to call for the production of the title of the lands in respect of which the prems were allotted.][2]

3. The purchaser shall send to the office of the vendor's solicitors [at Y afsd] his objections and requisitions, if any,

[1] This is a full form, with all the usual general clauses. Particular defects in title may render other clauses necessary in certain cases. See forms of Special Conditions of Sale, pp. 289–297, *infra*.

[2] This clause must, of course, be varied to suit the title of the particular property sold.

in respect of the title, the parties to or form of convce within twenty-one days after the delivery of the abstract, and any further objections or requisitions within fourteen days after the delivery of the replies in respect of which they are made, the title, except as so objected to, being considered as accepted, and in this respect time shall be of the essence of the contract: and if any objon or requon be insisted upon which the vendors shall consider themselves unable to remove or comply with, they shall be at liberty, notwithstanding any previous negotiation, to rescind the contract by notice in writing signed by their solicitors, and shall thereupon repay to the purchaser his deposit, but without interest, costs, or damages.

[*Here insert any special clauses that the title may render necessary.*]

4. The purchaser shall not require the production, or any copy of, or investigate or make any objon or requon in respect of any instrument dated previous to the said award, whether or not the same is recited in or referred to in any subsequent deed, or otherwise appears in the abstract, and every recital or statement in any document dated [fifteen] years prior to the day of the sale, shall be conclusive evidence of the facts, matters, and conclusions of law recited, stated, and implied therein; and the purchaser shall pay for all certificates, attested, official, or other copies of or extracts from any documents, and all declarations or other evidence required by him for any purpose whatever, and for the production and inspection of all deeds and evidences not in the possession of the vendors (and to the production of which the purchaser is entitled), and he shall bear the expense of deducing and getting in the title to any outstanding term or estate and of all searches, travelling and other incidental expenses incurred in respect of the matters aforesaid.

5. The property is believed and shall be taken to be correctly described, and is sold subject to all easements and outgoings. If any error or misstatement be discovered, it shall not annul the sale or entitle either party to compensation.

[6.[1] All deeds not properly registered in the county register shall, if required and practicable, be registered or re-registered at the purchaser's expense; but no other requon or objon shall be made in respect thereof.]

7. The purchaser shall bear the expense of stamping or re-stamping any unstamped or insufficiently stamped documents.

8. The purchase shall be completed at the office of the vendors' solicitors on the [date], up to which time the vendors will receive the rents and profits and pay the outgoings of the prems; but if from any cause whatever other than the wilful default of the vendors the purchase shall not be completed at that time the purchaser shall thenceforth pay interest on his pche-moy at £5 % per ann; until the actual payment thereof.

9. The vendors acknowledge receipt of a deposit of £ , and on pmt of the balance of the pche-moy at the time and place afsd, they will execute a proper conveyance of the said prems to the purchaser, but being only devisees in trust for sale, they will only enter into the usual separate covenants against incumbrances.

10. All deeds in the vendors' possession relating solely to the said prems will be delivered to the purchaser on the completion of his purchase, but the vendors will retain the probate of their testator's will [and will retain and enter into the usual limited covenant to produce all documents relating as well to the sd prems as to other property of their testator].

AS WITNESS, &c.

The SCHEDULE above referred to.

XI.

AGREEMENT *for* SALE *of* LEASEHOLD *Houses held by Underlease.*

CONCISE FORM—VERY STRINGENT.

AN AGREET made [date]. That A. B., of &c. (as vendor) agrees to sell, and C. D., of &c. (as purchaser) agrees to pche

[1] This clause is only required for property in Yorkshire or Middlesex.

for the sum of £—— the vendor's interest in the property described at the foot hereof. No evidence of identity shall be required beyond what deeds in the posson of the vendor afford, nor shall any objon be made in respect throf nor on account of any deed or document not being registered in Middlesex or owise, and the vendor shall not be bound to produce any deeds or documents not in his actual posson.

The requons (if any) to be delivered within seven days from the transmission of the abstract, and the title to be considered as accepted subject only to any requons or objons then made, whether such abstract be perfect or not, time in all respects being the essence of this contract. The pcher shall on the exon hrof pay to the vendor or his agent the sum of £—— as a deposit, and in part payment of the pche-moy, and shall pay the remainder of the pche-money and complete his pche on [date] at the office of the vendor's solrs and from that date the pcher to be entitled to the rents and profits or to posson. If delay in completion should arise from whatever cause the pcher to pay interest at 5 per cent. upon the balance of the pche-moy unless the vendor shall elect to take the rents and profits in lieu of such int. The pcher to pay to the vendor in addition to the pche-moy the proportion of any current rents, as also the proportionate amount of insurance under the existing policy. All deeds and documents to be accepted without objection whether unstamped or insufficiently stamped. Should any valid objon to the title be raised which the vendor may be unable, or by reason of expense or orwise decline, to remove, he shall be at liberty to put an end to this contract by returning the deposit paid without being liable to int or expenses of any description. The receipt for the ground rent last paid to be accepted as conclusive evidence of all covts stipulns and provons in the lease having been duly performed, and of all breaches of covenant whether continuing or not having been waived up to and including the day of completion. The assignment to be prepared by and at the cost of the pcher, and every assnce and act (if any) which shall be required by the pcher for getting in, surrendering, or releasing any outstanding este, right, title, or interest, or for completing or perfecting the vendor's title, or for any other ppse, shall be prepared, made, and done by and at the expense of the pcher. All attested official or other copies of or extracts from deeds, wills, proceedings, registers, or other documents, whr in the posson of the vendor or not, and all certificates, deeds of covt, declons, or evidence of title, and the prodon and inspection of any document or other evidence (if any) not in the vendor's possou, and all information not in the vendor's knowledge, whether required for the completion or verification of the title or the abstract, shall be sought for and obtained at the pcher's expense in all respects. The vendor to pay or allow all outgoings or proportions thereof payable by him up to the date from which the pcher takes the benefit of his purchase. The property is believed to have been faithfully described, but should any error inadvertently appear such shall be the subject of compensation (having regard to the pche money) to be ascertained by two referees in the usual manner, it being however understood that the pcher has satisfied himself as to the state of repair by inspection. Should the pcher fail to complete his pche at the time fixed the vendor to be at liberty to put an end to this contract without tendering an assignment, tho deposit in that case to be forfeited as ascertained and liquidated damages, and not by way of penalty, or at the vendor's discretion, he may enforce a specific performance of this contract.

DESCRIPTION OF THE PROPERTY.

Nos. 1, 2, 3, and 4, X. Street, Y., in the county of Middlesex, let to weekly tenants, landlord paying rates and taxes. The property is held by underlease for the residue of a term of   years from the [*date*], less forty days, at a net rent of £   a year, payable quarterly.

SPECIAL CONDONS.

The title shall commence with the underlease under which

the vendor holds, dated the 9th of February, 1863, which
shall be deemed and taken to be well granted, and no earlier
or other title shall be called for, inquired into, or objected to,
and no objection shall be made or taken by reason of any
superior lease having comprised other pres.

[Signatures.]

XII.

AGREEMENT *for* SALE *of* LEASEHOLD *Premises and*
STOCK *in Trade of a* LACE MANUFACTURER, *the*
Value of the Stock to be paid by Bills.

AN AGREET, made the   day of &c., between A. B.
of &c., of the one part, and C. D. of &c., of the other part,
as follows, namely :—

1. The said A. B. agrees to sell, and the said C. D. agrees
to buy, all that warehouse, situate &c. with the appurts
thrto belonging, as the same is held by the said A. B.,
under an indre of lease for a term of twenty-one years
from [*date*] at the yearly rent of £   , and subject to the
lessee's covenants and conditions in the said indre contained,
and now in the occupation of the said A. B., together with
the warming apparatus and all the fixtures thrn or thrto
belonging (except fixtures belonging to the landlord) : And
also all that factory situate &c., with the appurts thrto belonging, as the same are held by the said A. B. under an
indre of lease for a term of twenty-one years, from [*date*]
at the yearly rent of £   , and subject to the lessee's
covenants and conditions in the said indre contained, and
now in the occupation of the said A. B., together with all
the fixtures thrn or thrto belonging (except fixtures belonging to the landlord) : And also all that room at the said
factory, and all those other rooms situate at &c., with the
appurs, held by the said A. B. as a yearly tenant, at the
respective yearly rents of £   and £   together with all
and singular the fixtures thrin or thrto belonging (except
fixtures belonging to the landlord).

2. Each party shall on signing this agreet appoint a valuer, or in case eir party shall make default in so doing the other may appoint two valuers; the two valuers, immediately after their appointment, shall name an umpire to decide between them in case of dispute; such two valuers or their umpire shall, on the [*date*] proceed to fix and award the sum to be paid by the said C. D. to the said A. B. for the purchase of the said premises and fixtures, and the sum so fixed and awarded shall be final and conclusive.

3. The said purchase shall be completed and the purchase-money paid on the [*date*]; and in case default shall be made in the completion of the said purchase on that day, interest shall be paid on the amount of the said pche-moy at the rate of £5 per cent. per an. from the said [*date*] to the time the money shall be paid.

4. On the completion of the purchase the said C. D. shall be let into posson of the said prems, and entitled to the rents and profits throf as from the [*date*]; all outgoings up to which time shall be paid by the said A. B.

5. The title to the said prems shall commence with the several leases and agreets under which the same are resply held, and the said C. D. shall not call for the title of the lessors, nor make any objection whatever in respect thereto; and the production of the receipts for the payment of the rents in respect of the said premises up to the [*date*] shall be conclusive evidence of all the covts in the said respective leases and agreets having been duly performed, notwith-standing any prior breach may be shown.

6. The said A. B. also agrees to sell, and the said C. D. agrees to buy, upon the terms mentioned in paragraph 7 of this agreet, all the 1416 frames belonging to the said A. B.

7. The said C. D. shall on the completion of the purchase of the before-mentioned prems execute to the said A. B., his executors, administrators, and assigns, a bond prepared by the solicitors of the said A. B., but at the expense of the said C. D., in a sufficient penalty conditioned for the payment to the said A. B. during his life, by quarterly payments, of

a yearly annuity of £   , the first quarterly payment to
be made on the [date], and for the payment to E. B., the
wife of the said A. B., in case she shall survive him, during
her life of a yearly anny of £   : Provided always, that
said respective anns, or any aliquot portion thereof respectively, shall be redeemable by the purchase of a government
anny or other satisfactory anny or secy of like amount as
the anny or portion thof redeemed.

8. In case it shall happen that the purchase of the prems
mentioned in paragraph 1 hereof shall, through the neglect
or default of the said C. D., not be completed on the [date],
the said C. D. shall pay to the said A. B. or his wife, as the
case may be, the first quarterly payment of the said annuity on
the [date], and shall continue to make the said quarterly
payments until the above-mentioned bond shall have been
given.

9. The sd A. B. also agrees to sell, and the said C. D.
agrees to purchase, all the stock in trade, wares and merchandize of the said A. B. both manufactured and unmanufactured,
at the price following, that is to say, the manufactured
articles at the sums specified in the regular list of prices of
the said A. B., less five per cent. discount; and the unmanufactured articles, both in the warehouses and in the hands
of the workmen, at their nett prime cost, to be fixed by
reference to the business books of the said A. B.

10. The sd stock in trade, wares and merchandize shall
be paid for, with interest, as follows, namely, interest shall
begin to run in respect of such part of the purchase-money
thereof as shall remain unpaid from [date]. The said C. D.
shall, on the sd [date], accept bills drawn by the said A. B.
on him, and payable in manner following, that is to say, a
bill payable six months after date for one-fourth of the full
amount or value of the said stock in trade, wares and merchandize, ascertained as afsd; a bill payable nine months
after date for 1000l., and such further sum added thereto as
three months' interest on the value of the said stock in
trade, wares and merchandize, ascertained as afsd shall

amount to, after deducting the afsd one-fourth part thereof so paid as afsd ; a bill payable twelve months after date for £1000, and such further sum added thereto as three months' interest on the balance remaining of the said full value shall amount to, after deducting the amount so paid as aforesaid : a bill payable fifteen months after date for £1000, and such further sum added thereto as three months' interest on the balance then remaining of the said value shall amount to, after deducting the amounts so paid as aforesaid ; and such further bills for £1000 each, payable at every succeeding three months, with interest added thereto, calculated in manner afsd, as shall be requisite or necessary to make up the full value of the said stock in trade, wares and merchandize. The stamps on all the sd bills of exchange shall be paid for by the said C. D.

11. And for the due observance and performance of the stipulons and agreets herein contd on the part of the sd C. D., the sd C. D. doth hereby bind himself unto the said A. B. in the following sums, namely :—

For the performance of the agreet hnbfre contd for the pche of the sd warehouse and factory in the sum of £500 ; for the performance of the agreet hrnbfre contd for pche of the sd frames in the sum of £2,000 ; for the performance of the agreet hrnbfre contd for pche of the sd stock in trade, wares, and merchandize, in the sum of £2,000 ; all which said sums it is hereby declared and agreed shall be considered as liquidated damages, and not by way of penalties.[1]

As WITNESS the hands of the parties.

XIII.

AGREEMENT *for the* SALE *of a British* SHIP.

AN AGREET made &c., between [*parties* A. B. and C. D..]

The sd A. B. agrees to buy and C. D. to sell the ship or vessel called the Arno built at Newcastle upon Tyne of the

[1] As to the last clause, see *Kemble* v. *Farren*, 6 Bing. 141 ; *Reynolds* v. *Bridge*, 6 E. & B. 541.

measurement of 300 tons or thereabouts, now lying at Newport, Mon : for the sum of £—— of which £50 is now paid to the broker to bind the bargain; which sd ship or vessel hath been duly registered pursuant to an Act of Parliament for that purpose made and provided, and a copy of the certificate of such registry is set forth in the schedule hereto.

On payment of the pche-moy within one calr month from the date hereof, a legal bill of sale shall be made out and executed to the purchaser at his expense, and the sd ship with what belongs to her shall be delivered according to the inventory which has been exhibited, but the said inventory shall be made good as to quantity only. And the sd ship, together with all her stores, shall be taken with all faults, in the state and condition in which they now lie, without any allowance or abatement whatsoever, within one calendar month from the date hereof. But if default shall be made by the purchaser in the payment above mentd, the deposit shall be forfeited, and the sd A. B. shall be at liberty to put up and sell the said ship again, either by public or private sale, and the deficiency, if any, upon such resale shall be made good by the defaulting purchaser, who shall be responsible for risks of every description, subsequent to the present pche, and for all charges that may be incurred in consequence of noncompliance with this agreet; and neither the broker nor the sd A. B. shall be accountable for the forfeited deposit.

The said ship is declared to be at the risk of the purchaser immediately after he is put into possession of her.

As WITNESS, &c.

The SCHEDULE above referred to.

N.B.—*Here copy the Certificate of Registration with the endorsements on the back thereof.*

————

P

XIV.

Agreement for the Lease *or* Underlease *of a House
—Short Form.*

Agreement made the   day of &c., between A. B., of
&c., of the one part, and C. D., of &c., of the other part:—

1. The said A. B. agrees to grant, and the said C. D. to
take, a lease of the messe and prems, No. 9 in X. street, as
the same were late in the occupation of E. F., for seven years
at £65 per annum, payable quarterly.

2. The lease and a counterpart thereof shall be prepared
and engrossed by the sd A. B.'s solicitor at C. D.'s expense.

3. The said C. D. shall assume that the said A. B. has
full power to grant the sd lease, and shall not be entitled to
any abstract of or to investigate or make any objon or
requon in respect of the title of the said A. B. or any prior
or other title to the prems.[1]

4. The lease shall contain the following covenants by the
lessee, to pay rent, land tax, sewers and main drainage rates,
and all other outgoings (property tax excepted), to keep the
premises fully insured against fire in the sum of £1200, in
the usual manner, not to assign or underlet without lessor's
consent, but such consent not to be capriciously or without
reasonable cause withheld, to keep the premises in good
repair, and so to yield them up, and also all other usual [2]
covenants and provisions [including covenants similar to
those in the lease under which the sd A. B. holds the
prems].[2]

As witness &c.

[1] This clause is only necessary in an agreement for an underlease. In
granting any lease the title to the *freehold* cannot be called for. See
s. 2 (1) of the Vendor and Purchaser Act, 1874.

[2] As to what are usual covenants, see p. 91, *ante.*

XV.

AGREEMENT *for a* MORTGAGE.

AN AGEET made &c., between A. B., of &c., of the first part,
C. D., of &c., of the second part, and E. G., of &c., of the
third part, Whas, under the will of H. L., late of &c., deceased, dated, &c. the sd A. B. alleges that he will, upon
attaining of the age of twenty-five years, become absolutely
entitled in fee, free from incumbrances (except the annies
of &c., amounting in all to the yearly sum of £240) to an
undivided moiety of certain estates devised by the sd will
and thrn described as all the testator's estates resply called &c.,
situate in &c.: And whas the sd A. B. alleges that he is now
twenty-three years of age: And whas the sd A. B. also alleges
that the sd C. D. is now twenty-one years of age and that he
will also become entitled to the other moiety of the same estes
upon attaining the age of twenty-five years: And whas
the sd E. G. has agreed upon the said A. B. satisfying
him as to the value and title of the proposed secy to lend
the sum of £12,000 to the sd A. B., upon the secy of a
mtge of the sd moiety and of such policy of assce as hrnftr
mentd: And whas the sd C. D. has agreed to join in these
presents in manner hrnftr appearing: NOW THESE PRESENTS
WITNESS as follows:—

1. The sd A. B. shall forthwith, at his own expense,
deduce a good title to an undivided moiety of the estes
alleged to have been devised to him as afsd, to the satisfaction of the solicitor of the sd E. G.,[1] and also procure a
valuation thof by such valuer as the sd E. G. shall appoint.

2. As soon as the title of the sd A. B. to the sd moiety
shall have been approved of on behalf of the sd E. G., the
sd A. B. and all other necy parties (except the sd annants)
shall, upon the request of the sd E. G., but at the cost of
the sd A. B., convey the sd moiety to the use of the sd E. G.
in fee, free from incumbrances (except the sd annies) by

---

[1] As to this stipulation see *Hudson* v *Buck*, 7 Ch. D. 683.

way of mortgage for securing the pmt to him of the sum of £12,000 with int thon, at the rate of £5 per cent. per ann, and the said mortgage shall contain such power of sale, and such covenants and clauses as the solicitor of the sd E. G. shall reasonably require, including a clause sufficient to charge the whole of the sd annies upon the mansion and lands whof the sd A. B. is seised in fee, free from incumbrances, and now in his own occupation at, &c., with all other necy powers for enabling the sd E. G. to hold the sd moiety freed from the sd annies, and for exonerating not only the same moiety, but also (as between the sd parties hereto) the moiety of the sd C. D. from the sd annies, and every of them, and every part thof, and for indemnifying and protecting the sd E. G. and the entirety of the sd estes so devised as afsd during the continuance of the sd mtge secy, from the sd annies.

3. The sd A. B. shall, if required, at his own expense, effect an assce on his life for indemnifying the sd E. G. agnst all loss in the event of the death of the sd A. B. under the age of twenty-five years, such assce to be effected in the name of the sd E. G. in such office, for such sum, and upon such terms and condons as the sd E. G. shall reasonably require, and the premiums in respect of such assce shall be deducted from the amount of the proposed advance.

4. The sd E. G. shall, on the completion of the sd mtge, advance to the sd A. B. the sum of £12,000.

5. At any time after the sd [date], but before the completion of the sd mtge, the sd E. G. shall be at liberty to pay the sd £12,000, or any part thof, into the X bank to a deposit account in his own name but at the risk of the sd A. B. ; and from the date of such pmt (unless there shall be a delay in completion arising through the default of the sd E. G. or his solor), the sd A. B. shall pay to the sd E. G. interest on the sd sum of £12,000, or so much thof as shall be so paid in, at the rate of £5 per cent. per ann ; but the sd E. G. shall, in that case, account to the sd A. B. for all sums (if any) which he may receive from the bank by way of interest in respect thof.

6. If the sd mtge shall be completed, the sd C. D. shall concur with the sd A. B. in securing the interest of the sd mtge debt upon his moiety of the sd estes.

7. If the sd mtge shall not be completed on or before the [*date*], the sd E. G. may, at any time thaftr, and notwstndg any subsequent negons, by notice in writing, rescind these presents, and the sd A. B. shall, whether the sd mtge shall be completed or not, pay all the costs incurred by the sd E. G. in or about the negon for the sd mtge, and the preparon, engrossment, and exon hrof, and the investigon of the title to the sd estes, or in anywise incidental hrto.

8. In the meantime, and until the sd mtge shall be completed, the sd share and interest of the sd A. B. in the sd estes shall be a secy to the sd E. G. for all moys payable to him under this agreet, including all costs and expenses incurred in or about the prems.

As WITNESS, &c.

XVI.

AGREEMENT *for releasing an* ANNUITY *charged on* REAL ESTATE.

AN AGREET made [*date*], between A. B., of &c., of the one part, and C. D., of &c., of the other part: Whas E. F., late of &c., deceased, by her will, dated &c., devised her estate called A., in &c., to the sd A. B., in fee, charged with the pmt of the sum of £1 per week to the sd C. D. during her life: And whas the testatrix died on [*date*] without having revoked or altered her said will: And whas the sd A. B. is desirous of selling the said estate: Now, THEREFORE, it is hrby agreed as follows:—

1. The sd C. D. will, when required, by and at the cost of the sd A. B., and upon the sd A. B. complying with clause 2 hrof, join in the convce or convces of the sd este to the pchr or pchrs thof, or release the sd este from the sd anny.

2. The sd A. B. will, at his own cost, concurrently with

the exon of such convce or rele as afsd, execute and give to
the sd C. D. his bond in the penal sum of £900 conditioned
to be void on pmt to the sd C. D. during her life of the
weekly sum of £1, to commence from the date of the sd
bond ; and will at the same time pay all arrears of the sd
anny up to the date of the sd bond [and will also at the
same time deposit in the Bank of &c., at &c., in the names of
G. H. and I. K., of &c., the sum of £450, as a further secy
for the due pmt of such anny.

3. The sd sum of £450, when deposited, shall, together
with all interest thon, remain in the sd bank until default
shall be made in pmt of the sd anny, and thupon the sd
G. H. and I. K., or the svor of them, or the exors or admors
of such svor, shall, at the request of the sd C. D., eir pay the
sd anny and all arrears throut, or pay the arrears out of the
interest thof, if sufficient, and invest the sd sum of £450, or
a sufficient part thof, in the purchase for the sd C. D. of a
Government anny for her life of £1 per week, and pay the
residue (if any) of the said sum of £450 and interest (after
deducting all exps incurred by such pmt or pche as afsd)
unto the sd A. B.

4. The sd sum of £450 so to be deposited as afsd shall in
no way prejudice the right of the sd C. D. under the sd
bond, and nothing herein contained shall prejudice the right
of the said C. D. against the sd este, until the whole of the
arrangements hereby contemplated shall be carried out.]

5. All the costs of the sd C. D. of and incidental to the
sd arrngmt shall be pd by the sd A. B.

As witness &c.

XVII.

Agreement *for* Reference of Disputes *as to* Damage *by* Mining Operations.

An Agreet made &c., between A. B., of &c., of the one
part, and C. D., of &c., of the other part: Whas the sd A. B.
alleges that the messes, land and outbldgs belonging to him,

situate &c., have been shaken, sunk and cracked through
the mining operons of the sd C. D., and also that minerals
in, under and adjoining to the sd messes, land and outbldgs
belonging to the sd A. B. have been worked and taken by
the sd C. D., but which the sd C. D. denies: Now THESE
PRESENTS WITNESS, that, in order to finally settle the questions in dispute between them, the sd A. B. and C. D. hereby
refer all questions and disputes in reference to the mres
afsd to the arbitrament of E. F., of &c., upon the terms
following :—

1. The sd E. F. shall view the sd messes, land and oubldgs,
and inspect such plans, and examine such witnesses upon
oath as he shall think proper, and shall afterwards make his
award in writing under his hand, by which he shall determine
what (if any) damage has been caused to the sd messes,
lands and outbldgs through the mining operons of the sd
C. D., and what (if any) damages shall be pd in respect thof,
and what sum (if any) the sd A. B. shall rece as the value of
the minerals so alleged to be gotten, and shall fix the time
when the sd C. D. shall pay the same to the sd A. B., and
such award shall be binding on the sd A. B. and C. D.

2. The sd A. B. and C. D. shall afford every facility to
the sd E. F. for conducting his said view and examon, and
submit themselves for examon, and produce their plans at
such time as the sd E. F. shall require [but he shall not be
attended by counsel or solicitors].

3. The sd E. F. shall publish his award on or before
[date] &c., or within such extended time not exceeding one
calr month after that day, as he shall by writing under his
hand appoint.

4. The expenses of and incidental to this agreet, and of
the reference and of the award, shall be pd by such of the
parties hrto as the sd E. F. shall award.

5. This submon may be made a rule of any Division
of Her Majesty's High Court of Justice at the instance
of eir party, and shall not be revoked by the death of eir
party before the publishing of the sd award, and shall

be deemed a reference within the meaning of the Common Law Procedure Act, 1854.

As witness, &c.

***

XVIII.

AGREEMENT *for* REFERENCE *of an Action.*

An Agreet made [*date*], between A. B., of &c., of the one part, and C. D., of &c., of the other part; Whas on the [*date*] the said A. B. commenced an action in the Exchequer Division of the High Court of Justice agnst the sd C. D. to recover the sum of £—— : And whas the sd C. D. claims a set-off to the sd action, amounting to the sum of £—— : Now these presents witness that, in order to end all differences between them, the sd A. B. and C. D. hereby agree as follows:—

1. The sd action and set-off, and all other matters in difference betwn the sd A. B. and C. D. shall be referred to E. F., of &c., who shall make his award under his hand on or before the [*date*] or such further time, not later than three months from the date hrof, as he shall by writing indorsed hereon appoint.

2. The sd A. B. shall, within seven days from this date, deliver to the sd C. D. an account in writing of all the items of his claim; and within seven days after receipt thof the sd C. D. shall deliver to the sd A. B. an account in writing of all the items of his set-off, and in case of default by eir party as afsd, the arbitrator shall be at liberty to proceed as if the party making such default had abandoned his claim or set-off, as the case may be.

3. The sd A. B. and C. D. resply, and their respive witnesses, shall be examd on oath before the sd arbitrator, and shall produce all books and papers relating to the mres afsd in their posson.

4. If eir party shall make default in attending any appntmt made by the arbitrator, he shall be at liberty to

proceed *ex parte* as effectually as if such absent party were present.

5. The costs of the action shall abide the event of the award, and each party shall pay his own costs of this agreet, but the costs of the reference and award shall be in the discretion of the arbitrator.

AS WITNESS, &c.

XIX.

AGREEMENT *between a* MANUFACTURER *and his* SON *as to Services, the Son receiving a Salary and Percentage of Profits, but not being a Partner.*

THIS AGREET made the   day of, &c., between A. B., of &c., worsted manufacturer, of the one part, and C. B., of &c., worsted manufacturer, of the other part:

1. The sd C. B. shall for the term of five years from the 1st day of January, 1875, act as assistant to and serve the sd A. B. and his exs or ads and his and their partner or partners for the time being (hereinafter together designated as "the said A. B. & Co.") in the manufacturing departments of the worsted business of the said A. B. & Co. at the salary, with the powers, and upon the terms hrinafr mentioned.

2. The sd worsted business (hrinaftr called "the business") shall be carried on at X. Mill near, &c., and at such other place or places as the said A. B. & Co. shall think fit.

3. The amount of capital to be from time to time employed in the business shall be fixed by the sd A. B. & Co. in their uncontrolled discretion.

4. Subject to the other provisions hereof the sd C. B. shall have the management of the [spinning, preparing, and woolcombing] departments of the business, and in addition thereto he shall, as and when from time to time required so to do by the said A. B., aid and assist in any other department or departments of the business, but he shall not, without the

consent of the said A. B., dismiss any person employed in the business or increase the number of persons so employed, or increase the wages or salaries of any such persons, or make any change in the machinery employed in the business. The amount of goods to be manufactured shall from time to time be determined by the said A. B. in his uncontrolled discretion.

5. The sd C. B. shall not without the consent of the sd A. B. interfere in any way in the management of the financial department of the business or in the accounts thereof, and shall only buy or sell any raw material or manufactured article as and when from time to time required so to do under the control and directions of the sd A. B.

6. At all times during the sd term the sd C. B. shall diligently and faithfully employ his whole time, attention, and ability in and about the business as such assistant as aforesaid, and will conform to and govern himself by such orders, instructions, and directions as from time to time he may receive from the said A. B. ; and in all cases where he shall receive no special orders, instructions, or directions, will act in such manner as shall be to the greatest advantage of the sd A. B., and shall be just and faithful to the sd A. B. in all dealings and transactions in or about the business, and shall render a just and faithful account of all matters relating to the business whenever the same shall be reasonably required, and shall at the request of the sd A. B. give full information with respect to the business and process of manufacture or anything relating thereto, and shall also inform him of all letters, accounts, writings and things in anywise concerning the business and within the knowledge of the sd C. B., and shall not, either alone or in partnership with or as manager or assistant for any other person or otherwise howsoever, either directly or indirectly, engage in any other trade or business, and shall not, without the consent of the sd A. B., divulge or make known any of the trusts, secrets, or dealings of or relating to the business.

7. During the continuance of his engagement as such assistant the sd C. B. shall receive from the sd A. B. the fixed salary of £100 a year, payable half yearly, and shall

also receive in addition to such fixed salary £10 per cent. on the nett annual profits of the business, such share of profits to be paid at the end of one calendar month after the end of the year in respect of which the same shall have arisen.

8. If the sd C. B. shall die during the continuance of his employment as such assistant as afsd, his exs, ads, or assigns shall be entitled to receive from the sd A. B. a proportionate part of the fixed salary and of his share of the profits for the whole of the current year up to the day of his death, such proportionate part of the fixed salary to be payable immediately after the death of the sd C. B., and such proportionate part of his share of the profits for the whole of the current year to be payable at the time at which such last-mentioned share of profits would have been payable if the sd C. B. had lived and continued to act as such assistant as afsd to the end of such current year.

9. If the sd A. B. shall desire that the sd C. B. shall cease to act as such assistant as afsd before the sd term shall expire, and shall serve on him a notice to that effect, then at the expiration of three calendar months from the time of the service of such notice, or at any later time to be specified in such notice, the sd C. B. shall retire and cease to act as such assistant as afsd, but in such case the sd A. B. shall pay the sd C. B. such a proportionate part of his fixed salary and of his share of the profits down to the time of such retirement as his exrs or ads would have been entitled to if he had died on the day of such retirement, such proportionate part to be paid and ascertained at such time and in such manner respectively as if he had so died.

10. If the sd C. B. shall break any of his agreets herein contained, or shall, whether from illness or any other cause, without the consent of the sd A. B. absent himself from the business for more than fourteen days in the year, or for more than seven days at any one time, then and in every such case the sd A. B. may dismiss the sd C. B. from his employment as such assistant as afsd, and in such case the sd A. B. shall be entitled to the proportionate part of his fixed salary down to the time of his dismissal, to be paid

immediately after such dismissal, but not to any share of the profits for the current year, or to any other compensation whatsoever.

11. In ascertaining the nett profits of the business interest at the rate of £5 per cent. per annum on the capital from time to time employed in the business shall be deducted from the gross profits of the business, and a proper allowance shall also be made for the rent of any mills, warehouses, land, or buildings employed or occupied for the purposes of the business, for the expenses of all repairs, additions, and alterations of or to the same, and for all taxes, rates, assessments, payments for insurance against loss by fire, and other outgoings for and in respect of the same, and for all expenses incurred in or about the business, including salaries of clerks, workmen, and others, and for all moneys which shall become payable on account of the business, including the fixed salary of every assistant (but not his share of profits), and for all loss and damages which shall happen in relation thereto.

12. Proper books of account, which shall be constantly posted up, shall be kept at the office of the sd A. B., in which shall be entered all the dealings and transactions of the business. On the 26th day of December, or on such other day as shall be agreed upon between the parties, in every year during the continuance of the employment of the sd C. B. as such assistant as afsd, the sd books of account shall be balanced in the usual way by or under the direction the sd A. B. without any interference on the part of the sd C. B., his exs or ads, and a copy of the general balance-sheet and a statement of the nett profits of the business during the preceding year, signed by the sd A. B., shall be delivered to the said C. B., his exs or ads, within one calendar month from the taking of the sd accounts, and shall be final and conclusively binding on him or them, but so nevertheless that the sd C. B., his exs or ads, may within three calendar months after such delivery as afsd, by notice in writing to be served on the sd A. B., require him to verify such general balance-sheet and statement of profits during the preceding year by a statutory declaration.

13. Every notice to be given in pursuance of these presents shall be in writing and shall be served on the sd C. B., either by delivery to him personally, or by leaving the same at his usual or last known place of abode in England, or by sending the same through the post addressed to him at the place at which the business shall be carried on.

14. Nothing herein contained shall extend to or be construed or taken to extend to make the sd C. B. a partner in the business, or to give him any of the powers or rights of a partner therein, or to render him in any way liable to third persons for any of the debts or liabilities incurred in relation to the business.

15. Whenever any doubt, difference, or dispute shall hereafter arise between the parties hereto, or between any of them and the exs or ads of the others or other of them, or between their respective exs or ads, touching these presents or the construction thof, or any clause or thing herein contained, or any other thing in anywise relating to or concerning the business or the affairs thof, or the rights, duties, or liabilities of any party in connection therewith, the matter in difference shall be referred to two arbitrators, or their umpire, pursuant to and so as with regard to the mode and consequences of the reference and in all other respects to conform to the provisions in that behalf contained in the Common Law Procedure Act, 1854, or any then subsisting statutory modification thof.

As WITNESS, &c.

XX.

AGREEMENT *appointing* RESIDENT MANAGER *of Fireclay Works.*

AN AGREEMENT made the [*date*] between A. B., of &c. (hnftr called "the employer") of the one part, and C. D. of, &c. (hnftr called "the manager") of the other part.

1. The manager shall be employed to act as the resident manager of [the X. fireclay works situate at Z. afsd] (hnftr called " the works ") for one year certain from the date hereof, and thenceforth until this agreet shall be determined as hnftr mentd.

2. The manager shall, during the continuance of this agreet take the management and responsibility of the working of the works, together with all machinery thereon, but shall not interfere with the mercantile business thof, except as hrnftr specially provided.

3. All the plant, machinery, live and dead stock, required for the working of the works, or which shall be used in or about the same, shall be provided by the employer ; and no materials, plant, machinery, live and dead stock of any description shall be ordered or purchased by the manager without the special authority in writing of the employer [or some person by him duly authorized in that behalf], nor shall the manager in any way pledge the credit of the employer without the written authority of the employer [or some person duly authorized as aforesaid] ; but the manager shall have the entire charge of all such materials, plant, machinery, live and dead stock, and shall take proper care of and account for everything entrusted to his charge, and shall, at the termination of this agreet, deliver to the employer, or to such person as he shall direct, all materials, plant, machinery, live and dead stock, drawings, plans, accounts, papers, and other documents for which the manager shall then in due course of business be accountable.

4. The manager shall not sell or deliver any $\left[\begin{smallmatrix} \text{clay} \\ \text{bricks} \end{smallmatrix} \right]$ or other articles [or materials, whether manufactured or not], or any stock or effects of the works, upon credit to any person to whom the employer [or any person duly authorized as afsd] shall in writing have forbidden him to give credit.

5. The manager shall not, without such authority as afsd, erect any buildings or machinery, or otherwise incur outlay of a permanent character upon the works.

6. The manager shall from time to time engage, employ.

and discharge all such [*here specify the principal classes of workmen*] and other workmen, not exceeding the number for the time being prescribed by the employer, as he may think necessary for the proper working of the works, and shall during the continuance of this agreet keep a perfect supervision over all of them : Provided always, that the manager shall not, without the consent of the employer [or any person so authorized as afsd], engage or discharge any person who shall require or be receiving a higher remuneration than twenty shillings per week.

7. The manager shall, during the continuance of this agreet provide himself with a residence at Z. afsd at his own expense [*or* be entitled to reside rent free in the usual manager's house at X. collieries afsd, and shall be supplied by the employer with gas and fuel free of charge].

8. The manager shall during the continuance of this agreet diligently and faithfully observe and carry out all such instructions as he has already received and shall receive from his employer [or any person so authorized afsd], particularly in reference to the price of $\begin{bmatrix} \text{clay} \\ \text{bricks} \\ \text{pipes} \end{bmatrix}$ and other articles or materials [produced or made] at the works, and the credit, if any, to be given to customers, and in the absence of special orders, directions, or instructions, shall sell such $\begin{bmatrix} \text{clay} \\ \text{bricks} \\ \text{pipes} \end{bmatrix}$ and materials at the current market prices, without discount or deduction, and shall take all orders subject to a stipulon reserving to the employer the right of declining to execute such orders in case he shall not be satisfied with the credit of the customer, or the quantity of goods ordered, or the time over which the order is to extend or within which it is to be executed, and shall, in the absence of special orders, dirons, or instrons, honestly and diligently perform all the duties usually required of a manager of [fireclay works] to the utmost of his skill and knowledge, and shall work and manage the same in such manner as shall render the same as profitable as possible and best promote the interests of the employer, and shall at all times give to the person or persons having the charge of the mercantile business of the works

any informon relating to the working thereof which may be required of him.

9. It shall be the duty of the manager to travel to and from such places and so often as the employer [or such person authorized as afsd] shall require, for the purpose of obtaining orders and particulars of contracts for the supply and sale of materials and articles raw and manufactured from the works; but the employer shall provide the reasonable expenses of railway and other conveyance for the manager for such journeys.

10. The manager shall employ himself exclusively for the benefit of the employer, and devote his whole time to his duties, and shall not, during his employment by the employer, directly or indirectly sell or offer for sale, or solicit or take orders for, any materials or articles, raw or manufactured, on behalf of any person or company other than the employer.

11. The manager shall not, without express authority from the employer, compound or purport to compound for any debt, or receive any payment whatsoever from any customer, but all payments are to be made directly to the order of the employer, and, so far as may be, by cheque or post-office order payable at [specify bank or post-office].

12. The manager shall under no circes whatever directly or indirectly rece or accept for his own benefit any common, rebate, discount, gratuity, emolument, or profit whatsoever from any customer of the employer.

[14. The manager shall in no way whatsoever interfere with any manager or other official or servant engaged at any adjoining or other works of the employer.]

15. The employer shall pay to the manager the annual salary of [£200] by equal monthly payments upon the first day of each month, the first payment to be made on the [date].

16. This agreet may be terminated at any time after the [date] by either party giving to the other, at his last known place of residence in England, three months previous notice in writing of his intention to terminate the same,

or by either party paying to the other the amount of three months' salary in lieu of such notice, and such notice shall be sufficiently given if sent by post.

As WITNESS, &c.

Witness.

XXI.

AGREEMENT *between a* BREWER *and his* CLERK.

AN AGREET made [*date*] between J. B., of &c., of the one part, and J. H., of &c., of the other part:—

1. The sd J. H. will from the date hereof become the clerk of the sd J. B. in his trade of a brewer, and as receiver of the rents and profits of his messes, cottages, lands, tenements and heredits in the sd county of Y., and will give his whole time and attention to the sd trade and receivership, and will manage and improve the same to the utmost of his ability, and also will perform all such services as the sd J. B. shall from time to time direct.

2. The sd J. H. will not without the consent in writing of the sd J. B., divulge any of the trusts, secrets, accounts or dealings relating to the sd trade; and will be just and faithful to the sd J. B. in all his business dealings and transactions; and will render to the sd J. B. a just and true account of the same at all times when the same shall be required.

3. The sd J. H. shall also keep such books of accounts as shall be necessary, wherein he shall fairly write all moneys received and paid, and all goods bought or received in, or sold or delivered out upon credit or orwise, and the rates and prices at which the same shall be bought or received in or sold or delivered out, and all mres, circes and things necessary to manifest the state and condon of the sd trade; which sd books of acct shall always be kept in some convenient place on the prems where the sd trade shall be carried on, and be at all times open to the inspection of the sd J. B., or any person or persons appointed by him for that purpose.

4. The sd J. B. will pay to the sd J. H. by quarterly

payments on the usual quarter days, the clear yearly salary of £300, the first quarly pmnt thof to be made on the [*date*].

5. The sd J. B. will also from the [*date*], permit the sd J. H. to occupy the dwelling-house and prems which are now in the occupation of C. D., adjoining the brewery in X. afsd, free of rent and taxes; and also will, at the cost of the sd J. B., provide for the sd J. H. sufficient coals and beer for the use of himself and his family and domestic servants for the time being residing in the sd dwelling-house, and also will, at the like cost, keep a cow near the sd prems for the use of the sd J. H. and his family, and also a horse to be used by the sd J. H. in and about the necessary journeys on business of the sd trade.

6. In case of the death of eir of them, the sd J. B. and J. H., or in case eir of them shall be desirous to determine these presents, it shall be lawful for him so to do on giving to the other six calendar months' notice thof in writing; and in case such notice shall be given as afsd a proportionate part of the sd yearly salary from the last quarly day of pmnt thof up to the time of the expiron of the sd notice shall be paid by the sd J. B., his exors or admors, to the sd J. H., his exs or ads; and then these presents and everything herein contained shall cease, but without prejudice to any right of action, claim or demand by eir of them the sd parties, by reason of any previous breach or non-performance by the other of any of the covts or agreets herein contd.

As WITNESS, &c.

XXII.

AGREEMENT *between a* MANUFACTURER *and his* TRAVELLER.

AN AGREET, made the [*date*] between A. B. of &c., of the one part, and C. D., of &c, commercial traveller, of the other part :—

1. The sd C. D. will serve the sd A. B. as commercial traveller for the purpose of obtaining orders for the sale of

[*specify the goods*] manufactured by the said A. B. at his
works at X., in such counties, cities, towns, and places in
England as the sd A. B. shall determine [*or as may be
mutually agreed upon between the parties*] (hrftr called "the
travelling district").

2. It shall be the duty of the sd C. D. once in every
month to make the tour of the travelling district, and in
every such tour to visit as many of the cities, towns, and
places in the district being likely to prove remunerative
markets for the sale of the goods of the said A. B. on such
visit as can reasonably be visited in such tour, and he shall
use his best endeavours in making such visits to solicit and
procure orders for the sale of the sd goods as well among
existing customers of the sd A. B. as among new connections,
and to ascertain so far as possible whether all customers
visited (both old and new) are solvent and worthy of credit.

3. The sd C. D. shall devote his whole time to his aforesaid duty, and shall not during his employment by the sd
A. B. undertake any other business, and, in particular, shall
not either directly or indirectly sell or offer for sale, or
solicit or take orders for any article of merchandize on
behalf of any person or company other than the sd A. B.

4. The sd C. D. shall carry out all instructions which shall
be given to him by the sd A. B. as to the prices of the sd
goods, the credit, if any, to be given to customers, the
order in which any tour of the travelling district is to be
made, the visiting, or the omitting or ceasing to visit any
place or places, person or persons, in the sd district, and
generally as to the conduct of his employment; and in the
absence of express directions in writing to the contrary he
shall sell at the current monthly prices of the said A. B.
without discount or deduction [and shall take all orders for
goods, subject to a stipulon reserving to the sd A. B. the
right to decline to execute the order if not satisfied with the
reference or credit of the customer, and shall not enter into
any contract for a supply of goods without the consent in
writing of the sd A. B. to any such contract] and shall use
his best endeavours to promote the interests of the sd A. B.

5. The sd C. D. shall not [*take in clause* 11 *from Form XX.*].

6. The sd C. D. shall under no circumstances (*take in clause* 12 *from Form XX.*].

7. All expenses of the sd C. D. for travelling, board, lodging, and otherwise, shall be borne by the sd A. B. [*or* C. D. *according to arrangement*].

8. The sd A. B. will during his employment of the sd C. D. pay him the salary of £3 per week, the first payment to be made on [*date*], and also will at his own expense procure for the said C. D. a pass between all necessary stations on the lines of the X., Y., and Z. Railway Companies, and shall also pay to the sd C. D. a commission of 10 per cent. upon the invoice price of all goods sold through him. The said common shall only be payable upon sales which are adopted and ratified by the sd A. B., and shall be payable on the last day of the calr month in which the goods so sold shall have been delivered : [PROVIDED that if the sd A. B. shall fail to recover the whole of the price of any goods in respect of which any such common shall have been allowed or paid, the sd C. D. shall in such case allow in account or repay to the sd A. B., or permit him to deduct and retain out of the next monthly payment, the whole or, as the case may be, a proportionate part of the common allowed or paid in respect of such goods.]

9. The employment of the sd C. D. under this agreet shall commence from the date hereof, and shall continue for twelve calendar months determinable as hereinafter mentioned.

10. Either party shall be at liberty to put an end to this agreement at any time after [*date*], on giving to the other three calendar months previous notice in writing of his intention to do so, which notice shall be sufficient if sent by post addressed to the said A. B. at his commercial office, or to the sd C. D. at his address then last known to the said A. B. The said A. B. may also at any time peremptorily determine this agreet without previous notice upon paying or tendering to the sd C. D. three months salary at the rate of £3 per week in lieu of notice, and in the event

of such determination as last afsd the said C. D. shall only
be entitled to the common on sales effected up to the date
of such payment being made or tendered.

11. Upon the determination of this agreet the sd C. D.
shall immediately give up to the sd A. B. his railway passes
and all books, lists of customers, papers, memoranda, letters,
and documents relating to the business, and shall not retain
any copies of any such books, list of customers, papers,
memoranda, letters, or documents as afsd.

[12. In the event of this agreet being determined by the
sd C. D. he shall not for the space of twelve calendar months
thereafter directly or indirectly sell or solicit or take orders
for the sale of goods similar to those manufactured by the
said A. B. in the travelling district, or any part thereof,
either on his own account or for any other person or company without the previous consent in writing of the sd
A. B.]

As WITNESS, &c.

XXIII.

AGREEMENT *between* MANUFACTURERS *and a provincial*
AGENT.

AN AGREET made, &c., Between B. A. and D. A. (trading as
A. Bros.), of &c., of the one part, and C. D., of &c., of the
other part :—

1. The sd C. D. (hrnftr called "the agent") will act as
agent for the sd A. Bros. (hrnftr called "the principals")
for the sale, in the town of X., of articles and goods manufactured by them for the term of five years from the date
hereof, and will receive all such goods as may be consigned
or sent to him by the principals, and will use his best
endeavours to sell the same at such prices as shall be specified in writing by them, or such higher prices as can reasonably be obtained, and will at his own expense deliver such
goods to the respive pchers thof, the carriage from Sheffield
to X. being paid by the principals.

2. The agent shall sell only for ready money, or to psons of responsibility, and worthy to be trusted, and in selling upon credit shall be cautious and make due inquiries into the responsibility and position of intending pchers, and shall make a memdum of every such inqy and the result thof in a book to be kept by him for that purpose, and shall from time to time transmit a copy of the entries in such book to the principals with his monthly account hrnftr mentd.

3. The agent shall not give credit for goods exceeding the value of £100 to any pson, and shall not give credit to any pson for a greater length of time than three months, and shall give no credit to any pson whom the principals shall by notice in writing have forbidden him to trust.

4. The agent shall keep proper books of acct, in which he shall make plain and correct entries of all goods recd from the principals, and also of all goods sold or delivd by him as such agent as afsd, and also of all orders recd, and of all other transactions and mres in anywise concerning the agency, and shall on the first day of every month transmit to the principals a full, clear, and correct statement in writing of all such goods, orders, and transactions which shall have been recd, sold, or delivd, or which shall have taken place in relation to the agency during the preceding month, specifying the sales made for cash and on credit resply.

5. The agent shall on the first day of every month [or of March, June, September, and December, in every year] account for and transmit to the principals all moneys, bills, and securities for money recd by him during the preceding month [or three months], in respect of all goods sold by him as such agent as afsd.

6. The agent shall not, without the consent in writing of the principals, act as agent for any other person for the sale of goods of a nature similar to those manufactured [and supplied to him] by the principals.

7. The agent shall, in conducting the agency, in all respects conform to such instructions as he shall rece from the principals, and in the absence of special instructions

shall act in such manner as he shall judge to be most conducive to their interests.

[8. The agent shall not sell the goods recd by him from the principals in his own name, and shall cause the words " Agent for A. Bros., of Sheffield," to be placed, and shall keep the same during the agency in a prominent position (after his own name) upon the front of his principal place of business, and the same words shall be conspicuously printed at the head of every memorandum, invoice, and other similar document which shall be used by the agent in connection with the agency, and all letters, bills, and other documents relating to the goods of the principal, or to the agency written or signed by the agent shall be signed by him as such agent as afsd.]

9. The principals shall pay to the agent a common of £10 per cent. on the nett proceeds of all goods sold by him for them as such agent as afsd [and such common shall be allowed in account, and may be deducted by the agent from the amounts payable monthly [*or* quarterly] by him under clause 5 hrf.]

[10. The agent shall not be answerable for any loss or damage which may happen to any goods before they shall come to his hands, or within his custody, nor for any loss or damage which may happen to any which have actually come to his hands, unless such loss or damage shall happen through his own wilful default or neglect.]

11. The principals appoint the agent their attorney for them, and in their names to sue for, recover, and receive all sums of money owing on account of any goods sold by him as such agent as afsd, and to give receipts (which shall be sufficient discharges) for the same.

12. The agency may be terminated by either party upon giving six calr months previous notice in writing, and upon the expiration of such six months shall accordingly determine.

13. If the agent shall become insolvent, or commit any act of bankruptcy, the agency shall thereupon forthwith determine, and if the agent shall do anything contrary to

any of the stipulations or provisions herein contained, it shall be lawful for the principals forthwith by notice in writing to determine the agency, and if the agency shall be determined under the provisions of this clause, or clause 12 hrof, the accounts between the parties shall be adjusted and settled as if the sd term of five years had expired by lapse of time.

[14. All goods supplied to the agent by the principals shall remain their property until *bonâ fide* sold by him as their agent, and at the end or sooner determination of the sd term (from whatever cause), all such goods which shall remain then unsold, or be in his custody, shall be delivered up to the principals.]

15. If any dispute, question, or difference shall arise between the persons parties hereto, or their respive exs, ads, or assns, touching these presents, or any clause herein contained, or the construction hrof, or any matter in any way connected with these presents, or the operation hrof, or the rights, duties, or liabilities of either party in connection with the pres, then and in every or any such case the matter in difference shall be referred to two arbitrators or their umpire, pursuant to, and so as with regard to the mode and consequences of the reference, and in all other respects to conform to the provisions in that behalf contained in the Common Law Procedure Act, 1854, or any then subsisting statutory modification thof.

IN WITNESS, &c.

XXIV.

AGREEMENT *between a* PATENTEE *of* RAILWAY BUFFERS *and his* AGENT.

AN AGREET made the &c., between A. of &c., of the first part, and B., of &c., of the second part:—

1. The sd B. shall for the term of three years from the date hrof be employed by and act for the sd A. as agent for the sale of his patent rly buffers, manufactured by X. to the

several Ry Cos (or depts of Ry Cos as the case may be) specified in the first colm of the schedule hrto, upon the terms and condons herein contained, and shall use his best endeavours to procure the exclusive adoption by the sd Cos or depts resply of the sd buffers.

2. For every set of the sd buffers which shall be supplied by the sd X. during the continuance of these presents to any of the sd several Cos or depts, the sd A. shall, subject to clauses 3, 4, and 5 hrof, pay to the said B. a common of the amount set opposite the name of such Co or dept in the second colm of the sd schedule, whether the orders for the sd buffers shall be received direct from such Co or dept, or through the sd B.

3. As regards the supply to each of the said Cos and depts no common shall be payable to the sd B. during the first year of such supply, unless the number of complete sets of four buffers so supplied thereto during such year shall amount to the number set opposite to the name of such Co or dept in the third colm of the sd schedule; nor in any subsequent year in which the number of complete sets so supplied shall be less than the number set opposite to such name in the fourth col of the said schedule.

4. If any of the said Cos or depts, after having used or adopted the sd buffers, shall (from whatever cause) either cease to use the same, or adopt any other description of buffer not previously used by such Co or dept (as the case may be), either in substitution for or concurrently with the sd patent buffers; or shall for the space of six calr months give no orders for the sd patent buffers to the said X., then the sd A. may thrpon give to the sd B. three calr months' notice in writing to determine this agreet as regards such Co or dept only; and shall be at liberty at any time after the expiration of such notice to supply such Co or dept with the sd patent buffers either directly or through any agent or agents without the intervention of, or payment of any common to the sd B.

5. Notwithstanding anything hrn contd, the sd A. shall be at liberty to enter into any arrangements upon such

terms as he may think fit, for the manufacture of his sd patent buffers by the Z. Ry Co., at their works at S., for their own use, and in the event of any such arrangement being carried out, the sd A. shall pay to B. a common or royalty of 2s. 6d. for every complete set of the sd patent buffers which shall be manufactured in pursce thereof, and any such arrangement shall be without prejudice to the rights of the sd B. under these presents in respect of buffers supplied to the Z. Ry Co by the sd X.

6. The sd B. shall not during the sd term act as agent for the sale of or solicit orders for any rly buffers of any description whatsoever other than those patented by the sd A., and manufactured by the sd X., and if there shall be any breach of this clause these presents shall immediately thrpon determine without prejudice to the rights of the parties in respect of any of their past transactions.

The SCHEDULE above referred to.

IN WITNESS, &c.

XXV.

AGREEMENT *appointing* CONSULTING ENGINEER *of Colliery.*

AN AGREET made, &c., between A. B. of &c., of the one part, and C. D. of &c., of the other part:—

1. The sd A. B hrby appoints the said C. D. to be consulting engineer of the X. colliery at Y. afsd.

2. The sd C. D. shall act as such consulting engineer as afsd from the [*date*] until [*date*].

3. The sd C. D. during the continuance of this agreet shall reside at or near Y., and shall spend on an average at least three working days in each week at the sd colliery.

4. The sd C. D. shall devote the whole of such three working days in each week towards learning the workings and advising to the best of his ability as to the safe efficient working and development of the sd colliery, including any mines or working of ironstone or ore, brick, fire, or other

clays, or other minerals, and towards the general business and trade of the colliery and fire-clay works, including the advising as to the best and cheapest methods of purchasing materials, tools, and plant, and as to the prices to be charged for coals and bricks, &c., giving his best attention to the duties undertaken by him by this agreet.

5. The sd C. D. shall once at least in every month thoroughly and carefully inspect the sd colliery, mines, and workings to the utmost of his skill and knowledge, and during or immediately after every such inspection, shall give such directions and instructions to the resident manager as he shall consider necessary or desirable for the thorough and efficient working and development of the sd colliery, in conformity with the provisions of the Coal Mines Regulation Act, 1872, or any statutory modifications throf, or any substituted enactments which may from time to time be in force, and with the special rules of the colliery, established pursuant to the sd Act, and shall also within seven days after every such inspection furnish to the sd A. B., or as he shall direct, a detailed report in writing of the result of such inspection and of the directions and instructions then given by him to the resident manager as afsd, together with such additional remarks, recommendations, and advice as shall be necessary or desirable with reference as well to the further development as to the actual working of the sd colliery, mines and minerals, and he shall answer all such questions and give all such explanations relating to such inspection, and report on the subject-matter throf, as the sd A. B. shall require; and the sd reports of the sd C. D. shall give details as to the condon of the colliery as regards gas, water, and the general safety of the mine, and also as to its capabilities with regard to the daily output.

6. It shall also be the duty of the sd C. D., once at least in every three calendar months, to see that the manager of the mine duly and accurately plots on a draft plan to be kept at the office of the colliery the directions and nature of the workings then existing or intended to be carried on, and for such purpose to make an accurate survey of the under-

ground workings. The sd C. D. shall furnish to the sd A. B.
free of charge, all tracings of plans made by the said C. D.
which the sd A. B. shall from time to time require.

7. The sd A. B. shall pay to the sd C. D., the annual
salary of £——, by equal quarterly payments of £—— on
the usual quarter days in every year. The sd C. D. is not to
be entitled to any travelling expenses to or from the colliery.

8. Nothing hrin contd shall be deemed to authorize the
sd C. D. to give any order for the execution or erection of
any works, buildings, or machinery, or other outlay, without
the consent in writing of the sd A. B., unless such shall be
necessary to comply with the Coal Mines Regulation Act, or
such further enactment as afsd.

9. [*Same as Clause* 10 *in No. XXII.*]

XXVI.

AGREEMENT *appointing Certificated* RESIDENT MANAGER *of a* COLLIERY.

AN AGREET made &c., between A. B. of &c., of the one part
and C. D. of &c., of the other part:—

1. The sd C. D. is hrby nominated and shall be employed
by the sd A. B., and shall act as resident certified manager
of the X. Collieries, at Y. afsd, as from the [*date*], until this
agreet shall be determined as hrnftr mentd.

2. The sd C. D. shall during the continuance of this
agreet take the entire management and responsibility of the
working of the afsd colliery, including all mines and workings of ironstone, brick and other clays, and other minerals,
together with all machinery thereon, but shall not interfere
in any respect with the mercantile business throf.

3. It shall also be the duty of the sd C. D. to attend the
consulting engineer on his visits, and also once in every three
calendar months, duly and accurately to plot upon a draft
plan (to be kept at the office of the colliery as part of the
ppty of the sd A. B.), the directions and nature of the
workings then existing or intended to be carried on, and to
furnish to the sd A. B. free of charge all tracings that he

may require of any plans which the sd C. D. shall from time
to time make or procure to be made or possess of the sd
colliery and workings, or of any bldgs or machinery in
connexion thrwth

4. [*Same as Clause 3 in Form XX. p. 222.*]

5. [*Same as Clause 4 in Form XX., substituting "coals"
for "bricks."*]

6. [*Same as Clause 5 in Form XX.*]

7. [*Same as Clause 6 in Form XX.*]

8. [*Same as Clause 7 in Form XX.*]

9. [*Same as Clause 8 in Form XX., down to* "within which
it is to be executed," *and then proceed as follows:—*] and
shall keep the sd A. B., or any pson authorized by him
in that behalf, fully informed of the state and condon of the
sd mine, and shall keep a report book shewing such state
and condon, and shall faithfully, honestly and diligently
perform all the duties usually required of a resident certificated manager of a colliery, whether under the Coal Mines
Regulation Act, 1872, or orwise, to the utmost of his skill
and knowledge, and shall keep or cause to be kept all such
books of account, registers, plans, and records of workings
and other documents as shall be necessary for the proper and
lawful working of the sd colliery, and shall duly and punctually make all such returns relating thereto as are or shall
be required by the sd Act or any modification thof or substituted enactments, which may from time to time be in
force, and shall generally work and manage the sd colliery
with a due regard to the rights of adjoining owners, and in
such manner as shall be consistent with the provons of the sd
Act, or such modification or substituted enactment as afsd,
and of the special Rules of the sd colliery, and subject to
such rights and provons shall work and manage the same in
such manner as shall render the same as productive as possible and best promote the interest of the sd A. B., and
shall not do or permit to be done upon the sd colliery any
act or thing in contravention of any provision of the sd Act
or such enactment as afsd applicable to the sd colliery, nor
omit to do any act or thing which it may be his duty to do

as such certificated manager as afsd, in conformity with such Act or enactment, and shall employ himself exclusively for the benefit of the sd A. B. at the sd colliery.

10. The sd C. D. shall bear the expense of all fines, costs, and charges to which he or the sd A. B. shall be put in the course of any proceedings under the sd Act or such enactment as afsd, through or by reason of any negligence or wilful default of the sd C. D.

11. This agreet may be terminated at any time by eir party giving to or leaving at the last known place of residence in England of the other three calr months previous notice in writing of his intention to terminate the same, or by eir party paying to the other the amount of three months' salary in lieu of such notice, and if the certificate of the sd C. D. shall be cancelled or suspended, this agreet shall thereupon *ipso facto,* and without notice or payment of salary in lieu of notice, immediately determine.

XXVII.

AGREEMENT *between* a MINERAL WATER COMPANY *and a Provincial del credere* AGENT.

AN AGREET made &c., Between the A. Co., of &c. (hrnftr called "the Co"), of the one part, and C. B. of &c., of the other part :—

1. The sd C. B. is hrby appointed and will act as sole wholesale *del credere* agent for the sale in the town of X. and within a radius of ten miles as the crow flies from the X. Town Hall (which town and radius are hrnftr called "the agency district"), of the natural mineral water imported by the Co, and known as "The A. Natural Mineral Water," from the date hrof until such agency shall be determined as hrnftr mentioned.

2. The sd C. B. (hrnftr called "the agent") will use his best endeavours to sell the said water within the agency district at prices not exceeding those specified in the 1st schedule hrto for transactions with the trade, and not exceeding

those specified in the 2nd schedule hrto for transactions with private individuals, and will at his own expense cart from the X. Railway, Station, warehouse, and deliver such water to the respive pchers throf in carts or vans having the words "A. Water" conspicuously painted on one side throf, the carriage from London to X. being paid by the Co.

3. The Co may supply the sd water direct to any person in the agency district, but in every such case a memorandum of the water so supplied shall forthwith be sent by the Co to the agent, and all water so supplied shall be deemed to be supplied to or through the agent.

4. The agent shall during the agency occupy the Co's leasehold shop and office situate at X., afsd, rent free, but shall himself pay all rates and other outgoings in respect throf. The agent may sell on such prems artificial mineral waters of his own manufacture only, but shall not during the agency sell either there or elsewhere any natural mineral water except that supplied to him by the Co, and shall not act as agent for the sale of any mineral water whatsoever for any person or corporation except the Co, and shall publicly announce his appointment as agent to the Co by such advertisements, show-cards, invoices, and other printed stationery as the Co shall from time to time furnish him with.

5. The agent shall keep proper books of account and shall make therein plain and correct entries of all water received from the Co, and of all water sold by him as such agent as afsd, and of all orders reced and other transactions relating to the agency, and shall on the first day of every month transmit to the Co a full, clear, and correct written statement, copied from such books, of all water so reced and sold, and of all such orders and transactions during the then preceding calr month.

6. The agent shall be responsible to the Co for the amount of the invoice price of all water supplied by the Co to the agent or to any pson in the agency district. All water shall be invoiced to the agent at the prices specified in the 1st schedule hrto. The agent shall, on the first day of every month during the agency, account for and transmit to the

Co the amount of the invoice price of all water supplied by the Co to the agent or to any other pson within the agency district during the then preceding calr month.

7. The Co. shall in the first instance pay the rent of the sd shop and offices at X. afsd, and shall pay to the agent by equal quarterly payments the sum of £50 per annum for storage, cartage, and delivery of goods within the agency district, and a commission of 10 per cent. shall be calculated upon the wholesale prices (as specified in the 1st schedule hrto) of all water supplied by the Co to the agent or to any other pson within the agency district, and shall be paid or applied as follows (namely), if such commission shall exceed £120 per ann, the sum of £120 part throf shall be retained by the Co in repayment of the rent of the sd shop and office, and the balance throf shall be paid to the sd B., but if such commission shall not exceed £120 per ann the whole throf shall be retained by the Co in respect of such rent as afsd. Any commission payable to the agent under this clause shall be paid quarterly.

9. The Co shall not be answerable for any loss or damage which may happen to any goods consigned to the agent or any pson within the agency district after such goods have left the London warehouse of the Co.

10. The agency may be terminated at any time by either party upon giving to the other three months previous notice in writing to that effect.

11. If the agent shall become insolvent or commit any act of bankruptcy, the agency shall *ipso facto* determine, and if he shall break any stipulation hrin contained, the Co may forthwith, by notice in writing, determine the agency as from the date of such notice.

12. If the agency shall be determined upon any day other than the first day of any month, the accounts between the parties shall be adjusted from the then last monthly settlement.

As WITNESS, &c.

The 1st SCHEDULE above referred to.

The 2nd SCHEDULE above referred to.

XXVIII.

ARTICLES *of* CLERKSHIP.

AN AGREET made, &c., BETWEEN A. B. of &c , a solicitor
of the Supreme Court of the one part and and C. D., of &c.,
[*father of the clerk*], and E. D. of &c., of the other part,
WITNESSETH that the sd E. D. of his own free will and with
the consent and approbation of the sd C. D. DOTH hby place
and bind himself clerk to the sd A. B. to serve him from
the day of the date hrf during the term of five years, AND
the sd C. D. doth hby covt with the sd A. B. that the sd
E. D. will faithfully and diligently serve the sd A. B. as his
clerk in the profession of a solor of the Supreme Court
during the sd term of five years, And will not at any time
during such term cancel, obliterate, spoil, destroy, waste,
embezzle, spend, or make away with any of the books,
papers, writings, moneys, stamps, chattels, or other ppty of
the sd A. B. or of any of his clients or employers, which shall
be deposited in his hands, or which shall come or be entrusted to his care, custody, or posson, and that in case the
sd E. D. shall act contrary to the last ment covt, or if the sd
A. B. shall sustain or suffer any loss, damage, or prejudice,
by the misbehaviour, neglect, or improper conduct of the sd
E. D., the sd C. D. shall indemnify the sd A. B. and make
good and reimburse to him the amount or value thereof.
AND FURTHER that the sd E. D. will keep the secrets of the
sd A. B., and readily and cheerfully obey and execute his
lawful and reasonable commands, and shall not absent himself from the service or employ of the sd A. B. at any time
during the sd term without his consent first obtained, but
shall at all times during the sd term conduct himself with
all due diligence, honesty, and propriety. [AND that the sd
C. D. will during the sd term, at his own cost, find and provide the sd E. D. with food, lodging, suitable apparel, and
other necessaries.] AND the sd E. D. doth hby covt with
the sd A. B. that he will well and faithfully serve the sd

R

A, B. at all times during the sd term as a clerk ought to do in all things whatsoever. IN CONSIDERATION whof and of the sum of £200 by the sd C. D. to the sd A. B. paid at or before the excon of these presents (the receipt whof the sd A. B. doth hby acknowledge), the sd A. B. doth hby covt with the sd C. D. that he the sd A. B. will accept and take the sd E. D. as his clerk, and will by the best means he can, and to the utmost of his skill and knowledge, teach and instruct, or cause to be taught and instructed, the sd C. D. in the practice or profession of a solor. And also will at the expiron of the sd term use his best means and endeavours, at the request and cost of the sd C. D., and E. D., or eir of them, to cause and procure the sd E. D. to be admitted and sworn a solor of the sd Supreme Court, provided the sd E. D. shall have well and faithfully served his said intended clerkship, and shall have successfully passed all such examinations as articled clerks are by law or custom bound to submit to before being admitted to practise as a Solor. IN WITNESS, &c.

XXIX.

INDENTURE of APPRENTICESHIP.

THIS INDRE witnesseth, that A. B. doth put himself apprentice to C. D. to learn his art, and with him (after the manner of an apprentice) to serve from the date hrof until the end of five years thence next following, during which term the sd apprentice his sd master faithfully shall serve; his secrets keep; his lawful demands everywhere gladly do. He shall do no damage to his sd master, nor see it done by others, but shall forthwith give warning to his sd master of the same. He shall not waste the goods of his sd master, nor lend them unlawfully to any; nor contract matrimony within the sd term; nor buy nor sell without license of his sd master; nor haunt taverns or playhouses; nor absent himself from his sd master's service unlawfully; but in all things as a faithful apprentice he shall behave himself towards his master, and all his, during the sd term. He shall give a true and just account of his sd master's goods, chattels, and money committed to his charge, or which shall come to his hands, whenever required so to do. And the sd master by the best means that he can, shall teach and instruct, or cause to be taught and instructed, his sd apprentice in the art of [*specify the trade*]: finding him sufficient meat, drink, lodging, and all other necessaries during the sd term.

PROVIDED ALWAYS, and it is hrby agreed between the sd parties, that in case the sd apprentice shall at any time be wilfully guilty of disobedience or misconduct towards his sd master or any of his family or servants, it shall be lawful for his sd master immediately wholly to discharge such apprentice from his sd service, and it shall be lawful for him thenceforth, during the residue of the sd term, wholly to refuse to maintain, instruct, or receive his sd apprentice, [and he shall not be required to return any part of the sd premium.] [1]

IN WITNESS, &c.

[1] The last fourteen words will of course, be omitted where no premium is paid.

APPOINTMENTS.

XXX.

APPOINTMENT *of a Share of* RESIDUARY ESTATE.

To ALL TO WHOM THESE PRESENTS shall come, I, A. B. of &c., widow, send greeting:

Whas C. B. of &c., duly made his will, dated &c., and thby gave all his real and psnl este to R. S. and T. W. upon certain trusts thrn mentd, being in effect trusts for conversion and pmt of his debts, funeral and testamentary exps, and for the investment of the residue thof. And he thby directed the sd R. S. and T. W. to stand possd of such residue and the investments thof in trust to pay the income thof to me for my separate use for life, and after my death to hold the same residue and investments in trust for such one or more of his issue by me the sd A. B. and in such manner and form in every respect as I should so long as I shd remain his widow by deed or will or codicil appt. And whas the sd C. B. died on [*date*], and his will was duly proved by the sd R. S. and T. W., the exors thrn named. And whas the sd R. S. and T. W. duly converted the real and psnl este of the sd C. B. and paid thereout his funeral and testamentary exps, and the residue of his sd este is now represented by the sum of £20,000 Bank £3 per cent. Consolidated Annies standing in the names of the sd R. S. and T. W. in the books of the Governor & Co. of the Bank of England. And whas there was issue of the sd C. B. and myself five children, of whom one, namely, D. B., has recently attained the age of [twenty-four years, and is about to commence business on his own account], and I am desirous of making such appt as hrnftr contd.

Now KNOW YE and these presents witness, that I the sd A. B. in exercise of the power for this ppse given to me by

the sd will of the sd C. B. decd and of all other powers (if
any) enabling me in this behalf, DO HEREBY APPOINT that the
sd R. S. and T. W. shall stand possd of one equal tenth part
of the sd sum of £20,000 Bank £3 per cent. Consold
annies in trust for the sd D. B. his exors ads and ass
absolutely.

IN WITNESS, &c.

XXXI.

APPOINTMENT *of* NEW TRUSTEE *of a* *Will of* FREEHOLDS.

THIS INDRE, made &c., between A. B., of &c., and C. D., of
&c., of the one part, and E. F., of &c., of the other part:
Whas G. H., late of &c., deceased, by his will dated &c.,
devised all [*set out parcels from the will*] unto I. K. and the
sd A. B. and C. D., their heirs and assns, upon the trusts
thrin mentd. And he thrby declared, that if any of the
trees apptd by his sd will should die, or decline [*recite in the
past tense the power to appoint new trustees as set out in the
will, shewing that the power to appoint a new trustee is vested in
A. B. and C. D. as surviving trustees*]: And whas the sd G. H.
died without having revoked or altered his said will, which
was duly proved by the exors thrn named: And whas the
said I. K. died on the [*date*]: Now THIS INDRE WITNESSETH,
that, in exercise of the power given to them by the hrnbfre
recited will of the sd G. H. and of every other power enabling
them in this behalf, the sd A. B. and C. D. do hereby
appoint the sd E. F. to be a tree of the sd will in the place
of the sd I. K.: AND THIS INDRE ALSO WITNESSETH, that, in
conson of the prems, the sd A. B. and C. D. do hrby grant
unto the sd E. F. and his heirs all the freehold hdts comprised in and devised by the sd will of the sd G. H., which
are now vested in the sd A. B. and C. D., together with the
appurtenances to the sd hdts belonging, To HOLD the same
unto the sd E. F. and his hrs, to the use of the sd A. B.,
C. D., and E. F., their hrs and assns, upon, with, and subject

to such of the trusts, powers, provos and declons concerning the same declared by the sd will of the sd G. H. as are now subsisting and capable of taking effect.

And each of them the sd A. B. and C. D. [*covenant against incumbs. as in Form XXXII. below.*]

XXXII.

APPOINTMENT *of* NEW TRUSTEE *of a Settlement by* INDORSEMENT *under the Statutory Power where the Settlement contains no Power to appoint.*

THIS INDRE, made &c., between the within-named A. B. and the within-named C. D. of the one part, and G. H., of &c., of the other part: Whas the within-named E. F. died on [*date*]: NOW THIS INDRE WITNESSETH, that the sd A. B. and C. D., in execution of the power in this behalf given to them by the Act 23 & 24 Vict. c. 145, and of all other powers enabling them in this behalf, do hrby appt the sd G. H. to be a tree of the within-written Indre in the place of the sd E. F.: AND THIS INDRE ALSO WITNESSETH that, in conson of the prems, the said A. B. and C. D. do hrby grant unto the sd G. H. and his hrs the hdts comprised in and assured by the within-written indre, and which are now vested in the sd A. B. and C. D., to hold the same unto the sd G. H. and his hrs, to the use of the sd A. B., C. D., and G. H. their hrs and assns, upon, with, and subject to such of the trusts, powers, provons, and declons of the within-written indre as are now subsisting and capable of taking effect:[1] AND EACH of them, the sd A. B. and C. D. doth hrby for himself,

---

[1] Where a new trustee is appointed in the place of a retiring bankrupt trustee the following proviso may be useful:—

PROVIDED ALWAYS, and it is hrby expressly agreed and declared, that nothing herein contd shall operate to release the sd A. B. or his estate, or tree in liquon or bkcy, or any pson or psons from any liability which he, it, or they may have incurred, or may be under or from any claim which he, it, or they, may be liable to in respect of any breaches of trust committed by, or any misconduct of the sd A. B. as such tree as afsd or orwise or any other pson or psons.

his hrs, exors, and admors, covt with the sd G. H., his hrs and assns, that they the sd covtors resply have not done, executed, or knowingly suffered any act, deed, or thing whby the sd hdts are or can be in any manner incumbered [charged, or affected in title or orwise howsoever, or whby they are in anywise hindered from assuring the same in manner afsd.[1]]

XXXIII.

APPOINTMENT of GAMEKEEPER.

KNOW ALL MEN by these presents, that I, A. B., of &c., do hereby appoint C. D., of &c., to be my gamekeeper for my manor of X., to look after, take care of, and preserve the game therein, with full power to take and kill any hare, pheasant, partridge, or other game in and upon my sd manor [for his own use]: And also to seize all such guns, dogs, ferrets, nets, and engines for killing and taking conies, hares, pheasants, partridges, grouse, or other game, as within the precincts of my sd manor shall be used by any person or persons who by law is or are prohibited to keep or use the same: And also to do all other things belonging to the office of a gamekeeper, according to the several Acts of Parliament now or hrftr during his apptmt in force.

IN WITNESS, &c.

[1] The words within brackets, though usual, are unnecessary.

BONDS.

XXXIV.

Common MONEY BOND.

KNOW ALL MEN by these presents, that we A. B., of &c., and C. D. of &c., are bound to E. F., of &c., in the penal sum of £200, to be paid to the sd E. F., or his exors, admrs, or assns, for which payment we bind ourselves and each of us, our and each of our hrs, exors, and admors, jointly and severally by these presents. Sealed with our seals. Dated, &c.

The condon of the above written bond is such, that if the above-bounden A. B. and C. D., or eir of them, their or eir of their hrs, exors, or admors shall, on demand, pay to the sd E. F., his exors, admors or assns, the sum of £100 sterling, with interest for the same after the rate of £5 per cent. per ann, then the above-written bond shall be void, otherwise shall be in full force.

Signed, sealed, and delivered
in the presence of .

XXXV.

BOND *from the* MANAGER *of a* BREWERY *and his* Sureties.[1]

KNOW ALL MEN by these presents that we A. B., of &c., C. D., of &c., and E. F., of &c., are jointly and severally bound unto G. H., of &c., brewer, in the penal sum of £ , to be paid to the sd G. H., his exors, admors, or assns [*or* his or their attorney or attorneys] for which payment we bind ourselves jointly and each of us bindeth himself severally,

---

[1] This bond is supposed to be given by the manager appointed by Form XXI. p. 225, *supra*.

and our and each of our hrs, exors, and admors, and every of them, by these presents. Sealed with our respective seals. Dated, &c.

WHAS the above-named G. H. has taken the above-named A. B. into his employment as manager of his business of a brewer, and as receiver of the rents and profits of his messes, cottages, lands, and hdts in the county of X., and the above-bounden C. D. and E. F. have agreed to join with the sd A. B. in the above-written bond for his fidelity in the sd employ : Now the condon of the above-written bond is such that if the sd A. B. shall, so long as he shall be in the employment of the said G. H., faithfully account for, pay over, and deliver unto the sd G. H., his exors, admors, partners or assns [or to such other person or persons as he or they shall direct] all sums of money, books, papers, matters, and things belonging to the sd G. H. which shall from time to time be received by or come to the hands of the sd A. B., and also shall act and conduct himself at all times with fidelity, integrity and punctuality in and concerning the matters and things which may be reposed in or entrusted to him as such manager and receiver as afsd, and shall return and make good any such moneys, books, papers, matters or things as he may embezzle, take, or misemploy within the space of seven days after he shall have been justly accused thof, or in default thereof, if the sd C. D. and E. F., or eir of them, shall within fourteen days after he or they shall have had notice in writing from the sd G. H. of any such default, make due and sufficient repayment, restitution, or compensation for the loss or damage which the said G. H. shall have thereby sustained, then the above-written bond shall be void, otherwise the same shall remain in full effect.

Signed, sealed and delivered by the above-named A. B., C. D., and E. F.

in the presence of   .

XXXVI.

BOND *for replacing a* SUM *of* STOCK, *and the Payment of Annual Sums in lieu of Dividends.*

KNOW ALL MEN, &c. [*as in Form* XXXIV., binding A. B. to C. D. in penal sum of £5000].

WHAS the above-bounden A. B. has requested the sd C. D. to lend him the sum of £2,300 stock of Consolidated £3 per Cent. Bank Annuities, the sd C. D. hath sold the same and paid the proceeds thof, amounting to the sum of £2500, to the above-bounden A. B. (which he doth hrby acknowledge) : Now the condition of the above-written bond is such, that if the above-bounden A. B., his hrs, exors, or admors, or any or eir of them, shall on or before the [*date*], purchase the sum of £2300 stock of Consolidated £3 per Cent. Bank Annuities, and transfer the same into the name of the sd C. D., or of his exors, admors or assns [or into the name or names of such other person or persons as he or they shall direct or appoint] and pay to the sd C. D., his exors, admors or assns, in lieu of the divds thof, such sums of moy as the sd C. D., his exors, admors or assns would have been entitled to receive as the dividends of the said sum of £2300 stock, in case the same had continued standing in his name, at such time as the sd divds would have been payable in case the same had not been sold in manner afsd, then the above-written bond is to be void and of no effect, otherwise to be in full force.

Signed, &c.

CERTIFICATE OF ACKNOWLEDGMENT.

XXXVII.

ACKNOWLEDGMENT *to be indorsed on* DEED *to which a Married Woman is a Party.*

MEMORANDUM, that on the [*date*], this deed was duly acknowledged before me at X., in the county of Y., by A. B., therein named, to be her deed, previous to which acknowledgment the sd A. B. was examined by us separately and apart from her husband, touching her knowledge of the contents of the said deed and her consent thereto, and declared the same to be freely and voluntarily executed by her.

C. D., of &c.
E. F., of &c. } Perpetual Commissioners to take the Acknowledgments of Married Women in the county of Y.

CONDITIONS OF SALE.

XXXVIII.

CONDITIONS OF SALE *of a* FREEHOLD HOUSE *in Mid-dlesex or Yorkshire* (*with possession*) *in one Lot with Special Stipulations.*

I. No person is to advance less than £10 at each bidding or to retract a bidding. The highest bidder (subject to a right which is hereby reserved for the vendors to bid by themselves or their agents) shall be the purchaser, and if any dispute shall arise concerning a bidding the property shall be put up again and re-sold.

II. The purchaser is immediately after the sale to pay a deposit of £10 per cent. of his purchase-money into the hands of the auctioneers and to sign the subjoined agreement.

III. The vendors are to deliver to the purchaser or his solicitor an abstract of the title to the property subject to the stipulations contained in these conditions.

IV. The purchaser is within twenty-one days from the actual delivery of the abstract, to deliver at the office of [Mr. A. C., No. 7, F. I., E.C.] a statement in writing of his objections and requisitions (if any) in respect of the title, or the form of or the parties to the conveyance, and upon the expiration of such period of twenty-one days the title is to be considered as approved of and accepted by the purchaser subject only to such objections and requisitions (if any); and a similar statement is to be delivered within fourteen days after the delivery of answers to any previous statement (whether such answers do or do not include any supplemental abstract) the title being considered as approved of and accepted except as appearing by such similar statement; and every objection or requisition not so delivered shall be

considered as absolutely waived notwithstanding any subsequent negotiation or litigation, and time shall in these
respects be considered as of the essence of the contract and
for the purpose of any objection or requisition an abstract
shall be deemed to be perfect if it supply the information
suggesting the same although otherwise defective; and if
the purchaser shall insist on any objection or requisition
which the vendors shall consider themselves unable or on
the ground of expense or for any other reason shall decline
to remove or comply with, the vendors shall, notwithstanding
any intermediate negotiation or litigation, and although they
may have insisted that such objections or requisitions are
untenable, be at liberty by notice in writing signed by their
solicitor to rescind the contract, and shall thereupon return
to the purchaser his deposit but without any interest, cost
of investigating the title, or other compensation or payment
whatever.

V. The abstract of title shall commence [as to a portion of
the property with an indenture dated, &c., and made between
G. H. J. L. of the first part, M. A. D. of the second part,
and J. R. H. of the third part; as to another portion, with an
indenture dated, &c., made between J. S. D. of the one part,
and T. C. of the other part; and as to the remainder, with
an indenture dated, &c., and made between T. C. of the one
part and F. W. S. of the other part.]

VI. The purchaser shall not be at liberty to require,
investigate, or object to any title or evidence of title or any
other matter whatsoever prior to the respective commencements, notwithstanding any reference to or notice of any
prior documents; and every abstracted document of title
dated more than [15] years prior to the day of sale shall
be accepted as conclusive evidence of the facts, matters, and
conclusions of law recited, stated, assumed, or implied therein,
and also of the material contents and due execution of all
instruments therein recited or noticed, and of which the
vendors have neither the original nor attested copies,
whether the vendors have covenants for the production
thereof or not; and no objection or requisition shall be

made in respect of the non-production of the original or an attested or other copy of any instrument so recited or noticed or of any instrument enrolled for safe custody and accessible to the purchaser, or of any instrument of which the vendors shall produce what purports to be an attested copy ; and no abstract in chief shall be required of any documents so recited or noticed and of which the vendors have neither the originals nor a copy ; and no objection or requisition shall be made on the ground of the absence or imperfection of any covenants for title or covenants for the production of muniment of title.

[VII. As respects any securities given to or released, reconveyed or transferred by persons acting or described in the deeds of mortgage, release, or transfer, or any receipt indorsed on any mortgage or transfer and intended to operate as a release or re-conveyance as trustees of any benefit building society, it shall be assumed that such persons were the duly appointed and only trustees for the time being of a duly constituted benefit building society as therein referred to, and had full power to accept, release, re-convey, or transfer (as the case may be) the said securities respectively.   And the rules of any such society, or any documents or proceedings relating to the constitution of the same or the appointment of the trustees thereof shall not be called for.]

[VIII. The purchaser shall assume that every former owner of any part of the property whose wife or widow (if any) might be entitled to dower and is not mentioned in the title was unmarried at the time when he died or ceased to be the owner of the estate conferring the right to dower.]

IX. As respects any deed, will, or other document which may not have been registered or properly registered in the county register, the same shall (if required and practicable) be registered or re-registered at the expense of the purchaser, who shall not make any other objection or requisition in respect thereof, nor shall the completion of the purchase be delayed with a view to such registration or re-registration.

X. The property is believed and shall be taken to be correctly described as to quantity and otherwise, and is sold subject to all chief and other rents, rights of way and water and other easements (if any) charged or subsisting thereon, and if any error, mis statement, or omission in the particulars be discovered the same shall not annul the sale nor shall any compensation be allowed by the vendors or purchaser in respect thereof.

XI. The purchaser shall admit the identity of the property with that comprised in the muniments offered by the vendors as the title to such property upon the evidence afforded by a comparison of the descriptions in the particulars and the muniments. And the vendors shall not be required to account for the discrepancy (if any such exists) between present measurements and those given in the abstracted muniments of title.

[XII. The purchaser shall, within twenty-four hours after the sale, give notice in writing at the office aforesaid, whether he elects to take any (and if so, what part) of the fittings mentioned in the particulars or not; and if he elects to take the same or any portion thereof, he shall pay for the same as hereinafter provided, and shall assume that the vendor has power to sell the same, and to give an effectual receipt for the purchase-money thereof.

XIII. The valuation referred to in the particulars is to be made in the following manner (that is to say): each party (vendor and purchaser, or their respective solicitors) is, within twenty-four hours after the sale, to appoint by writing one valuer, and give notice in writing to the other party of such appointment, and the valuers so appointed are to make such valuation; but before they commence their valuation they are to appoint an umpire by writing, and the decision of such valuers if they agree, and of such umpire if they disagree, is to be final; and in case the purchaser shall neglect or refuse to appoint a valuer, and give notice thereof in the manner and within the time hereby specified, the valuation is to be made by the valuer appointed by the vendor alone, and his valuation is to be final.]

XIV. If the purchaser may consistently with these conditions require and shall require an abstract or the production of any deed or document not in the possession of the vendors, or any office, attested, or other copy of or extracts from any deed, will, or other document, whether in their possession or not, and whether for the purpose of verifying the abstract or of accompanying or completing the title or otherwise, or any affidavit, statutory declaration, certificate, or other evidence not in the possession of the vendors as to seisin, identity of parcels, or any other matter, or any information not in the vendors' possession or knowledge, the expense of complying or attempting to comply with any and every such requisition shall be borne by the purchaser, who shall also bear the expense of tracing and getting in all outstanding legal estates (if any) and of stamping or re-stamping any unstamped or insufficiently stamped muniments of title should any such there be (which, however, is not known or believed to be the case) and of all searches, inquiries, and journies, for the above purposes or any of them. The purchaser shall not require any incumbrances to be discharged otherwise than by the incumbrancers joining in such purchaser's conveyance, or make any claim for costs in respect thereto.

XV. The purchaser shall pay the remainder of the purchase-money, [and the value of the said fixture, in case he shall elect to buy them,] on the [twelfth day of August] next, at the office aforesaid to the vendors, or as they shall direct, and upon such payment the vendors will execute, or procure to be executed, by all necessary parties, a proper assurance to the purchaser of the property purchased by him, but such assurance and every other assurance and act (if any) which shall be required by the purchaser for getting-in, surrendering, or releasing any outstanding estate, right, title, or interest, or for completing or perfecting the vendor's title, or for any other purpose, shall be prepared, made, and done, by and at the expense of the purchaser, and every such assurance shall be left not less than ten clear days before the said [twelfth day of August] next, at the office aforesaid, and the expenses of the perusal on behalf of, and execution and acknowledgment by all parties (if any) other than the vendors of all such assurances shall be borne by the purchaser.

XVI. Possession will be retained and the outgoings discharged by the vendors up to the said [twelfth day of August] next; and as from that day the outgoings shall be discharged and the possession taken by the purchaser, and such outgoings shall (if necessary) be apportioned between the vendors and purchasers for the purpose of this condition.

XVII. If from any cause whatever (other than the wilful default of the vendors) the purchase shall not be completed on the said [twelfth day of August] next, the purchaser shall pay interest on the remainder of the purchase-money at the rate of £5 per cent. per annum from that day until the purchase shall be completed.

XVIII. Such of the deeds and muniments of title in the possession of the vendors as relate exclusively to the property, will, upon completion of the sale, be delivered over to the purchaser ; as respects such deeds and muniments as do not relate exclusively to the property the vendors will retain the same, and will at the purchaser's expense enter into covenants with him for their production, such covenants to be so framed as to bind, as far as may be practicable, such deeds and muniments in the hands of the actual owners for the time being, but not so as to subject any covenantor or his representative to liability except in respect of his or their individual acts and defaults, during such time as he or they shall be in the actual possession of, or entitled to, the custody of such deeds and muniments respectively.

LASTLY.—If the purchaser shall fail to comply with the above conditions his deposit shall be forfeited, and the vendors shall be at liberty to re-sell the property at such time, in such manner, and subject to such conditions as the vendors may think fit, and any deficiency in price which may happen upon, and all expenses attending the re-sale, shall immediately afterwards be paid by the purchaser to the vendors, and in case of non-payment shall be recoverable by the vendors as liquidated damages.

CONTRACT.

IT IS HEREBY AGREED AND DECLARED that   of
has this day purchased by public auction of the vendors

s

(insert names of vendors)[1] the property described in the within particulars, for the sum of £—— under and subject to the conditions of sale within specified, and has paid down the sum of £—— as a deposit and in part payment of the said purchase-money; and that the said purchase shall be completed and the remainder of the purchase-money paid according to the terms of the said particulars and conditions.[2]

As witness the hands of the respective parties this day of   1878.

Purchase-money	£	.,	,,	Purchaser.
Deposit paid	£	,,	,,	Vendor's Agent.
Balance	£	,,	,,	

XXXIX.

CONDITIONS OF SALE *of* FREEHOLDS *in two Lots.*

I. No person is to advance less than £10 at each bidding, or to retract a bidding. The highest bidder (subject to a right which is hereby reserved for the vendors to bid by themselves or their agents) shall be the purchaser, and if any dispute shall arise concerning a bidding, the property shall be put up again and re-sold.

II. Each purchaser shall, immediately after the sale, pay a deposit of £10 per cent. of his purchase-money into the hands of the auctioneers, and sign the subjoined agreement.

---

[1] It is *always* advisable to insert the *names* of the vendors, unless they are named in the conditions.

[2] Where property put up for sale is in mortgage, and not sold by the mortgagee under his power of sale, it is necessary in some part of the particulars or conditions of sale to give notice to the purchaser of the property being in mortgage; otherwise he could require the vendor either to get in the mortgage by a separate deed, or to pay any costs occasioned by the extra length of his conveyance consequent upon the necessity of the recital of the mortgage in the conveyance, and of making the mortgagees parties to it.

III. The vendors will deliver to each purchaser, or his solicitor, an abstract of the title to the property purchased by him, subject to the stipulations contained in these conditions. No purchaser of two lots held wholly or partially under the same title shall be entitled to more than one general abstract, except at his own expense.

IV. Each purchaser is, within fourteen days from the actual delivery of the abstract to deliver at the offices of B. at &c., a statement in writing of his objections and requisitions (if any) in respect of the title, or the form of, or the parties to the conveyance, and upon the expiration of such period of fourteen days the title is to be considered as approved of, and accepted by such purchaser, subject only to such objections and requisitions (if any), and a similar statement is to be delivered within seven days after the delivery of answers to any previous statement (whether such answers do or do not include any supplemental abstract) the title being considered as approved of and accepted, except as appearing by such similar statement; and every objection or requisition not so delivered shall be considered as absolutely waived, notwithstanding any subsequent negotiation or litigation, and time shall, in these respects, be considered as of the essence of the contract; and for the purpose of any objection or requisition, an abstract shall be deemed perfect if it supply the information suggesting the same, although otherwise defective, and if any purchaser shall insist on any objection or requisition, which the vendors shall consider themselves unable or, on the ground of expense, or for any other reason, shall decline to remove or comply with, the vendors shall (notwithstanding any intermediate negotiation or litigation, and although they may have insisted that such objections or requisitions are untenable) be at liberty by notice in writing signed by their solicitor, to rescind the contract, and shall thereupon return to the purchaser his deposit, but without any interest, costs of investigating the title, or other compensation or payment whatever.

[V. The property was formerly part of the estate of the

See of Winchester, and the title shall commence with the last lease thereof for lives dated, &c., granted by the late bishop [*name*], and with a conveyance dated &c., of the reversion in fee simple expectant on such lease to trustees for the bishop. with the concurrence of the Church Estates Commissioners.]

VI. No purchaser shall be at liberty to require, investigate, or object to any title, or evidence of title, or any other matter whatsoever (either in respect of the fee or of any lease on the determination of which the aforesaid lease appears to have been granted) prior to such respective commencements, notwithstanding any reference to or notice of any prior documents, and every abstracted document of title dated more than [twelve] years prior to the day of sale shall be accepted as conclusive evidence of all facts, matters, and conclusions of law recited, stated, assumed, or implied therein, and also of the material contents and due execution of all instruments therein recited, of which the vendors have neither the originals nor attested copies, whether they have covenants for the production thereof or not, and no objection shall be made in respect of the non-production of the original, or an attested, or other copy of any instrument so recited, or of any instrument inrolled for safe custody and accessible to the purchaser, or of which the vendors shall produce what purports to be an attested copy, and no abstract in chief shall be required of any document so recited, and of which the vendors have neither the original nor a copy, and no objection or requisition shall be made on the ground of the absence or imperfection of any covenants for title or for the production of muniments of title.

[VII. The vendors are trustees selling under a power of sale in the will of the late J. N., Esq. On the [*date*] an action (*N.* v. *N.*, 187-, N. No. 98), was commenced in the Chancery Division of the High Court of Justice, to obtain the sanction of the Court to a compromise relating to certain real estate of the testator not comprised in the present sale, and the plaintiffs claimed in the alternative a declaration of the rights of the plaintiffs and defendants in such real estate and also administration of the testator's real and personal estate, if and so far as necessary for the purposes aforesaid. An order was made sanctioning such compromise. No purchaser shall be entitled to require the sanction of the Court to be obtained to the present sale, or to make any objection or requisition in respect thereof, or in respect of such action or any of the proceedings therein, or the effect thereof, nor to require the concurrence in his conveyance of any of the persons beneficially interested. The vendors will only enter into the usual trustees' covenants against incumbrances.]

[VIII. The whole of the property is sold and is believed to be free from land tax, but no evidence thereof shall be required beyond that furnished by the reservation in the above-mentioned lease of rent in respect of redeemed land tax.]

IX. Each purchaser shall admit the identity of the property purchased by him with that comprised in the muniments offered by the vendors as the title to such property, upon the evidence afforded by a comparison of the descriptions in the particular and muniments. And the vendors shall not be required to account for any discrepancy between present measurements and those given in any of the abstracted muniments of title.

X. The property is believed and shall be taken to be correctly described as to quantity and otherwise, and each lot is sold subject to all rights of way, and water, and other easements (if any) subsisting thereon, and to the leases mentioned in the particular; and if any error, mis-statement, or omission in the particular be discovered, the same shall not annul the sale, nor shall any compensation be allowed in respect thereof. [The part of Lot 2 called "C. Alley," was formerly called by that name, and was subject to a public right of way, said to have been closed long since by the Commissioners of the Clink Pavement. It was also subject to a private right of way, but this is believed to have ceased. The use only of the alley was granted by the said lease of the [date], but the site was conveyed by the said indenture of the [date], and it shall be admitted that the fee simple of the said alley passed by such conveyance, and the same is

sold and shall be conveyed subject to all existing rights
of way, whether public or private, over the same if any
there be.]

XI. The counterpart, or a copy of each of the leases
mentioned in the particular will (if required) be produced
at the sale, and each purchaser shall therefore be deemed to
buy with full notice of the contents and effect thereof respectively, and as regards each lot the purchaser shall also
be deemed to buy with full notice of the lessees' rights
(if any) to fixtures and otherwise, and of the state of the
property as respects repairs, insurance, and all other matters.

XII. If any purchaser may, consistently with these conditions, require and shall require an abstract, or the production of any deed or document not in the possession of
the vendors, or any office, attested, or other copy of or
extracts from any deed, will, or other document, whether in
their possession or not, and whether for the purpose of
verifying the abstract or of accompanying or completing the
title or otherwise, or any affidavit, statutory declaration,
certificate, or other evidence not in the possession of the
vendors, as to seisin, identity of parcels or any other matter,
or any information not in the vendors' possession or knowledge, the expense of complying or attempting to comply
with any and every such requisition shall be borne by the
purchaser requiring the same, who shall also bear the expense
of tracing and getting in all outstanding legal estates (if
any) and of stamping or re-stamping any unstamped or
insufficiently stamped muniments of title, should any such
there be (which, however, is not known or believed to be the
case), and of all searches, inquiries, and journeys for the
above purposes, or any of them.

XIII. Each purchaser shall pay the remainder of his
purchase-money on the [*date*] at the offices aforesaid, to the
vendors, or as they shall direct, and upon such payment the
vendors will execute, or procure to be executed by all necessary parties, a proper assurance to each purchaser of the
property purchased by him, but such assurance, and every
other assurance and act (if any) which shall be required by

any purchaser for getting in, surrendering, or releasing any outstanding estate, right, title, or interest, or for completing or perfecting the vendors' title, or for any other purpose, shall be prepared, made, and done by and at the expense of such purchaser, and every such assurance shall be left not less than seven clear days before the said [*date*] next at the offices aforesaid, and the expense of the perusal on behalf of and execution and acknowledgment by all parties (if any) other than the vendors of all such assurances, shall be borne by the purchaser.

XIV. The rents will be received and the outgoings discharged by the vendors up to the said [24th of June] next, and as from that day the outgoings shall be discharged and the rents taken by the respective purchasers, and such rents and outgoings, shall (if necessary), be apportioned between the vendors and purchasers for the purpose of this condition. If from any cause whatever (other than the wilful default of the vendors) the purchase of either lot shall not be completed on the said [24th of June] next, the purchaser of such lot shall pay interest on the remainder of his purchase-money, at the rate of £6 per cent. per annum, from that day until the purchase shall be completed.

XV. The purchaser of the larger part in value of property held under the same title, shall be entitled, after the completion of the sale of all such property, to the custody of the muniments of title relating thereto, and shall, at the expense of the other purchaser, enter into usual covenants with him for the production and furnishing copies of such muniments. If either lot shall not be sold at this sale, the vendors shall retain the said muniments until both lots shall be sold, and the purchaser of the lot sold shall in the meantime be entitled at his own expense to the production of such muniments and to copies of them, but the vendors will not enter into any covenant in relation thereto.

LASTLY. If either purchaser shall fail to comply with the above conditions his deposit shall thereupon be forfeited, and the vendors shall be at liberty to re-sell the property bought by such purchaser, at such time, in such manner, and subject to such conditions as the vendors shall think fit, and any deficiency in price which may happen on, and all expenses attending the re-sale, shall immediately afterwards be paid by the defaulter to the vendors, and in case of non-payment shall be recoverable by the vendors as liquidated damages.

[The contract will be the same as in the last preceding form.]

XL.

CONDITIONS OF SALE *of a* LEASEHOLD HOUSE (*with possession*) *in one Lot.*

I.
II.
III.   } *These will be the same as in Form* XXXVIII., *p.* 252.
IV.

V. The abstract of title shall commence with the lease under which the property is held (the same being an under-lease) dated the 27th of March, 1841, the lessor being Mr. William Woods; and the purchaser shall not be entitled to investigate, object to, or require the production of the title of the lessor, or any title prior to or other than the said lease, whether such lessor's or prior or other title appear by recital, statement, or otherwise, or do not appear at all, and the said lease shall be deemed valid and well granted.

VI. Inasmuch as the original or a copy of the said lease will be produced and may be seen at any time prior to the day of sale at the office aforesaid, the purchaser shall be deemed to have full notice of the contents thereof. And the production of the receipt for the rent which last accrued due under the said lease, or satisfactory evidence of the payment thereof, shall be accepted as conclusive evidence that all covenants and conditions of such lease, as well as of any prior or superior lease, have been fulfilled, or all breaches (if any) of such covenants or conditions or any of them, whether appearing by the abstract or otherwise, or not, have

been effectually waived down to the time of completion of
the purchase, including the interval between the contract for
sale and such completion, and that such lease is then valid
and subsisting, and no evidence shall be required of the fact
of the persons receiving such rent being entitled so to receive
the same, and no objection or requisition shall be made in
respect of the fact (should it be one) of such superior lease
having comprised other property under a joint liability to
rent and covenants.

[VII. The property was assigned by the original lessee to
Mr. W. S. H., in 1842, by a deed-poll which contains the
usual covenants for title on the part of the assignor. No requisition or objection shall be made in respect of such
assignment not having been made by indenture.]

[VIII. The property was formerly known as No. 4, A.
Terrace, and was changed to No. 5 in 1841 or 1842. The
statement of this fact in the last-mentioned deed shall be
accepted as conclusive evidence thereof. The property is
now known as No. 7, and the purchaser shall be satisfied
with such evidence of the change from No. 5 to No. 7 as the
vendors may be able to adduce.]

IX. Every abstracted document of title dated more than
15 years prior to the day of sale shall be accepted as sufficient evidence of the facts, matters, and conclusions of law
recited, stated, assumed or implied therein, and also of the
material contents and due execution of all instruments therein
recited or noticed, and of which the vendors have neither the
original nor attested copies, whether the vendors have covenants for the production thereof or not, and no objection or
requisition shall be made in respect of the non-production of
the original, or an attested or other copy of any instrument
so recited or noticed, or of any instrument enrolled for safe
custody and accessible to the purchaser; or of any instruments of which the vendors shall produce what purports to
be an attested copy, and no abstract in chief shall be required of any documents so recited or noticed and of which
the vendors have neither the original nor a copy ; and no
objection or requisition shall be made on the ground of the

absence or imperfection of any covenants for title or covenants for the production of muniments of title.

X. As respects any deed, will, or other document which may not have been registered or properly registered in the county register, the same shall (if required and practicable) be registered or re-registered at the expense of the purchaser; but the purchaser shall not make any other objection or requisition founded on the fact of such non-registration or insufficient registration, nor shall the completion of the purchase be delayed with a view to such registration or re-registration.

XI. The purchaser shall admit the identity of the property with that comprised in the muniments offered by the vendors as the title to such property upon the evidence afforded by a comparison of the descriptions in the particular and the muniments, and of a declaration to be made (if required) at the purchaser's expense that the property has been enjoyed according to the title from the date of the stipulated commencement. And the vendors shall not be required to account for the discrepancy (if any such exists) between present measurements and those given in the abstracted muniments of title.

XII. The property is believed to be and shall be taken to be correctly described as to quantity and otherwise, and is sold subject to all rights of way and water and other easements (if any) charged or subsisting thereon; and if any error, misstatement, or omission in the particular be discovered the same shall not annul the sale, nor shall any compensation be allowed by the vendors or purchaser in respect thereof.

XIII. If the purchaser may, consistently with these conditions, require and shall require an abstract or the production of any deed or document not in the possession of the vendors, or any office, attested, or other copy of or extracts from any deed, will, or other document, whether in their possession or not, and whether for the purpose of verifying the abstract or of accompanying or completing the title or otherwise, or any affidavit, statutory declaration, certificate, or other evidence not in the vendor's possession as to any matter whatever, or any information not in the vendor's possession or knowledge, the expense of complying with or attempting to comply with any such requisition shall be borne by the purchaser, who shall also bear the expense of tracing and of getting in all outstanding legal estates (if any), and of stamping or re-stamping any unstamped or insufficiently stamped muniments of title should any such there be (which however is not known or believed to be the case), and of all searches, inquiries, and journeys for the above purposes or any of them.

XIV. The purchaser shall pay the remainder of his purchase-money on the 1st day of August next, at the office aforesaid, to the vendors, or as they shall direct; and upon such payment the vendors will execute or procure to be executed by all necessary parties a proper assurance of the property to the purchaser, or as he shall direct; but such assurance and every other assurance and act (if any) which shall be required by the purchaser, for getting in, surrendering, or releasing any outstanding estate, right, title, or interest, or for completing or perfecting the vendors' title, or for any other purpose, shall be prepared, made and done by and at the expense of the purchaser; and every such assurance shall be left, not less than 10 clear days before the said 1st day of August, at the office aforesaid, and the expenses of the perusal on behalf of and execution by all parties, other than the vendors, of all such assurances shall be borne by the purchaser.

XV. The sale being made under powers of sale contained in two mortgage deeds, the purchaser shall not require the concurrence of any person interested in the equity of redemption, and shall not require any other covenants to be entered into than the usual covenant against incumbrances.

XVI. The possession will be retained and the outgoings discharged by the vendors up to the said 1st of August next, and as from that day the outgoings shall be discharged and the possession taken by the purchaser, and such rents and outgoings shall (if necessary) be apportioned between the vendors and purchaser for the purpose of this condition.

XVII. If from any cause whatever (other than the wilful default of the vendors) the purchase shall not be completed on the said 1st of August next, the purchaser shall pay interest on the remainder of the purchase-money at the rate of £5 per cent. per annum from that day until the purchase shall be completed.

XVIII. Such of the deeds and muniments of title in the possession of the vendors as relate exclusively to the property will, upon completion of the sale, be delivered over to the purchaser. As respects such deeds and muniments as do not relate exclusively to the property, the vendors will retain the same, and will, at the purchaser's expense, enter into covenants with him for their production. Such covenants to be so framed as to bind, as far as may be practicable, such deeds and muniments in the hands of the actual owners for the time being, but not so as to subject any covenantor or his representatives to liability, except in respect of his or their individual acts and defaults during such time as he or they shall be in the actual possession of or entitled to the custody of such deeds and muniments respectively.

LASTLY. If the purchaser shall fail to comply with the above conditions his deposit shall be forfeited, and the vendors shall be at liberty to resell the property, at such time, in such manner, and subject to such conditions as they may think fit, and any deficiency in price which may happen upon and all expenses attending the resale, shall, immediately afterwards, be paid by the purchaser to the vendors, and in case of non-payment shall be recoverable by the vendors as liquidated damages.

[The contract may be in the same form as in the two previous forms.]

XLI.

Short Form *of Conditions of Sale of* Leasehold Property *in Lots.*

I.
II. } *These conditions may be taken from Form* XXXIX.,
III. } *supra, p.* 258.

IV. The title to lot 1 shall commence with an indenture of lease dated, &c., and that to lot 2 with an indenture of lease dated, &c., and the purchaser of such lots respectively shall not be entitled to call for the production of, or to investigate, or make any objection to or requisition in respect of the title of the lessors respectively, or their right to grant such leases respectively; and it shall not be a ground of objection that the property comprised in lot 1 is held by the vendor under a derivative lease; and the production of a receipt for the last payment of rent accrued on each of the said lots respectively, previously to the completion of the purchase, shall be conclusive evidence that all the covenants and conditions in the said leases respectively have been respectively performed and observed up to the completion of the purchase of the said lots respectively.

V. The purchaser of each lot shall, within ten days after the delivery of the abstract of title, give the vendor, or his solicitor, a statement in writing of the objections or requisitions (if any) not precluded by these conditions to or on the title of the lot purchased by him, and every objection not taken and so communicated within such period shall be deemed waived, the title shall be deemed absolutely accepted and the purchaser precluded from objecting thereto. And if any purchaser shall insist on any objection or requisition made within the time limited, which the vendor shall be unable or unwilling to remove or comply with, the vendor may, by notice in writing, to be given to such purchaser or his solicitor, at any time, notwithstanding any negotiation in respect of any objection or requisition, annul the sale, and the auctioneer shall thereupon return to such purchaser his deposit, but without any interest, costs or compensation whatever.

VI. The leases of the property will be produced for inspection on the day of sale, and the purchaser or purchasers shall not afterwards refuse to perform his, her or their contract or contracts, on the ground of any covenants, stipulations, restrictions, conditions, matters or things therein respectively contained.

VII. No purchaser shall be entitled to call for the production of, or make any objection on account of the non-production of, any deeds or muniments of title of which the vendor shall produce attested copies.

VIII. All extracts, attested, official, or other copies of deeds, wills, or other instruments, and all certificates, statutory or other declarations, and other documents which may be required either for the purpose of verifying the abstract, identifying property, or persons, or otherwise, are to be procured, made, furnished, and obtained at the expense of the purchaser requiring the same.

IX. Upon payment of the remainder of the purchase-money, at the office aforesaid on the [date], the vendor will execute a proper assurance to the purchaser, such assurance to be tendered or left at the offices aforesaid for execution by the vendor ten days at least before the said [date].

X. In case both lots shall be sold, the purchaser of the larger lot in value shall be entitled to the custody and possession of such of the title deeds as have reference to and include both of the said lots, and shall enter into a covenant for their production to the purchaser of the other lot; but in case either lot shall remain unsold, such deed shall remain in the custody of the vendor, who in that case shall enter into the usual defeasible covenant for the production of the same; and such covenant, and all substituted deeds of covenant and all other deeds required for the assignment of the respective lots, shall be prepared by and at the expense of the purchasers.

LASTLY. If any purchaser shall fail to comply with the above conditions, his deposit shall thereupon be forfeited to the vendor, and the vendor shall be at liberty to re-sell the lot bought by such purchaser, either by public auction or private contract, at such time and generally in such manner as the vendor shall think fit; and the deficiency in price (if any) which may happen on such second sale, and all costs and expenses attending the same, shall immediately after such second sale be made good and paid to the vendor by such defaulter at this present sale, and in case of non-payment, the whole or such part of the deficiency and expenses as shall not be paid shall be recoverable by the vendor, as and for liquidated damages; [and it shall not be necessary for the vendor to tender any assignment to the purchaser,] and any profit at such second sale shall belong to the vendor.

[The purchase contract may be taken from Form XXXVIII., p. 258.]

XLII.

CONDITIONS OF SALE *of* FREEHOLD GROUND RENTS.

I.
II. *These will be the same as in Form* XXXIX., *p.* 258,
III. *supra.*
IV.

V. The title of the vendor to the several lots sold shall commence with a conveyance from [A.B., dated, &c.] The purchaser shall not require the production of, or be entitled to investigate or object to, the prior title, notwithstanding there is a covenant for the production of title-deeds of prior date.

VI. No evidence shall be required for identifying any of the lots with the description, either general or particular, in any of the abstracted deeds or other documents, or in the printed particular. Any certificate or statutory declaration that may be required for making out or evidencing the vendor's title, and the obtaining all information relating thereto, are to be procured at the expense of the purchaser requiring the same.

VII. If any error, misstatement, or omission in the particular shall be discovered, compensation shall be allowed or given by the vendor or purchaser, as the case may require; and such compensation shall be settled, regard being had to the amount of the purchase-money, by the auctioneer at the present sale.

VIII. On payment of the remainder of the purchase-money, the vendor will execute a proper conveyance to the purchaser of the lot or lots sold, subject to the existing lease or leases thereof, such conveyance to be prepared by the purchaser's solicitor at his expense, and the engrossment thereof with the draft to be left at the office of the vendor's solicitor three days prior to the day named for completion. The vendor will retain the above-mentioned conveyance of the [date], and the conveyance to the purchaser shall contain a covenant on the part of the vendor to produce the same indenture to the purchaser, his heirs and assigns, such covenant to be determinable on the vendor parting with the said indenture, and procuring the person or persons to whom it shall be delivered to enter into at the purchaser's expense a like covenant with the person or persons who may then be entitled to the benefit of the vendor's covenant.

LASTLY. If any purchaser neglect or refuse to observe or comply with these conditions, the deposit-money is to belong absolutely to the vendor, who may re-sell the property without previously tendering a conveyance of the lot or lots sold, or giving any notice to such purchaser, and either by public auction or private contract, and subject to these or any altered particulars or conditions, as the vendor may think fit; and any deficiency on such re-sale, with all expenses attending the same, are to be made good by the purchaser at this sale, and recoverable by the vendor as liquidated damages without relief in equity.

[The contract may be taken from Form XXXVIII., p. 258]

XLIII.

PARTICULARS *and* CONDITIONS OF SALE *of a* REVERSION *in two Sums of Stock and a House by Trustee in Bankruptcy.*

PARTICULARS.

LOT 1.

THE EQUITABLE LIFE ESTATE

Of a Gentleman now aged 49, in ONE MOIETY
of the Income of a

SUM OF £11,000

(Now invested in and consisting of £12,482 5s. 6d. Consolidated Three per Cent. Bank Annuities),

IN REVERSION expectant on the Death of a Lady now aged 69 Years; and also in the OTHER MOIETY thereof in REVERSION expectant on the Death of the same Lady and a Lady now aged 47 Years.

LOT 2.

THE EQUITABLE LIFE ESTATE

Of the same Gentleman in a

MESSUAGE OR DWELLING HOUSE,

GARDEN AND HEREDITAMENTS,

SITUATE AT

CLEVEDON, IN THE COUNTY OF SOMERSET,

AND ALSO IN A

SUM OF £1,000

CONSOLIDATED THREE PER CENT. BANK ANNUITIES,

Both expectant on the Death of a married Lady, of unsound mind, now aged 49 Years.

T

CONDITIONS OF SALE.

I. }
II. } *Same as in Form* XXXIX., *p.* 258.

III. The vendor (the trustee in bankruptcy of the person entitled to the property) is to deliver to each purchaser or his solicitor an abstract of the title to the property purchased by him subject to the stipulations contained in these conditions.

IV. [*Same as IV. in Form* XXXIX., *p.* 258].

V. The abstract shall commence, as to lot 1, with the will of A. B., dated, &c., and inasmuch as a copy of such will will be produced at the sale, and may be inspected for seven days prior to the sale at the office aforesaid, the purchaser shall accept the same as a good root of title, and as containing a valid and effectual bequest of the life interest comprised in lot 1, according to the description thereof contained in the particulars of sale, and shall not require any further or other title thereto, or make any objection or requisition whatsoever in respect of the said will.

VI. The abstract shall commence, as to lot 2, with an indenture of settlement, dated the 31st day of July, 1852, and made previous to the marriage of C. D. with E. D., by which the said messuage and the said sum of £1000 consols was settled in trust after the death of the said E. D., for the said C. D. for life. The said indenture shall be accepted as conclusive evidence of all facts, matters, and conclusions of law recited, stated, assumed, or implied therein.

VII. The vendor will produce a letter, dated, &c., written by the solicitors of the present legal personal representatives of the testator A. B., and the purchaser of lot 1 shall accept such letter as conclusive evidence that the said sum of £11,000 is now invested as stated in the particular, in the names of such legal personal representatives. The purchaser of lot 2 shall be satisfied with such evidence of the present state of investment of the said sum of £1000 consols as the vendor may be able to produce.

VIII. The vendor will produce certificates of baptism of

the persons referred to in the particular of sale, and a certificate of the marriage of the persons mentioned in condition 6, and such certificates shall be deemed conclusive evidence of the ages of such persons respectively, and of the solemnization of such marriage.

IX. No purchaser shall require any other covenant for title than the usual covenant that the vendor has not encumbered.

X. [*Same as XII. in Form* XXXIX., *p.* 262.]

XI. Each purchaser shall pay the remainder of his purchase-money on the 2nd day of April next at the office aforesaid, to the vendor, or as he shall direct, and upon such payment the vendor will execute or cause to be executed by all necessary parties a proper assurance to such purchaser of the property purchased by him, but such assurance and every assurance and act (if any) which shall be required by any purchaser for getting in, surrendering, or releasing any outstanding estate, right, title, or interest, or for completing or perfecting the vendor's title, or for any other purpose, shall be prepared, made, and done by and at the expense of the purchaser, and every such assurance shall be left not less than ten clear days before the said 2nd day of April, at the office aforesaid, and the expense of the perusal on behalf of and execution by all parties (if any) other than the vendor and the bankrupt of all such assurances, shall be borne by the purchaser.

XII. If from any cause whatever (other than the wilful default of the vendor) any purchase shall not be completed on the [*date*] next, the purchaser shall pay interest on the remainder of his purchase-money at the rate of £5 per cent. per annum, from that day until the purchase shall be completed.

LASTLY. [*Same as in previous forms.*]

XLIV.

CONDITIONS OF SALE *of* LEASEHOLDS *in Lots under a Judgment of the Chancery Division of the High Court of Justice.*

I. No person is to advance less than £5 at each bidding.

II. The sale is subject to a reserve bidding for each lot which has been fixed by the Judge to whose Court this cause is attached.

III. Each purchaser is, at the time of the sale, to subscribe his name and address to his bidding (in the bidding paper) and the abstract of title, and all written notices and communications and summonses are to be deemed duly delivered to and served upon the purchaser by being left for him at such address unless or until he is represented by a solicitor.

IV. Each purchaser is, at the time of sale, to pay a deposit of £10 per cent. on the amount of his purchase-money to Mr. A. B., the person appointed by the said Judge to receive the same.

V. The Chief Clerk of the said Judge will after the sale proceed to certify the result, and Monday, the [*date*], at twelve of the clock at noon is appointed as the time at which the purchasers may, if they think fit, attend by their solicitors at the Chambers of the said Judge, No. 11, New Square, Lincoln's Inn, in the county of Middlesex, to settle such certificate. The certificate will then be settled and will, in due course, be signed and filed and become binding without further notice or expense to the purchasers.

VI. The vendors (the plaintiffs in the cause) are, within ten days after such certificate has become binding, to deliver to each purchaser, or his solicitor, an abstract of the title to the premises purchased by him subject to the stipulations contained in these conditions. No purchaser of two or more lots, held wholly or partially under the same title, shall be entitled to more than one general abstract except at his own expense.

VII. Each purchaser is, within fourteen days after the

actual delivery of the abstract, whether the same be delivered within the above-mentioned ten days or not, to deliver at the office of Messrs..F. & S., No. 14, G. Street, in the city of London, a statement in writing of his objections and requisitions (if any) in respect of the title or the form of or parties to the conveyance. And upon the expiration of such period of fourteen days the title is to be considered as approved of and accepted by such purchaser, subject only to such objections and requisitions (if any), and a similar statement is to be delivered within fourteen days after the delivery of answers to any previous statement (whether such answers do or do not include any supplemental abstract) the title being considered as approved of and accepted, except as appearing by such similar statement, and every objection and requisition not so delivered shall be considered as absolutely waived, notwithstanding any subsequent negotiation or litigation, and time shall, in these respects, be considered as of the essence of the contract, and for the purpose of any objection or requisition an abstract shall be deemed to be perfect if it supply the information suggesting the same, although otherwise defective. And if any purchaser shall insist on any objection or requisition which the vendors shall consider themselves unable, or, on the ground of expense or for any other reason which the Judge shall consider sufficient, shall decline to remove or comply with, the vendors, with the sanction of the said Judge shall, notwithstanding any intermediate negotiation, be at liberty, by notice in writing signed by their solicitor, to rescind the contract upon such terms, in all respects, as the said Judge shall be pleased to direct.

VIII. The abstracts of title shall commence with the leases under which the premises respectively are held (the same being underleases), dated respectively the 18th, 19th, 20th, and 21st days of, &c., and the lessor being in each case Mrs. M. A.

IX. The purchasers respectively shall not require the production of, or investigate the title of the lessor, or any title prior to or other than the leases under which the property described in the particulars is held by the vendors, and all such leases shall be deemed valid and well granted. And inasmuch as the originals or copies of all the leases above referred to will be produced and may be seen at any time prior to the day of sale at the office aforesaid the purchaser shall be deemed to have full notice of their respective contents. And as respects each lot, the production of the receipt for the rent which last accrued due under the lease thereof above-mentioned or satisfactory evidence of the payment of such rent shall be accepted as conclusive evidence that all the covenants and conditions of such lease, as well as of any prior or superior lease or leases, have been fulfilled, or all breaches (if any) of such covenants and conditions or any of them (whether appearing by the abstract, or otherwise, or not) effectually waived down to the time of completion of the purchase, including the interval between the contract for sale and such completion, and that the said lease is then valid and subsisting, and no evidence shall be required of the fact of the parties receiving such rent being entitled so to receive them. And no objection or requisition shall be made in respect to the fact (should it be one) of such superior leases or any of them having comprised other property under a joint liability to rent and covenants.

X. All facts or matters admitted, proved, or proceeded on in the above-mentioned suit of *M.* v. *B.*, or certified by the Chief Clerk of the Judge to whose Court that suit is attached shall be deemed thereby conclusively evidenced, and no objection or requisition shall be made on the ground of the absence or imperfection of any covenants for title or covenants for production of muniments of title.

XI. As respects any deed, will, or other document which may not have been registered or properly registered in the county register the same shall (if practicable) be registered or re-registered at the expense of the purchaser requiring the same, but no purchaser shall make any other requisition or objection founded on the fact of such non-registration, or insufficient registration, nor shall the completion of the purchase be delayed with a view to such registration or re-registration.

XII. Every purchaser shall admit the identity of the property purchased by him with that comprised in the muniments offered by the vendors as the title to such property upon the evidence afforded by a comparison of the descriptions in the particulars and muniments, and of a declaration to be made (if required) at the purchasers' expense that the purchased property has been enjoyed according to the title abstracted since the date of the lease above referred to under which the same is held.

XIII. Every lot is believed and shall be taken to be correctly described as to quantity and otherwise and is sold subject to all chief and other rents, rights of way and water, and other easements (if any) charged or subsisting thereon, and if any error, misstatement, or omission in the particular be discovered, the same shall not annul the sale, nor shall any compensation be allowed by the vendors or purchaser in respect thereof.

XIV. Lots 1 and 2 appear to have been mortgaged in the year 1866 to persons who are described as trustees for the National Bank. These mortgages were paid off or discharged in the year 1867. It shall be assumed (as is believed to be the fact) that the parties receiving and giving discharges for the mortgage moneys were competent so to do, and no abstract, copy, or extract of or from any deed of settlement or other documents of or relating to the said bank or the constitution thereof or the appointment of the trustees shall be required.

XV. As respects those lots which are not in hand the purchasers shall be satisfied with such evidence of the terms of the tenancies as the vendors may be able to adduce. And the expense of stamping or re-stamping any unstamped or insufficiently stamped tenants' agreements or duplicate thereof shall be borne by the purchaser requiring the same. And the purchasers shall also be deemed to buy with full notice of the tenants' rights (if any) to fixtures and of the state of the different lots as respects repairs, insurance (if any) and all other matters.

XVI. If any purchaser may, consistently with these conditions, require and shall require an abstract or the production of any document not in the possession of the vendors, or any office, attested, or other copy of or extract from any document whether in their possession or not, and whether for the purpose of verifying the abstract or of accompanying or completing the title or otherwise, or any affidavit, statutory declaration, certificate, or other evidence not in the vendors' possession as to identity of parcels or any other matter, or any further evidence or information as to the suit of *M.* v. *B.* than a print of the bill and an abstract of the order for sale, the expense of complying or endeavouring to comply with any and every such requisition, including the expense of obtaining a conveyance or vesting order of or as to any legal estate and any administration shall be 'borne by the purchaser, and the purchaser shall bear the expense of tracing and getting in all outstanding legal estates (if any) and of stamping or re-stamping any unstamped or insufficiently stamped muniments of title should any such there be (which however is not known or believed to be the case) and of all searches, inquiries, and journeys for the above purposes or any of them.

XVII. No purchaser shall require from any conveying party any further or other covenant than a covenant that such party has not incumbered, nor require for any purpose the concurrence of any person in respect of any equitable or beneficial interest bound by the order of sale, nor require the production of any abstract or copy of any documents relating solely or so far as the same only relate to any interests so bound, whether such documents are or are not stated in the said bill, nor require any decree or order to be enrolled.

XVIII. Such of the deeds and muniments of title in the possession of the vendors as relate exclusively to any of the lots and have not already been covenanted to be produced will, upon completion of the sale of the lot or lots to which the same relate, be delivered over to the purchaser of the lot, or as the case may be, the largest purchaser in value of the lots to which the same relate, but every purchaser to whom any deeds or muniments relating to other lots or another lot shall be so delivered, shall, if required in that behalf, enter into a covenant for the production of all or any of the same deeds and muniments with the purchasers or purchaser of such other lots or lot, any such covenant to be determinable upon the deeds or muniments to which the same relate being parted with to any person or persons undertaking to enter into a like covenant with the person or persons then entitled to the benefit of the original covenant, and every such covenant, whether original or substituted, to be prepared by and at the cost of the covenantee, who shall also pay the expenses attending its perusal and execution by and on behalf of the covenantor and all other necessary parties (if any), and no purchase shall be delayed with a view to giving or procuring such covenant. In the meantime the vendors will retain such deeds and muniments and will produce the same, and also such deeds and muniments as do not relate exclusively to the said lots or any of them, or which have already been covenanted to be produced to any other person by the vendors or any person through whom they claim, to and at the expense of the several purchasers, but will not enter into any covenant in relation thereto. The vendors, however, reserve the right of making, with the approval of the Judge, any substituted or other arrangement in respect of the muniments of title or any of them.

XIX. Each purchaser is under an order to be obtained by him, or in case of his neglect by the vendor, at the cost of the purchaser, upon application at the Chambers of the said Judge, to pay the amount of his purchase-money, after deducting the amount paid as a deposit, into Court to the credit of the cause, *M.* v. *B.*, 1879, M. 3, proceeds of mortgaged property, Nos. 5, 6, 7, and 8, D. V., on or before the [*date*], and if the same is not so paid then the purchaser is to pay interest on his purchase-money at the rate of £5 per cent. per annum, from the said [*date*], to the day on which the same is actually paid, deducting property tax. Upon payment of purchase-money in manner aforesaid the purchaser is to be entitled to obtain possession or to the rents and profits as from the said [*date*], down to which time all outgoings are to be paid by the vendors, and if necessary such rent and outgoings shall be apportioned between the vendors and purchasers.

LASTLY. If the purchaser shall not pay his purchase-money at the time above specified, or at any other time which may be named in any order for that purpose, and in all other respects perform these conditions, an order may be made by the said Judge upon application at Chambers for the resale of the lot purchased by such purchaser, and for payment by the purchaser of the deficiency (if any), in the price which may be obtained from such resale, and of all costs and expenses occasioned by such default.

XLV.

CONDITIONS OF SALE *incorporating the Common Form Conditions of the* BIRMINGHAM LAW SOCIETY.

1. These condons shall be deemed to incorporate the common form condons of the Birmingham Law Society, a copy whof is hrto annexed, and the same shall be construed together, and if there be any variance or inconsistency between the provons of these condons and the common form condons, the provons of these condons shall prevail. The expression "the vendor" and "the purchaser" shall apply as well to one pson (including a corporation) as to several psons. The expressions "the auctioneer" and "the vendor's solr" shall mean the pson or psons or firm named in these condons as resply filling those offices. The expression "the parlars" shall mean the parlars of sale, and shall include the plan (if any). Words importing the masculine gender shall be deemed to include the feminine, and the singular shall be deemed to include the plural.

2. The auctioneers are, &c.

3. The vendor's solr is, &c.

4. The ppty is sold subject to all rights of way, water, light, and other easements, including, &c.

5. The deposit shall be at the rate of £10 per cent. upon the pche money.

6. The pche shall be completed on [*date*], at the office of the vendor's solr, situate at, &c.

7. The abstract shall be delivered or sent by post to the pcher or his solr on or before the [*date*].

8. Objections and requons on the title shall be sent within fourteen days from the delivery of the abstract, and all further objections and requons arising out of the replies to any former requons shall be sent within seven days from the delivery of such replies.

9. The draft assurance shall be sent to the vendor's solr ten days, and the draft and engrossment three days, before the day named for completion.

10. The title shall commence, &c.

[*Here insert any special conditions that may be necessary. Then will follow the*

Common Form Conditions of the Birmingham Law Society.[1]

1. The vendor reserves to himself the following rights, viz. (1) A right to bid by himself or his agent; (2) A right to withdraw the ppty from sale either in the event of a disputed bidding or without offering the same for competition or declaring the reserve price (if any); (3) A right to arrange the ppty in other lots than those shewn in the parlars, and to consolidate two or more lots into one.

2. The amount of each bidding shall from time to time be prescribed by the auctioneer, and no bidding shall be retracted; subject to the rights hrinbefre reserved to the vendor the highest bidder shall be the pcher, and if any dispute shall arise concerning a bidding the auctioneer. whose decision shall be final, shall determine the same.

3. The pcher shall immediately after the sale pay to the vendor's solr, in the character of stakeholder for both parties, a deposit of £10 per cent. upon the amount of his pche

---

[1] These conditions are copyright, and are printed here by permission of the Committee of the Birmingham Law Society.

money, and also sign an agreement acknowledging himself to be the pcher subject to the condons of sale, and undertaking to complete the pche at the time and place named in the condons. The pche shall be completed at the time and place named in the condons of sale, and if from any cause whatever, other than the wilful default of the vendor or his capricious refusal to deduce a title or assure the ppty, the pcher fails to complete his pche at such time and place, he shall pay to the vendor interest on the balance of the pche money, and also on the value of the timber upon the ppty purchased by him if by the condons of sale such timber is to be taken at a separate price after the rate of £5 per cent. per ann from that time until completion ; or if the delay in completion arise from the default of the vendor (not being wilful on his part or a capricious refusal by him to deduce a title or assure the ppty) until the pcher shall appropriate the balance of his pche money for the purpose of completing the purchase, and shall give notice in writing of such appropriation to the vendor or his solicitor ; but this stipulation shall not affect the provons of the 10th of these condons. Upon completion of the pche the vendor and all other necessary parties (if any) shall, by a proper assurance to be prepared by and at the expense of the pcher, convey or assign the ppty to the pcher or as he may direct, the draft of such assurance being submitted to the vendor's solr for perusal and approval, and the engrossment sent to him for exon on or before the respive dates named in the condons of sale. The rents or posson will be received or retained, and the outgoings discharged by the vendor up to the time appointed for completion, all current rents and current outgoings up to that date being, for the purposes of this stipulation, apportioned between the vendor and pcher, such apportionment in case of dispute being made by the auctioneer, whose decision shall be final. As from the time appointed for completion the rents or posson shall belong to the pcher, but (unless orwise provided by the condons of sale) he shall not be let into the actual posson or receipt of the rents until the completion of the pche.

4. A tree, incumbrancer, or other pson who sells or concurs in any assurance merely in a fiduciary capacity shall only be required to enter into the usual covenant that he has not incumbered.

5. The vendor shall, by the time named in the condons of sale, deliver or send by post to the pcher or his solr an abstract of his title to the ppty, and any limitation of the title to be deduced by such abstract shall be named in the condons of sale, but no pcher of two or more lots held wholly or partially under the same title shall be entitled to more than one abstract of the common title except at his own expense. No earlier title than is named in the condons of sale as the commencement of the title shall be required by the pcher, nor shall he be entitled to make any objection whatever in respect of any earlier title or in respect of any deed or matter prior to the date of the deed forming the stipulated commencement of the title, notwithstanding that he may have notice of such earlier title, deed, or matter by recital or orwise. No objection shall be made by the pcher on the ground of any existing covenant for the prodon of muniments of title not running with the land, or being in cases of trees or incumbrancers covenanting personally binding upon them and their representatives so long only as they have the actual custody of the muniments of title covenanted to be produced. Where the ppty sold is subject to any incumbrance, the vendor shall not be obliged to procure a release thereof by a separate instrument, nor to make any allowance to the pcher on account of the assurance being increased in length or rendered complicated by the incumbrancer joining therein. The pcher of two or more lots held under a common title shall, if he so elect, be entitled to several assurances of such lots. All recitals or statements in any abstracted muniment of title twenty years old and upwards shall be considered conclusive evidence of the matters or things stated, recited, or noticed therein or to be implied thrfrom. The vendor shall, at his own expense, verify the title by the prodon of all such muniments and evidences of title as are in his posson or power, and give to

the pcher all such information relative thereto as is within the knowledge of the vendor, the expense incurred by the pcher with reference to the examination by him of any deed, will, or muniment of title, whether in the posson of the vendor or produced by any incumbrancer or under covenant for prodon or orwise, and of all journeys for such purpose, as also the expense of making and obtaining any official, attested, or other copies of deeds, wills, or other muniments of title, whether in the vendor's posson or not, whether required for verification of the abstract or completion of the pche, shall be borne by the pcher.

6. Where the ppty is of leasehold tenure the title of the lessor named in the lease (whether original or derivative) which by the condons of sale is made the root of title, shall be considered as admitted without the same being deduced or inquired into. The receipt for the last payment of ground rent accrued previously to the completion of the pche shall be accepted by the pcher as conclusive proof that the rent reserved by, and the covts and condons contd in, as well the original lease as the derivative lease (if any) under which the ppty is held, have been paid and performed up to the time of the completion of the pche, or that any breaches of such covts and condons to that time have been waived, and no evidence shall be required as to the right of the pson by or on whose behalf such receipt was given to receive the rent thrin expressed to be paid. The lease, whether original or derivative, by the condons of sale made the root of the title, or a copy throf, shall be produced, and may be examined at the office of the vendor's solr at any time between the hours of 10 A.M. and 4 P.M. on the three days immediately preceding the day of the sale, and shall also be produced at the time of sale, and the pcher, whether he examines the same or not, shall be deemed to have bought with notice of the covts and condons thrin contd.

7. Such of the muniments of title as relate exclusively to any two or more lots mentioned in the parlars if all such lots be not sold, and also such of the muniments of title as relate to any lot or lots mentioned in the parlars, and also

to other ppty belonging to the vendor, shall be retained by him. Such of the muniments of title as relate exclusively to any one lot shall be delivered to the pcher of that lot, and such as relate exclusively to any two or more lots mentioned in the parlars, shall, on the completion of all the pches to which the same relate, be delivered to the largest pcher in value, whether he buy at the present sale or previously or subsequently thrto. Every pson having the custody of muniments of title under this condon shall enter into the usual defeasible covt for the prodon thof to every pcher of ppty comprised in such muniments of title who shall require the same. Such covt shall be prepared by and at the expense of the covenantee, but the covenantor shall bear the expense of the perusal on his part and of the execution throf by him. Where a vendor or other pson being a tree or incumbrancer, or orwise acting in a fiduciary capacity, enters into such covts, the same shall be qualified so as to be personally binding upon him and his representatives so long only as he or they retain the actual custody of the muniments of title comprised thrin.

8. Within the time limited by the condons of sale the pcher shall send to the vendor's solr a statement in writing specifying the objections and requons (if any) to or in respect of the title or the evidence throf wch the pcher may be entitled to make consistently with these condons and the condons of sale, and in default of such objections or requons (if none), and subject only to such (if any), he shall be deemed to have accepted the title, and time shall in this respect be considered as of the essence of the contract, and for the purpose of any objection or requon an abstract shall be deemed to be perfect if it supply the information suggesting the same, although orwise defective. And if the pcher shall insist on any objection or requon (not being a claim for compensation falling within the 9th of these condons) wch the vendor shall be unable, or on the ground of expense shall decline to remove or comply with, the vendor shall, notwithstdg any intermediate or pending negotiation, or any litigation which the pcher may have commenced, or any

attempt to remove or comply with such objection or requon, be at liberty, by notice in writing signed by him or his solr and delivered to the pcher or his solr, to rescind the contract with such pcher unless within ten days after delivery of such notice the pcher shall, by notice in writing signed by him or his solr, withdraw such objection or requon, and upon such rescission the pcher shall be entitled to receive back his deposit-money, but without interest, costs of and incident to the investigation of the title, or other compensation, except costs of suit allowed by the Court on any litigation.

9. If any error, misstatement, or omission in the description of the ppty by the parlars be discovered, the same shall not annul the sale, but if pointed out before the completion of the pche, and not orwise, shall form the subject of compensation, such compensation to be allowed by the vendor or pcher as the case may require, and the amount throf to be settled by the auctioneer, whose decision shall be final.

10. Should the pcher neglect or fail to comply with any of the condons of sale or of these condons, his deposit-money shall be forfeited to the vendor, who without being obliged previously to tender an assurance to the pcher, shall be at liberty to resell the ppty bought by him either by public or private sale, and with or without any special or other condons as to title, evidence of title, expense, or orwise, and at such time and generally in such manner as the vendor may think fit, and the deficiency in price (if any) on such second sale, together with all charges attending such second sale, shall be made good by the pcher at this present sale, and shall be recoverable from him by the vendor as and for liquidated damages.

VARIOUS SPECIAL CONDITIONS.[1]

1. *As to* AUCTIONEER *fixing Amount of* ADVANCES.

THE auctioneer shall before commencing the sale of each lot
fix the advance to be made on each bidding in respect of
that lot, and no person shall retract a bid.[2]

2. *As to* WILL *being* ROOT *of* TITLE.

THE abstract of title shall commence as to lots 3 and 4
with a devise expressed in general terms (but with reference
to the locality) in the will dated, &c., and proved in the
following year, of A. B., the testator in the cause, whose
seisin in fee shall be presumed.

3. *As to* COMMENCEMENT *of* ABSTRACT *of* FREEHOLD *and* LEASEHOLD *Property, and a Freehold* RENT-CHARGE.

THE title to all the freehold property shall commence with
certain indentures of lease and release dated respectively,
&c. The title to lot 3 shall commence with the will of
A. B., dated the &c. (by which will the rent-charge was
created), and no earlier title shall be required; and the title
to lot 4 shall commence with the lease under which it is held,
and the purchaser of such lot shall not be entitled to the
production of, or to inquire into, or on any ground to object
to, the title of the lessors in such lease, whether appearing
thereby to be freeholders or only leaseholders, nor shall any
objection be taken, or any indemnity required, in consequence
of such lot being, together with other property, subject to
any superior or other ground rents or covenants; and the

[1] These conditions are intended for insertion among the forms of general
conditions previously given, in cases where they are respectively applicable.
[2] Sometimes the conditions fix the amount of each advance; but where
there are several lots of varying size and value this form of condition is
preferable.

U

production of the last receipt for the rent reserved by the lease shall be deemed conclusive evidence of the satisfactory performance and observance of all the lessee's covenants in the leases up to the time of the completion of the purchase of such lot, including the interval between the contract and completion, and a waiver of all breaches of covenant (if any), and of all right of entry consequent upon any such breaches.

------

4. *As to* ROOT *of* TITLE *of* LAND *originally acquired by a* PARISH.

IN the year 1870 the vendor bought the property and now sells it subject to the following condition, namely, that it was acquired by the parish in or about the year 1856 in or by way of exchange for other parish property near X , given up by the parish. A statement of facts collected from the entries in the vestry and other parochial minute books, and from the court rolls of the manor of Y., relating to the property, with a copy of the opinion of counsel thereon as to the power of the parish to sell the premises, may be seen by the purchaser before the sale, at the office of Messrs. A. B. & Co. at &c.; and a copy of such statement and opinion will be furnished to the purchaser if required, at his or her expense, but the purchaser must accept the title of the parish thereto without further investigation, and without requiring the vendor to give any further evidence or proof of title whatever, or proof of any statement contained in the case submitted to counsel as aforesaid; and the abstract of title to be furnished by the vendor shall commence with a conveyance from the guardians, churchwardens and overseers of the parish of X., dated &c, and such shall be accepted as sufficient root of title to the premises, without it being incumbent on the vendor to abstract, produce, or verify any earlier muniments or facts of title, whether recited or otherwise noticed or not in the abstracted documents, the purchaser being bound not to investigate or object to the earlier title.

5. *As to Evidence of* INTESTACY *and* HEIRSHIP.

THE purchaser shall accept as sufficient evidence that A. B. (who in [*date*] sold and conveyed the premises to a purchaser in fee) was heir-at-law of C. B. (letters of administration to whose effects were granted in [*date*] to X. Y. and the said A. B.) a document in the vendor's possession, purporting to be an affidavit of X. Y. (therein noticed to be the half-brother of the said A. B.), sworn before a master extraordinary in Chancery in or about the same year; and every recital or statement in a deed, will, or other document of title, dated twenty years or upwards prior to the day of sale, shall be sufficient evidence of the instrument or matter recited or stated; and neither the production nor a covenant for the production of any such instrument shall be required. The purchaser shall not require any further or other evidence relating to the suit of A. *v.* B. than a short statement, to be contained in the abstract, of the decree, certificate, and order of sale, and shall assume that such order is in all respects regular and binding.

---

6. *As to* ACCEPTING VENDOR'S TITLE.

THE pcher of lot 3 shall take it with the title under which it is now held by the vendors. An abstract of this title will be produced, and may be seen at the office afsd at any time prior to the day of sale.

---

7. *As to* TITLE *being considered* NOT MARKETABLE.

IF the counsel for the purchaser shall, on the examination of the title, be of opinion that a good title and conveyance cannot be made of the purchased premises within the time limited by these conditions, in that case these conditions shall be at an end, and the purchaser shall be entitled to a return of the deposit, without interest or costs.

---

8. *As to* SHORT ABSTRACTS *for small Lots.*

As respects any lot the pche-money of wch will not exceed
£100, the pcher, except at his own expense, shall be entitled
only to a short abstract commencing with the will of the testator [in the cause] : but such pcher may, at his own expense,
have an abstract of such prior title (if any) as he would be
entitled to an abstract of in case his pche-money exceeded
£100. The vendor, however, will furnish to the pcher of any
lot the pche-money of which is not more than £100 a conveyance of such lot in a short form settled by [the Judge in
Chambers and] at a cost of £2 2s. for each conveyance exclusive of the stamp duty, [and also exclusive of the costs
of obtaining the order for the payment into Court of the
pche-money by the pcher].

In every case where, under the previous condons, the pcher
may, if he pleases, have an abstract of the prior title at his
own expense, such option, if exercised by him, shall be so
exercised by his leaving a notice in writing to that effect at
the office afsd within seven days after the delivery of such
abstract as under these condns he is entitled to at the vendor's
expense; such notice to be signed by the pcher, and to contain
an undertaking to receive such abstract of prior title and to
pay on delivery for the same.

9. *As to* LOSS *of Mesne* ASSURANCE.

AN indre whrby A. B., one of the original lessees, is believed
to have released his interest in the property to his co-lessees,
C. D. and E. F., cannot now be found, and the vendors have
no office, attested, or other copy of such deed. The vendors
will (if required) make or obtain a statutory declon that for
upwards of twenty years prior to the day of sale the rents of
the ppty have been received by the vendors or the psons
through whom they claim, and the pcher shall presume that
the interest of the said A. B. was duly assured to the said
C. D. and E. F., and that the legal estate in the property
was on the [*date*] vested in the said E. F. (*the survivor*) alone.

10. *As to* SURRENDER OF OLD LEASE.

THE purchaser shall not be entitled to require the vendors to procure the surrender of a lease for twenty-one years from October, 1858, of certain part of the property, but shall be satisfied with the production of the original lease and an agreement (which was confirmed by the Court of Chancery) for the assignment of such lease.

11. *As to* AGE *of* CESTUI QUE VIE.

THE lease of the 12th of February, 1877, is determinable on the death of the lessor or of a lady now aged eighty-two, and the whole of the property will, after the death of such lady, be held under the lease of the 22nd of March, 1877. The statement of the age of such lady in the first-mentioned lease shall be conclusive evidence of her age.

12. *As to* ORIGINAL LEASE *comprising* OTHER PROPERTY.

THE property now offered for sale is subject, along with other tenements, to the rent and covenants reserved and contained in the original demise of the entire premises, dated &c., granted by A. B to C. D. and others, but the purchaser shall not require any evidence of the discharge of the premises hereby offered for sale from the said rent and covenants, nor make any requisition or objection as to the same not being sufficiently secured by the other part of the premises charged therewith, neither shall the purchaser require any indemnity in respect of such rent and covenants, nor be entitled to any evidence as to whether the covenants comprised in such original lease have been observed and performed.

13. *As to* UNDERLEASE *taking effect as* ASSIGNMENT.

IN the years 1865 and 1866 respectively the testor purported by four several indres to demise a portion of lot 4, and the

whole of lot 5, for the whole residues of the terms for which
he held the same resply at the rents stated in the parlars. It
is apprehended that such indres operated as assignments, but
it is believed that the rents thrby resply reserved have been
duly paid since the dates of the said indres resply, and the
purchasers of these lots shall not make any objection or
requon in respect of the matters afsd.

———

14. *As to* Underlease *operating as* Assignment.

The original lease comprised the adjoining hdts hrinbefre
referred to at an entire rent of £   per annum, under a
joint liability to rent and covts.

By an indre dated &c. (and which was probably intended
to take effect as an underlease) A. B., in whom the entire
property comprised in the original lease was then vested,
demised such adjoining hdts to W. X. at the rent of £30 per
annum, and for a term which (as is supposed) was intended
to terminate ten days prior to the determination of the original lease, but which in fact will not terminate by effluxion
of time until nearly three months after that date.

It is considered that such indre operated as an assignment
of the said adjoining property for the residue of the said term
granted by the original lease, and at a rent of £30 per annum
secured by the covt of the said W. X., but without any reversion being left in the said A. B. The purchaser shall be
entitled to an assignment of such rent, with the benefit of
such remedies for the recovery of the same as the vendors are
able to confer, and shall not make any objection or requisition
in respect of any of the matters referred to in this condition.

———

15. *As to* Breach *of* Covenant *to Assign without Licence.*

The lease contains restrictions against alienation without
licence of the wardens and keepers of London Bridge and
the clerk comptroller of the works and revenues of the same

bridge first had and obtained, and also requires that all deeds of alienation should be prepared by the comptroller. Some of the original lessees have released or assigned their interests in the ppty to their co-lessees, and certain tenancy agreements relating to the ppty have from time to time been executed. No licences in respect of such instruments have, in fact, been obtained. The pcher shall not make any objection or requon on account of such licences not having been obtained, nor in consequence of any instruments relating to the ppty not appearing to have been prepared by the comptroller. It is believed that a licence will not be refused in the case of a sale to a pcher of known respectability. Should it, however, be refused in the case of the pcher at the present sale, the vendors shall be at liberty to rescind the sale upon payment to the pcher of his deposit, but without interest, costs, or compensation of any kind.

16. *As to* MORTGAGE *to Trustees for a* BANK.

LOTS 1 and 2 appear to have been mortgaged in the year 1866 to persons who are described as trees for the X. bank. These mortgages were paid off or discharged in the year 1872. It shall be assumed (as is believed to be the fact), that the parties receiving and giving discharge for the mortgage moneys were competent so to do, and no abstract, copy, or extract of or from any deed of settlement or other documents of or relating to the said bank or the constitution thereof or the appointment of the trees shall be required.

17. *As to* RENTS *for* EASEMENT.

THE Co has recently opened certain windows through a wall on the north-west side of the property (which wall belongs to the owners of the adjoining ppty), and have also passed certain bolts and supports for a boring machine through the same wall. The conveyance to the Co contains a reservation of a rent of 20s. per annum in respect of these matters, and a reservation of a right for the adjoining owners to interfere with the access of light to such windows, and also certain covts relating to the user of the sd wall by the Co. The pcher shall not be entitled to make any objections or requons in respect of these matters, and inasmuch as the originals or copies of the conveyance above referred to [and of the above-mentd lease of [*date*], and of the lease by which the ground rents referred to in the parlars are reserved], will be produced and may be seen at any time prior to the day of sale at the office afsd, the pcher shall be deemed to have full notice of their respive contents.

----

18. *As to* IDENTITY *and* CHANGE *of Name.*

THE purchaser shall admit the identity of the property with that comprised in the muniments offered by the vendors as the title to such property upon the evidence afforded by a comparison of the descriptions in the particulars and muniments and of a declon to be made (if required) at the pcher's expense that the property has been enjoyed according to the title for twenty years prior to the day of sale. The ppty was formerly known as No. 5 A. Road, and is now known as No. 115 O. Road, and the pcher shall be satisfied with such evidence of the change of name as the vendors may be able to adduce.

----

19. *As to* TENANCIES.

THE purchaser shall be satisfied with such evidence of the terms of the tenancies as the vendors may be able to adduce, and shall be deemed to buy with full notice of the tenants' rights (if any) as to fixtures and of the state of the property as respects repairs, insurance (if any), and all other matters.

----

20. *As to the* MORTGAGEE *not* JOINING *in* LEASES.

No objection shall be made by any purchaser of that part of the property now sold, which may be subject to leases or agreements granted or made by the vendor's testator, on account of such leases or agreements, or any of them, being liable to be defeated by reason of the mortgagee not having joined in the granting such leases or agreements, all of which will be delivered to the purchasers.

---

21. *As to* COST *of* CERTIFICATES *and other Evidence.* (SHORT FORM.)

THE purchaser shall bear the expense of procuring all certificates of births, deaths, and marriages, and all declarations and other evidence which he may require for the purpose of verifying the title the abstract or otherwise, and of all searches, inquiries, and journeys for the above purposes or any of them.

---

22. *As to* COPYHOLDS *being distinguished from* FREEHOLDS.

THE purchaser of lot 1 shall assume that the copyholds comprised in the admittance of [*date*] form part of that lot; and he shall make no objection founded on any want of apparent identity, nor require the vendors to shew which portion of such lot is the freehold or copyhold portion resply.

CONVEYANCES AND ASSIGNMENTS.

(a) COMPLETE FORMS.

XLVI.

CONVEYANCE *of a Plot of* FREEHOLD LAND *by Owner* IN FEE—CONCISE FORM.

THIS INDRE made &c., between A. B., of &c., of the one part and C. D., of &c., of the other part, WITNESSETH, that in conson of £50 to the sd A. B. paid by the sd C. D. (the receipt whof is hrby acknldgd), the sd A. B. grants to the sd C. D. and his hrs the hdts described in the schedule hereto and delineated on the plan drawn hereon [Together with all rights, easements, and appurts thereto in fact or by reputation belonging. And all the estate and interest of the said A. B. thrn.],[1] to hold the prems unto and to the use of the sd C. D., his hrs and assns; AND THE sd A. B. covts with the sd C. D., his hrs and assns, that [notwithstanding any thing by the sd A. B., done, omitted or knowingly suffered, he has power to grant the prems to the use afsd. And that][1] the same shall henceforth be quietly enjoyed accordingly free from incumbrances and interruptions by the sd A. B. AND THAT the sd A. B. and every person claiming through or in trust for him will, at all times, at the cost of the pson requiring the same, execute and do every such further assce and act for better assuring the prems to the use of the sd C. D., his hrs and assns, as by him or them shall be reasonably required.[2]

IN WITNESS whof the parties hereto have hereto set their hands and seals the day and year first above written.

---

[1] The words in brackets may be omitted where extreme brevity is desired.

[2] Add covenant for production of deeds if necessary, see p. 305.

The SCHEDULE above referred to.[1]

A piece of land situate at the corner of High Road and King's Lane in the parish of X., in the county of Y., containing 100 square yards or thereabouts.

XLVII.

CONVEYANCE *of Freehold* COTTAGE *with Right to use Pump*—VERY CONCISE FORM.

THIS INDRE made &c. between A. B., of &c., of the one part and C. D., of &c., of the other part:

WHAS[2] the sd A. B. (hrnftr called "the vendor") is seised in fee free from incumbs of the hdts hereby granted and has agreed to sell the same to the sd C. D. (hrinftr called "the purchaser"), for the sum of £50.

NOW THIS INDRE WITNESSETH that in conson of £50 pd by the pchr to the vendor (the receipt whereof is hrby ackgd), the vendor hrby grants unto the pchr, his hrs and asss, ALL THAT piece of land with the messe thron situate and being No. 5, on the south side of X. Street, Y., in the county of Z., contng in width fronting the sd street 18 feet, and in the rear throf 22 feet, and in depth on each side throf 41 feet, TOGER with all rights, easements, and appurts thrto in fact or by reputation belonging [and in particular the right to use the well and pump on the piece of land adjoining the said hdts on the west side throf, in common with such other psons as are entitled to the use throf subject to the pmnt of a fair proportion of the expense of keeping the sd well and pump, and the machinery and tackle throf in repair.]   And all the este and interest of the vendor in the prems To HOLD the prems hby granted unto and to the use of the pchr, his hrs and assns.

---

[1] On the plan should be marked the dimensions of the property.

[2] This recital is inserted in order that the conveyance may be conclusive evidence of the vendor's seisin after twenty years have expired, under sect. 2 of the Vendor and Purchaser Act, 1874.

AND THE VENDOR covts with the pchr, his hrs and assns, that notwithstanding anything by the vendor done, omitted, or knowingly suffered, the vendor has power to grant all the sd prems to the use afsd.[1] And that the same shall be quietly enjoyed accordingly free from incumbs [and interruptions], by the vendor. And that the vendor and every person claiming through or in trust for him will at all times at the cost of the pchr, his hrs or assns, execute and do all such assces and acts for further assuring the prems or any part throf to the use afsd as by him or them shall be reasonably required.

IN WITNESS, &c.

XLVIII.

CONVEYANCE *of Freeholds by* INDORSEMENT[2]—VERY CONCISE FORM.

THIS INDRE made, &c., between the within-named A. B. of the one part and C. D. of &c., of the other part,

WITNESSETH that in conson of £60 pd by the sd C. D. to the sd A. B. (hby ackngd) the sd A. B. grants unto the sd C. D. and his hrs, all and singular the prems comprised in and assured by the within-written indre, To HOLD the same unto and to the use of the sd C. D., his heirs and assns. And the sd A. B. [*covenants for title as in Form* XLVII., *supra.*]

[1] The covenant for power to convey, although usually inserted, is of very little (if any) practical value, and may be omitted where brevity is an object.

[2] Freeholds are seldom (if ever) conveyed by an indorsed deed, although leaseholds often are. In simple cases, especially where the same solicitor acts for both parties, and therefore has the conveyance to the vendor in his possession, there seems no reason why this course should not be adopted.

XLIX.

CONVEYANCE *in Fee of Part of a* FREEHOLD FARM, *a* LESSEE *joining to* MERGE *his Term*—FULL FORM.[1]

THIS INDRE made, &c., between A. B., of &c., of the first part, and C. D., of &c., of the second part, and E. F., of &c., of the third part:

WHAS the sd A. B. has agreed with the sd E F., for the sale to him of the hdts hrinafr described, and the inhance throf in fee simple in posson free from incumbs, at the price of £3500.

AND WHAS the sd hdts are part of a farm of which the sd C. D. is tenant, under a lease dated &c., for a term which will expire on the [*date*] and the sd C. D., at the request of the sd A. B., has agreed to concur in these presents for the ppse and in manner hrinafr appearing.

NOW THIS INDRE witnesseth that in pursee of the sd agreet in this behalf and in conson of the sum of £3500 upon the exon of these presents paid by the sd E. F. to the sd A. B., with the privity and approbon of the sd C. D. (the receipt &c.). He the said A. B. doth hrby grant and convey, and at his request the sd C. D., for the purpose of merging the residue of the sd term in the hdts hrnafr described, doth hrby assign and surrender unto the sd E. F., his hrs and assns.

ALL THOSE fields [*short description*].

All which said fields or closes of land, are more particularly described with their dimensions in the schedule hereto and are delineated with the abuttals throf in the map drawn in the margin of these presents and therein coloured pink, the numbers in the said schedule referring to corresponding numbers on the said map, TOGETHER WITH all buildings, erections, fixtures, commons, mines, minerals, hedges, ditches, fences, ways, waters, watercourses, liberties, privileges, ease-

[1] This conveyance contains the full forms of general words and covenants for title usually inserted in conveyances of large properties. They are considerably longer than there is any necessity for. Compare the two previous forms.

ments, advantages, and appurts whatsoever to the said hdts
or any of them appertaining, or with the same or any of
them now or heretofore demised, occupied, or enjoyed, or reputed or known as part or parcel of them or any of them, or
appurtenant thereto.   And all the estate, right, title, interest,
property, claim, and demand whatsoever of them the sd A. B.
and C. D., and each of them, into and out of the same prms
and every part throf.   [And particularly with full liberty for
the said E. F., his hrs and assns, and his and their agents and
tenants, and the owners and occupiers for the time being of
the hdts hby assured, and the servants and workpeople of him
and them resply, from time to time and at all times, for all
purposes, to go, return, pass and repass, with and without
horses, carts, waggons and other carriages, laden or unladen,
and also to drive cattle and other beasts in, through, along,
and over a certain road or way of four yards wide at the
least, to be forthwith laid out, levelled and formed by the sd
A. B., across the land of the sd A. B., in the course and direction shewn in the said plan, and thrn coloured brown].

To HAVE AND TO HOLD the said fields or closes of land and
hdts, and all and singular other the prems hereby assured
unto the sd E. F. and his hrs, freed and discharged from the
residue of the said term of years,

To the use of the sd E. F., his hrs and assns, for ever.

AND THE SD A. B. doth hereby for himself, his hrs, exors,
and ads, covt with the sd E. F., his hrs and assns, that
notwithstanding anything by him the sd A. B., or any
pson through whom he derives title orwise than by way
of pche for valuable conson, done or knowingly suffered, the
sd A. B. and C. D. now have full power to assure all and
singular the sd pres by them hrby assured, to the uses hrinbefre decld ; and that the same pres shall at all times remain
and be to the uses hrinbefre decld, and be quietly entered
into and upon, and held and enjoyed, and the rents and profits
thof reced by the sd E. F., his hrs and assns accordingly,
without any lawful interruption or disturbance by the
sd A. B., or any pson claiming or to claim through or in
trust for him, or through or in trust for any pson through

whom he derives title orwise than as afsd. And that free and discharged from or orwise by the sd A. B., his hrs, exs, or ads, suffly indemnified against all estates, incumbs, claims, and demands created, occasioned, or made by the sd A. B., or any pson or psons through whom he derives title otherwise than as afsd, or any pson claiming through or in trust for him, them, or any of them.

And further, that the said A. B., and every pson claiming any estate, right, title, or interest in or to the said prems, or any of them, through or in trust for the sd A. B., or through or in trust for any pson through whom he derives title orwise than as afsd, will at all times, at the cost of the sd E. F., his hrs or assns, execute and do every such lawful assurance and thing for the further or more perfectly assuring all or any of the sd pres to the uses hrinbefre decld as by him or them shall be reasonably required.

[AND that the sd A. B., his hrs, exors, admors, or assns, will at his and their own cost forthwith lay out, level, and form, and afterwards at all times maintain and keep in repair in a good, substantial and workmanlike manner, a road or way of four yards wide at the least for the whole length thof over and across the land of the sd A. B., in the course and direction shewn and delineated in the sd plan, and thrn coloured brown.]

AND HE, the sd C. D., so far as relates to his own acts and deeds, doth hrby for himself, his hrs, exors, and ads, covenant with the said E. F., his hrs and assns, that he the sd C. D. has not executed or done, or knowingly suffered, or been party or privy to any deed or thing whrby or by reason or means whrof the pres hrinbefre assured, or any of them, or any part throf, are, is, or may be impeached, charged, affected, or incumbered in title, estate, or orwise howsoever, or whrby or by reason or means whrof he the sd C. D. is in anywise hindered from assuring the same pres or any of them, or any part throf in manner afsd.

IN WITNESS, &c.

———

L.

CONVEYANCE *of Freeholds by* APPOINTMENT *and* GRANT, *with Covenant to produce Deeds*—CONCISE FORM.

THIS INDRE, made &c., between A. B. (*the vendor*) of &c., of the one part, and C. D. (*the purchaser*) of &c., of the other part: Whas by an indre dated &c., and made between Y. Z. of the first part, the sd A. B. of the second part, and W. X. of the third part, the hdts hrinftr described were assured unto the sd A. B. and his hrs, to such uses as the sd A. B. should appoint; and in default of apptmt to the use of the sd A. B. and his assns for life, with remr to the use of the sd W. X. his exors and admors during the life of the sd A. B., in trust for the sd A. B. and his assns, with remr to the use of the sd A. B., his hrs and assns: And whas the sd A. B. has agreed with the sd C. D. for the sale to him of the sd hdts, and the inhance thof in fee in posson, free from incumbs, at the price of [£500]. And whas the documents specified in the schedule hereto relate as well to the hdts hrnftr described as to other hdts of the sd A. B. Now THIS INDRE WITNESSETH, that, in conson of the sum of [£500] to the sd A. B. paid by the sd C. D. on [or before] the exon hrof (the rect whof the sd A. B. doth hrby acknge), he the sd A. B , in exercise of all powers enabling him in this behalf, doth hrby appt that all and singular the hdts hrnftr described shall henceforth go, remain, and be to the uses hrinftr declared concerning the same: AND THIS INDRE ALSO WIT- NESSETH, that, for the consons afrsd, the sd A. B. doth hrby grant and confirm unto the sd C. D. [*purchaser*] and his hrs, all, &c. [*parcels*], together with all rights, easements, and apprts thrto in fact or by reputation belonging, To HOLD the sd hdts unto and to the use of the sd C. D., his hrs and assns [And the sd C. D. doth hrby declare that no widow whom he may leave shall be entitled to dower out of the sd hdts];[1] AND THE SD A. B. doth hrby for himself, his hrs,

---

[1] This bars the wife's right to dower as against the heir of the purchaser in the event of the latter dying intestate. It is a harsh clause and its insertion cannot be recommended.

exors, and ads, covt with the sd C. D., his hrs and assns,
that notwithstanding anything by the sd A. B. done, omitted,
or knowingly suffered, he the sd A. B. now hath full power
to assure the sd hdts in manner afsd [*Covenant for quiet
enjoyment from Form XLVII. should be inserted here*], free
from incumbs; And that the sd A. B., and every person
claiming [any estate or interest in the said hereditaments]
through or in trust for him will from time to time, at the
request and cost of the sd C. D., his hrs or assns, execute
and do every such further assurance and thing for better
assuring the sd hdts in manner afsd, as he or they shall
reasonably require: and also will (unless prevented by fire
or other inevitable accident), at all times, upon the like
request and cost, produce and shew in England, as occasion may require, the deeds and writings specified in the
schedule hereto, for the proof of the title of the sd C. D.,
his hrs or assns, to the sd hdts; and will, upon the like
request and cost, from time to time furnish to the sd C. D.,
his hrs or assns, attested or other copies, abstracts, or extracts of or from the same; and will, in the meantime, keep
the same safe, whole, and uncancelled.

Provided that in case the sd A. B., his hrs or assns, shall
deliver the sd deeds, evidences, and writings to any pchr
of the hdts to which the same relate, or any part throf,
and shall, at his or their expense, procure such pcher to
enter into a similar covt with the sd C. D., his hrs and assns,
to that lastly hrin-before contd, then the sd covt lastly
hinbfre contd shall cease and be void.[1]

IN WITNESS, &c.

[1] This proviso cannot be insisted upon by the vendor without express
stipulation.

X

LI.

CONVEYANCE *in Fee by* MORTGAGOR *and* MORTGAGEES *of* FREEHOLDS *in the City of* LONDON *in Mortgage to the Trustees of a* LOAN SOCIETY.

THIS INDRE, made &c., between A. B. of &c. (hrnftr called "the vendor") of the first part, C. D. of &c., and E. F. of &c. [*mortgagees*], (trustees of the X. society established and inrolled under the Friendly Societies Acts, and hereinafter called "the trees") of the second part, and G. H. of &c., of the third part: Whas the vendor being seised in fee of the hdts hrinftr described, did by an indre dated &c., and made between the vendor of the one part and the trees of the other part, in consideration of £1500 advanced by them to him, demise to the trees, their successors and assigns, the sd hdts [and which in the indre now in recital were by mistake called No. 4, instead of No. 5, Y. Street] with the appurts, to hold the same unto the trees, their succors, and assns, for the term of 500 years, subject to a proviso for redemption on payment by the vendor to the trees, their succors, or assns, of £1500: together with interest thon at £5 per cent. per ann. as thrn mentd: And whas the sd G. H. has agreed with the vendor for the purchase of the sd hdts, and the inheritance thereof in fee simple in possession, free from incumbrances, for the sum of £3000: And whas there is now due to the trees under the hrnbfre-recited indre the sum of £1000, all interest for the same having been paid up to the date hrof; and it has been agreed that the sd sum of £1000 shall be pd to the trees out of the sd sum of £3000: Now THIS INDRE WITNESSETH, that, in conson of £3000 upon the exon hrof by the sd G. H. pd, as to £1000 part thof, to the trees by the diron of the vendor (the receipt whof the trees hereby acknowledge), and as to £2000 residue thof to the vendor (the receipt whereof the vendor doth hrby ackndge), he the said vendor doth hrby grant, and the sd trees, by the diron of the vendor, do and each of them doth hrby assign unto the sd G. H., his hrs and assns, ALL THAT messge or tenement situate and being No. 5, X. Street, in the City of London, together with all rights, easements, and appurtes thereto in fact or by reputation belonging, or used, occupied or enjoyed therewith, To hold the sd prems unto and to the use of the sd G. H., his hrs and assns. And the vendor doth hrby for himself, his heirs, exors, and admors, covt with the sd G. H., his hrs and assns, that notwithstanding anything by the vendor or the trustees [or any person through whom the vendor derives title orwise than by way of pche for valuable conson][1] done, omitted, or knowingly suffered, the vendor and trees, or some of them, have or one of them now has, power to assure the prems unto and to the use of the sd G. H., his hrs and assns, And that the same prems shall accordingly be quietly enjoyed by the sd G. H., his hrs or assns, without interruption from the vendor [or any person through whom he derives title orwise than as a purchaser for valuable conson][1] or any person claiming through or in trust for him [or any such person as last afsd],[1] free from incumbrances ; and that the *vendor* and every person claiming through or in trust for him [or through or in trust for any such person as afsd],[1] will from time to time, and at all times hrftr, upon the request and at the cost of the sd G. H., his heirs or assigns, do and execute every such further assce and thing for further or more perfectly assuring the prems to the use of the sd G. H., his heirs and assigns, as by him or them shall be reasonably required. And each of them the trees doth hrby for himself, his hrs, exors, and admors, covt with the sd G. H., his hrs and assns, that they the trees resply have not done, or omitted, or been party or privy to any act or deed, whby or by means whof the said hereditaments can or may be in any manner incumbered or prejudicially affected, or whby or by means whof they are in anywise hindered from assuring the same in manner afsd.

IN WITNESS, &c.

---

[1] These words must be inserted where the vendor claims under a will or settlement.

LII.

Conveyance *in Fee by a* Mortgagee *under his* Power of Sale.

This Indre, made &c., between C. D. of &c., of the one part, and C. K. of &c., of the other part : Whas by an indre dated &c., and made between A. B. of the one part and C. D. of the other part, in consideration of £   paid by the sd C. D. to the sd A. B., the sd A. B. granted unto the sd C. D. and his hrs the hdits hrnftr described [and intended to be hrby granted], To hold unto and to the use of the sd C. D., his hrs and assns, subject to a provo for reconveyance of the sd hdts on payment by the sd A. B., his hrs, exors, or adors, unto the sd C. D., his exors, adors, or assns of the sd sum of £   with interest thron, on the [*date*]. And it was thrby declared [*set out the power of sale and receipt clause, and clause protecting the purchaser from the necessity of inquiring, &c., as in Form XCVII., p.* 395, *infra*]. And whas the sd sum of £   was not paid on the sd [*date*], and the same still remains due to the sd C. D., together with an arrear of interest thron : And whas the sd C. D. has agreed with the sd C. K. for the sale to him of the hdts comprised in the sd indre of mtge, and the inhance thof in fee simple in possession, free from incumbrs, for the sum of £   : Now this Indre witnesseth, that, in condon of £   to the sd C. D. paid by the sd C. K. on the exon hereof (the receipt whof the sd C. D. doth hrby acknge), the s l C. D. doth hrby grant unto the sd C. K. and his hrs, all [*parcels, general words, and " all the estate " clause*], To hold the sd hdts and prems unto the sd C. K. and his hrs (freed and discharged from the sd sum of £   and all interest due in respect of the same, and all moneys secured by the hrinbfre-recited indre of mtge), To the use of the sd C. K., his hrs and assns : And the sd C. D. doth hrby for himself, his hrs, exors and adors, covt with the sd C. K., his hrs and assns, that the sd C. D. has not done, omitted, or knowingly suffered any thing whby or by reason or means whof the sd hdts or any part thof are, is, or can be in any manner incumbered or prejudicially affected, or whby or by reason or means whof he is in anywise hindered from granting the same in manner afsd.

IN WITNESS, &c.

LIII.

CONVEYANCE *in Fee by* TENANTS IN COMMON *of Undivided Shares in* FREEHOLD *Property with* COVENANT *that an* INFANT *shall* CONVEY *his presumptive Share on* ATTAINING MAJORITY.

THIS INDRE, made &c., Between A. B. of &c., of the first part, C. B. of &c., of the second part, and E. F. of &c., of the third part :

WHAS X. B. died on [*date*], seised in fee of the hdts hrnftr described, having duly made his will dated &c., whrby he devised all his real este in the county of Y. unto and to the use of such one or more of his children as being male shd attain the age of twenty-one years, and being female shd attain that age or marry, and if more than one in equal shares. And whas the sd X. B. had three children and no more, namely, the sd A. B. and C. B., who have both attained the age of twenty-one years, and D. B. who attained the age of nineteen years on the [*date*] last. And whas the sd A. B. and C. B. have agreed with the sd E. F. for the sale to him of the hdts hrnftr described for the sum of £3000. And whas purst to an agreet in that behalf the sum of £1000, being the pche-moy for the expectant undivided third part of the sd D. B. of and in the sd hdts, has been invested in the joint names of the sd A. B., C. B., and E. F. [*specify the invest-ment*] and the sd A. B. and C. B. have agreed to enter into the covts hrnftr contd.

NOW THIS INDRE WITNTH that in pursce of the sd agreet in this behalf, and in conson of the sums of £1000 and £1000 now pd by the sd E. F. to the sd A. B. and C. B. resply, and the sd sum of £1000 invested as hrnbfre recited (the rect

and investment of which sums of £1000, £1000 and £1000,
making together the sd pche-moy of £3000, the sd A. B. and
C. B. hby acknge), They the sd A. B. and C. B. do, and
each of them doth, hby grant and convey to the sd E. F. and
his hrs All those the two undivided third parts or shares
and all other the parts or shares, whether vested or contingent, of them the sd A. B. and C. B. and each of them, of
and in ALL THAT [*parcels, describing the property*] TOGETHER
WITH [*general words from Form XLVI. or XLIX.*]

To HAVE AND TO HOLD the same prems unto and to the use
of the sd E. F., his hrs and assns.

AND THEY the sd A. B. and C. B. do hby for themselves,
their hrs, exors, and ads[1] [*covenants for title as in Form
XLVII or XLIX.*]

And also that the sd D. B. will, at the request and cost of
the sd E. F., his hrs or assns, when and so soon as the sd
D. B. shall have attained the age of twenty-one years, or at
any time thereafter, within twelve calendar months after
being thereunto required, execute and deliver to the sd E. F.,
his hrs or assns, a proper assce to him or them of the undivided third part or share of the sd D. B. of and in the sd
prems; and also, that in case the sd D. B. shall die without
having attained the age of twenty-one years, or without
having signed, sealed, and delivered such assce as afsd, the
sd A. B. and C. B., their hrs or assns, will at any time after
such decease of the sd D. E. as afsd, and whenever thereunto
required by the sd E. F., his hrs or assns, and at the cost of
the pson requiring the same, execute such further assces for
better assuring the sd prems to the use of the sd E. F., his
hrs and assns, as by him or them shall be reasonably required.

And the sd E. F. doth hby for himself, his hrs, exors, adors,
and assns, covt with the sd A. B. and C. B., their hrs and
assns, that if the sd D. B. shall attain the age of twenty-one
years and execute such assce to the sd E. F. as afsd, the sd
E. F. will, upon the exon of such assce, concur with the sd

---

[1] In an ordinary conveyance by tenants in common they would only
covenant as to their respective undivided shares; but in a case like the
present, each ought to covenant as to the entirety.

A. B. and C. B. in transferring the sd sum of £1000 so invested as afsd into the name of the sd D. B., and that if the sd D. B. shall die under the age of twenty-one years, and the sd A. B. and C. B. shall thereupon execute such further assce of the prems to the sd E. F. as by him shall be reasonably required, the sd E. F. will, upon the exon of such further assce, transfer the said sum of £1000 into the names of the sd A. B. and C. B. only.[1]

IN WITNESS, &c.

LIV.

CONVEYANCE *in Fee of Freeholds by* CLERK OF THE PEACE *to* TRUSTEES *of a Settlement.*

THIS INDRE, made, &c., between A. B., of &c., in the county of Y., the clerk of the peace for the said county of Y., of the first part; Sir C. D., of &c., knight, of the second part; and E. F., of &c., and G. H., of &c., of the third part: Whas by an indre dated, &c., and made between X. Y. of the first part, the mayor, aldermen and burgesses of the borough of Z. afsd of the second part, and the sd A. B. of the third part, the hdts hrnftr described and assured were (with other hdts) assured unto and to the use of the sd A. B., as such clerk of the peace afsd, his succors and assns, in trust for the justices of the peace for the county of Y. for the ppses of the sd county; and whas the sd hdts are not required for the ppses of the sd county. And whas by an indre of stlmt dated, &c., and made between O. D., since

---

[1] It is only very rarely that a conveyance in this form is required. An ordinary purchaser would not accept a title depending upon the contingency of an infant attaining his majority; but the writer has known cases where special circumstances have induced a willing and friendly purchaser to do so. Nor is it often that vendors who are *sui juris* would enter into such a covenant as the above; for if the infant on attaining twenty-one refused to concur in conveying his undivided share, the purchaser could recover damages for breach of covenant against the other vendors. Having regard to the Infants Relief Act (37 & 38 Vict. c 62) the infant is not made a party to the conveyance.

deceased (the late father of the sd C. D.), and the sd Sir
C. D. of the first part, L. M. and the sd G. H. of the second
part, certain hdts now stand limited to the use of the sd
C. D. for life; and it was thby declared, that it should be
lawful for the sd C. D. and L. M., or other the trees of the
sd indre of stlmt at any time thftr, at the request of the
person who should for the time being be entitled under the
indre now in recital to the first estate of freehold in the
hdts thby settled, every such request to be signified by deed,
to sell and dispose of the hdts thby settled or any part
thof, and that the sd trees should with the like consent
apply the moneys to arise from any such sale (among other
ppses) in the purchase of freehold hdts situate in England or
Wales or orwise as thrn mentd, to be settled to the same
uses, upon the same trusts and subject to the same powers
and provisoes as were in and by the sd indre of stlmt expressed concerning the hdts thby settled in strict stlmt, or
as near thto as the deaths of parties and other circes would
admit; And whas the sd L. M. died on [*date*], and by an
indre dated, &c., and made between the sd Sir C. D. of the
first part, the sd E. F. of the second part, and the sd G. H.
of the third part, the sd G. H. was (pursuant to a power for
that ppse in the sd indre of stlmt contd) appointed a tree of
the same indre, in the place of the sd L. M.; and all the
hdts then subject thrto were duly vested in the sd E. F. and
G. H. upon the trusts thof then subsisting; And whas sales
have been made by the sd trees of portions of the sd settled
hdts pursuant to the powers contd in the sd indre of stlmt;
And whas the sd E. F. and G. H., as trees of the sd indre of
stlmt, have, at the request of the sd Sir C. D. (testified by
his executing these presents), agreed with the sd A. B., as
such clerk of the peace for the county of Y., for the purchase
of the piece of land hrnftr described and the inhauce thof in
fee simple in possession, at the price of £1700: And whas
the sd contract was at the Michaelmas Quarter Sessions, 1880,
for the said county of Y., duly confirmed by the justices of
the peace for the sd county: NOW THIS INDRE WITNESSETH,
that in conson of the sum of £1700 upon the exon of these

presents pd to the sd A. B. by the sd E. F. and G. H. out of
moneys in their hands which have arisen from such sales a
afsd, with the consent of the said Sir C. D. (the receipt whof
the sd A. B. doth hby ackdge), he the sd A. B., in pursce of
the power given to him by the statute 21 & 22 Vict. c. 92,
doth hrby grant unto the sd E. F. and G. H. and their hrs,
ALL THAT, &c. [*parcels, general words, and all the estate clause*],
To HOLD the same unto the sd E. F. and G. H. and their hrs,
To such uses, upon such trusts and subject to such powers
and provons as are in and by the sd indre of sltmt declared
of and concerning the freehold hdts thby limited, or as
near thto as the deaths of parties and other circes will
now admit.   And the sd A. B. doth hrby for himself, his hrs,
executors, and administrators, covt with the sd E. F. and
G. H. their hrs and ass [*covt against incumbs as in Form LII.*]
    IN WITNESS, &c.

A certified copy of the justices' confirmation and approval of the sale
should be obtained and annexed to the conveyance.

LV.

CONVEYANCE IN FEE *of a Plot of Land subject to
a Yearly* RENT - CHARGE *and* RESERVATION *of*
MINERALS.

THIS INDRE, made &c., between A. B., of &c. [*grantor*] of
the one part, C. D., of &c. [*grantee*] of the other part,
WITNESSETH, that, in conson of the rent hrinftr limited,
and of the covts and agreets hrinftr contained on the part
of the sd C. D., his hrs, exors, admors, and assns, the sd
A. B. doth hrby grant unto the sd C. D. and his heirs,
ALL THAT plot of land situate at &c., and which said plot
of land contains in the whole 230 superficial square yards
of land or thrbts, and is, with the boundaries and dimensions thof, more fully delineated in the plan drawn in
the margin of these presents, and therein coloured red, and
also all and singular the dwelling-house and other bldgs

already erected by the sd C. D. on the said plot of land, or
any part thereof, with the appurtes to the sd plot of land
belonging (save and except out of these presents all mines,
minerals, and materials lying within or under the said plot
of land, with liberty to get and dispose of the same, as well
as the mines lying under any other lands, leaving sufficient
pillars to support the surface of the same plot and any erections now erected or hereafter to be erected thron), To HOLD
the prems hrby granted unto the sd C. D. and his hrs, to
the several uses and upon the trusts hrinftr limited and
declared concerning the same (that is to say), to the use
that the sd A. B., his hrs and assns, may out of the sd
premises for ever hrftr receive and take one clear rent of
£10 sterling, to be issuing and payable throut by two equal
half-yearly payments, on the [*dates*] in every year, free from
all deductions, the first half-yearly payment whof will become due on [*date*].   And to the further use, that if the sd
yrly rent-charge or any part throf shall be in arrear and
unpaid for the space of twenty days after the same shall
become due, then it shall be lawful for the sd A. B., his hrs
and assns, to enter into and upon the sd prems, and to distrain
for the sd rent in arrear, and the distress or distresses so
taken to sell and dispose of according to law as landlords are
authorized to do in respect of distresses for arrears of rent
upon leases for years, so that the sd A. B., his hrs or assns,
may be paid and satisfied the sd yearly rent, or so much
throf as shall then remain due and unpaid, and all costs and
expenses occasioned by the nonpmt thof: And to the further
use, that in case the sd yrly rent charge or any part thof
shall be in arrear and unpaid for the space of forty days
next after the same shall become due, then (although no
legal demand shall have been made thof) it shall be lawful
for the sd A. B., his hrs and assns, into and upon the said
prems to enter, and rece and take the rents thof for his
and their own use, until not only all arrears of the sd yearly
rent but also all such rent as shall accrue during such posson,
and all exps incurred on account of such entry or entries
and rect of rents shall be fully paid, and such posson when

taken shall be without impchmt of waste : [And to this further use, that if it shall happen that the sd yearly rent or any part thereof shall be behind or unpaid for the space of two years next after any of the sd days or times of payment on which the same ought to be paid as afsd, and no sufficient distress or distresses can or may be found in or upon the sd prems, it may be lawful for the sd A. B, his hrs or assns, into and upon the sd prems, or any part thof in thé name of the whole, to re-enter and the same to have again, re-possess and enjoy, and receive and take the rents and profits for his and their own benefit as in his or their first and former estate] ; and subject to and charged with the sd yearly rent and the remedies hrby provided for recovery thof, and to the several limons afsd to the use of the sd C. D., his hrs and assns : And the sd C. D. for himself, his hrs, exors, and admors, doth hrby cort with the sd A. B., his hrs and assns, that he the sd C. D., his hrs and assns, will yearly for ever hrftr pay unto the sd A. B., his hrs and assns, the sd yearly rent of £10, by equal half-yearly payments, upon the days and in manner afsd, without any deduction (the property tax in respect of the sd yearly rent only excepted), And the sd A. B. doth hrby for himself, his hrs, exors, and admors, covt with the sd C. D., his hrs and assns, that, notwithstanding anything by him done, omitted, or knowingly suffered, he A. B. now hath full power to grant the sd prems to the uses and in manner afsd, And that the same may be quietly entered into and enjoyed by the sd C. D. his hrs and assns, free from incumbs by the sd A. B. his hrs and assns ; and that the sd A. B., and every person claiming through or in trust for him, will at all times hrftr, at the cost of the pson requiring the same, do and execute all such acts and assurances for more effectually assuring the sd prems to the uses afsd (subject, nevertheless, as hrin mentd), as by the sd C. D. his hrs or assns shall be reasonably required.

IN WITNESS, &c.

LVI.

CONVEYANCE *of* LIFE INTEREST *in Real Estate.*

THIS INDRE, made &c., between A. B., of &c., of the one part, and C. D., of &c., of the other part: Whas J. S., late of &c., deceased, by his will dated &c., devised the hdts hrnftr described unto the sd A. B. for his life with remainder over; and whas the said J. S. died on &c. without having revoked or altered his said will, which was on [*date*] duly proved by the exors thrn named: And whas the sd A. B. has agreed to sell to the sd C. D. for the sum of £735 his life estate in the sd hdts; Now THIS INDRE WITNESSETH, that, in conson of £735 on or before the exon hrof paid to the sd A. B. by the sd C. D. (the receipt whof the sd A. B. doth hrby acknge), the sd A. B. doth hrby grant unto the sd C. D., his hrs and assns, ALL THAT piece of land containing 20A. 3R. 16P. or thereabouts, situate at X., in the county of Y., on the east and south of a messe belonging to the sd C. D. and now in his occupon, as the same with the abuttals thrf is delineated in the plan drawn in the margin hrof and thrn cold pink. To HOLD the prems hby assured unto and to the use of the sd C. D., his hrs and assns, during the remainder of the life of the sd A. B. AND THE SD A. B. doth hby covt with the sd C. D., his hrs and assns, that notwithstanding anything by the sd A. B. done, omitted, or knowingly suffered, the sd A. B. has power to grant all the prems to the use of the sd C. D. during the life of the sd A. B. And that the same may be quietly enjoyed accordingly during the life of the sd A. B. free from interruption or incumbs by him. And that the sd A. B. and every pson claiming through or in trust for him will, at all times, at the cost of the sd C. D., his hrs and assns, execute and do all such assces, acts for further assuring the prems, or any part thrf, to the sd C. D., his hrs and assns, during the life of the sd A. B. as by him or them shall be reasonably required.

IN WITNESS, &c.

LVII.

CONVEYANCE *of Land for* BURIAL GROUND *under*
43 *Geo.* 3, *c.* 108.

THIS INDRE, made &c., between [*donor*] of the first part,
[*ordinary*] of the second part, and [*vicar*] of the third part:
Whas the sd [*donor*] is seised in fee of the piece of land
hrnftr described and granted, with the appurts; And whas
the churchyard of the vicarage of X. and diocese of R. is too
small for the burial of the parishioners of the sd vicarage;
And whas the sd piece of land adjoins to the churchyard of
the sd vicarage, and is convenient to be added thereto, and
the sd [*donor*] is desirous and, with the consent and approbation of the sd [*ordinary*], as the ordinary of the sd
vicarage, intends to give and vest in the sd vicar and his
succors the sd piece of land to be applied for the enlarge-
ment of the sd churchyard, and for ever hrftr to be used as
a burial ground for the parishioners of X. afsd, pursuant to
the statute passed in the forty-third year of the reign of his
late Majesty King George the Third, intituled " An Act to
promote the building, repairing, or otherwise providing of
Churches and Chapels, and of Houses for the Residence
of Ministers, and the providing of Churchyards and Glebes:"
Now THIS INDRE WITNETH, that, in conson of the prems, he
the said [*donor*], in pursce of the power given by the sd
statute, and of every other power enabling him in this
behalf, and with the consent and approbation of the sd
[*ordinary*] (testified by his being a party hereto), doth hby
grant to and vest in the sd [*vicar*] and his succors, vicars of
X. afsd, ALL THAT piece of land, part of a close called
the churchyard piece, adjoining the churchyard, of the sd
vicarage of X., and delineated on the map in the margin
hrof, and thrn coloured blue. To HOLD the sd piece of land
unto the sd [*vicar*] and his succors, vicars of X. afsd, for
ever, as and for additional burial ground, and to be added to
the churchyard of the afsd vicarage for ever for the inter-
ment of the inhabitants of the afsd parish of X.: And the

sd [*donor*] doth hby for himself, his hrs, exors, and admors, covt with the sd [*vicar*] and his succors, vicars of X. afsd, that he the sd [*donor*], and every person claiming through or in trust for him, will at all times, at the cost of the pson requiring the same, execute and do such further assces and acts for more satisfactorily conveying the sd piece of land unto and to the use of the sd [*vicar*] and his succors, vicars of X. afsd, for ever, for the ppse afsd, as by him or them shall be lawfully required. IN WITNESS whereof to these presents the sd [*donor*] and [*vicar*] have set their hands and seals, and the sd [*ordinary*] has set his hand and caused his episcopal seal to be affixed, the day and year first above written.

[*In the margin of the deed insert the following*:—Taken and acknowledged by the said [*donor*] at W. in the county of Y. this   day of   , 1880, who desired that the same might be enrolled in the Chancery Division of the High Court of Justice.

Before me E. F., a commissioner to administer oaths in the Supreme Court of Judicature in England.]

LVIII.

SURRENDER *of Copyhold Hereditaments.*

Manor of } BE IT REMEMBERED, that out of court on [*date*], X. } A. B., of &c., a copyhold tenant of this manor, and M. B. his wife came before Y. Z., steward of the sd manor, and in consideration of £700 to the sd A. B. pd by C. D. of &c., on the passing of this surrender (the receipt whof the sd A. B. doth hereby acknowledge), they the sd A. B. and M. B. his wife (the said M. B. joining herein, for the purpose of passing all her right or title to dower, and being first examined by the sd steward, apart from her sd husband, according to the custom of the sd manor) did surrender into the hands of the lord of the sd manor, by the hands and acceptance of the sd steward, by the rod, according to the custom of the sd manor, ALL THAT [*parcels*] (all of which sd hdts and prems are holden of the sd manor of X., and are

situate at W., in the parish of V., in the county of Middlesex)
together with the easements and appurces to the sd hdts
belonging, to the use of the sd C. D., his heirs and assigns
for ever, at the will of the lord, according to the custom of
the sd manor, by and under the suit and services, rents, fines
and heriots therefor due and of right accustomed.

Taken, together with the separate examination
of the sd M. B., the day and year afsd, by me,

Y. Z., Steward.

LIX.

DEED OF COVENANTS *for Title to accompany Surrender of* COPYHOLDS.

THIS INDRE, made, &c., between A. B. of &c., of the one part,
and C. D. of &c., of the other part : Whas the sd A. B. agreed
with the sd C. D. for the sale to him of the hdts hrnftr
described, with their appurts and the inhance thof in posson,
according to the custom of the manor of which the same are
holden free from incumbs, except the rents, fines, heriots,
suits, and services therefor due and of right accustomed, for
the sum of £700 and upon the treaty for the sd sale it was
agreed that the sd A. B. should enter into such covts as are
hrnftr contd ; And whas, in pursce of the sd agreet, the sd
A. B. and M. B. his wife did out of court, immediately before
the exon hrof, surrender into the hands of the lord of the
manor of X. by his steward, and according to the custom of
the sd manor, ALL THAT [*parcels from surrender*], (all which
sd hdts and prems are holden of the manor of X., in the
county of Middlesex, and are situate at W., in the parish of
V., in the sd county), together with the appurs, to the use of
the sd C. D., his hrs and assns, according to the custom of
the sd manor, and by and under the suits and services, rents,
fines and heriots therefor due and of right accustomed : Now
THIS INDRE WITNESSETH, that, in conson of the sd sum of
£700 pd to the sd A. B. by the sd C. D. on the exon of the
sd surrender, he the sd A. B. doth hby for himself, his hrs,
exors, and admors, covt with the sd C. D., his hrs and assns

that, notwithstanding any thing by the sd A. B. done, omitted,
or knowingly suffered, the sd A. B. and M. B. had at the
time of making the sd surrender or one of them' had full
power to surrender the sd hdts to the use of the sd C. D., his
hrs and assns, according to the custom of the sd manor and
free from incumbs, but under and subject to the rents, fines,
heriots, suits, and services therefor due and of right accustomed and that the same prems may henceforth be quietly
enjoyed by the sd C. D. his hrs and assns, free from interruptions and incumbs by the sd A. B. and M. B. or eir of
them or by any person claiming through or in trust for them
or eir of them.   And that the sd A. B. and M. B. and every
such person as afsd will at all times, upon every reasonable
request, by and at the cost of the sd C. D., his hrs or assns,
do and execute such acts and assces for more perfectly surrendering and assuring the sd hdts to the use afsd, as by him
or them shall be reasonably required.

IN WITNESS, &c.

LX.

DEED OF ENFRANCHISEMENT *of Copyholds with Grant
of* RIGHTS *of* COMMON.

THIS INDRE, made, &c., between A. B., of &c., lord of the
manor of X., of the one part, and C. D., of &c., a copyhold
tenant of the sd manor, of the other part : Whas the sd A. B.
is seised of the sd manor of X., for an estate of inhance in fee
simple in posson free from incumbs ; And whas the sd C. D.
is seised to him and his hrs, according to the custom of the
sd manor, of the hdts hrnftr described, being part of the copyhold hdts of the sd manor ; And whas the sd C. D. has agreed
with the sd A. B. for the enfranchisement of the sd hdts for
the sum of £   : NOW THIS INDRE WITNESSETH, that, in
conson of £   to the sd A. B. pd by the sd C. D. on the
excon hof (the rect whof the sd A. B. doth hby acknge), the
sd A. B. doth hby grant unto the sd C. D. and his hrs ALL
[*parcels*], together with [*general words, and estate clause,
p.* 298, *supra*], To hold the sd hdts unto the sd C. D. and his

hrs, to the use of the sd C. D., his hrs and assns, freed, enfranchised, and discharged from all and all manner of customary and other rents, fines, heriots, fealty, suit of court, forfeitures, duties, services or customs whatsoever, which according to the custom of the sd manor of X. the sd hdts hrnbfre grantd are or have been subject or liable to or charged with, or which would but for these presents be paayble or to be done and performed in respect of the same hdts or any of them, or any part thof: [AND THIS INDRE ALSO WITNESSETH,[1] that for the consons afsd, and in order to preserve to the sd C. D., his hrs and assns, all such rights of common in, upon, and over the waste lands of the sd manor of X. as he the sd C. D., or any of his predecessors in title, have at any time hrtfre used or enjoyed as belonging or appurtenant to the hdts and prems hrnbfre described, notwithstanding the en-franchisement of the same respve prems, he the sd A. B. doth hby grant unto the sd C. D., his hrs and assns, all such commonage and right of common of what nature or kind soever, in, upon, or over all or any of the wastes, commons, and commonable lands of or belonging to the sd manor of X. as he the sd C. D. immediately before the excon of these presents or as any of his predecessors in title at any time hrnbfre held, possessed, or enjoyed in respect of and as appur-tenant or belonging to the sd hdts and prems hby granted, and the freehold and inhance of all such commonable rights as afsd, in as large, ample, and beneficial a manner to all intents and purposes as he the sd C. D., or any of his sd predecessors, have hrtfre used and exercised all or any of the sd rights or privileges, or as he or his customary hrs could or might have used and exercised the same if these presents had not been executed.] [*Add covenants by the lord of the manor for title as in a conveyance of freeholds.*]

IN WITNESS, &c.[2]

---

[1] If there are no common rights in the manor, or if it is not intended to reserve common rights to the copyholder after the enfranchisement, the grant of common rights will of course be omitted.

[2] A covenant on the part of the lord of the manor for production of title-deeds should be added or taken by a separate document.

Y

LXI.

SURRENDER *of Copyholds to the* TRUSTEES *of a Settlement.*

Manor of X. ⎱ BE IT REMEMBERED, that out of court on the [*date*] A. B., of &c., a cyhold tenant of this manor came before T. W., steward of the sd manor, and in pursce of a covt contd in a certain indre, dated &c., made between &c. (being a settlement executed in conplon of the marre of the sd A. B. with the sd C. B.), did surrender into the hands of the lord of the sd manor by the hands and acceptance of the sd steward by the rod, according to the custom of the sd manor, all [*parcels*] (which sd hdts are holden of the manor of X. in the county of Y.), togr with the easements and appurts to the sd hdts belonging or appurtenant, to the use of the sd E. F. and G. H., their hrs and asns, at the will of the lord, according to the custom of the sd manor, by and under the suit and services, rents, fines and heriots therefor due and of right accustomed [upon the trusts and subject to the provisions contained in and declared by the sd indre of the [*date*].] [1]

LXII.

CONVEYANCE *of* FREEHOLDS *and Covenant to surrender* COPYHOLDS.

THIS INDRE, made &c., between A. B., of &c., of the one part, and C. D., of &c., of the other part: WITNESSETH, that, in conson of the sum of £800, paid by the sd C. D. to the sd A. B. on the exon hrof (the rect whof he doth ackdge) the sd A. B. doth hby grant unto the sd C. D. and his hrs, all &c. [*parcels of freehold land*] together with all appurts to the sd hdts in fact, or by reputation, belonging. To hold the same unto and to the use of the sd C. D., his hrs and

---

[1] If the steward does not object to the words within brackets, they had better be inserted; but some stewards will not allow a reference to any trusts to appear on the court rolls.

assus: AND THIS INDRE ALSO WITNESSETH, that, in consideration of the sum of £50 pd by the sd C. D. to the sd
A. B. on the execution hrof (the rect whof he doth ackndge)
the sd A. B. doth hby for himself, his hrs, exors, and admors,
covt with the sd C. D. and his hrs, that he, the sd A. B.
will forthwith surrender into the hands of the lord of the
manor of O. in the county of Y. all, &c., [*parcels of copyhold
land*] [to which hdts the sd A. B. was on the [*date*] admitted
tenant in fee simple in possession] to the use of the sd C. D.,
his hrs and assns, at the will of the lord according to the
custom of the sd manor, subject to the rents, suits, and services therefor due and of right accustomed: And the sd
A. B. doth hby for himself, his hrs, exors, and admors,
covenant with the sd C. D., his hrs and assns, that he, the
sd A. B., now has power to convey and surrender the sd freehold and copyhold hdts resply, in the manner and to the
uses afsd, And that the same resply shall henceforth be
quietly enjoyed by the sd C. D., his hrs and assns, free from
incumbrances and interruptions by the sd A. B., his hrs or
assns, and also that the sd A. B., and all persons claiming
through or in trust for him, will at all times, at the request
and cost of the sd C. D., his hrs or assns, execute and do all
such deeds and things for more effectually assuring the sd
hdts and every part thereof to the uses aforesaid, as he or
they shall reasonably require.

IN WITNESS, &c.[1]

[1] The better course is to surrender the copyholds before the deed is
executed, and if this be done the deed should be thus varied. Recite the
contract for sale and the apportionment of the purchase-money, viz., £800
for the freeholds and £50 for the copyholds, and then proceed thus :—"And
whas the sd A. B. has this day surrendered into the hands of the lord of
the manor of O. in the county of Y., all [*give a short description of the
copyholds*] to the use of the sd C. D., his hrs and assns." Then resume
with " Now THIS INDRE WITNESSETH," and continue to the end of the
habendum of the freeholds : omit the covenant to surrender the copyholds ;
proceed with the covenants for title, making the vendor covenant that he
" has power to convey the sd freehold hdts, and at the time of surrendering the sd copyhold hdts had power to surrender the same to the uses afsd,
according to the intent hereof and of the sd surrender resply, free from all

LXIII.

ASSIGNMENT *of* LEASEHOLDS *by Independent Deed.*

THIS INDRE, made &c., between A. B. of &c., of the one part, and C. D. of &c., of the other part: WHAS by an indre dated &c., and made between X. Y. of the one part, and T. W. of the other part, ALL [*here copy the parcels from the lease verbatim*], with their appurts, were demised to the sd A. B., his exors, admors, and assigns, from [Michaelmas-day then last] for the term of [ninety-nine] years, at a yearly rent of £[150] and subject to the lessee's covenants thrin contd : AND WHAS by virtue of divers mesne assmts and acts in the law, and ultimately by an indre dated &c., and made between S. Z. of the one part, and the sd A. B. of the other part, the prems comprised in and demised by the sd indre of lease are now vested in the sd A. B. for the residue of the said term : AND WHAS the sd A. B. has agreed with the sd C. D. for the sale to him of the sd prems for the residue of the sd term at the price of £   : NOW THIS INDRE WITNTH, that in conson of £   now pd to the sd A. B. by the sd C. D. (the recpt whrof the sd A. B. doth hby ackdge) the sd A. B. doth hby assign unto the sd C. D., his exors, admors, and assns, all the prems comprised in and demised by the hrinbfre-recited lease, TO HOLD the sd prems unto the sd C. D., his exors, admors, and assns, for the residue of the sd term, subject to the payment of the rent and the performance of the lessee's covts therein reserved and contd resply : And the sd A. B. for himself, his hrs, exors, and admors, covts with the sd C. D., his exors, admors, and assns, that (notwithstanding anything by him done, omitted, or knowingly suffered) the rent reserved by and the lessee's covts contained in the sd indre have been

---

incumbrances," and then resume with the covenant for quiet enjoyment and go to the end as before.

The deed conveying the freeholds will only require an *ad valorem* stamp on the apportioned amount of purchase-money, and the surrender will require an *ad valorem* stamp on the residue of the purchase-money.

paid, observed, and performed up to the date hrof, and that, notwithstanding any such thing as afsd, the sd A. B. now has power to assign the prems for the term and in manner afsd ; and also that the same may be quietly enjoyed by the sd C. D., his exors, admors, and assns, for the residue of the sd term free from incumbrances and interruptions by the sd A. B., or any pson claiming through or in trust for him. And that the sd A. B., and any such person as afsd, will at all times during the sd term, at the request and cost of the pson requiring the same, execute and do all such acts and asces for further assuring the prems unto the sd C. D., his exors, adms, and assns, for the term afsd, as he or they shall reasonably require : AND THE sd C. D. doth hby for himself, his hrs, exors, or assns, covt with the sd A. B., his exors, and admors, that the said C. D., his exors, admors, or assns, will henceforth pay and perform the rent reserved by and lessee's covnts contained in the sd indre of lease ; and indemnify the sd A. B., his hrs, exors, and admors, against all consequences of the non-payment and non-performance thof resply.

IN WITNESS, &c.

LXIV.

ASSIGNMENT *of Leaseholds by* INDORSEMENT.

THIS INDRE made, &c., between the within-named A. B., of the one part, and C. D., of &c., of the other part, witnesseth, that, in conson of £   now paid by the sd C. D. to the sd A. B. (the receipt whof the sd A. B. doth hby acknge), the sd A. B. hby assigns unto the sd C. D., his exors, admors, and assns, all the premises comprised in and demised by the within-written indre, To HOLD the same unto the said C. D., his exors, admors, and assns, henceforth for the residue of the term of [ninety-nine] years by the within-written indre demised, subject to the rent and lessee's covts and condons thn conted : And the sd A. B. for himself, his hrs, exors, and admors, hby covts with the sd C. D., his exors, admors, and assns, that, notwithstanding anything by him done or knowingly suffered, the rent reserved by and the lessee's covts and condons in and by the within-written indre resply reserved and contd have been paid, observed, and performed up to the date hrof, and that, notwithstanding any such thing as afsd, the sd A. B. now has power to assign the prems unto the sd C. D., his exors, admors, and assns in manner afsd, and that the prems may be quietly enjoyed by the sd C. D. during the sd term free from incumbs and interruptions by the sd C. D., or any pson claiming through or in trust for him. And that the sd A. B., and all such persons as last afsd, will, at all times during the sd term, execute and do all such further assurances and things for more perfectly assigning the prems unto the sd C. D., his exors, admors, and assns, for the residue of the sd term, as by him or them shall be reasonably required: AND THE sd C. D. doth hby for himself, his hrs, exors, and admors, covt with the sd A. B. his exors and admors, that the sd C. D., his exors, admors, or assns, will henceforth pay the rent reserved by and perform the lessee's covts contained in the within-written indenture, and indemnify the sd A. B., his hrs, exors, and admors, against all consequences of the non-payment and non-performance of the same resply.

IN WITNESS, &c.

LXV.

ASSIGNMENT *of* LEASEHOLDS *by* MORTGAGOR *and* MORTGAGEE.

THIS INDRE, made &c., between A. B., of &c., of the first part, C. D. of &c., of the second part, and E. F., of &c., of the third part: WHAS by an indre, dated, &c. [*recite lease for ninety-nine years to A. B. as in Form LXIII. p. 324, supra, setting out parcels verbatim*]: AND WHAS by an indre dated, &c., and made between the sd A. B. of the one part, and the sd C. D. of the other part, in conson of £   paid by the sd C. D. to the sd A. B., the sd A. B. assigned the prems demised

by the sd indre of lease, together with the two several messes
then built thereon, and which are now known as Nos. 2 and 4,
X. Street afsd, to the sd C. D., his exors, admors, and assns,
for the then residue of the sd term of ninety-nine years,
subject to a proviso for re-assignment thof on payment by
the sd A. B., his exors, admors, or assns, to the sd C. D., his
exors, admors, or assns, of £   with interest as thrn
mentd.   AND WHAS the said A. B. has agreed with the sd
[*purchaser*] E. F. for the sale to him of the prems hrnble
described for the residue of the sd term for the sum of
£   : AND WHAS [*recite amount due to mtgee and his
agreement to concur, as in Form LI., p. 306, supra*]: Now
THIS INDRE WITNESSETH, that in consideration of £   to
the sd A. B., and of £   to the sd C. D. now pd by the
sd E. F. (the receipt of which several sums of £
and £   , making together £   , the sd A. B. and
C. D. hby resply acknge), the sd C. D. at the request of
the sd A. B. doth hby assign, and the sd A. B. doth hby
assign and confirm unto the said E. F., his exors, admors, and
assns, all and singular the prems comprised in and demised
by the sd indre of lease, TOGETHER WITH the sd two messes
now built thereon, and all rights, easements, and appurts
thereto in fact or by reputation belonging, And all the
estate and interest of the sd A. B. and C. D. thrn, To
hold the prems unto the sd E. F., his exors, admors, and
assns, for the residue of the sd term, subject to the rent
reserved by, and the lessee's covenants and condons contd
in the sd indre of lease: And the sd A. B. doth hby for
himself, his hrs, exors, and admors, covt with the sd E. F.,
his exors, admors, and assns, that (notwithstanding anything by the sd A. B. and the sd C. D., or either of them
done or knowingly omitted), the rent reserved by and the
lessee's covenants contained in the sd indre of lease have
been paid and performed up to the date hrof; and that
notwithstanding any such thing as afsd the sd A. B. and C. D.,
or one of them, now has power to assure the prems for the
term and in manner afsd; and that the same may henceforth during the sd term be quietly enjoyed by the sd E. F.,

his exors, admors, and assns, free from interruption and incumbs by the sd A. B. and C. D. or eir of them, or any person claiming through or in trust for them or eir of them, and that the said A. B. and C. D. and every such person as last afsd, will at all times during the said term, at the request and cost of the person requiring the same, execute and do all such assces and things for better assuring the premises unto the sd E. F., his exors, admors, and assns, for the term and in manner afsd, as he or they shall reasonably require: And the said C. D. [*covenant against incumbrances, see p. 308, supra*] doth hby for himself, his hrs, exors, admors, and assns, covt with the sd A. B., his exors, and admors, that he [*covenant to pay rent and perform covts, as in Form LXIII.*]

IN WITNESS, &c.

———

LXVI.

ASSIGNMENT *of Leaseholds by a* MORTGAGEE *under his* POWER OF SALE.

THIS INDRE, made &c., between A. B., of &c., of the one part, and C. D., of &c., of the other part: Whas by an indre dated the &c. [*recite lease, as in Form LXIII., p.* 324.]

AND WHAS by an indre dated [*recite mortgage by assignment to A. B. as in Form* LXV. *p.* 327, *and continue as follows:*—]

And by the same indre it was provided that if default should be made in the payment of the sd sum of £   on the sd [*date*], it should be lawful for the said A. B., his exors, admors, or assns, at any time thftr, without any further consent on the part of the sd [*mortgagor*], his exors, admors, and assns, to sell the prems thby assigned, or any part thof. eir togr or in parcels, and eir by public auction or private contract, and subject to such condons of sale, and generally in every respect as the said A. B., his exors, admors, or assns, should deem fit, and upon such sale to assign the prems sold to the purchaser or purchasers, or as

he or they might require : And by the sd indre it was also
declared that every receipt which should be given by the sd
A. B., his exors, admors, or assns, for any moneys to be
derived from any such sale or sales or owise under the same
indre, should be an effectual discharge to the person or
persons to whom the same should be given : And whas, by a
memorandum dated &c., and indorsed on the last-recited
indre, the sd [*mortgagor*] acknged to have received from the
sd A. B., on the secty created by the sd indre, the further
sum of £   , together with an arrear of interest thrn : And
whas the sd A. B. agreed with the sd C. D. for the sale to
him of the prems comprised in the sd indre of lease, for the
residue of the sd term for £   : Now this Indre witnesseth, that in consideration of £   sterling pd by the
sd C. D. to the sd A. B. (the rect whof is hrby acknged), he
the sd A. B. doth hby assign unto the sd C. D., his exors,
admors, and assns, all that parcel of land and all other the
prems comprised in and demised by the hrnbfre-recited
indre of lease, togr with [*general words and " all the estate "
clause as in Form XLVI., p.* 298]. To hold the prems unto
the sd C. D., his exors, admors, and assns, for the residue of
the sd term of   years granted by the hrnbfre-recited
indre of lease, freed from all claims and demands in respect
of the moneys secured by and from all right or equity of
redon under the hrnbfre-recited indre of the [*date*], but
subject to the rent reserved by the lessee's covenants and
condons contained in the hrnbfre-recited lease : And the sd
A. B. doth hby for himself, his hrs, exors, and admors,
covt with the sd C. D., his exors, admors, and assns, that he
the sd A. B. has not done, omitted, or knowingly suffered,
or been party or privy to anything whereby or by reason or
means whrof the prems hby assigned, or any of them, or any
part thof, are, is, or may be in anywise charged, affected, or
incumbered in title, estate, or owise howsoever, or whereby
or by reason or means whof he is in anywise hindered from
assigning the same in manner afsd.

In Witness, &c.

LXVII.

ASSIGNMENT *of* LEASEHOLDS *to be indorsed on a* MORTGAGE *pursuant to Covenant for* FURTHER ASSURANCE.[1]

THIS INDRE, made &c., between A. B. of &c., of the first part, and C. D. of &c., of the second part.

Whas the within recited indre of assmt to the mtgor (the date of which is omitted, but which is in fact dated the 6th day of March, 1875) of the hdts and prems comprised in the within recited indre of lease, dated [*date*] (and thby demised to the within named X. Y.) had not been executed at the date of the exon of the within written indre, and therefore it is considered that no legal estate in the hdts and prems demised by the sd indre of lease passed to the mtgee by virtue of the within written indre.

And whas the sd indre of assmt as within recited has been duly executed since the exon of the within written indre, namely, on the 6th day of March, 1875, and the hdts and pres comprised in the sd indre are now vested in the mtgor for the residue now unexpired of the within mentioned term of ninety-nine years subject as in the within written indre is mentd.

And whas the mtgor at the request of the mtgee and in pursce of the covt for furr assee in the within written indre contd has agreed to execute such assee to him of the sd hdts and prems comprised in the sd indre of lease as is hrnftr contd.

NOW THIS INDRE WITNESSETH that in pursce of the sd agreet, and for the consons in the within written indre mentd

He, the sd A. B., doth hby demise unto the sd C. D., his exors, admors, and assns,

---

[1] A. B. mortgaged leaseholds in Surrey to C. D. by indre dated 11th September, 1874, to secure £8000 and further advances. A. B. had purchased these leaseholds from X., and they had all been assigned to him before the 11th of September, 1874, except the portion comprised in this demise, about the title of which there had been some difficulty, and the assignment by X. to A. B. of this portion was not executed till 1875, though the assignment had been recited in the mortgage without a date.

ALL THAT piece of land with the messuages, cottages, and outbuildings, hdts, rights and easements, appurts, and prems comprised in and demised by the sd indre of lease of the [*date*],

To HAVE AND TO HOLD all and singular the sd hdts and prems hby demised unto the said C. D., his exors, admors, and assns, for the residue now to come of the sd term of ninety-nine years granted by the sd indre of lease of the [*date*], except the last two days thof, subject to the provo for redon thof in the within written indre contd.

To the intent that the hdts and prems hby demised may form part of the security for the within mentd sum of £   , and further advances in the same manner as if the sd indre of assmt of the 6th day of March, 1875, had been duly executed before the exon of the within written indre.

AND THE SD A. B. doth hby for himself, his hrs, exors, and ads, covenant with the mtgee [*that lease is valid, &c., and for right to demise.*]

And also that all the covts for title and for payment of rent and observance of lessees' covts, and all other the covts, and all the powers (including the power of sale and powers ancillary thto), provos, trusts, declons, agrects, and stipulons, in the within written indre contd with regard to the hdts and prems thby assured shall extend and be applicable to the hdts and prems hby demised in as full a manner in all respects as if the sd indre of assmt of the 6th day of March, 1875, had been duly executed before the 11th day of September, 1874, and the hdts and prems hby demised had been actually comprised in and demised by the within written indre as such security as afsd.

IN WITNESS, &c.

LXVIII.

ASSIGNMENT *of* DEBTS.

THIS INDRE, made &c., between A. B., of &c., of the one part, and C. D., of &c., of the other part: Whas the sd A. B. has for some time carried on the business of [*specify it*] at X.

afsd, and in the course of such business the several psons whose names are mentd in the Schedule hereto have become and are now indebted to him in the several sums of money set opposite to their respive names in such schedule, and he has agreed with the sd C. D. for the absolute sale of the same debts for the sum of £ : Now this Indre witnesseth, that, in conson of £ to the sd A. B. now paid by the sd C. D. (the receipt whof is hby acknged), he the sd A. B. doth hby assn unto the sd C. D., his exors, admors, and assns, all and singular the debts and sums of moy specified in the Schedule hereto, To have, receive and take the sd debts and prems hby assigned unto and by the sd C. D., his exors, admors, and assns, for his and their own absolute use and benefit; And the sd A. B. doth hby for himself, his hrs, exors, and admors, covt with the sd C. D., his exors, admors, and assns, that the sd several debts hby assigned are now due and owing to him, and that he, his exors or admors, will at all times, on the request and at the cost of the sd C. D., his exors, admors or assns, do and execute all such further acts and assurances for more effectually assuring unto the sd C. D., his exors, admors and assns, the sd several debts and prems, and enabling him or them to recover and rece the same resply as by him or them shall be reasonably required.[1]

In witness, &c.

The Schedule above referred to.

Name of Debtor.	Amount of Debt.	Name of Debtor.	Amount of Debt.

[1] Before the Judicature Act, 1873, came into operation it would have been necessary for A. B. to give C. D. a power of attorney to sue in his name, and for C. D. to covenant to indemnify A. B. from costs, &c., in respect of any action brought in his name. But now, a simple notice to each of the scheduled debtors renders these clauses unnecessary, and they are therefore omitted.

LXIX.

ASSIGNMENT *of* REVERSIONARY INTEREST *in a Sum of Stock.*

THIS INDRE, made &c., between A. B. of &c., widow, of the one part, and C. D. of &c., of the other part: Whas E. F., late of &c., deceased, made his will dated &c., and thereby bequeathed unto G. H. and K. L. (whom he appointed exors thof), their exors, admors and assns, his personal estate upon certain trusts, being in effect trusts for payment of debts and funeral exps, and subject thereto for the benefit of his wife M. F. during widowhood, and after the decease or second marre of his sd wife he directed his trees to sell such part of his residy psnal este as should not have been previously sold, and he declared that his trees should stand possessed of the moneys to be produced from such sales, and also the stocks or funds in which any part of his residy psnl este, if sold during the widowhood of his sd wife, should be invested, and all other his trust moys, upon trust to pay, assn, and transfer the same unto the three children of his sd wife by her former husband in the proportions following (viz.), three equal seventh parts thof to Y. Z., his exors or admors, three other equal seventh parts thof to W. X. for her separate use, and the remaining one equal seventh part thof to the sd A. B. for her separate use; or in case of her death during the widowhood of his sd wife, to such pson or psons, and in such shares and proportions as the sd A. B. should, notwithstanding coverture, by deed or will appoint: And whas the sd E. F. died on the [*date*] without having altered or revoked his sd will, which was duly proved by the sd exors in the Probate Division of the High Court of Justice: And whas the testator's residy psnal este has been sold and called in by the sd G. H. and K. L, and the proceeds thof, after payment of his debts, funeral and testy exps, have been invested, and the same now consist of the sum of £1768 New £3 per Cent. Annies, standing in the names of sd G. H. and K. L. in the books of the Governor and Company of the Bank of England: And whas the sd M. F. (the widow of the testator) is still living, and is of the age of seventy years or thereabouts; And whas the sd A. B. caused the one seventh part or share to which she is entitled in reversion expectant on the death of the sd M. F., in the sd sum of £1768 New £3 per Cent. Annies, to be offered for sale by public auction at the Auction Mart in the city of London, on the [*date*]; and at the sd sale the sd C. D. was the highest bidder for, and declared to be the purchaser of, the same for the sum of £ :[1] Now THIS INDRE WITNESSETH, that in order to effectuate the sd sale, and in conson of £ sterling to the sd A. B. pd by the sd C. D. on the exon of these presents (the receipt of wch the sd A. B. doth hby acknowledge), she the sd A. B. doth hby assn, appoint and confirm unto the sd C. D., his exors, admors, and assns, all that the one seventh part or share, and other the part, share, and interest to wch she is entitled in reversion, expectant upon the decease of the sd M. F., of and in the sd sum of £1768 New £3 per Cent. Annies, and of and in all and singular the stocks, funds or securities in or upon wch the same or any part thof may from time to time be invested, and all the divds, interest, and income thof from and after the decease of the sd M. F., To have, receive, and take the sd part or share hby assured of and in the sd sum of £1768, New £3 per Cent. Annies, and other the moy and prems hrnbfre mentd, unto and by the sd C. D., his exors, admors and assns: And the sd A. B. doth hby for herself, her hrs, exors, and admors, covt with the sd C. D. his exors, admors, and assns, that notwithstanding any act, deed, or thing whatsoever by her or any pson through whom she claims orwise than as a pcher for valuable conson done, permitted, or knowingly suffered, she now has power to assure the sd part or share and prems hby assured, in manner afsd free from incumbs; and also that she the sd A. B., and every other pson

---

[1] Unless there is some special reason for it, a sale by auction is seldom recited in this form: it is usually sufficient to recite it as an ordinary contract for sale; but in the case of a reversion the fact that it was purchased at a sale by public auction may properly appear in the assignment in order to prevent any future question whether the sale was at an undervalue.

claiming through or in trust for her, or through or in trust for any such pson as afsd, will at all times upon the request, and at the expense of the sd C. D., his exors, admors, or assns, do and execute such acts and assces as may be necessary for more effectually assuring the prems unto the sd C. D., his exors, admors, or assns, or for enabling him or them to recover and receive the same.

IN WITNESS, &c.[1]

LXX.

ASSIGNMENT *of a* REVERSIONARY INTEREST *in Residuary Estate and a* POLICY OF ASSURANCE *by* MORTGAGEE *under* POWER *of Sale.*

THIS INDRE made &c., between A. B. of &c., of the one part, and C. D. of &c., of the other part.

Whas [*recital of will of Z. giving one-fifth of residy este to each of sons subject to life estate of Y.*]

And whas [*recite death and probate*].

And whas the testator had five children who survived him or died in his lifetime leaving issue, and X. hrinafr mentioned is one of such children, And whas the sd Y. is still living.

And whas by a policy of assce under the hands of three of the dircctors of the Royal Assce Corporation, dated &c., and numbd &c., the sum of £   is assured to be pd to the exors,

---

[1] In the above instance the assignor was a widow. If her husband had been living, he would not have been a necessary party to the deed, as the share was bequeathed to the assignor for her separate use. If, however, in such a case the husband be living and is willing to concur in the deed, it is as well to procure his concurrence, in order that he may enter into the usual covenants, a married woman not being able to bind herself by a covenant except in equity, and then only so far as concerns her separate estate.

Notice of the deed should be given to the trustees immediately after its execution. Such notice will complete the transfer of the legal estate to the purchaser so as to render a power of attorney unnecessary. A Notice in lieu of *distringas* should also be placed on the stock. See form of Affidavit, p. 95, *supra*, and of Notice to the Bank, p. 404, *infra*.

ads, or assns of the sd X., within three calendar months after proof of his death, subject to the annual premium of £ .

And whas by an indre of mtge dated &c., and made between the sd X. of the one part, and the sd A. B. of the other part, in conson of the sum of £ pd by the sd A. B. to the sd X., he the sd X. assigned to the sd A. B., his exs, ads, and assns, *First*, All that one equal eighth part or share or other the part and share, and all other the estate and interest of the sd X. under or by virtue of the will of the sd Z. decd (expectant on the decease of the sd Y.) of and in all and singular the residuary psonal estate and effects of the sd Z., deceased, and the proceeds thof, and of and in the stocks, funds, and securities by which the same or any part thereof might be represented, howsoever the same resply might be invested or circum- stanced, and the income and acculons throf resply: And secondly, all the hrinbefre recited policy of assce and the sd sum of £ thereby assured, and all other moneys to become payable thrunder by way of bonus or othwise, sub- ject to a provo in the indre now in recital contd for the redon and reassignment of the said pres thrby assigned on pay- ment on the [*date*], by the sd X., his hrs, exs, ads, or assns to the sd A. B., his exs, ads, or assns, of the sd sum of £ , with int thron at the rate of £5 per cent. per annum, computed from the date of the indre now in recital. And it was by the indre now in recital provided and agreed that in case [*power of sale verbatim, including power to assure to pcher*]. And it was by the same indre agreed, and the said X. did for himself, his exs and ads, direct that [*pcher not to be liable to see to application of pche-money, and that receipts of A. B. should be good discharge*].

And whas default was made in the payment of the sd sum of £ and int, on the [*date*], &c., there is now due and owing to the sd A. B. on the secy of the hrinbefre recited indre of mtge for pcl, int, and costs the sum of £ .

And whas the sd A. B. in exercise of the power in the said indre of mtge contd, and of all other powers in anywise enabling him has agreed with the sd C. D., for the sale to him of the sd pres comprised in the sd indre of mtge for the sd sum of £   .

Now this Indre witnesseth that in pursuance of the sd agreement, and in conson of the sum of £   upon the exon of these presents pd by the sd C. D. to the sd A. B. (the receipt [&c.]): He the sd A. B. doth hereby assign unto the sd C. D., his exs, ads, and assns,

All those pres comprised in and described by the hrinbefre recited indre of mtge, and the full benefit throf. And all the right, title, interest, claim, and demand of the sd A. B. in to and upon the same,

To have and to hold all the sd pres hrinbefre described and intended to be hrby assured unto the sd C. D. his exs, ads, and assns,

Freed and discharged from all right and eqy of redon, and from the sd mortgage debt of £   , and int, secured by and from all claims and demands under the hrinbefre recited indre of mtge, but subject as to the sd residuary estate to the life interest of the sd Y. therein.

And the sd A. B. doth [*covt against incumbs, see p.* 329.]

In witness, &c.

LXXI.

Assignment *of the* Goodwill *of the* Business *of a Clock and* Watch Maker, *and the Clock Winding connected therewith.*

This Indre, made the &c., between A. B., of &c., watch maker, of the one part, and C. D., of &c., watch maker, of the other part: Whas the sd A. B. has for some time past carried on the trade or business of a clock and watch maker, at X. Street aforesaid, and is now employed in winding the clocks of the several persons whose names appear in the Schedule hereto for the yearly remunerations set opposite to their respective names in the same Schedule: and whas

z

the sd A. B. has agreed with the sd C. D. for the sale to him of the goodwill of the sd business of a clock and watch maker, and the clock winding connected therewith, for the sum of £ : Now THIS INDRE WITNESSETH, that in conson of £ now paid by the sd C. D. to the sd A. B. (the receipt whof the sd A. B. doth hby acknge), he the sd A. B. doth hby assign unto the sd C. D., his exors, admors, and assns, the goodwill of the sd business of a clock and watch maker, as carried on by the sd A. B. at X. Street aforesaid, together with the clock winding connected therewith, expressly including the winding of the clocks of the several persons whose names appear in the schedule hereto, and all the interest of the sd A. B. therein, To have hold and enjoy the sd goodwill, custom and prems hby assigned unto the sd C. D., his exors, admors, and assns absolutely: And the sd A. B. doth hby for himself, his hrs, exors, and admors, covt with the sd C. D., his exors, admors, and assns, that, he the sd A. B. has good right to assign the sd goodwill and prems in manner afsd, and that the same shall be enjoyed by the sd C. D., his exors, admors, and assns, free from any interruption or incumbrance by the sd A. B. or any pson claiming through or in trust for him, and that the sd A. B. his exors and admors, and every such pson as afsd, will at all times at the cost of the pson requiring the same, do and execute such deeds and things for further assuring the prems to the sd C. D., his exors, admors, and assns, as by him or them shall be reasonably required; and also that he the sd A. B. will not within a period of seven years from the date hereof, either alone, or jointly with or as agent, journeyman or assistant for any pson or company, either directly or indirectly, or upon any account or pretence set up, exercise or carry on, or be employed in carrying on, the business of a clock or watch maker or clock winder, within ten miles as the crow flies from No. , X. Street afsd, and will not, either alone or by or with any pson or company, do or cause to be done any wilful act or thing to the prejudice of the sd business and prms hby assigned, but, on the contrary, will to the utmost of his power endeavour to promote the interest of the sd C. D. amongst the customers of the sd A. B. and owise.

IN WITNESS, &c.

The SCHEDULE above referred to.

(b) RECITALS IN CONVEYANCES.

1. RECITAL *of* SEISIN *in fee.*

WHAS the sd A. B. is seised in fee of the hdts hrnftr described and hrby granted.

----

2. RECITAL *of* SEISIN *in fee.*

WHAS the sd A. B. is seised of the fee simple and inhance in posson, free from incumbs, of and in the hdts hrnftr described and hby granted.

----

3. RECITAL *of* CONVEYANCE *to Uses to bar* DOWER.

WHAS by an indre dated &c., and made between A. B. of the first part, C. D. of the second part, and E. F. of the third part, the hdts hnftr described and hereby granted were assured to such uses, upon such trusts and in such manner generally as the sd C. D. should by any deed or deeds appt; and in default of and subject to any such apptt, to the use of the sd C. D. and his assns for life, with remr to the use of the sd E. F., his exors and admors, during the life of the sd C. D., in trust for him and his assns, with remr to the use of the sd C. D., his hrs and assns.

----

4. GENERAL RECITAL *of* CONVEYANCE *in fee.*

WHAS by an indre dated &c., and made between A. B. of the one part, and C. D. of the other part, the hdts hrnftr described and hby assured, were assured unto and to the use of the sd C. D., his hrs and assns.

----

5. Particular Recital *of* Conveyance *in fee*.

And whas by an indre dated &c., and made between the sd
A. B. of the one part, and C. D. of the other part, the sd
A. B. granted the hdts hrnftr described, and hby assured,
unto and to the use of the sd C. D., his hrs and assns.

---

6. Recital *of* Lease.

Whas by an indre dated &c., and made between A. B. of
the one part, and C. D. of the other part: the sd A. B.
demised unto the sd C. D. all [*copy the parcels verbatim
from the lease*], with their rights, easemts, and appurts, to
hold the same unto the sd C. D., his exors, admors, and
as-ns, from the [*date*] for   years, subject to the payment of the yearly rent of £   , and to the performance
of the lessee's covts and condons thrn contd.

---

7. Recital *of* Assignment *of Lease*.

And whas by an indre dated &c., and made between A. B.
of the one part and C. D. of the other part, the prems comprised in and demised by the hrnbfre-recited indre of lease,
were assigned [by the sd A. B.] to the sd C. D., for all the
residue of the sd term of   years created by the sd
indre of lease, subject to the pmnt of the rent reserved by
and to the performance of the lessee's covts and condons
contained in the same indre.

---

8. Recital *of* Mesne Assignments *of Lease*.

And whas by divers mesne assignments [and acts in the
law], and ultimately by an indre dated &c., and made
between A. B. of the one part and C. D. of the other part,
the prems comprised in and demised by the sd indre of
lease became vested in the sd C. D. for all the residue of
the term thby granted, subject to the pmnt of the rent

thby reserved, and to the performance and observance of the lessee's covts and condons therein contained.

---

9. RECITAL *of* MORTGAGE *of* LEASEHOLDS *by demise*.

AND WHAS by an indre dated &c., and made between the sd A. B. of the one part, and C. D. of the other part, in conson of £   pd by the sd C. D. to the sd A. B., the sd A. B. demised the prems comprised in the sd indre of lease to the sd C. D., his exors, admors, and assns, for the residue of the term granted by the sd indre of lease (except the last ten days throf), by way of mtge to secure the repmt of the sd sum of £   .

---

10. RECITAL *of* POLICY OF ASSURANCE *for Life*.

AND WHAS by a policy of assurance under the hands of the directors of the P. Assurance Society, dated &c., and numbered &c., the sum of [£500] is assured to be pd to the exors, admors, or assns of the sd A. B. within [3] calr months after proof of his death, subject to the annual premium of [£9].

---

11. RECITAL *of* MORTGAGE *in fee*.

AND WHAS by an indre dated &c., and made between A. B. of the one part, and C. D. of the other part, in conson of £   pd by the sd C. D. to the sd A. B., the sd A. B. granted the hdts hrnftr described and hby assured unto and to the use of the sd C. D., his hrs and assns, subject to a provo for redon of the same prems by the sd A. B., his hrs, exors, admors, or assns, on pmnt by him or them to the sd C. D., his exors, admors, or assns, of £   with int for the same at the rate, on the day, and in the manner thin mentd.

---

12. RECITAL *of* FURTHER CHARGE.

AND WHAS by an indre dated &c., and made between the sd A. B. of the one part, and the sd C. D. of the other part, in conson of the sd sum of £   then due to the sd C. D., by virtue of the last-recited indre, and of the further sum of £   then lent by the sd C. D. to the sd A. B., the hdts comprised in the sd last recited indre were charged as well with the pmnt of the sd sum of £   as of the sd sum of £   with int for the same sums respy to the sd C. D., his exors, admors or assns.

------

13. RECITAL *of* FURTHER CHARGE *by Indorsement.*

AND WHAS by a deed poll dated &c., under the hand and seal of the sd A. B., indorsed on the hrinbfre recited indre of mtge, the hdts comprised in the sd indre of mtge were charged with the pmt of the further sum of £   with int, to the sd C. D., his exors, admors, or assns.

------

14. RECITAL *of* AMOUNT DUE *on Mortgage.*

AND WHAS there is now due to the sd C. D. on the secy of the sd indre of mtge the sum of £   [together with int thron from [*date*]] *or* [in respect of principal, but all int thron has been paid up to the date hrof.]

------

15. RECITAL *of* TRANSFER *of Mortgage.*

AND WHAS by an indre dated &c., and made between the sd A. B. of the first part, the sd C. D. of the second part, and the sd E. F. of the third part, in conson of the sum of £ pd to the sd A. B. by the sd E. F., all that the sd pcl sum of £   secured by the hrnbfre recited indre of mtge, and all secs for the same, were assigned unto the sd E. F., his exors, admors and assns : [*If the mortgage was of lease-holds, proceed thus :*] and all the prems comprised in and demised by the hrnbfre-recited indre of lease were assured to the sd E. F., his exors, admors, and assns for the residue of the sd term of   years, subject to such equity of redon as was then subsisting in the same prems under the sd indre of mtge : [*If the mortgage was in fee substitute this clause for the last :*] and all the hdts and prems comprised in the sd indre of mtge were assured to the use of the sd E. F., his hrs and assns, subject to such equity of redon as was then subsisting in the same by virtue of the sd indre of mtge.

---

16. RECITAL *of* DEATH *of* MORTGAGEE INTESTATE *as to Mortgaged Estate.*

AND WHAS the sd A. B. died on &c., intestate, so far as relates to the legal estate in the sd hdts comprised in the hrnbfre-recited indre of mtge [leaving the sd J. B. his eldest son and heir-at-law], or [and letters of admon to his estate and effects were, on the [*date*] granted to the sd J. B. his eldest son and one of his next of kin.] [1]

---

17. RECITAL *of* SEISIN *of Testator and* WILL.

WHAS A. B. being seised [or entitled] for an estate of in-hance in fee simple in posson [or an estate equivalent thrto] of [or to] the hdts hrinafr described and intended to be hby assured, duly made his will dated, &c., and thereby gave, devised, and bequeathed [*&c., follow the words of the devise.*]

---

18. RECITAL *of* CODICILS *not affecting Devise of Realty.*

AND WHAS the sd testator made several codicils to his sd will, none of which revoked or in any manner affected the devise of his real estates contd in his sd will.

---

19. RECITAL *of* TENANCY BY CURTESY.

AND WHAS the sd A. B. died on the [*date*] leaving the sd B. B., her eldest son and heir-at-law, and on her death the sd H. B., as the surviving husband of the sd A. B.,

---

[1] See s. 4 of the Vendor and Purchaser Act, 1874 (37 & 38 Vict. c. 78).

became tenant for his life by the curtesy of England of the sd hdts.

---

20. RECITAL *of* LETTERS OF ADMINISTRATION.

AND WHAS the said A. B. died [*date*], and letters of admon of the estate and effects of the sd A. B., were on [*date*] granted to the sd C. D. by the principal registry [*or* by the district registry at W.] of the Probate Division of the High Court of Justice.

---

21. RECITAL *of* LIMITED ADMINISTRATION.

AND WHAS letters of admon of the estate and effects of the sd A. B., so far as relates to or concerns, &c., were on, &c., granted to the sd C. D. [*proceed as above*].

---

22. RECITAL *of Appointment of* NEW TRUSTEES.

AND WHAS by an indre dated &c., and made between &c., the sd A. B. and C. D., in exon of the power for that purpose contd in the hrnbfre-recited indre of the [*date*], appointed the sd E. F. to be a tree of the sd indre in the place of the sd G. H.

---

23. SHORT RECITAL *of Death of Old and* APPOINTMENT *of* NEW TRUSTEES.

AND WHAS the sd A. B. and C. D. died on [*dates*] resply, and by virtue of a power for that purpose contd in the hrnbfre-recited will of the said E. F. [*or* by virtue of the power in that behalf contd in the Act 23 & 24 Vict. c. 145], the said G. H. and I. K. were duly apptd trees throf [*or* of the sd will of the sd E. F.] [*or as the case may be*], in the stead of the sd A. B. and C. D.

---

24. RECITAL *of* REVOCATION *of Appointment of* EXECUTOR *and Appointment of* SUBSTITUTE.

AND WHAS the sd A. B. made a codicil dated &c., to his sd will, and thereby revoked the apptmt of the sd C. D. as exor and tree of his sd will, and apptd the sd E. F. an exor and tree throf in the place of the sd C. D.

---

25. RECITAL *of* AGREET FOR SALE.

WHAS the sd A. B. has agreed with the sd C. D. for the sale to him of the hdts hrnftr described and intended to be hby granted, and the fee simple and inhnce throf in posson, for the sum of £   .

---

26. SHORT RECITAL *of* AGREET FOR SALE.

AND WHAS the sd A. B. has agreed with the sd C. D. for the sale to him of the hdts hrnftr described for the sum of £   .

---

27. RECITAL *of* CONTRACT FOR SALE *of Lands, and that no* CONVEYANCE *made*.

AND WHAS the sd A. B. some time since agreed with the sd D. F. for the sale to him of the sd hdts, [so devised to the sd A. B. by the sd will of the sd C. B. as afsd,] for the sum of £   , but no convce has been executed in pursce of such agreet.

---

28. RECITAL *of* AGREEMENT *for* PURCHASE, *subject to Incumbrances*.

AND WHAS the sd A. B. has agreed with the sd C. D. for the pche of the sd hdts for the sum of £   , subject to the hrinbfre recited indre of mtge.

---

29. RECITAL *of* SUB-CONTRACT.

AND WHAS the sd D. F. has agreed with the sd G. H. to give up to him the sd G. H. the benefit of his sd contract.

---

30. *Another Form of* RECITAL *of* SUB-CONTRACT.

AND WHAS the sd D. F. hath agreed that the sd G. H. shall have the benefit of the sd contract upon the terms of paying the sd sum of £ [*the original purchase money*] to the sd A. B., and the sum of £ [*the premium*] to the sd D. F.

---

31. RECITAL *of* PURCHASE *by* AGENT.

AND WHAS the sd A. B. pched the sd hdts, as agent for and on behalf of the sd C. D., as they the sd A. B. and C. D. do hby resply declare.

---

32. RECITAL *of* AGREEMENT *for* SALE *of* LEASEHOLDS.

AND WHAS the sd A. B. has contracted with the sd C. D. for the sale to him of the prems demised by the sd indre of lease, subject to the rent reserved by and to the observance and performance of the lessee's covts and the condons contd in the sd indre, for the sum of £ .

---

33. RECITAL *of Contract for* LICENCE *to use* PATENT INVENTION.

AND WHAS the sd A. B. has agreed with the sd C. D. for the sale to him of the licence to make, use and exercise the sd invention within the sd town of X. for the term of four years upon the terms hrnftr contd for the sum of £ .

---

34. Recital *of* Agreement *to make* new Conveyance *and to join in* confirming *same.*

And whas the sd A. B. has agreed to make a new convce of the sd prems, and the sd C. D. and E. F. have agreed to join thrn for the ppse of confirming and giving effect to the same.

---

35. Recital *of* Agreement *by* Heir *to effectuate Ancestor's Contract by* joining in Conveyance.

And whas the sd A. B. has agreed to carry into effect the sd recited contract, and for that ppse to join in these presents in manner hrinftr appearing.

---

36. Recital *of Agreement by* Persons interested *in Purchase-Money to* join in Conveyance.

And whas the sd A. B. and C. B. his wife, and D. E. and F. E. his wife, being (tgor with the sd E. G. and R. M. G. in their own respve rights, and with the sd E. G. and G. B. as the personal reprves of the sd R. G., deceased) interested in the sd pchse-moy under the trusts of the sd will, have resply agreed to join in these presents in manner hruftr appearing.

---

37. Recital *of Erection of* Buildings since Conveyance.

And whas since the exon of the hrnbfe-recited indre, the sd A. B. has built upon the sd piece of land certain messes, with suitable offices and outbuildings.

---

38. Recital *of Agreement by Executor to* Assent to Legacy.

And whas the sd A. B. has requested the sd C. D. to join in these presents for the ppse of assenting to the sd legacy of

£——, so bequed to him by the hrnbfre recited will, which the sd C. D. has agreed to do.

---

39. Recital *of* Abortive Sale *of Trust Property.*

And whas the sd A. B. and C. D., as such trees as afsd, lately caused the hdts by the sd will directed to be sold to be put up for sale by public auction, but no adequate price having been bid for the same, the sd hdts were bought in.

LXXII.

CONFIRMATION *of a* DEED *to which either a* WIDOW *or a* SPINSTER *was a Party, but who* MARRIED *before she executed the Conveyance.*

THIS INDRE, made &c., between A. B., of &c. [*husband*], and C. B. his wife (formerly the within-named C. K.) of the one part, and the within-named E. F. of the other part: Whas since the engrossment of the within-written indre and before the exon throf by the sd C. B., the sd C. B. intermarried with the sd A. B., And whas the sd A. B. and C. B. have agreed to execute these presents for the purposes hrnftr appearing: NOW THIS INDRE WITNESSETH, that in conson of the prems and in pursce of the sd agreet the sd A. B. and C. B. do and each of them doth hby ratify and confirm the within-written indre and the several covts and provons thrin contd, To the intent that the within-written indre shall notwithstanding the sd marre have the same effect as if the sd indre had before such marre, and with the privity and consent of the sd A. B. been duly executed by the sd C. B. by her then name of C. K.

IN WITNESS, &c.[1]

LXXIII.

DEED OF CONFIRMATION *by a* MARRIED WOMAN *to be indorsed on* ASSIGNMENT OF LEASEHOLDS *which, by mistake, had not been* ACKNOWLEGED *by her.*

THIS INDRE, made &c., between A. B. and C. B. his wife of the first part, and E. F. and G. F. his wife of the second

[1] N.B.—If this deed relates to real estate or any interest therein it must be acknowledged by the wife.

part, and I. J. of the third part: Whas the within mentd
W. X. duly made his will dated, &c., and thby (*inter alia*)
devised and bequed all the real and persnl este of or to which
he should at his dece be scised, possed, or entitled, or over
which he should have any general power of testy disposition
(except estes vested in him by way of mtgc or upon any
trust) Unto and to the use of his wife V. X. and the sd T. J.
upon certain trusts in the sd will mentd, And he apptd his
sd wife and the sd T. J. exix and exor of his sd will.

AND WHAS [*death and probate*].

AND WHAS the sd V. X. died on [*date*].

AND WHAS the este of the sd W. X. is in course of admon
by the High Ct of Justice in an action in which M. N. and
ors are plts, and the sd T. J. is deft, and by an order made
in the sd action on [*date*] the pres comprised in the within-
written indre have been directed to be sold.

AND WHAS the within-written indre has not been acknowledged by the sd within named C. B. and G. F., in pursce of
the Fines and Recoveries Abolition Act, and doubts are
entertained as to whether the sale or arrangement in the
nature of or purporting to be a sale recited in the within-
written indre is binding upon the sd C. B. and G. F. or eir
of them.

AND WHAS the sd C. B. and G. F., with the concurrence of
their respive husbands, and at the request of the sd T. J.,
and for the ppse of enabling him to carry into effect the sd
order for sale, have agreed to execute and ackndge these
presents by way of confirmon of the title of the sd T. J. to
the within-mentd hdts and pres.

NOW THIS INDRE WITNESSETH that in pursce of the sd
agreet in this behalf and in conson of the pres she the sd
C. B., with the concurrence of the sd A. B., and she the sd
G. F., with the concurrence of the sd E. F., do and each of
them doth hby assign, release, and confirm, and the sd A. B.
and E. F. do hby also resply release and confirm unto the
sd T. J. his exors, admons, and assns, ALL THE hdts and
pres in the within-written indre described and expressed to
be thrby assured TOGETHER WITH [*general words comprising*

the interest of A. B., C. B., G. F, and E. F. in the pres.] To
HAVE AND TO HOLD the sd hdts and pres hrby assured
(Freed and discharged from all claim or equity to a settlement by the sd C. B. and G. F. or either of them, and from
all other claims or demands whatsoever by them or their
respive husbands or cir of them).

UNTO the sd T. J., his exors, admons, and assns, for all the
residue now to come of the within-mentd term of ninety-nine
years.

UPON the trusts upon which the same ought to be held
under or by virtue of the sd will of the sd W. X. and the
sd order for sale.

AND EACH of them the sd A. B., C. B., E. F., and G. F.,
so far as relates to his or her own acts and deeds (and as
respects each of them the sd C. B. and G. F. for the purpose
of binding, so far as may be practicable, her separate este in
equity) doth hby [*covt against incumbrances, see p.* 329].

IN WITNESS, &c.[1]

---

[1] This deed must be separately acknowledged by C. B. and G. F.

DEEDS OF COVENANT.

LXXIV.

COVENANT *to produce* DEEDS.

THIS INDRE, made &c., between A. B., of &c., of the one part, and C. D., of &c., of the other part: Whas [*recite conveyance to C. D.*]; And whas the several deeds and writings mentd in the schedule hereto are in the posson of the sd A. B., and concern the title not only of the said messe, farm and lands at X. afsd, but also of certain lands and hdts of the said A. B., situate at Y. in the county of Middlesex: Now THIS INDRE WITNESSETH, that in pursuance of an agreement in this behalf, he the sd A. B. for himself, his hrs, exors, and admors, doth hby covt with the sd C. D., his hrs and assns, that he the sd A. B., his hrs or assns, will at all times (unless prevented by fire or other inevitable accident), upon every reasonable request and at the cost of the sd C. D., his hrs or assns, produce and show to the sd C. D., his hrs or assns, or to such pson or psons as he or they shall require, or to his or their counsel, agents, or solicitors, or to or before any court or courts of law or equity, or otherwise as occasion shall require, the several deeds and writings mentd and described in the schedule hereto, or any of them; and will at the like request and cost at all times, unless prevented as afsd, make and deliver to the sd C. D., his hrs or assns, fair, true, and attested copies, abstracts, or extracts from such several deeds, or any of them, and permit the same to be examd and verified with the originals either by the sd C. D., his hrs or assns, or any other pson or psons whom he or they shall appt for that ppse: And that the sd A. B. will in the meantime, unless prevented by fire or other inevitable accident, keep the same deeds and writings safe, whole, and uncancelled [provided always, and it is hby agreed and decld, that if the sd A. B., his hrs or assns, shall at any time hrftr sell and dispose of the sd estate to which the sd several deeds and writings relate as afsd, or any part thof, and shall procure the pcher or pchers thof to enter into a like covenant to that which is hrnbfre contd with the sd C. D., his hrs or assns, for the prodon and delivery of copies of the sd several deeds and writings in manner afsd, then the covt hrnbfre contd for that ppse shall from thenceforth cease and be void; and these presents shall, at the request of the sd A. B., his hrs, exors, or admors, be delivered up to be cancelled].

IN WITNESS, &c.

LXXV.

MUTUAL COVENANTS *by Purchasers of* BUILDING LAND *where it is intended the* BUILDINGS *shall be* UNIFORM.[1]

THIS INDRE, made &c., between [owner], of the one part, and [purchasers] and the several other persons who shall at any time hrftr execute these presents, of the other part: Whas the sd [owner] is seised in fee in posson of a piece of land containing   acres, situate on the South Cliff, at Ramsgate, part of which he has laid out in separate lots or divisions for the erection of a row of houses thron, intended to be called Nelson's Crescent, and the form of the front building line of the sd houses is delineated in a ground plan appearing in these presents, and contains, including the curve, 400 feet in front towards the south-east; and whas, in order to preserve some degree of similarity and uniformity

----

[1] The above is the form of the indenture in *Whatman* v. *Gibson*, 9 Sim. 196. An injunction will be granted to restrain a breach of the above deed; but in the different conveyances to the purchasers this indenture must be plainly referred to, so as to fix the several sub-purchasers with notice of it, otherwise the court will not interfere as against them. Nor will the court grant an injunction against persons with notice who claim under a purchaser without notice of such a covenant: *Attorney-General* v. *Biphosphated Guano Co.* 26 W. R. 533.

of appearance in such intended row of houses, the sd [*owner*] has determined that it shall be a general and indispensable condon of the sale of all land intended to form any part of such row, that the several proprietors of such land resply for the time being shall observe and abide by the several stipulons and restrictions hrnftr contd in regard to the several houses to be erected thron, and in all other parlars; and that the sd [*owner*] and his hrs shall at all times observe the like stipulons and restrictions as to such of the lots or divisions of the same land as for the time being shall remain unsold by him or them; And whas the sd [*purchasers*] have severally agreed to purchase of the sd [*owner*] Lots 1 to 10 part of the sd intended row, and appearing on the sd plan, subject to the proposed stipulons and restrictions: Now THIS INDRE WITNESSETH, that, in conson of the prems and in pursce of the condons afsd, and for effectuating the plan afsd, it is hereby mutually agreed by and between the sd [*owner*], [*purchasers*] and the several other psons who shall at any time or times hrftr execute this indre (the respive times of the excon thof by the several parties being expressed in the several attestations thof), and each and every of them the sd [*owner*,] [*purchasers*] and such several other psons as afsd, mutually and reciprocally, in manner following (that is to say), that the front wall of every house in the sd intended row shall be brought immediately up to, but shall not in any case project beyond, the building line shown on the sd plan; and also that none of the houses in the sd intended row shall have bow windows of any sort; and also that the area in front of the sd houses shall be of the width of five feet in the clear, and shall extend the whole length thof, and that the forecourt in front of each house shall be surrounded by a uniform railing of iron or wood, which shall not extend beyond the height of four feet from the surface of the ground there; and also that the wall of partition between the several houses and the areas in front of the yard and garden behind such houses respectively shall be placed equally on the ground of the two proprietors of adjoining houses or ground, and shall at all times be considered as

party-walls, and shall be built at the joint expense of the
two proprietors of the adjoining houses or ground; but if
any of them shall be first and originally built at the sole expense of eir of the proprietors of the adjoining houses or
ground, then the proprietor who shall so first and originally
build such walls shall build a brick party-wall nine inches
thick, and at the height of seven feet from the surface of the
ground from the front building ground throughout, and one
half of the expense thof shall be paid to the proprietor who
shall have so built the same, by the proprietor of the adjoining house or ground, within three calendar months after the
proprietor of the adjoining house or ground shall begin to
erect his or her house in the principal front; and also that
the proprietor of such adjoining house or ground shall also
pay one half part of the expense of so much of the residue
of the party-wall as he shall make use of and build to, within
one calendar month after he shall make use of and build to
the same, and the expense in both cases, if any difference
shall arise thereon, shall be determined by admeasurement
and value; and also that none of the proprietors of the
houses or grounds in the sd intended row shall lay any
chalk or mould which shall be dug out of any of the lots of
land appearing on the sd plan, on the foot, horse, or carriage
way in front of the sd row, or on the land lying between
the sd way and the edge of the sea cliff; and also that the
piece or slip of land of the breadth of twenty-nine feet,
intended to be mentd in the conveyances to the several purchasers, beyond the area steps of entrance and forecourt,
shall at all times hrftr remain open and unincumbered as
and for a free foot, horse, and carriage way in front of the
sd intended row, and shall be formed, made, maintained, and
kept repaired at the expense of the several proprietors of the
sd houses in the sd row, in propon to the extent of front
towards the south-east of each respve house; and also that
none of the proprietors of any of the lots for the time being
shall at any time or times, or on any account whatsoever,
erect or suffer to be erected on any of the several lots which
shall resply belong to them for the time being, or on any

part of them, any public livery stables or public coach house, or use, exercise, or carry on, or suffer to be used, exercised, or carried on, through or on any part thereof, the trade or business of a brass founder, tobacco pipe maker, common brewer, tallow chandler, soap boiler, distiller, innkeeper, common ale-house keeper, brazier, working smith of any kind, butcher, or slaughterman, or any other noxious or offensive trade or business whby the neighbourhood might be in any respect endangered or annoyed, or burn or make, or suffer to be burnt or made, on any of the sd lots or on any part of them, any bricks or lime; and also that no other building or buildings than good dwelling-house or dwelling-houses or lodging-houses shall be erected on the said lots or any of them.

IN WITNESS, &c.

_____

LXXVI.

DEED OF COVENANT *by* RIPARIAN OWNERS *to preserve the* RIVERS A. AND W. *and the* WATER *therein within certain Limits* PURE *and free from Rubbish.*[1]

WHAS the several psons whose names and seals are hereto resply subscribed and affixed (hrnftr called "the parties hrto"), are the owners of property situate on the banks of or contiguous to that part of the rivers A. and W. resply,

_____

[1] Persons having a common interest may agree to unite in a defence, but the agreement must not go beyond the common object; and, therefore, an agreement by several owners and occupiers of land in a parish to concur in defending any actions that may be commenced against any of them by the present or any future rector for the tithes of articles covered by certain specified moduses or any other moduses, binding themselves not to compromise or settle, and not limited to their continuance in the parish or to any particular time, is illegal. *Stow* v. *Yea*, Jacob, 427.

Millowners bound themselves by a bond to stop their mills pursuant to resolutions passed by the majority (the object in fact being to prevent strikes by their workpeople). Held, that the bond was illegal at common law, as being contrary to public policy, and in restraint of trade, and of the free action of individuals, and was incapable of being enforced by action. *Quære*, whether the entering into such a bond is an indictable offence? *Hilton* v. *Eckersley*, 4 W. R. 326.

which, commencing as to the A. at B., and as to the W. at
C., extends as to both to D., all in the county of Y.: And
whas the parties hrto for the ppse of preventing injury to
their ppty afsd by the deposit in or discharge into the sd
rivers within the limits afsd of any stones, clay, soil, or
ashes, dirt, rubbish, or other refuse matter, or from obstruc-
tions or nuisances caused or created in the sd rivers resply,
have agreed to enter into the covts hrnftr contd : Now THIS
INDRE WITNETH, that, in pursce of the sd agreet and in
conson of the prems, each of them the parties hrto, so far as
the covts hrnftr contained are to be performed by him, his
hrs, exors, or admors, doth for himself, his hrs, exors, and
admors, covt with the others of them the parties hrto, thr
exors and admors, and also with any two or any greater
number of the ors of them the parties hrto, thr exors and
admors, and also with each of the ors of them, the parties
hrto, his exors and admors, in manner following (that is to
say), that they the parties hrto will not at any time during
the period of fifteen years commencing from the day of the
date hrof, deposit or discharge any stones, clay, soil, ashes,
dirt, rubbish, or other refuse matter in or into the sd rivers
within the respive limits afsd, nor will at any time during
the period afsd do or suffer to be done any act or thing
whatsoever which may tend to the obstruction of the sd
rivers or eir of them within the limits afsd, or which may be
or become a nuisance, detriment, or annoyance to any other
of the parties hrto, or whereby any one or more of them
may during the period afsd be prevented from enjoying
the full benefit and advantage of the water of the sd rivers
resply within the limits afsd, or be in anywise prejudicially
affected ; and also that the parties hrto resply will at all
times during the period afsd to the best of thr respive
ability prohibit and prevent all persons from discharging
any stones, clay, soil, ashes, dirt, rubbish, or other refuse
matter into the sd rivers or eir of them within the limits
afsd, or from doing any thing whereby the supply of water
to the parties hrto resply may be in anywise obstructed
or lessened, or rendered impure, or whereby the este or

effects of them, or any of them, may be in anywise prejudicially affected; and also that the parties hrto resply,
thr respive heirs, exors, and admors, will give all the aid
and assistance in thr respive power (both by subscribing
from time to time such sums of money not exceeding upon
any one occasion the sum of £5, or by any other means
that may be considered most advisable by a majority of
them, or of the parties for the time being interested under
these presents to be assembled at any meeting after due
notices in writing have been given to them resply or left at
thr respive usual or last known places of abode at least one
week before the sd meeting) to or towards any proceeding at
law or orwise against any pson or psons whomsoever who
shall discharge any stones, clay, soil, ashes, dirt, rubbish, or
other refuse matter into the sd rivers, or eir of them within
the limits afsd; and also will upon the determon and ap-
plicon of such majority as afsd do all such further or other
lawful and reasonable acts, and also enter into such further
deeds, as may be considered necessary for the further,
better, and more perfectly prohibiting or preventing the
discharge of any stones, clay, soil, ashes, dirt, rubbish, or
other refuse matter into the sd rivers, or eir of them, within
the limits afsd; and also for the further and more perfectly
prohibiting or preventing any other pson or psons from discharging any stones, clay, soil, ashes, dirt, rubbish, or other
refuse matter into the sd rivers, or eir of them within the
limits afsd, or orwise annoying or prejudicially affecting the
parties hrto, or any of them, thr or any of thr hrs, exors, or
admors, or thr or any of thr estates or effects, by obstructing
the course or lessening the quantity of or rendering impure
the water of the sd rivers, or eir of them, within the limits
afsd: and also all such other things as may be considered
necessary or expedient by such majority as afsd: and also
that each of them the parties hrto, his exors and admors, will
at all times during the period afsd defend and keep indemnified all and each of the ors and other of them the parties
hrto, thr and his exors and admors, and thr and his estate and
effects, from and against all actions, suits, accounts, reckon-

ings, costs, damages, claims, and demands whatsoever, which they or he may incur or sustain by reason of thr or his commencing or prosecuting any proceeding at law or orwise under this indre, and for the ppse of effectuating the same: Provided always, that all moneys that shall be required for the ppse of carrying these presents or anything hrn contd or relating thereto into exon or effect shall, subject to the provon hrnftr contd, be contributed in equal shares by the parties hrto, thr respive exors or admors: Provided always, that no one of the parties hrto, his hrs, exors, or admors, shall be liable to pay any greater sum of money, or bear or be put unto any greater risk in proportion to the value of his property or interest than the other or ors of them, thr or his hrs, exors, or admors, unless it shall be declared or resolved orwise by a majority of the parties hrto assembled at any meeting to be called as afsd: Provided also, that no proceeding at law or orwise shall be commenced or prosecuted by any of the parties hrto, thr or any of thr hrs, exors, or admors, unless and until the party so taking, commencing, or prosecuting the same shall have first obtained an authority in writing so to do, signed by the majority present at a meeting to be called as afsd for the ppse of conferring such authority.

In witness, &c.

DISCLAIMERS.

LXXVII.

DISCLAIMER *of* TRUSTS *of* *Will*.

To ALL TO WHOM these presents shall come, A. B., of &c., sends greeting: Whas C. D., late of &c. by his will, dated &c., appointed the sd A. B. and E. F. trees and exors thereof; and also appted his wife and the sd A. B. and E. F. guardians of his infant children; and he thrby also bequd his leasehold messe X., unto the sd A. B. and E. F., their exors, admors, and assns, upon the trusts thrn declared; and also devised and bequd unto the sd A. B. and E. F., their hrs, exors, admors, and assns. all and singular his freehold and leasehold estes, and the residue of his personal este, To hold the same unto the sd A. B. and E. F., their hrs, exors, admors, and assns, according to the nature and quality thof resply, upon the trusts thrin declared; And whas the sd C. D. died [*date*] without having revoked or altered his sd will, and the same was proved by the sd E. F. alone on the [*date*], the Principal Registry of the Probate Division of the High Court of Justice, the sd A. B. having first renounced probate thof; And whas the sd A. B. has in nowise administered to the este of the sd testator nor acted or interfered in the exon of the trusts of the sd will, or as guardian of the children of the sd testator. NOW THESE PRESENTS WITNESS, that he the sd A. B. doth renounce and disclaim all and singular the sd leasehold messe and premises in X., and all and singular the sd testator's freehold, leasehold este, and the residue of his personal este, and all and singular other the real and personal este and effects whatsoever given, devised, or bequd by the sd will, and all devises, bequests, legacies and benefits made or given to him by the sd will, and also the sd office of tree and exor of the sd will and guardian of the children of the sd testator, and all trusts, powers, authorities, rights, and privileges whatsoever under the sd will.

In witness, &c.

LXXVIII.

Disclaimer *of* Trusts *of Will*—Short Form.

To all to whom these presents shall come, A. B., of &c., sends greeting: Whas C. D., late of &c., made his will, dated &c., and thby apptd the sd A. B. and T. S., of &c., exors, and devised and bequeathed all his real and psnl estes unto the sd A. B. and T. S., their hrs, exors, admors, and assns, upon the trusts and for the intents and ppses thrn mentd; And whas the sd C. D. died on &c., without having revoked or altered his sd will; and whas the sd A. B. has not acted in the trusts and exorship of the sd will or accepted any of the devises or bequests thrby made to him: Now this Indre witnth, that the sd A. B. doth disclaim all the devises and bequests to him made, and all the trusts, powers, and discretions reposed or vested in him in and by the sd will, either jointly with the sd T. S. or otherwise.

In witness, &c.

LXXIX.

Disclaimer *by Trustees of* Copyholds *in order that One of their Number only may take Admittance.*

This Indre, made &c., between [*disclaiming trustees*], of the one part, and [*continuing trustee*] of the other part: Whas [*here recite will, death of testator, and proof of will as in two previous forms*]; And whas no person has since the decease of the testator been admitted to the sd copyhold hdts holden of the manors afsd, or any of them; And whas the sd [*disclaiming trustees*], and also the sd [*continuing trustee*], are resply desirous that the sd copyhold hdts holden of the manors afsd should be vested in the sd [*continuing trustee*], solely to the intent that he alone may be admitted thrto, and for that ppse the sd [*disclaiming trustees*] have resply agreed to execute the disclaimer and release hrnftr contd: Now THIS INDRE WITNTH, that in pursuance of the sd agreet they the sd [*disclaiming trustees*] do hby disclaim all and singular the copyhold hdts devised by the sd will of the testator, and holden resply of the manors of &c. [except as to the sd C. D. the power of appmt and the beneficial interest for her life resply given to her by the sd will]: AND THIS INDRE FURTHER WITNTH, that, in further pursce of the sd determon, they the sd [*disclaiming trustees*] do and each of them doth hby release unto the sd [*continuing trustee*] and his hrs ALL AND SINGULAR (if any), thr right to be admitted, or other thr right, este and interest, if any, of and in the sd cyhold hdts held of the sd manors of &c., with the rights, members, and appurts thrto belonging [except as to the sd C. D. the power of apptmt and beneficial interest for her life resply given to her by the sd will] to the intent that, by virtue of the sd disclaimer and, if need be, of this rcle, the right to be admitted to and to hold the sd hdts and all and singular the prems may be vested in the sd [*continuing trustee*], and his hrs, as sole tenant or tenants thof, according to the customs of the sd manors resply.

IN WITNESS, &C.[1]

[1] As to the above disclaimer, see *Lord Wellesley* v. *Withers*, 24 L. J. Q. B. 139.

LXXX.

DISENTAILING DEED *by Tenant in Tail, with the* CONSENT *of the* PROTECTOR.

THIS INDRE, made &c., between C. D., of &c. [*tenant in tail*] of the first part, E. D., of &c. [*protector*] of the second part, and G. H., of &c. [*releasee*] of the third part: Whas by indres of lease and rele, dated resply &c., release being made between [*parties*], the hdts hrnftr assured were limited to the use of the sd A. B. and his assns for his life, without imphmt of waste, with remr to the use of the sd E. D. and his assns for his life, without impchmt of waste, with remr to the use of the sd I. K. and his hrs during the lives of the sd A. B. and E. D., and of the survor of them, in trust for them, and to prเserve contingent remrs, with remr to the use of the first and other sons of the sd E. D. on the body of L. M. begotten or to be begotten successively, according to their resive seniorities, in tail, with divers remrs over; And whas the sd C. D. was the first and eldest son of the sd E. D. on the body of the sd L. M. begotten, and he attained the age of twenty-one years on [*date*]; And whas the sd A. B. died on [*date*]; And whas the sd C. D. is desirous of barring the sd este tail, and all other estes tail of him the sd C. D. of or in the hdts hnftr assured, and all remrs, revons, estes, rights, interests, and powers, to take effect after the determon or in defeazance of such este tail or estes tail, and of assuring the same hdts to the uses, upon the trusts, and subject to the power hrnftr contd (subject to the estes by the sd indre limited, which precede the este tail thby limited to the first son of the sd E. D., and to the powers and privileges to the same preceding estes annexed, so far as the same estes, powers, and privileges are now subsisting or capable of taking effect) ; And whas the sd E. D. as protector of the sd stlmt, has agreed to concur in these presents for the purpose of giving his consent to the disposon intended to be hby made by the sd C. D.

Now this Indre witnesseth, that for effectuating the sd desire of the sd C. D., and in conson of the prems, he the sd C. D., with the consent of the sd E. D., testified by his being a party to and executing these presents, doth hby grant unto the sd G. H. and his hrs, all [*parcels*], and also all other the hdts (if any) which are now subject to the subsisting uses of the sd indre of &c., To hold the sd hdts unto the sd G. H. and his hrs, subject to the estes by the sd indre of &c., limited, which precede the este tail by the same indre limited to the sd C. D., and to the powers and privileges to the same precedent estes annexed during the continuance thof, so far as the same are now subsisting or capable of taking effect, but freed and discharged from the sd este tail, and all other estes tail of the sd C. D., and all remrs, revons, estes, rights, titles, interests, and powers, to take effect after the determon of such este or estes tail.

To the use of the sd C. D. his hrs and assns.

And the sd E. D., so far as relates to his este for life in the prems, doth hby for himself, his hrs, exors, and admors, And the sd C. D., so far as relates to his remr in fee expectant upon the same life este, doth hby for himself, his hrs, exors, and admors, covt with the sd G. H., his hrs and assns, that notwithstanding anything by the sd now covenanting parties resply, or any person through whom they resply derive title orwise than by way of pche for valuable conson, done, omitted, or knowingly suffered, &c. [*covenants for title as in Form XLIX., p. 302.*]

In witness, &c.

LXXXI.

AGREEMENT *for* TENANCY *of a small* HOUSE *for Three Years.*[1]

AN AGREET made the [*date*], between A. B , of &c., of the one part, and C. D., of &c., of the other part :—

1. The sd A. B. lets, and the sd C. D. takes, from the date hrof, for the term of three years, all that messe known as No. 1, X. Street, in the parish of Y., with the yard, garden, outbuildings, and appurtenances thrto (as the same were lately in the occupation of G. H.) at the yearly rent of £20.

2. The sd C. D. shall pay the sd rent quarterly (the first qtr's pmnt to be made on the [*date*]), and shall also pay all rates, taxes, and other outgoings whatsoever in respect of the prems (except only property tax).

3. The sd A. B. shall, during the term, keep the prems in tenantable repair.

4. The prems shall be used by the sd C. D. as a private dwelling-house only, and no structural alteration shall be made by him in the same, nor shall any trade or occupation be carried on thrin, nor shall the sd C. D. allow any sale by auction to take place on the prems.

AS WITNESS, &c.

LXXXII.

TENANCY *Agreement of* HOUSE *for less than Three Years*—CONCISE FORM.

AN AGREET made &c., between A. B., of &c. (hrnftr called the landlord) of the first part, and C. D., of &c. (hrnftr called the tenant) of the second part.

[1] This agreement takes effect as a lease, and must be stamped as such. See pp. 9, 101.

The landlord agrees to let and the tenant agrees to take the prems hrnftr described upon the terms hrnftr expressed.

PREMISES.—[*insert description.*]

TERM.—For nine months certain, commencing from the [*date*], since which time the tenant has been in posson.

RENT.—£120, payable quarterly, on the 24th March, 25th June, and 29th September; the first payment to be made on the 25th March next, but the last quarter to be paid twelve days before Michaelmas; landlord to bear and pay all rates, taxes, assessments, and outgoings of all kinds, except gas rate.

USE.—Premises to be used as a private residence only, but this not to interfere with the profession of a physician or surgeon carried on by the tenant, and nothing to be done or carried on therein to vitiate any insurance or to increase the premium; tenant not to assign or underlet without landlord's permission in writing.

REPAIRS.—Tenant to repair broken windows, to clean out gutters, pipes, and make good all damages caused by non-removal of snow, as well as any other wants and amendments which may be rendered necessary through the tenant's neglect or default.

VIEW.—Landlord or his agent, workmen, or servants, may at all reasonable times enter to view the prems to do all repairs he may think requisite (but landlord not to be requested to do any repairs), and for all other necessary purposes.

RE-ENTRY.—If any quarterly payment of the afsd rent be at any time in arrear for twenty-eight days, or if the prems at any time be left vacant, or the tenant become bankrupt or insolvent, or shall break or make default in any of the stipulons hrnbfr contd, the landlord may, after one weeks' notice (signed by himself or his agent) to be left at or affixed to the door or some other conspicuous part of the prems, but without any other formality, retake posson of the prems as if this agreet had not been made, but without prejudice to any other remedies he may have.

BILL "TO LET."—Landlord to be at liberty one month previous to the expiration of the tenancy to put a bill in the front drawing-room window for reletting the prems, and the tenant to keep the same always exposed to view, and to afford facilities for intending tenants to view the prems at all reasonable hours.

EXPENSES.—Tenant to pay £2 towards the expenses of this agreement.

AS WITNESS, &c.

___

LXXXIII.

AGREEMENT *for* WEEKLY TENANCY *of a Cottage between a* MANUFACTURER *or Colliery Owner and his* WORKMEN.

AN AGREET made the   day of, &c., between A. B., of X. Mills, &c. [or colliery] (hrinftr called the landlord) of the one part, and C. D., of &c., afsd (hrinftr called the tenant) of the other part, whereby the landlord agrees to let and the tenant agrees to take the cottage or tenement known as No. 1 W. Street, at X., in the parish of Y., in the county of Z., with its appurts, upon the following terms (that is to say):—

1. The tenancy shall commence on the   day of &c., and continue for one week and thenceforward from week to week until the same shall be determined by a week's notice to quit in writing, terminating with a current week to be given either by landlord or tenant to the other, and which notices may resply be given by causing the same to be left in the case of notice by the landlord, at the cottage afsd, and in case of notice by the tenant at the office of X. Mills [or colliery] afsd.

2. The rent shall be 5s. per week, and shall be payable weekly without deduction, and in case of notice to quit being given on either side the rent for the last week of the tenancy shall be payable in advance.

3. It shall be lawful for the landlord to stop and deduct out of any wages for the time being payable by him to the tenant as his overlooker, woolsorter, spinner, weaver,

mechanic, pitman, miner, workman, artificer, servant, or orwise, any sum or sums which shall be payable for the time being by the tenant to the landlord for rent of the sd prems.

4. The tenant shall, at his own expense, keep clean, in good order and condon the privy used with the sd cottage, and also such part of the waste land in the rear of the sd cottage as is immediately opposite thereto, and sweep the chimneys when necessary, and keep the sd cottage in clean, wholesome, and decent condon. And the tenant shall also, at his own expense, repair, or make good, all broken windows and other glass, locks, bolts, hooks, door handles, bells, bell wires, hinges, latches, window fastenings, and sash lines, and also all damage, waste, spoil, and unreasonable wear and tear done or committed wilfully, negligently, or carelessly by the tenant, his family, or lodgers, and in case the tenant after being required to do any of the things by this clause agreed by him to be done shall for the space of seven days neglect or omit to do the same the landlord may do the same and the tenant shall repay to the landlord all sums expended by him in so doing within seven days after that such sums shall have been so expended, after which lastmentd period of seven days such sums so expended shall be deemed to be rent in arrear and shall be recoverable accordingly by distress or by deduction from wages as afsd, or by any other legal remedy.

5. Save as afsd, the landlord will at his own expense keep the prems in tenantable repair.

6. The landlord and all persons authorized by him may at all reasonable hours in the daytime enter upon the prems and every part thereof, to view the state thereof, and to repair the same.

7. The prems shall not be used as a shop for any trade or business.

8. The tenant shall not assign, underlet or part with the possession of the prems or any part thof without the written consent of the landlord, but this clause is not to prevent the tenant from taking lodgers.

9. Upon determination of his tenancy the tenant shall

peaceably give up possession of the prems and fixtures to the landlord in a clean condition, and if the tenant shall neglect or refuse so to give up possession, the landlord may take possession of the sd prems and expel the tenant forcibly if necessary.

10. The tenant performing his part of this agreement may quietly enjoy the prems during his tenancy without any eviction, interruption, or disturbance, by the landlord or any person claiming through or in trust for him.

As WITNESS, &c.

LXXXIV.

LEASE *of a* HOUSE.

THIS INDRE, made &c., between A. B., of &c., of the one part, and C. D., of &c., of the other part, WITNETH, that, in conson of the rent hereby reserved, and the covts hrnaftr contd, the sd A. B. doth demise unto the sd C. D., ALL &c. [*Insert description of house*], To hold unto the sd C. D., his exors, admors, and assns, for twenty-one years from [*date*], yielding and paying therefor yearly unto the sd A. B., his hrs and assns, the rent of £ by quarterly pmts on the usual quarter days, the first pmt to be made on [*date*]; AND THE SD C. D. doth hby for himself, his hrs, exors, admors, and assns, covt with the sd A.B., his hrs and assns, that the sd C. D., his exors, admors, and assns, will during the sd term pay unto the sd A. B., his hrs and assns, the rent hereby reserved in manner hrnbfe mentd, without any deduction (except landlord's property tax); and also will pay all taxes, rates, duties, and assmts, whether parochial, parly, or orwise, now charged or hrftr to be charged on the prems or the lessor on account thof (except only the ppty tax); and also will during the sd term well and sufficiently repair, maintain, pave, empty, cleanse, amend, and keep the demised prems and every part thof, with the appurts, in good and substantial repair and condition; and also will in every third year of the sd term paint

2 B

all the outside wood work and iron work belonging to the
prems with two coats of proper oil colours in a workmanlike manner; and also will in every seventh year paint the
inside wood, iron, and other work now or usually painted with
two coats of proper oil colours in a workmanlike manner:
and also repaper with paper of such quality as at present
such parts of the prems as are now papered; also wash, stop,
whiten, or colour, such parts of the prems as are now plastered,
and also will forthwith insure and keep insured the prems in
the sum of [£1500] in some respectable insurance office in
the joint names of the sd A. B. and C. D., and will upon the
request of the sd A. B., his hrs or assns, or his or their
agent, show the receipt for the last premium paid for such
insurance for every current year, and as often as the prems
shall be burnt down or damaged by fire all and every the
sums or sum of money which shall be recovered or recd by
the sd C. D., his exors, admors, or assns, in respect of such
insce shall be laid out by him or them in building or repairing the demised prems, or such parts thof as shall be burnt
down or damaged by fire; [AND it is hrby declared and
agreed, that in case the prems hrby demised, or any part
thof, shall at any time during the sd term be burnt down or
damaged by fire so as to render the same unfit for habitation, then and so often as the same shall happen the rent
hby reserved, or a proportionate part thof, according to the
nature and extent of the injury sustained, and all remedies
for recovering the same, shall be suspended and abated
until the prems shall have been rebuilt and made fit for
habitation.] And also that it shall be lawful for the sd
A. B., his hrs or assns, and his or their agents, at all season-
able times during the sd term to enter the demised prems,
to take a schedule of the fixtures and things made and
erected thereupon, and to examine the condition of the sd
prems, and that all wants of reparation which upon such
views shall be found, and for the amendment of which notice
in writing shall be left at the prems, the sd C. D., his exors,
admors, and assns, will within three calr months next after
every such notice well and sufficiently repair and make good
accordingly; [and also will not convert, use, or occupy the

sd prems, or any part thof, into or as a shop, warehouse, or other place, for carrying on any trade or business whatsoever, or suffer the sd prems to be used for any such purpose or orwise than as a private dwelling-house.]   [And also will not during the sd term assn, transfer, or underlet the demised prems, or any part thof, without the consent in writing of the sd A. B., his hrs or assns.][1]   And also will at the expiron or sooner determon of the sd term peaceably yield up the demised prems with the appurts and all additions thrto unto the sd A. B., his hrs or assns, together with all buildings and fixtures thereon, in good and substantial repair and condition in all respects: PROVIDED ALWAYS, that if the rent hby reserved or any part thof shall be unpaid for twenty-one days after any of the days on which the same ought to have been paid (although no formal demand shall have been made thereof), or in case of the breach or non-performance of any of the covts hrn contd on the part of the sd C. D., his exors, admors, and assns, then and in either of such cases it shall be lawful for the sd A. B., his hrs or assns, at any time thftr into and upon the demised prems or any part throf in the name of the whole to re-enter, and the same to have again as in his or their former este:[2] AND THE SD A. B. doth hby for himself, his hrs, exors, admors, and assns, covt with the sd C. D., his exors, admors, and assns, that he and they, paying the rent hby reserved and performing the covts hrnbfre on his and their parts contd, may peaceably enjoy the demised prems for the term hby granted without any interruption or disturbance from the sd A. B., or any person lawfully claiming through or in trust for him. [*In an underlease the following covenant should be added*:] AND that the sd A. B., his exors, admors, and assns, will during the sd term (if not prevented by fire or other inevit-

---

[1] Instead of this, the following clause may be used :—

AND that the sd C. D., his exors, admors or assns, shall not at any time during the sd term, assn or underlet the prems hby demised, or any part thof, without the previous consent in writing of the sd A. B., his hrs or assns, provided, nevertheless, that it is hby declared that such consent shall not be unreasonably or capriciously withheld.

[2] See *Phillips* v. *Bridge*, L. R. 10 C. P. 48.

able accident), at the request and cost of the sd C. D., his exors, admors, or assns, produce unto him or them, or as he or they may direct in [England], the sd indre of lease of the [*date*] and will at the like request and cost furnish to the sd C. D., his exors. admors, or assns, such copies or extracts (attested or orwise) of or from the same indre as he or they may require.

In witness, &c.

LXXXV.

Lease *of a* Public-house.

This Indre, made &c., between A. B., of &c., of the one part, and C. D., of &c., of the other part, Witneth, that, in conson of the rent hby reserved and of the covts and agrects hrnftr contd, the sd A. B. doth demise unto the sd C. D., his exors, admors, and assns, all that messe or public-house known by the sign of the White Horse, situate in X. Street, in the parish of F. in the county of Msex, as the same is now in the occupon of the sd C. D., togr with all easements, vaults, cellars, yards, and appurts to the prems belonging or appertng, To hold the prems, with the appurts, unto the said C. D., his exors, admors, and assns, for twenty-one years from the [*date*], Yielding and paying [*reservation of rent as in Form LXXXIV., p.* 369, *supra*]. And the sd C. D. doth hby for himself, his hrs, exors, admors, and assns, covt with the said A. B., his hrs and assns [*for payment of rent, rates, &c., as in Form LXXXIV., p.* 369, *supra*]; and also will, at all times during the sd term, sufficiently repair and maintain, and keep in repair with good materials, the prems hby demised [together with the glass and other windows, window shutters, doors, locks, fastenings, bells, partitions, ceilings, chimney-pieces, pavements, pitchings, privies, drains, sinks, cesspools, cisterns, pumps, wells, pipes, water-closets, and water-courses, to the sd premises belonging] and all buildings, improvements, and additions at any time during the sd term erected or made by the sd C. D., his exors, admors, or assns, upon the sd prems; and will [*here insert covenants from Form LXXXIV., pp* 370–1, *supra, for painting, in-suring, re-instating, and for lessor to be at liberty to inspect and give notice of wants of repairs, &c., and for delivery up at end of term*] ; [And also, that the sd C. D., his exors, admors, or assns, will not, during the sd term, use, exercise, or carry on, or permit or suffer to be used, exercised, or carried on, in or upon the sd prems, any noxious or offensive trade or business, without the consent in writing of the sd A. B., his hrs or assns.] [And also that the sd C. D., his exors, admors, and assns, will not during the sd term, without the consent in writing of the sd A. B., his hrs or assns, convert the prems hby demised, or any part thereof, into a shop, ware-house, shed, or place of sale for goods or merchandize, or into a private dwelling-house, or open or use or suffer the same to be opened or used for any other purpose than as an hotel or inn, public-house or tavern : And also that the sd C. D., his exors, admors, and assns, or such other person or persons as shall for the time being conduct the business of the sd public-house, will during the sd term keep and conduct the same in a regular and proper manner in every respect, and will immediately apply for and use his and their best endea-vours to obtain a certificate, licence, or permission of Her Majesty's justices of the peace for the vending of wines, spirituous liquors, and beer on the prems, and shall not knowingly or willingly do any act whby the same may be-come legally or justly abrogated, forfeited, or refused : And also will at all times during the sd term manage or conduct the business of the said public-house, hotel or inn, under the name of and constantly keep up the effigy or sign of the " White Horse "; and will at the end or sooner determon of the sd term, upon demand by the sd A. B., his hrs or assns, or his or their incoming tenant, deliver up the said several certificates, licences, or permissions of her sd Majesty's jus-tices of the peace granted during the then current year, for the vending of any wines, spirits, liquors, beer, ale, or tobacco upon the demised prems, and also all and every the excise licences for the unexpired term they may have then to run.] PROVIDED ALWAYS [*power of re-entry on non-pay-*

*ment of rent or breach of covenant as in Form LXXXIV.,
p. 371*]. [PROVIDED ALSO, that if the sd A. B. or C. D., their
respive exors, admors, or assns, shall be desirous to determine
this demise at the end of the first seven or fourteen years
of the sd term, and of such his or their respve desire shall
give six calr months' notice in writing to the other or others
of them resply before the expiron of the sd seven or fourteen
years, then and in that case the term hereby granted shall,
at the expiration of the said seven or fourteen years, cease
and determine, in like manner as if the whole of the sd term
of twenty-one years had expired.] AND THE SAID A. B. [*covenant by lessor for quiet enjoyment, as in Form LXXXIV., p.* 371].

IN WITNESS, &c.

LXXXVI.

AGREEMENT *for Tenancy from* YEAR TO YEAR *of*
AGRICULTURAL *Land.*

AN AGREET, made the [*date*], between A. B. of the one
part, and C. D. of the other part.

1. The sd A. B. agrees to let, and the sd C. D. to take ALL
[*parcels at length*], and now in the occupation of the sd C. D.,
from the   day of   last (from which time he has had
the posson), for one year, and so from year to year, until such
notice shall be given for determining the sd term as hrnfter
mentd, at the yearly rent of £——, by half-yearly payments,
on the [*date*] and the [*date*] in every year, the half-year's rent
which became due on the [*date*] last to be paid within ten
days next after the date hereof, and the next half-yearly
payment of rent to be made on the [*date*] next:

2. The sd C. D. will duly pay the sd rent in the manner
aforesaid, and also the land tax and all other rates, taxes,
tithes, and rent-charge in lieu of tithes, and other outgoings
whatsoever payable or charged on the landlord or tenant in
respect of the premises:

3. The sd C. D. will also keep in good and tenantable repair
and condition the fences, hedges, gates, stiles, and boundaries,
and will scour out the ditches as often as the hedges shall be

cut, and will not cut the hedges under seven years' growth, and will not cut, stock, or injure the timber or timber-like trees, tellers, saplings, or trees likely to become timber, but use his best endeavours to preserve the same, and will dung, manure, and cultivate the land in a good and husbandlike manner, and not waste, destroy, impoverish, or make barren the same, and will deliver up the same accordingly at the determination of the tenancy :

4. If the sd rent, or any part thof, shall be in arrear for twenty-one days, or if breach shall be made in any of the tenant's agreets afsd, it shall be lawful for the sd A. B. to re-enter upon the sd prems and repossess the same, and remove the sd C. D. and all other occupiers thof :

5. If the sd A. B. shall be desirous that the sd C. D. shall quit the sd prems, or if the sd C. D. shall be desirous of quitting the same, then one half-year's notice shall be given by eir party to the other, and until such notice shall be given this agreet shall be in full force.

6. The Agricultural Holdings Act shall not apply to this tenancy.

IN WITNESS, &c.

[The above is a lease, and requires the same stamp as a lease.]

- - -

LXXXVII.

LEASE *of a small* FARM *from Year to Year*—CONCISE FORM.[1]

THIS INDRE made the [date] between A. B. of &c. (hrnftr called "the landlord") of the one part, and C. D. of &c. (hrnfter called "the tenant") of the other part, WITNESSETH as follows :—

1. The landlord demises to the tenant the farm described in the first schedule hereto with the appurts (except the wood, mines, and minerals, and the right to cut, get, and carry away the same) as yearly tenant, as to the land from the 2nd day of February, 1880, and as to the buildings, from

[1] This form has been used for many years on an estate in the West Riding of Yorkshire.

the 1st day of May, 1880, at the yrly rent of £20, payable on the 21st day of June. And also at the additional yrly rents specified in the 2nd schedule hereto, such additional rents resply to be payable immedly upon the doing of the respive acts giving rise to the same resply, and to be payable yrly during the rest of the tenancy.

2. The tenant covts with the landlord to pay the rents afsd in the manner afsd, and all outgoings chgble on the prems, and to observe all the stipulons contd in the 3rd schedule hrto, and to keep the prems in good repair and condon, and so yield up the same at the determinon of the tenancy and not to underlet or assign the prems or any part throf.

3. The landlord may at all times enter and inspect the prems and may enter and determine the tenancy on breach of any of the tenant's covts hrn contd.

4. If during the tenancy the landlord, his agent, hrs, or assns, shall distrain to obtain pmt of rents hrnbfe reserved, he or they may sell any crops distrained to be consumed upon the prems, and the pchr or pchrs thof shall have the use of the farm bldgs for a reasonable time from such sale free of charge.

5. The landlord covts with the tenant that the tenant observing his covts hrn contd may occupy the prems without interruption by the landlord.

6. The Agricultural Holdings Act shall not apply to this tenancy.

IN WITNESS, &c.

The First SCHEDULE above referred to.

A farm and prems called " C. Farm," situate in the township of H. in the county of York, containing by estimon nine acres, and consisting of house, farm bldgs, yard, and four closes of land, called resply West Green, Middle Field, Belle Isle, and Low Pasture.

The Second SCHEDULE above referred to.

£15 yearly for every acre or part of an acre of meadow land ploughed or turned up, or sown with corn, grain, or roots.

£5 yearly for every acre or part of an acre of pasture land ploughed or turned up without the consent in writing of the landlord.

£5 yearly for every cartload or part of a cartload of hay, straw, grass, turnips, or manure, sold or carried off the prems.

£1 each for every horse, mule, foal, cow, calf, sheep, lamb, or other animal put upon the meadow or pasture lands during the last year of the tenancy more than the number usually kept upon such lands.

The Third SCHEDULE above referred to.

To consume all the hay, straw, clover, grass, roots, and fodder grown or produced upon the prems. To cultivate the lands according to the most approved modes of husbandry. To spread all ashes, manure, dung, muck, or compost made on the prems upon the meadow land (except what is made during the last year of the tenancy, which shall be left in the usual dung or midden stead, free of charge, and which the landlord may cart or take away at any time during the last five months of the tenancy). To put at his own cost two tons of lime on the meadow or pasture land in each year if directed by the landlord. To put at his own cost three tons of lime on every acre of pasture land turned up or ploughed.

LXXXVIII.

LEASE *of a* FARM *and Cottages in* YORKSHIRE.

THIS INDRE made &c., between A. B., of &c. (hrnftr called "the landlord") of the one part, and C. D., of &c. (hrnftr called "the tenant") of the other part, WITNESSETH that the landlord hby demises unto the tenant his exors, admors and assns, ALL [*Insert description of farm with cottages*]. TOGETHER with the appurtenances thto belonging, RESERVING unto the landlord, his heirs and assigns, all timber and other trees which during the term hby created may grow

on the sd premes, and all stone and other minerals in or
under the sd premes; AND the right at all times to enter
and be upon the sd prems to mark, peel, cut down, lop, grub
up, dispose of, and carry away the sd timber and other trees,
and to search for, get, dig for, dispose of and remove the sd
stone and other minerals; AND the right at all times to
enter and be upon the sd prems to inspect the same, and to
plant and prune trees, and alter, build and make fences and
drains therein, and make improvements therein; AND ALSO
RESERVING unto the landlord, his hrs and assns, all the game
which during the sd term may be in or upon the sd prems,
with exclusive liberty for him and them, and his and their
gamekeepers, and all other persons by his and their permission at all times to hunt, course, shoot in or upon the
prems; To HOLD the sd prems (reserving as afsd) unto the
tenant, his exors, admors and assigns, for the term of five
years, as to the land from the 2nd day of February, 1880,
and as to the buildings hby demised from the 1st day of
May, 1880: YIELDING AND PAYING therefor unto the landlord, his hrs or assns, during the sd term the yearly rent of
£150 without deduction, payable by equal half-yearly payment, on the [dates], in every year, the first of such payments being due on the [date], and the last payment to be
made in advance on the [date] next preceding the expiration of the sd term: AND ALSO YIELDING AND PAYING in
like manner at the times afsd, the additional yearly rent of
£5 for every £100, and so in proportion for any less sum
which during the sd term shall be expended by the landlord,
his hrs or assns, with the consent of the tenant, his exors,
admors, or assns, in draining, fencing and enclosing the sd
prems or any part thof, or erecting buildings thon, or orwise
improving the same, such additional rent to commence and
be computed from such one of the sd half-yearly days of
payment as shall immediately precede the period at which
such outlay shall be made, and the first payment thereof to
be made on such one of the same half-yearly days of payment, as shall first happen after such outlay, and to continue
payable during the residue of the sd term, and the last pay-

ment to be made in advance on the sd [*date*] next preceding
the expiration of the sd term; AND ALSO YIELDING AND
PAYING in the event of and immediately upon the sd term,
being determined by re-entry under the proviso hrnftr contained a proportionate part of the sd several rents for the
fraction of the current half-year up to the day of such re-
entry; [AND ALSO YIELDING AND PAYING unto the landlord,
his hrs or assns, in addition to the rent afsd, £10 for every
acre of pasture land hby demised which shall be mown
contrary to the covts in that behalf hrnftr contd, and £10
for every acre of the land hby demised, which shall be
ploughed, graven or turned up, or sown with corn or other
grain, or planted with esculent roots contrary to the covts in
that behalf hrnftr contained, and £5 for every ordinary cartload of hay, grass, clover, straw, turnips, potatoes, or other
esculent roots, fodder bedding, manure, or compost, which
shall not be eaten, consumed, laid, spread, bestowed and spent
in accordance with the covts in that behalf hrnftr contd, and
so in proportion for any less quantity than an acre or a cartload, such last-mentd additional rents resply to commence
and be payable immediately after the same shall resply be
incurred, and be recoverable by distraint as rent in arrear];
AND the tenant doth hby for himself, his hrs, exors, admors
and assns, covt with the landlord, his hrs and assns, that he
the tenant, his exors, admors or assns, during the sd term,
will pay the rents hby reserved on the days and in manner
afrsd, AND will pay the land tax and all rates, taxes, tithes,
tithe composition, lords' rents and other outgoings whatsoever (except property tax) which may become payable in
respect of the sd prems or the occupon thof; AND will keep
the sd prems, with all additions thereto and improvements
thrin, in good condon and complete repair; AND will preserve
all game upon or in the sd prems exclusively for the landlord, his hrs and assns, and all persons authorized by him or
them, and will warn off the sd prems all trespassers thereupon
in pursuit of game, and immediately upon the discovery of
each such trespass inform the landlord, his hrs and assns,
thof, and of the name and address of each person committing

such trespass, so far as the same can be ascertained, and will permit the landlord, his hrs or assns, to bring any action or other proceeding in the name of the tenant, his exors, adms, or assns, against any person or persons who may trespass upon the sd prems in pursuit of game, [AND will not without the written consent of the landlord, his hrs or assns, and then only upon the terms and subject to the condons expressed in such consent, assign, underlet or part with the posson of any of the sd prems (except the said cottages) or the winter eatage theof, or any part thof, or mow any of the pasture land hby demised, or plough, grave, or turn up, or sow with corn or other grain, or plant with esculent roots, any of the said closes called [*insert names of permanent pastures*]; AND will, after taking a white crop from any of the lands hby demised, and before taking another white crop therefrom, effectually clean and sufficiently manure the same lands and take a grass crop therefrom; AND will mow or destroy in every year all docks and thistles and such like weeds on the sd prems before the same grow to seed; AND ALSO will in all other respects cultivate, manure and manage the lands hby demised in a good and husbandlike manner, and according to the most improved system of agriculture, keeping them in good heart and condition and in a perfectly clean state; AND will observe every reasonable direction in writing as to the mode of cultivation, manuring, and management to be given by the landlord, his hrs or assns, or his or their agent or steward; AND will not without the written consent of the landlord, his hrs or assns, and then only upon the terms and subject to the condns expressed in such consent, sell, give, exchange or carry away, or suffer to be sold, given, exchanged or carried away from the sd prems, or advertise or offer or suffer to be advertised or offered for sale, exchange or gift (except upon the terms that they shall be consumed on the sd prems) any hay, grass, clover, straw, turnips, potatoes or other esculent roots, fodder or bedding, grown, gathered or brought on the sd prems, or any manure or compost arising from the same hay, grass, clover, straw, turnips, potatoes, or other esculent roots, fodder or bedding, or otherwise made or gathered on the sd prems, but will eat, spend, and consume on the sd prems the same hay, grass, clover, straw, turnips, potatoes and other esculent roots, fodder and bedding, and lay, spread, bestow, and consume the same manure and compost upon some part of the meadow land hby demised at proper times and in a husband-like manner; AND will at the expiron or sooner determon of the sd term leave in the yards of the sd prems for the use of the landlord, his hrs or assns, or his or their incoming tenant, and without compenson therefor, all such of the sd manure and compost, both liquid and solid, as shall not have been laid and spread pursuant to the covt in that behalf hrnbfre contd, and yield up the sd prems with all additions thereto and improvements thron in such good condon and complete repair, and in fair and proper order as afrsd, unto the landlord, his hrs or assns, without receiving or requiring or being entitled to any valuation, allowance, remuneration, or compenson for tenant-right, tillage, labour, or improvements in or on or additions (if any) to the sd prems : PROVIDED ALWAYS that if and whenever any part of the rents hrnbfre reserved shall be in arrear for twenty-one days, whether the same shall have been legally demanded or not, or if and whenever the tenant, his exors, admors, or assns, shall be adjudicated bankrupt, or take proceedings for liquidation by arrangement or composition, or compound with his creditors, or any execution shall be levied upon him or his goods or chattels, or upon the sd prems, or if and whenever any breach shall be made in any of the covts by the tenant condons and agrects hrin contd, the landlord, his hrs or assns, may re-enter upon the sd prems and repossess and hold the same as if this demise had not been made; AND IT IS HEREBY AGREED that the landlord, his hrs or assns, or his or their incoming tenant, may at any time after the month of December next preceding the expiron or determon of the sd term enter upon the sd prems and carry, cart, lead, spread and bestow into and upon the lands hby demised any dung, compost, or manure, and plough and do all other acts of husbandry for preparing the crops of the succeeding year ;

AND that if during the sd term the landlord, his hrs or assns, shall distrain upon the sd prems in order to obtain payment of the rents hby reserved, or any part or parts thof, he or they may sell and dispose of any crops distrained upon to be consumed on the prems, and for this purpose the person or persons purchasing the same shall have reasonable use and occupancy of the demised farm buildings for three calendar months next following the time of such sale : [PRO-VIDED ALSO that the land'ord, his hrs or assns, may at any time during the sd term resume possession of any part or parts of the sd prems which may be required for planting, building, change of occupation, or any other purpose, making compenson in respect thrf to the tenant, his exors, admors, or assns, either by payment of a sum in gross, or by a reduction of rent, or by a demise of other lands in lieu of what may be so taken, and that in case posson of any part or parts of the sd prems shall be so resumed the provons hrin contd with reference to the whole of the sd prems shall, so far as the same may be applicable, continue in force and apply to such part of the same as shall be left in the possession of the tenant, his exors, admrs, or assns in the same manner as if such part only had originally been included herein, and the reduced rent or rents (if any) had been herein inserted instead of the principal rent hby reserved ;] [1] AND the land-

---

[1] Instead of this clause the following may be used :—

PROVISO in Lease requiring LESSEE TO GIVE UP any PART of demised premises ON NOTICE from Lessor.

[PROVIDED always, and it is hby agreed, that in case the sd [lessor], his hrs or assns, shall at any time during the sd term be desirous of having any part, not exceeding [four] acres, of the sd pieces of land hby demised delivered up to him or them, and of such his or their desire shall give three calr months' notice in writing to the sd [lessee], his exors, admors or assns, at his or their last or usual place of abode, or upon the sd demised premises, then at the expiron of such notice the sd [lessee], his exors, admors, or assns, will yield and surrender such part or parts of the sd piece of land as shall be mentd in such notice as afsd, the sd [lessor], his hrs or assns, paying to the sd [lessee], his exors, admors, or assns, a reasonable compenson in respect of the moys which may have been laid out by the sd [lessee], his exors, admors, or assns, in improving the condon of so much of the sd land as shall be so given up, and thenceforth the rent reserved

lord doth hby for himself, his hrs and assns, covt with the tenant, his exrs, adms, and assns, that he or they paying the rent hby reserved, and performing and observing the several covts by the tenant hrnbfre contd may peaceably hold and enjoy the sd prems during the sd term, without any interruption by the landlord, his hrs or assns, or any person lawfully claiming through or in trust for them, or any of them ; [PROVIDED ALWAYS that if any dispute, question, difference, or controversy shall arise between the sd parties hereto, or their respive hrs, exors, admors, or assns, or any of them, touching these presents, or any clause, matter, or thing hrin contd, or the construction hrof, or anything to be done under any of the provisions hrin contd, or any matter in any way connected with these presents or the operation herof, or the rights, duties, or liabilities of either party in connection with the prems, then and in every such case the matter in difference shall be referred to two arbitrators or their umpire, pursuant to and so as with regard to the mode and consequences of the reference and in all other respects to conform to the provons in that behalf contained in the Common Law Procedure Act, 1854, or any now subsisting or future statutory modification thereof :] PROVIDED ALWAYS, and it is hereby agreed and declared that the Agricultural Holdings (England) Act, 1875, shall not nor shall any provision thereof apply to the contract of tenancy by these presents made, confirmed, or perfected.

IN WITNESS, &c.

LXXXIX.

BUILDING LEASE *with usual Clauses and* RESERVATION *of* WATER *in a Well.*

THIS INDRE, made &c., between A. B. of the one part, and C. D. of the other part : WITNESSETH, that, in conson of the

---

by this indre shall be reduced at the rate of £2 for each acre (and so in proportion for a less quantity than an acre), of the sd land that may be so given up.]

rent, covts, and condons hrnftr reserved and contd, the sd
A. B. doth hrby demise unto the sd C. D., his exors, admors,
and assns, ALL &c., situate at &c. ; and which plot or parcel
of land forms part of a piece of land called &c., and contains
in the whole by admeasurement   square yards or thr-
abouts ; and is more particularly delineated in the plan drawn
in the margin hrof, and thrn colrd pink, together with the
appurtenances to the same belonging, [except and reserved
out of this demise all mines, veins, beds, and seams of coal
and cannel, and all other minerals, with liberty for the sd
A. B., his hrs and assns, and his and their tenants, agents,
servants, workmen, and others, with his and their permission
and authority, to win, work, get, and carry away the same,
when and as he and they shall think proper ; and also to
erect engines and machinery, and make roads, and do all
such acts and exercise all such powers and privileges as
shall be necessary for the more profitable winning, working,
getting and carrying away of the sd mines and minerals,
when and as he and they shall think fit.   EXCEPT also and
reserved unto the sd A. B., his hrs and assns, and the occupier
and occupiers of the prems colrd green on the sd plan, full
and free liberty of ingress, egress, and regress, in, to, from,
and out of the sd pieces of land, colrd blue in the sd plan, to
take in common with the sd C. D., his exors, admors, and
assns, and his and their under-tenants of the prems hby demised, the water from the well therein sunk, and to sink any
other well or wells, and make any tank or reservoir in or
upon the sd pieces of land colrd blue, and to take and lay
down any pipes or aqueducts in and through any part or
parts of the prems hby demised, not being the site of any
building, for conveying the water therefrom in order to
supply with water any other messes of the sd A. B., his hrs
or assns ; and also, except and reserved unto the sd A. B.,
his hrs and assns, and the occupier and occupiers of the
prems colrd green as afsd, the free passage of water and soil
in, by and through the channels and drains belonging or to
be made upon or through the sd hby demised prems, or any
part thof,] To HOLD the prems hby demised with their

appurts unto the sd C. D., his exors, admors, and assns, from
the date hrof, for the term of ninety-nine years thence next
ensuing ; Yielding and paying therefor [*reservation of rent
as in Form LXXXIV., p.* 369].   And the sd. C. D. for himself, his hrs, exors, admors, and assns, doth hby covnt [*to pay
rent, rates, &c., as in Form LXXXIV., p.* 369].   AND ALSO,
that the sd C. D., his exors, admors, and assigns, will, at his
own cost, within two years from the date hrof, in a good
substantial and workmanlike manner, build and completely
finish, fit for habitation and use, upon the land hby demised,
one or more messe or messes, to be built with the best sound
material of all sorts, and will roof and cover in such messes
with good blue slate ; and also will fence off the land hby
demised, on the [north and east] sides thof resply, by a good
brick wall, six feet in height at the least, from other parts of
the land adjoining, and will make no door or other communication from the N. and E. sides of the prems hby demised
to the lands immediately adjoining or contiguous thto :
And such messe or messes, when so built as afsd, shall be
worth, to let to a tenant or tenants, by the year, not less
than double the amount of the yearly rent hby reserved :
and also that he tho sd A. B., his exors, admors, and assns,
will, as occasion shall require, during the sd term, well and
sufficiently repair, maintain, pave, empty, cleanse, amend,
and keep the sd prems, with the appurts, in such good and
substantial repair as is necessary for the occupon of a tenant
or tenants at rack rents ; and the sd prems, being in all
things repaired, maintained, paved, emptied, cleansed,
amended and kept as afsd, at the end or sooner determon
of the sd term will quietly yield up unto to the sd A. B.,
his hrs or assns, together with all chimney-pieces, windows,
doors, fastenings, water-closets, cisterns, partitions, fixed
presses, shelves, pipes, pumps, rails, locks and keys, and
all other things which at any time during the last seven
years of the sd term shall be fastened to the sd demised
premises and come within the denomination of fixtures :
[And also, that it shall be lawful for the sd A. B., his hrs
or assns, and any persons deputed by him or them, at any

reasonable hours, in the daytime, during such last seven years, to enter upon all and every the sd demised prems, and take a schedule or schedules of the same fixtures and things resply.] And also [*covenants to paint, as in Form LXXXIV., p.* 370]. [And also, that the sd C. D., his exors, admors, and assns, will, on demand, pay to the sd A. B., his hrs and assns, one-half the expense of making and forming an intended new street of ten yards wide, and now forming part of other land belonging to the sd A. B.; and also of making a covered drain or drains, from the front of the sd messe or messes, and leading from the common sewer: And shall bear the like propon of laying down and paving the sd street, so far as the same shall run co-extensively with the prems hby demised, such street, drain, and pavement to be made to the satisfaction of the surveyor for the time being of the sd A. B., his hrs or assns, and also will at his own cost, and to the satisfaction of the sd A. B., his hrs or assns, pave with good flagging stones, the footways to be made on the side of the sd intended new street as afsd before the fronts of the said messes, and lay down edging-stones to the afrsd foot-paths, resply, so far as such foot-paths run co-extensively with the hby demised prems, and also will during the sd term repair and keep in repair the whole of the sd foot-paths in the front of the sd mess or messes so far as the same resply run co-extensively with the sd prems; and also will bear, pay, and discharge one-half of the expenses of making, supporting, repairing, and amending all party walls and gutters, which during the sd term shall belong to the sd prems, or which shall be used in common by the sd C. D., his exors, admors, or assns, and the takers or occupiers of the adjoining or contiguous prems resply.] And, moreover, that it shall be lawful for the sd A. B. [*to enter, view, and give notice to repair, as in Form LXXXIV., p.* 370.] [And that the sd C. D., his exors, admors, and assns, shall not exercise, or carry on, or permit or suffer to be exercised or carried on, upon any part of the prems hby demised, the trade of a boiler of horse flesh, slaughterman, soap maker or boiler, melter of tallow, distiller, brewer, victualler, beer shop or alehouse keeper, blacksmith, boiler maker, or any other noisome, dangerous, or offensive trade or business whatsoever, without the express consent in writing of the sd A. B., his hrs or assns; nor do, or cause or knowingly suffer to be done, any act or thing on the sd demised prems which may grow to the annoyance, damage, or disturbance of the sd A. B., his hrs or assns, or his or their tenant or tenants.] AND ALSO [*to insure and rebuild, as in Form LXXXIV., p.* 370.] And that in case the sd C. D., his exors, admors, or assns, shall sell, assn, or underlet the land hby demised, or any part thof, or part with this indre, then and in any or either of the sd cases he or they will within twenty-one days thftr deliver a true copy of such assignment, under-lease, or other assce to the sd A. B., his hrs or assns; [and that the sd C. D, his exors, admors, or assns, shall not during the last seven years of the sd term sell, assn, demise, or make over or part with the sd prems or any part thereof, for all or any part of the residue of the sd term, without the consent in writing of the sd A. B., his hrs or assns]: PRO-VIDED ALWAYS [*power of re-entry on non-payment of rent or breach of covt, as in Form LXXXIV., p* 371]. AND THE SD A. B. [*covenant for quiet enjoyment, as in Form LXXXIV., p.* 371].

IN WITNESS, &c.

LICENCES.

XC.

LICENCE *by Lessor to* ASSIGN *Lease.*

WHAS by indre dated &c., and made between the undersigned A. B. of the one part, and C. D. of the other part,
the said A. B. did demise to the said C. D. certain prems
situate in the parish of X., in the county of Y., for the
term and at the yearly rent thin mentd, and the sd C. D.
theby covtd that he would not assign, demise, underlet, or
orwise part with the posson of the sd prems without the
licence in writing of the sd A. B.; Now the sd A. B. doth
hby give license unto the sd C. D. to assign the sd lease and
all his este and interest therein, unto Y. Z., of &c.[1]

XCI.

LICENCE *by Lessor to Lessee to permit* SALE BY AUCTION *on Premises.*

WHAS by indre of lease dated the &c., made between the
undersigned S. B. of the one part, and J. H. of the other
part, the sd S. B. demised the prems thin mentd for the
term and at the yearly rent thin mentd; and the sd J. H.
thby covenanted that he would not permit or suffer any
auction or sale to be made in or upon the sd prems without
the licence in writing of the sd S. B.: Now the sd S. B.
doth hby give full licence unto the sd J. H. to make sale by

---

[1] Lord St. Leonards' Act (22 & 23 Vict. c. 35), § 1, enacts, that such a
licence as the above shall only extend to the particular assignment mentioned in the licence.

auction of the sd lease and also of his present household goods, furniture and effects in and upon the sd prems within [six] weeks from the date hrof; nevertheless the licence hby given shall not extend to permit the sd J. H. to make any future sale in or upon the sd demised prms without the like licence of the sd S. B., his exors, admors, and assns.

Dated &c.

MEMORIALS.

XCII.

MEMORIAL *of a* CONVEYANCE.[1]

B.   ⎫ A MEMORIAL to be registered of   .
to   ⎬   An Indenture, bearing date the [*date*], made be-
D.   ⎭ tween [*parties verbatim as in deed*] : Whereby the sd
A. B. did grant unto the sd C. D. ALL [*parcels verbatim*],
with their rights, easements, and appurts, To HOLD the
same unto and to the use of the sd C. D., his hrs and assns,[2]
and which sd indre, as to the execution thof by the sd A. B.
is witnessed by E. F. of &c., and as to the execution thof by
the sd C. D. is witnessed by G. H. of &c., and the same is
hereby required to be registered by the sd C. D.

As witness his hand and seal.   (L.S.)

Signed and sealed in the presence of

[*Two witnesses.*]

---

[1] If the deed and memorial are executed in the country, the following
memorandum should be indorsed :—

I hereby certify that the within-named E. F. made oath of the signing
and sealing of this memorial, and of the due execution of the deed to
which it refers, before me,

K. L., a Commissioner to administer Oaths in the
Supreme Court of Judicature in England.

[2] N.B.—If the conveyance is to the ordinary uses to bar dower, then,
instead of the above limitation, it will be as follows : " To uses for the
benefit of the said C. D. his heirs and assigns, being the ordinary uses to
bar dower."

XCIII.

MEMORIAL *of an* ASSIGNMENT.

B.
to
D.

A MEMORIAL to be registered of   .
An Indre, bearing date &c., made between [*parties verbatim as in deed*]: After reciting an indre of lease whereby [*parcels from the lease as set out in the recital of that document in the assignment*] were demised to A. B., it was by the memoralising indre witnessed, that the sd A. B. did assign unto the sd C. D. ALL [*parcels verbatim from the body of the assignment*] with their rights, easements, and appurts, To HOLD unto the sd C. D., his exors, admors, and assns, for the remainder of a term of ninety-nine years created by the sd indre of lease, subject to the pmnt of the rent reserved by and to the performance of the condons contd in the same indre, which sd indre as to the execution thof by the sd A. B. is witnessed by E. F. of &c., and as to the execution thof by the sd C. D. is witnessed by G. H. of &c., and the same is hby required to be registered by the sd C. D.

As witness his hand and seal.   (L.S.)
Signed and sealed in the presence of
[*Two witnesses.*]

XCIV.

MEMORIAL *of a* MORTGAGE.

B.
to
D.

A MEMORIAL to be registered of   .
An Indre, bearing date &c., made between [*&c., as in Form XCII., down to end of habendum*], subject to a proviso for re-conveyance of the said hereditaments on payment by the sd A. B., his hrs, exors, or admors, unto the sd C. D., his exors, admors, or assns, of the sum of £—— with interest, after the rate, on the day, and in the manner therein mentioned, which sd Indre [*&c., as in Form XCII.*]

XCV.

MEMORIAL *of a* LEASE.

B.   )   A MEMORIAL to be registered of   .
to   }   An Indre of lease, bearing date &c., made between
D.   )   A. B., of &c., of the one part, and C. D., of &c., of
the other part: Whereby all [*insert parcels from the lease
verbatim*], with their rights, members, and appurtenances,
were demised by the sd A. B. to the sd C. B. for twenty-one
years, and which sd indre, as to the execution thereof by the
sd A. B., is witnessed by E. F., of &c., and the same is
required to be registered by the sd A. B.

AS WITNESS, &c.   (L.S.)

XCVI.

MEMORIAL *of an* INDORSED DEED.

A MEMORIAL to be registered of   .

An Indre, dated the &c. (indorsed on an indre, dated
the   day of   , 18   , made between A. B., of &c.,
of the one part, and C. D., of &c., of the other part: A
memorial whereof was registered on the   day of
18   , B., No.   ) The indre, of which this is a memorial, is
made between the therein within-named C. D. of the one
part, and E. F. of &c., of the other part: Whereby, for the
considerations therein mentioned, the sd C. D. did assign
unto the sd E. F. [all and singular the messuages or tenements and other hereditaments comprised in and demised by
the therein within-written indre with the appurtenances]:
And which premises are in the therein within-written indre
described to be situate in the parish of X., in the county of
Middlesex. To hold [*&c., as in previous Forms*].

XCVII.

MORTGAGE *of* FREEHOLD HOUSES *to one or several Mortgagees.*

THIS INDRE, made &c., between A. B., of &c., of the one part, and C. D., of &c., [*or* C. D., E. F., and G. H., of &c.] of the other part: Whas the sd A. B. is seised in fee of the hdts hrnftr described and granted; and whas the sd C. D. has [*or* C. D., E. F. and G. H., have] agreed to lend the sd A. B. £200 [out of money belonging to them on a joint account]¹ on having the repayment of the same with int secured as hrnfter appears: NOW THIS INDRE WITNESSETH, that in conson of [£200] to the sd A. B. pd by the sd C. D. [*or* C. D., E. F., and G. H.], the rect whof the sd A. B. hby acknges, the sd A. B. hby for himself, his hrs, exors, and admors, covts with the sd C. D., his [*or* with the sd C. D., E. F., and G. H. their] exors and admors, that the sd A. B., his hrs, exors, or admors will, on the [*six months from date of mortgage*] pay to the sd C. D., his exors, admors, or assns [*or* to the said C. D. and E. F., or the survors or survor of them, or the exors or admors of such survor, their or his assns] (hinftr called the mtgees) the sum of [£200] with int for the same in the meantime at the rate of £5 per cent. per ann, and in case the whole of the same sum shall not then be paid, will thenceforth pay to the mtgees int for the same sum or for so much thof as for the time being shall remain unpaid at the rate afsd by equal halfyearly payments on every [*date*] and [*date*]: AND THIS INDRE ALSO WITNESSETH that in conson of the prems the sd A. B. hby grants unto the sd C. D., his hrs and assns [*or* the sd C. D., E. F.,

---

¹ These words should be inserted where the mortgagees are trustees.

and G. H., their hrs and assns], all those messuages situate and being Nos. 2 and 4, X. Street, in the city of London, togr with all easements and appurtenances in fact or by reputation thereto belonging, To HOLD the prems unto and to the use of the sd C. D., his hrs and assns [*or* the sd C. D., E. F., and G. H., their hrs and assns]: PROVIDED ALWAYS, that if the sd A. B., his hrs, exors, admors or assns, shall pay unto the mtgees the sum of [£200] with int for the same in the meantime at 5 per cent. per ann, on the [*date*], then the mtgees will, upon the request and at the cost of the sd A. B., his hrs, exors, admors or assns, reassure the prems hby assured to the use of the sd A. B., his hrs and assns, or as he or they shall direct [free from incumbs by the mtgees]: AND IT IS HBY declared that it shall be lawful for the mtgees at any time after the sd [*date fixed for repayment*], without any further consent on the part of any pson, to sell the prems for the time being comprised in this secy togr or in parcels, and eir by public auction or private contract, with power upon any such sale to make any stipulons which the mtgees shall deem proper, and also with power to buy in or rescind any contract for sale, and resell without being responsible for loss occasioned thby, and for the ppses afsd, or any of them, to execute and do all such assces and things as they shall think fit: [And on any sale under this power by any pson not having the legal este in the prems sold, the person in whom such legal este shall be vested shall assure the same as the pson making such sale shall direct:] Provided always, that the sd power of sale shall not be exercised unless and until default shall have been made in pmt at the time hrnbfre appointed for pmt thof of some peal moy or int hby secured, and the mtgees shall have given a notice in writing to the sd A. B., his hrs, exors, admors or assns, requiring him or them to pay off the moys for the time being owing on this secy, or left a notice in writing to that effect at or upon some part of the sd prems, and default shall have been made in pmt of such moys, or some part thof, for six calendar months from the time of giving or leaving such notice, as the case may be; but no purchaser at any such sale shall be concerned to inquire whether such notice has been given, or whether such default as afsd has been made, or whether any moy remains on this secy, or into the regularity or propriety of such sale : [And notwithstanding any irregularity or impropriety in such sale the same shall, so far as regards the purchaser, be valid] : And it is hby further agreed and declared, that the pson or psons exercising the sd power of sale shall, out of the proceeds thof, in the first place pay or retain all the costs and expenses incurred in or about such sale, or orwise in respect of the prems, and in the next place apply such proceeds in or towards satisfon of the moys owing on this secy, and pay the surplus (if any) unto the pson who immedly before such sale was entitled to the equity of redon in the prems sold. [And that the powers afsd may be exercised by any pson entitled to give a discharge for the pchemoy hby secured, and that no pson exercising the same shall be liable for involuntary loss thby incurred.] AND THE SD A. B. for himself, his hrs, exors and admors, hby covts with the mtgees that the sd A. B. has power to assre the sd prems in manner afsd free from incumbs ; and that all the prems may be quietly entered into, held, and enjoyed by the sd C. D., his hrs and assns, without interruption. And that the sd A. B. and every other pson having any este or int in the prems, will at all times (at the cost of the sd A. B., his hrs, exors or admors, until foreclosure or sale, and afterwards of the pson requiring the same) execute and do every such assrce and thing for more perfectly assuring the sd prems to the use afsd, as by the mtgees shall be reasonably required, and also that the sd A. B., his hrs, exors, admors, or assns will, so long as any money shall remain on this secy, keep the sd messes and bldgs insured in some respectable office in London or Westminster against loss or damage by fire in the sum of £250 at the least, and punctually pay all premiums and sums of moy necessary for such ppose, and will on demand deliver to the mtgees the policy or policies of such insurance, and the receipt for every such pmt ; and that if default shall be made in keeping the said prems so insured, the mtgees may keep insured the same sd prems in any sum not exceeding £250 ; and that the sd A. B., his exors, admors, or assns, will repay to the mtgees every sum of moy expended for that ppose by him or them, with int thron at the rate afsd, from the time of the same resply having been so expended, and that until such repayment the same shall be a charge upon the prems hby assured.

In witness, &c.

XCVIII.

MORTGAGE *of* FREEHOLDS—*Short Form adopting the Statutory Powers.*

This Indre made &c., between A. B., of &c., of the one part, and C. D., of &c., of the other part, WITNESSETH that in conson of the sum [*continue covenant to pay principal and interest, as in Form XCVII., p.* 393.]

And this Indre also witnesseth that in conson of the prems the sd A. B. grants to the sd C. D. and his hrs ALL THAT [*parcels as in a conveyance*] To hold the prems unto and to the use of the sd C. D. his hrs and ass [subject to the provo next hrnftr contd.]

PROVIDED ALWAYS [*proviso for redemption, as in Form XCVII., p.* 394.]

PROVIDED ALSO, that the powers given to mtgees by the Act 23 & 24 Vict. c. 145, shall apply to this secy except that the power of sale may, subject to the provons of s. 13 of the sd Act, be exercised at any time after the [*date* [1]] AND THE SAID A. B. [*covenants for title, as in Form XCVII., p.* 395.]

In witness, &c.

[1] This date is usually six months from the date of the mortgage.

XCIX.

Conditional Surrender *of Copyholds by way of* Mortgage.

The Manor of X. in the county of Y.

Be it remembered, that out of court on the day of 18 , A. B., of &c. (one of the customary tenants of the sd manor) came before C. D., gentleman, steward of the sd manor, and in conson of £—— to the sd A. B. pd by E. F. of &c., did surrender by the rod into the hands of the lord of the sd manor, by the acceptance of the sd steward, according to the custom of the sd manor, ALL [*parcels*], together with all [trees, hedges, ditches, fences, ways, waters, watercourses, lights, easements, privileges, fixtures], rights, members and appurts to the sd hdts belonging, To the use of the sd E. F., his hrs and assns, at the will of the lord, according to the custom of the sd manor, by the rents, customs and services therefor due and of right accustomed : Provided always, that if the s l A. B., his hrs, exors, admors, or assns, shall pay or cause to be pd to the sd E. F., his exors, admors, or assns, the sum of £—— together with int for the same at the rate of £5 per cent. per annum on [*date*], then this surrender shall be void, but otherwise shall remain in full force and virtue.

Taken and accepted the day and year above written by me,

C. D., *Steward of the said manor.*

————

C.

Deed *of* Covenant *to accompany conditional* Surrender *of* Copyhold.

This Indre, made &c., between A. B., of &c., of the one part, and E. F., of &c., of the other part : Whas the sd A. B. did out of court, immediately before the excon hrof, in conson of of £—— to him pd by the sd E. F., surrender into the hands of the lord of the manor of X., in the county of Y., by his steward, according to the custom of the sd manor, ALL [*parcels*], with their rights, easements, and appurts, to the use of the sd E. F., his hrs and assns, by and under the rents, fines, heriots, suits and services therefor due and of right accustomed, but subject to a condon for making void the same on pmnt by the sd A. B., his hrs, exors, admors, or assns, unto the sd E. F., his exors, admors, or assns, of £——, with int thron at £5 per cent. per ann, on [*date*] ; And whas on the treaty for the sd advance it was agreed that the sd A. B. should execute these presents : NOW THIS INDRE WITNESSETH, that, in conson of the prems, he the sd A. B. doth hby for himself, his hrs, exors, and admors, covt with the sd E. F., his exors and admors, that he the sd A. B., his exors or admors, will pay [*covenant for payment of principal and interest, as in Form XCVII., p.* 393. AND IT IS HBY DECLARED that it shall be lawful [*power of sale with ancillary clauses down to and including trusts of purchase-money, as in Form XCVII., p.* 394.] AND THE SD A. B. doth hby for himself, his hrs, exors, and admors, covt with the sd E. F., his hrs and assns, that he the sd A. B. had at the time of making the sd surrender power to surrender the hdts therein comprised to the use of the sd E. F., his hrs and assns, according to the custom of the sd manor and in manner afsd, free from incumbrances (except the rents, fines, heriots, suits and services therefor due and of right accustomed); [*Further covenants for title, as in Form XCVII., p.* 395, *including covenant for further assurance*], according to the custom of the sd manor, and subject and in manner aforesaid, as by him or them shall be reasonably required.

IN WITNESS, &c.

CI.

WARRANT *to enter* SATISFACTION *on Conditional Surrender.*

I, A. B., of &c., do authorize and require you or your lawful deputy for the time being to enter full satisfaction and discharge on the court rolls of the manor of X. on and for a conditional surrender, dated &c., made by C. D., of &c., of certain hdts in the sd surrender described, to the use of me, my hrs and assns, for securing to me the sum of £   in manner therein mentd.

Dated, &c.   A. B.

To the steward of the manor of X.

CII.

MORTGAGE *of* LEASEHOLDS *for a Sum certain by* DEMISE.

THIS INDRE [*date*] between A. B , of &c., of the one part, and C. D., of &c., of the other part: Whas by an indre, dated &c., and made between [*lessor*] of the one part, and [*lessee*] of the other part, ALL [*copy parcels from lease verbatim*], with the appurts thrto belonging, were demised unto the sd [*lessee*], his exors, admors, and assns, from [*date*], for the term of   years, at the yearly rent of £——, and subject to the covts and agreets thrn contd ; And whas by divers mesne assmts, and ultimately by an indre, dated &c., and made between X. Y. of the one part, and the sd A. B. of the other part, the prems comprised in the sd lease became vested in the sd A. B., his exors, admors, and assns, for all the residue of the sd term, subject to the sd rent, covts, and agreets ; and whas the sd C. D. has agreed to advance the sd A. B. £500 on having the same with int secured in manner hrnftr appearing :

NOW THIS INDRE WITNETH, that, in conson of £500 sterling on the exon hrof pd by the sd C. D. to the sd A. B., the receipt whof the sd A. B. hby ackndges [*covenant by A. B. to pay principal and interest, as in Form XCVII., p. 393*].

AND THIS INDRE ALSO WITNETH that for the conson afsd the sd A. B. hby demises to the sd C. D., his exors, admors, and assns, all the prems comprised in and demised by the sd indre of lease with the easements and appurts thrto belonging or enjoyed thrwth To HOLD the sd prems with their appurts, unto the sd C. D., his exors, admors, and assns, for the remainder of the sd term of   years granted by the sd indre of lease, except the last ten days thereof.

PROVIDED ALWAYS, that if the sd A. B., his exors, admors, or assns, shall on or before the [*date*] next pay to the sd C. D., his exors, admors, or assns, the sum of £500, with int for the same in the meantime, after the rate of £5 per cent. per ann, then the sd C. D., his exors, admors, or assns, will thrpon, at the request and cost of the sd A. B., his exors, admors, or assns, surrender the sd prems unto the sd A. B., his exors, admors, or assns.

AND IT IS HBY DECLARED [*power of sale as in Form XCVII., p. 394, including power to execute assurances and clause as to assurance of legal estate.*] And that after any sale under the afsd power the sd A. B., his exors, admors, and assns, shall stand possed of the last ten days of the sd term upon trust for the pchr of the prems sold ; And shall be a tre e or trees throf for such pchr within the Trustee Acts, 1850 and 1852. PROVIDED ALWAYS [*powers not be exercised until after default and notice, but purchaser need not inquire, as in Form XCVII., p. 394.*] AND IT IS HBY declared [*trusts of proceeds of sale, as in Form XCVII., p. 395*]. And the said A. B., for himself, his hrs, exors, and admors, hby covts with the sd C. D., his exors and admors, that the rent and lessee's covts in and by the sd indre of lease resply reserved and coutd have been paid, observed, and performed up to the date hrof; and that the sd A. B. has power to demise the prems unto the sd C. D., his exors, admors, and assns, in manner afsd free from incumbs; and that the same may be quietly entered into, held, and enjoyed by the sd C. D., his exors, admors, and assns, without interruption; And that the sd A. B. and all psons claiming any estate or interest in the prems will (at the cost until foreclosure of the sd A. B., his exors, admors, or assns, and afterwards of the person requiring the same) do and execute every such assurance and thing for better assuring the prems unto the sd C. D., his exors, admors, and assigns, for the residue of the term hby demised as he or they shall require; and that the sd A. B., his exors, admors, or assns will so long as any money shall remain on this secy pay, perform, and observe the rents, lessee's covts (and particularly the covt for insurance against loss or damage by fire) in and by the sd indre of lease reserved and contd, and keep the sd C. D., his exors, admors, and assns, indemnified against all claims and actions in respect of the nonpayment or nonperformance of the same resply; and will at the request of the sd C. D., his exors, admors, or assns, produce to him or them the rect for the premiums payable on such insurance for the then current year. And that if default shall be made in keeping the prems so insured the sd C. D., his exors, admors, and assns, may so insure or keep insured the same, and the moneys expended in so doing shall be repaid to the sd C. D., his exors, admors, or assns, by the sd A. B., his exors, admors, or assns, on demand, and shall until repaid be a charge upon the prems.

IN WITNESS, &c.

CIII.

MEMORANDUM OF DEPOSIT *of Deeds with Limited* BANKING COMPANY *to secure Balance of current Trade Account.*

MEMORANDUM that A. B. and C. D., both of &c, carrying on business in partnership under the style of and hrinftr called B. & D., having recently opened a banking account with the X. Bank, Limited, hrinafter called "the company," E. F., of &c. [*or* the sd A. B., *or* the sd B. & D] has [*or* have] this day deposited with the Co the muniments of title mentioned in the schedule hereto, as a security to the Co for payment of all such sums of money as the Co has pd, advanced, or lent, or hrftr shall pay, advance, or lend, or has or shall become responsible or liable to pay to or for the use, or by the order or direction, or for the credit or on acct of the sd B. & D., or eir of them, eir alone or togr with any other pson or psons, eir as their or his partner or partners in trade or orwise. And also such further or other sums of money as at any time hrftr may be found due or owing from or payable by the said B. & D., or eir of them, eir alone or togr with any such other pson or psons as afsd, or from or by their or his hrs, exors, or ads, to the Co on any acct whatsoever. And also to indemnify and protect the Co at all times hrftr from and against all losses, costs, damages, claims, and demands which may arise or be incurred for or by reason or means or on acct or in respect of the non-pmnt of any notes, drafts, orders, cheques, bills of exchge, or other negotiable instruments which now are or hrftr may be held by the Co, or upon which the Co now is or hrftr may become liable, and upon which the sd B. & D. or eir of them, their or his hrs, exs, or ads, eir alone or together with any other pson or psons, are, is, or shall be liable antecedently to or in relief of the Co. And also to secure to the Co the costs and exps incurred or to be incurred in preparing, completing, and carrying into effect this memdum, or in obtaining or attempting to obtain the pymt of the moys for the time being owing to the Co by the sd B. & D., or eir of them, their or his hrs, exs, or ads, eir alone or together with any other pson or psons as afsd : PROVIDED ALWAYS, that the secy of the Co upon the sd muniments and the property to which the same relate is to be limited to the sum of £2000, nevertheless the sd secy is to be a continuing secy and to extend to cover the ultimate balance not exceeding the sd sum of £2000 due from the sd B. & D., or eir of them, their or his hrs, exs, or ads, eir alone or togr with any other pson or psons as afsd, after giving credit for any divd or divds, composition or compositions, which may be recd from them or him, or on account of their or his estates or estate, and that notwithstanding that the Co may have recd any moys from them or him after the date of this agreet. And that the sd secy is intended not to be discharged, varied, or affected by any change or changes which at any time or times hrftr may take place in the shareholders of the Co or in the partner or partners or trade or trades of the sd

B. & D. or eir of them. [And that the sd E. F. shall not be entitled to stand in the place of the Co or to use any remedies available in any action or other proceeding in order to obtain from or through the Co indemnification for the loss sustained by the sd E. F. in consequence of the giving of the sd secy, or to claim any other benefit or relief under the Mercantile Law Amendment Acts or any of them.] And it is hrby declared that the powers and incidents by the Act of 23 & 24 Vict. c. 145, § 2, conferred and made incident to mtges shall be exercisable and take effect in relation to the property comprised in the sd muniments, except that the power to sell (with all ancillary powers and provons) shall be exercisable by the Co or its assns at any time or times hftr without giving or affixing the notice mentioned in § 13 of the sd Act or any other notice whatever.

Dated, &c.

The SCHEDULE above referred to.

NOTICES.

CIV.

NOTICE *as to* STOCK *under R. S. C. Ord. XLVI.*[1]

To the X. Company [Limited].

TAKE NOTICE that the stock comprised in and now subject to the trusts of the [settlement] [*or* will] referred to in the affidavit to which this notice is annexed, consists of the following (that is to say) [*here specify the stock*].

This notice is intended to stop the transfer of the stock only, and not the receipt of dividends [*or* the receipt of the dividends on the stock as well as the transfer of the stock].

(*Signed*)   A. B.

CV.

NOTICE *of* DISSOLUTION *of Partnership.*

NOTICE is hby given, that the partnership lately subsisting between us the undersigned A. B., C. D., and E. F., as merchants at X., in the county of Y., under the firm of A. & Co., was on the 31st day of December last dissolved by mutual consent, so far as regards the sd A. B., who on that day retired from the business; and that all debts due and owing to or by the late firm will be received and paid by the sd C. D. and E. F.

As witness our hands this [*date*].

(*Signed*) { A. B.
C. D.
E. F.

Witness, G. H.

[1] This Notice, and the Affidavit on p. 195, have the same operation as a Writ of Distringas formerly had. See R. S. C. Ord. XLVI., R. 26.

CVI.

NOTICE TO QUIT, *from Landlord to* TENANT.

To Mr. J. P., or whom else it may concern:

I hby give you notice, that I require you to quit and deliver up to me on or before the [*date*] the peaceable and quiet possession of all that messe or tenement, outbuildings, garden, and arable land, situate in the parish of E., in the county of M., which you now hold of me as tenant, or orwise that you deliver up the sd prems to me at the end of the year of your tenancy which shall expire next after the end of one half year from the dated hrof. Dated, &c.

Yours, &c., A. B.
[By C. D., his agent.]

CVII.

NOTICE TO QUIT, *and for* DOUBLE RENT.

To Mr. A. B., or whomsoever else it may concern:

I hby give you notice to quit and deliver up to me, or to the landlord for the time being, posson of the several pieces of land and hdts situate in the parish of X., in the county of Y., which you now hold as tenant from year to year, and which are more particularly described in the schedule hrto, on the [*date*], or at the end of the year of your tenancy which shall expire next after the end of one half-year from the date hrof, and on failure thof I shall require you to pay thenceforth double the former rent, or double the yearly value of the sd several pieces of land and hdts, according to the form of the statute in that case made and provided. Dated, &c.

Yours, &c.,
A. B.,
Solicitor and agent for the landlord or
landlords of the said prems.

The SCHEDULE above referred to.

[*Description of property.*]

CVIII.

Notice to Quit, *from Tenant to* Landlord.

To Mr. J. P., or whom else it may concern :

I hby give you notice that it is my intention to quit and deliver up to you on the [*date*], possession of all that messe or tenement, outbuildings, garden, and land, situate in the parish of E., in the county of M., which I now hold of you as tenant. Dated &c.,

Yours, &c.
A. B.

CIX.

Notice *to Lessee to* abate Nuisance.

To Mr. C. D., or whom else it may concern : Whas by indre dated, &c., and made between, &c., a piece of land with the messe and bdgs thon, situate in the parish of X., in the county of Y., was demised to you for the term of forty years, at the yearly rent of £60, and subject to the covts on your part to be observed and performed, and in the sd indre is contd a covt to the effect that you would not erect on the sd piece of land any new or additional erection or bldg, nor use, or exercise, or permit or suffer to be used or exercised in or upon the sd messe and prems thby demised, any trade or business without the consent in writing of the sd A. B., his hrs or assns : Now we hby give you notice, and require you within fourteen days from the date hrof, to take down the cart-shed and stable you have lately erected on the sd prems, contrary to the covt contd in the sd lease, and we also require you immedly to discontinue the trade or business of a greengrocer now carried on upon the sd prems by you or on your account, contrary to the sd covt in the sd lease; and we further give you notice, that the sd A. B. will enter upon the demised prems, and make void the above-mentd lease, if you disregard this notice, and do not observe and perform the covts on your part in the sd indre contd.

Dated, &c.,

M. and N.,

Solors for the above-named A. B.

CX.

NOTICE BY MORTGAGEE *to Tenant to* PAY RENT *to him.*

I HBY give you notice, that by an indre dated &c., made between &c., the house and prems at X. now in your occupation was mortgaged to me for securing £1000 and int, and the sd house and prems are now vested in me by virtue of the sd indre: And I require you to pay to me or to my authorized agent all rent now due and hrftr to become due in respect of the same prems. Dated, &c.,

To Mr. C. D.   [*Signed*]   A. B.

CXI.

NOTICE *by* SECOND MORTGAGEE *to First Mortgagee.*

I HBY give you notice, that by indre dated &c., made between A. B. of the one part, and me the undersigned C. D. of the other part, the hdts now in mortgage to you situate at X., were assured to me by the sd A. B. for securing the sum of £200 and int. Dated &c.

[*Signed*]   C. D.

To Mr. [*first mortgagee*].

CXII.

NOTICE *by* MORTGAGEE TO TRUSTEES *of Mortgage of* LEGACY.

To Messrs. G. H. and I. K.,

    Gentlemen,

      I hby give you notice that by an indre dated &c., and made between A. B., of &c., of the one part, and C. D., of &c.,

of the other part, the sd A. B. assnd unto the sd C. D., his exors, admors, and assns, the legacy or sum of £2000, and the stocks, funds, and securities upon which the same may be invested, and to which under the will of E. F., late of &c., deceased, the sd A. B. is absolutely entitled, subject to the life interest in the divds, int, and annual income thof of the sd testor's sister L. F. for her life, and which sd sum of £2000 is now invested in the names of you the sd G. H. and I. K., as the trees and exors of the sd will of the sd E. F. in the Three per Cent. Consolidated Annes, by way of mtge for securing to the said C. D., his exors, admors, and assns, the repmnt of the sum of £700, with int thron at the rate of £5 per cent. per annum.   Dated &c.,

Yours, &c.,

Y. Z.

Solr for the sd C. D.

CXIII.

NOTICE *of* SALE *by Mortgagee.*

To Mr. A. B. and whom else it may concern:

I hby request pmnt of the sum of £1000, with int thron, from [*date*], owing to me by virtue of the indre of mtge executed by you, dated &c.; and I hby give you notice, that unless the same be pd within three calr months from the delivery hrof, I shall proceed to a sale of the hdts in the sd indre comprised, in excon of the power thby vested in me. Dated &c.

CXIV.

Partnership Deed between two Traders, with usual Clauses.

This Indre, made &c., between A. B., of &c., of the one part, and C. D., of &c., of the other part: Whas the sd A. B. has for some time past carried on the business of &c., at X. street, Z., in the county of Y.; and whas the sd A. B. has agreed to admit the sd C. D. into ptshp in the sd business as from the [*date*], for the term and upon the condons hnftr contd; and whas upon the treaty for the sd ptshp it was agreed that the value of the stock in trade, plant, and materials used in carrying on the sd business should be taken at the sum of £5000, and that the sd C. D. should pay to the sd A. B. the sum of £2500 for the purchase of one moiety of the sd business, and the stock in trade, plant and materials used in carrying on the same; and whas the sd C. D. has immediately before the excon hrof pd to the sd A. B. the sd sum of £2500, as he doth hby acknge: Now this Indre witnesseth, that, in consideration of the prems, each of them the sd A. B. and C. D., as far as the covts and agreets hrnftr contd are to be observed or performed by him, his hrs, exors, or admors, doth hby covt with the other of them, in manner following; (that is to say,)

1. The sd A. B. and C. D. will be partners in the business of [*specify it*] for the term of seven years, from [*date*], if they shall so long live.

2. The firm of the ptshp shall be " A. B. & Co."

3. The business of the ptshp shall be carried on at Z., or at such other place or places as the partners shall hraftr determine.

4. The sd A. B. shall, when required by the sd C. D., at the expense of the ptshp, execute such assurance for vesting the prems where the ptshp business is carried on in the sd A. B. and C. D. jointly for the remainder of the term therein, subject to the payment of the rent and performance of the lessee's covts, as the said C. D. may require.

5. The sd C. D. shall be at liberty, if he shall think proper, to use and occupy the dwelling-house at No. 10, X. street aforesaid [in the same manner as he has for some time past used and occupied the same] for the residence of himself and his family, without paying any rent or taxes for the same ; and the rent of the houses and prems where the ptshp business shall be carried on, and all repairs, additions, and alterations of, to, in, or about the same, and all taxes, rates, assessments, payments for insurance and other outgoings whatsoever for or in respect of the same, and the salaries, wages, or maince of all clerks, travellers, workmen, servants, or apprentices who shall be employed in or about the business of the ptshp, and all charges and expenses which shall be incurred in or about the business of the ptshp, and all losses and damages which shall happen in or about the same, shall be paid out of the profits, or in case the same shall become deficient, then by the ptners out of their respve separate estates, in the proportions to which they are entitled to the profits of the ptshp.

6. The capital of the ptshp shall consist of the stock in trade, plant, and materials now in, upon, or belonging to the prems where the sd business is carried on, and also the lease of the sd prems, and of advances to be made by the ptners as hrnftr mentd.

7. Each ptner shall within one month from the date hrof advance to the ptshp the sum of £1000, and all future capital required for carrying on the sd business shall be advanced by the ptners in equal shares, and they shall be considered as creditors of the ptshp in respect of such advances, and shall be allowed interest for the same at the rate of £5 per cent. per annum.

8. The sd A. B. and C. D. shall at all times during the

ptshp diligently employ themselves in and about the business of the ptshp, and carry on, manage, and conduct the same for the greatest benefit and advantage of the ptshp.

9. Neither of the ptners shall either directly or indirectly engage in any trade, manufacture, or business, except upon the account and for the benefit and advantage of the ptshp, nor take any apprentice, or hire or dismiss any clerk, traveller, workman, or servant in the business of the ptshp without the consent of the other, nor go any journey for or on account of the ptshp or otherwise, without such consent, and if eir of them shall, at any time during the ptshp, go any such journey without such consent as afsd, he shall for such time as he shall be upon any such journey forfeit a proportionate part of his share in the profits of the ptshp, or the sum of £50, at the option of the other ptner.

10. Each of the ptners shall be just and faithful to the other and to the partnership in all dealings and transactions in or about the business of the ptshp, and shall give to the other a faithful and just account thof when and so often as the same shall be reasonably required, and shall at all times during the ptshp, upon any reasonable request of the other, inform him the other of all letters, accounts, writings and other things which shall come into his hands or knowledge in anywise touching or concerning the ptshp business.

11. Neither of the partners shall, without the consent in writing of the other, employ any of the moneys, goods or effects of the ptshp, or engage the credit thof, except upon the account and for the benefit of the ptshp; and in all cases where there shall be occasion to give any bond, note, bill, or other security, or sign any cheque for the payment of any money on account of the ptshp, the same shall be signed or executed by both partners [or in the name of the firm.]

12. Neither of the partners shall lend any of the moneys or deliver upon credit any of the goods of the ptshp to any person whom the other shall previously by notice in writing have forbidden him to trust; and in case either partner shall after such notice as afsd lend any money or deliver

upon credit any goods of the ptshp, the partner so doing shall pay to the ptshp the ready money amount or value of the money or goods which he shall so lend or deliver upon credit as afsd.

13. Neither partner shall, without the previous consent in writing of the other, enter into any bond or become bail, surety, or security, with or for any person, or subscribe any policy of insurance, nor do or willingly suffer to be done any thing whereby any property of the ptship may be seized, attached, extended, or taken in execution.

14. Each partner shall duly and punctually pay all debts now or hrftr during the ptshp owing from him; and shall keep the other and the property of the ptshp, indemnified against his private debts and engagements, and all actions and expenses on account thereof.

15. The partners shall keep proper books of account of all moneys received and paid, all contracts entered into, and all business transacted on account of the ptshp, and all other matters of which accounts are usually kept in similar businesses, which accounts, together with all deeds, securities for money, and papers belonging to the ptshp, shall be kept at the principal place where the sd business shall be carried on; and shall at all reasonable times be open to the inspection of both partners.

16. As soon as conveniently may be after the 31st of December in every year during the ptshp the partners shall make a full account in writing of all such goods as shall have been bought and sold in the business (in the first of such general accounts from the day of the commencement of the ptshp, and in each of such subsequent general accounts from the day of the last preceding account), and of all moneys, stock in trade, goods and effects, belonging or due, or owing to or by the ptshp, and of all the liabilities thof, and of all such matters and things as are usually comprehended in general accounts of the like nature taken by persons engaged in similar businesses, and cause such account to be written in two books, to be resply signed by the partners within one calr month after the time appointed for taking

thof resply ; and after such signature each of them shall take one of the sd books into his custody, and shall be bound by every such account, save that if any manifest error shall be found therein within twelve calr months after the same shall have been so signed, and shall be signified by cir of them to the other, then such error shall be rectified.

17. On the making up of every such yearly account all interest which shall be due to either partner for such sums of money as they shall resply advance to the ptshp, shall in the first place be deducted, and the clear profits shall be divided between them [in equal shares].

18. The sd A. B. shall be at liberty to draw out of the business any sum not exceeding £6 per week for his own use, and the sd C. D. shall be at liberty to draw any sum or sums not exceeding £5 per week for his own use, but in case at the end of the year it shall appear, upon making the general annual account hrnbfre directed to be made, that the nett profits of such year shall not have amounted to the aggregate sum drawn out by the partners, then each partner shall immediately after such general annual account shall have been made and settled, repay to the ptshp the difference between the amount of the sums which he shall actually have received in respect of such weekly payment, and the sum which he shall have been entitled to receive as his share of the nett profits.

19. Within six calr months after the expiration or determon of the ptshp, a full and general account in writing shall be made and taken by the partners of all moneys, stock in trade, debts and effects belonging to and of all the liabilities of the ptshp, and a just valuation shall be made of all the particulars included in such account which require and are capable of valuation, and immediately after such last-mentd acct shall have been so taken and settled, the partners shall forthwith make due provision for meeting all the liabilities of the ptshp, and, subject thereto, all the moneys, stock in trade, debts, effects and things then belonging to the ptshp shall be divided between the partners in the propons afsd, and such instruments in writing shall be executed by them for facili-

tating the getting in of the outstanding debts and effects of the ptshp, and for indemnifying each other touching the prems, and for vesting the sole right in the respive shares of the ptshp stock and property in the parties to whom the same resply shall upon such division belong, and for releasing to each other all claims on account of the ptshp as are usual in cases of the like nature.

20. If either partner shall die during the ptshp, his share in the ptshp shall be taken to be the amount which appeared as his share of the capital in the last preceding balance-sheet, and his exors or admors shall be entitled to rece from the surviving partner such amount, together with or less by any sum which may be due from or to the firm to or from the deceased partner at the time of his death in respect of moneys owing to or by the ptshp, by or to such deceased partner, in respect of profits or orwise from the date to which the last preceding balance-sheet shall have been made, up to the time of death, together with interest after the rate of £5 per cent. per ann on the sd aggregate amount from the day of the death of such deceased partner until payment; and the surviving partner shall, within two months next after the death of the deceased partner, give such security as the exors or admrs of the deceased partner shall reasonably require for the payment and discharge of the debts and liabilities of the ptshp due at the time of the death, and for indemnifying the estate and effects of the deceased partner therefrom; and also for securing to such exors or admors the payment of such aggregate amount as afsd by three equal yearly instalments, payable resply at the expiration of one, two and three years after the death of the deceased partner, and with each of such instalments the sum due at the date of each such payment in respect of such interest as afsd on the sd aggregate amount, or on so much thof as shall for the time being remain unpaid; and until such security shall be so given the sd aggregate amount and interest shall be the primary charge on all the estate and effects of the ptshp at the time of the death of the sd partner, after payment of the liabilities thof, and when the whole of the sd aggregate amount and

interest, and liabilities, shall have been fully paid and discharged, then, or at any time thftr, the exors or admors of
such deceased partner shall, at the request and cost of the
surviving partner, his exors or admors, execute to him or
them a sufficient release of the sd security so to be given as
afsd, and also from all claims and demands respecting the
ptshp.

21. [For the purpose of giving proper effect to the last
preceding clause, in the event of the death of either partner
during the first year of the ptshp, it is agreed that the profits
of the ptshp for such year shall be fixed at the sum of £1500,
and in the event of such death taking place during the second
year of the sd ptshp, then the sd profits shall consist of the
nett profits of the preceding year (as appearing by the
balance-sheet of that year), and the hinbfre mentioned sum
of £1500 added thto.]

22. If any dispute, doubt, or question shall arise between
the partners, or their respive hrs, exors, or admors, either on
the construction of these presents, or respecting the accounts,
transactions, profits, or losses of the ptshp business, every
such dispute, doubt, or question shall be referred to the arbitration of two [*remainder of arbitration clause, as in Form
XXIII., p. 232*]; and this submission to reference may be
made a rule of the Chancery Division of the High Court of
Justice, on the application of either of the parties to the
reference.

POWERS OF ATTORNEY.

CXV.

POWER OF ATTORNEY *to* EXECUTE *a* DEED.

KNOW all men by these presents that we A. B. of &c., and C. D. of &c., hby appoint E. F. of &c., and G. H. of &c., attorneys and attorney in our respive names and stead and on our behalf to receive from X. Y. of &c., or his agent or attorney, the sum of £600, being the price agreed to be paid by the sd X. Y. for all our estate and interest in certain leasehold messges known resply as [*insert description*], and upon the receipt of the sd sum of £600 in our respive names and stead and on our behalf, and as our respive acts and deeds, to sign, seal, and deliver a certain indre already prepared and engrossed, or intended to be shortly engrossed, bearing or intended to bear date on or about the 31st day of December, 1880, and made or intended to be made between I. K. of the first part, the sd E. F. of the second part, ourselves of the third and fourth parts resply, and the sd X. Y. of the fifth part, and being or intended to be an assurance of the sd messges to the sd X. Y., his exors, adms, and assns. And also in our respive names and stead, and on our behalf, to indorse and sign on the sd indre a proper or effectual receipt for the sd sum of £600, and to execute and do all other deeds and things which our sd attorneys or attorney shall consider expedient or necessary for assuring the sd messges, and all the estate or interest thrin of us and each of us to the sd X. Y., his exors, adms, or assns, we hereby resply undertaking to ratify, confirm, and allow all that our sd attorneys or attorney shall do or cause to be done, or purport to do or cause to be done, by virtue of these presents.

IN WITNESS, &c.

CXVI.

POWER OF ATTORNEY *under the* TITHE COMMUTATION ACT.

WE the Reverend A. B., of &c., and C. D., of &c., hby appoint E. F., of &c., to be our and each of our attorney, to act for us and each of us, in the execution of an Act passed in the 6th and 7th years of his late Majesty King William the 4th, intituled "An Act for the Commutation of Tithes in England and Wales." Dated &c.

$$(Signed) \quad \left\{ \begin{array}{l} \text{A. B.} \\ \text{C. D.} \end{array} \right.$$

Witness,
    E. F., of &c.

CXVII.

POWER OF ATTORNEY *under the General* INCLOSURE ACT.

WE A. B., of &c., and C. D., of &c., hby appoint E. F., of &c., our and each of our attorney for all the purposes of an Act passed in the 8th & 9th years of her present Majesty, intituled "An Act to facilitate the Inclosure and Improvement of Commons and Lands held in common, and the division of intermixed Lands, to provide remedies for defective or incomplete Executions and for the non-execution of the powers of General and Local Inclosure Acts, and to provide for the revival of such Powers in certain Cases." Dated &c.

$$(Signed) \quad \left\{ \begin{array}{l} \text{A. B.} \\ \text{C. D.} \end{array} \right.$$

Witness,
    E. F. of &c.

CXVIII.

POWER OF ATTORNEY *to recover a* DEBT.

To ALL TO WHOM these presents shall come, I, A. B., of &c., send greeting : Whas C. D., of &c., is indebted to me in the sum of £257 : Now KNOW YE, that I hby appoint E. F., of &c., my attorney, to demand of the sd C. D. the sd sum of £257, and on non-payment thof, or any part thof, to commence and prosecute any action for the recovery of the same in my name, and generally to do all acts, deeds, and things in or about the prems as fully and effectually as I could do if personally present, I hby ratifying and confirming all the sd E. F. shall do or cause to be done in or about the prems by virtue hrof.

IN WITNESS, &c.

CXIX.

RELEASE *to Executors* BY *a* RESIDUARY LEGATEE.

THIS INDRE, made &c., between A. B., of &c., of the one part, and C. D., of &c., and E. F., of &c., of the other part: Whas G. II., late of &c., deceased, by his will, dated &c., bequeathed unto the sd C. D. and E. F. all the residue of his psnl este upon trust (after pmnt throut of a legacy of £100 to I. K., and a legacy of £100 to L. M.) for the sd A. B. absolutely; And whas the sd G. H. died without having revoked or altered his sd will, which was duly proved on the [*date*] by the sd C. D. and E. F.: And whas the whole of the residue of the psnl este of the sd G. II. has been got in by the sd C. D. and E. F., and after pmnt throut of the expenses incidental to getting in the same, and the sd legacies of £100 and £100, there remains in their hands the sum of £25,763: And whas the accts of the sd C. D. and E. F., shewing the gross amount of the psnl este of the sd G. II., and the pmnts throut, have been handed to and fully inspected by the sd A. B., and signed by him in order to express his approbation of the same: And whas the sd C. D. and E. F. have before the excon hrof paid to the sd A. B. the sd sum of £25,763, being the balance appearing by the sd accts to be due to him in respect of the sd psnl este: NOW THIS INDRE WITNESSETH, that in conson of the prems, he the sd A. B. doth hby release the sd C. D. and E. F. and each of them, their and each of their hrs, exors, and admors, from the residue of the psnl este of the sd G. II., and from all trusts declared by his sd will, and from all actions, accts, claims, and demands on acct of or in relation to the este or effects of the sd G. H., or in relation to any act, matter, or thing in anywise incidental to or connected with the same: [And the sd A. B. doth hby covt with the sd C. D. and E. F., and each of them, their and each of their exors or admors, that in case the sd C. D. and E. F., or eir of them, their or eir of their exors or admors, shall hrftr be called upon to pay any debt or sum of money owing from the sd G. H., not already discharged, the sd A. B. will immediately pay or reimburse the sd C. D. and E. F. and each of them, their and each of their exors and admors, such debt or sum as afsd, togr with all costs and expenses which they or he shall have paid on account or in consequence of the demanding or recovery of such debt or sum, as afsd, or in anywise relating thrto.]

In witness, &c.

REQUEST.

CXX.

REQUEST *by Cestuis que Trustent* TO TRUSTEES TO
SELL OUT STOCK *for a* LOAN.

To A. B. and C. D., trustees of an indre of stlmnt dated, &c.

I, the undersigned E. H., do hereby (with the consent of
the undersigned A. H., my wife) request that so much of the
£3 per Cent. Consd Bank Annies standing in your names as
such trees as afsd as will realize the sum of £1000 sterling
may be sold, and that the sd sum of £1000 may be advanced
and lent to me, the undersigned E. H., upon secy of my
bond, payable on demand, with int in the meantime at the
rate of £5 per cent. per ann, pursuant to the power for that
purpose contd in the sd indre. Dated &c.

SETTLEMENTS.

CXXI.

SETTLEMENT, *on Marriage, of* REAL ESTATE.[1]

THIS INDRE, made &c., between A. B., of &c., of the first part, C. D., of &c., of the second part, and E. F., of &c., and G. H., of &c., of the third part: Whas the sd A. B. is seised in fee free from incumbs of the hdts intended to be hby granted; And whas a marre has been agreed upon, and is intended shortly to be solemnised between the sd A. B. and C. D., and upon the treaty for such marre the sd A. B. agreed to settle the sd hdts to the uses, upon and for the trusts and subject to the provons hrnftr declared concerning the same: NOW THIS INRE WITNESSETH, that, in conson of the prems, the sd A. B. grants unto the sd E. F. and G. H. and their hrs, ALL &c. [*set out parcels*], To HOLD the sd hdts unto the sd E. F. and G. H., their hrs and assns, to the use of the sd A. B., his hrs and assns, until the solemnisation of the sd intended marre; and after the solemnisation thof, to the use of the sd A. B. and his assns for his life, without impeachment of waste; and after his dece to the use of the sd C. D. for her life for her separate use, without power of anticipation, and after the dece of the svor of them, the sd A. B. and C. D., to the use of all or such one or more exclusively of the other or others of the children of the sd intended marre, for such estes or este, intcrests and interest, and if more than one in such shares, and under and subject to such charges, powers, provos, and limons for the benefit

---

[1] In this form the powers of maintenance, accumulation, appointing new trustees, and giving receipts, are omitted in reliance on the statutory powers.

of all, or any one or more of the sd children, and in such manner as the sd A. B. and C. D. shall by deed, with or without power of revocation and new apptmt, appt, and in default of, and so far as any such apptmt shall not extend, then as the svor of them shall in like manner, or by will appt; and in default of, and so far as any such apptmt shall not extend, to the use of all and every the children of the sd intended marre, and their respive hrs and assns, as tenants in common; and if there shall be only one such child, then to the use of such only child, his or her hrs and assns; and in default of such children, to the use of the sd A. B., his hrs and assns: PROVIDED ALWAYS, and it is hby declared, that it shall be lawful for the sd A. B. during his life, and after his death, for the sd C. D. during her life, to demise all or any of the sd prems for any term not exceeding twenty-one years in posson, so that there be reserved in every such lease the best yearly rent or rents, to be incident to the immediate reversion that can be reasonably obtained without any premium, and so that there be contd in every such lease a condition for re-entry on non-payment within a reasonable time to be thrin specified of the rent or rents thby reserved, and so that the lessee or lessees execute a counterpart thof: PROVIDED ALWAYS, and it is hby agreed, that it shall be lawful for the sd E. F. and G. H., or the svor of them, or his hrs, or their or his assns, but during the lifetime of a tenant for life only with his or her consent in writing, to sell the sd hdts or any part thof, by public auction or private contract, and subject to such condons, and generally in such manner as to them or him shall seem desirable, and to stand possed of the nett proceeds of such sale, upon the same trusts as are hrnbfe declared, and in the same manner as if no such sale had taken place.

In witness, &c.

CXXII.

SETTLEMENT, *on Marriage, of* PERSONALTY.

THIS INDRE, made &c., between A. B., of &c. [*intended husband*] of the first part, C. D., of &c. [*intended wife*] of the second part, and E. F., of &c., and G. H., of &c. [*trustees*] of the third part: Whas the sd C. D. is entitled to a sum of £1000 £3 per Cent. Consolidated Annies, lately standing in her name in the books of the governor and company of the Bank of England; And whas a marre has been agreed upon between the sd A. B. and C. D., and in psce of an agrt in that behalf made upon the treaty for the sd marre the sd sum of £1000 £3 per cent. Consolidated Annies has been transferred into the names of the said E. F. and G. H.

NOW THIS INDENTURE WITNESSETH, that, in conson of the sd intended marrge, it is hby agreed and declared that the sd E. F. and G. H., their exors, admors, and assns, shall stand possed of the sd sum of £1000 £3 per Cent. Consolidated Annies, in trust for the sd C. D., until the solemnisation of the sd intended marre, and after the solemnisation thof, upon trust that they the said E. F. and G. H., and the survor of them, his exors or admors, their or his assns (hrnftr called "the trustees"), shall either permit the whole or any part of the sd annies to remain in its present state of invest-ment, or shall at any time with the consent in writing of the sd A. B. and C. D. during their joint lives, and of the survor of them during his or her life, and after the death of the survor of them at the discretion of the trees, sell the same, and invest the proceeds thof in their names in any of the parliamentary stocks or public funds of Great Britain, or at interest upon government or real securities in England or Wales (but not in Ireland), or on the debentures or stock of any such railway, canal, or other incorporated company in Great Britain as the trustees shall think well established and sound; with power with such consent or at such discretion as afsd to vary or transpose any such investments; and shall, during the joint lives of tho sd A. B. and C. D., pay the income of the sd annies, and of the investments for the time being representing the same (hrnftr called "the trust fund"), unto the sd C. D., for her separate use, independently of the sd A. B., without power of anticipation; and after the death of such one of them the sd A. B. and C. D. as shall first die, shall pay the income of the trust funds unto the survor of them during his or her life, and after the death of such survor, the trustees shall stand possed of the trust funds, in trust for all or such one or more exclusively of the others or other of the children of the said C. D. in such manner generally as the sd C. D. shall by deed with or without power of revocation and new appointment, or will, or codicil, appt, and in default of any such apptmt, and so far as any such apptmt shall not extend, in trust for such one or more of the children of the sd C. D., as being a son or sons shall attain the age of twenty-one years, or being a daughter or daughters shall attain that age or marry, and if more than one, in equal shares: PROVIDED ALWAYS, that no child or children taking any part of the trust funds under any apptmt to be made in pursuance of the power herein contained, shall be entitled to any share in the unappointed part of the trust funds without bringing his, her, or their appointed share or shares into hotchpot and accounting for the same accordingly: AND IT IS HEREBY declared, that it shall be lawful for the trustees at any time or times after the decease of the survor of the sd A. B. and C. D., or in the lifetime of them or of the survor of them, in case they, he, or she shall so direct in writing, to raise any part not exceeding half of the then expectant or presumptive or vested share of any child under the trusts hrnbfre declared, and to pay or apply the same to him or her, or for his or her advancement or benefit, as the trustees shall in their discretion think fit: AND IT IS HEREBY DECLARED, that in case there shall be no child of the sd marre, who being a son shall attain the age of twenty-one years, or being a daughter shall attain that age or marry, the trustees shall stand possed of the trust fund, or of so much thof resply as shall not have been applied under any of the trusts or powers herein contd, upon the trusts following, that is to say, in case the sd A. B. shall die in the lifetime of the sd C. D., then in trust for the sd C. D., her exors, admors, and assns: but in case the sd C. D. shall die in the lifetime of the said A. B., then, after the decease of the said A. B. and such default or failure of children as afsd (which shall last happen), upon such trusts as the sd C. D. shall, by will or codicil, appt; and in default of such apptmt, and so far as any such apptmt shall not extend, in trust for such person or persons as at the decease of the sd C. D. would have become entitled thereto under the statutes for the distribution of the personal estes of intestates, in case the sd C. D. had died possed thof intestate and without having been married, such persons, if more than one, to take as tenants in common in the shares in which they would have been entitled under the same statutes.

AND IT IS HBY declared that the power of apptg a new tree of these presents shall be exercisable by the said A. B. and C. D. during their joint lives and by the svor of them during his or her life and afterwards by the surviving or continuing trees or by the last retiring tree, and upon every apptmt the number of trees may be augmented or reduced, but not so as to reduce their number to less than two.

IN WITNESS, &c.

TESTIMONIUM.

CXXIII.

Testimonium *to Instrument executed* by Attorney.

In Witness whereof the said A. B. has set his hand and seal, and by virtue of a power of attorney enabling him in that behalf, a copy whereof is hereto annexed, has set the hand and seal of the sd C. D. this [*date*].

A deed executed under a power of attorney should always be signed in the name of the principal, thus:—

"C. D.
by A. B. his attorney."

WILLS.

CXXIV.

Will *giving* ALL *Testator's* Property *to his* Wife *and appointing her* Executrix.[1]

This is the last will of me, A. B., of &c. I give [devise and bequeath] all my [real and personal] estate and effects, unto [and to the use of] my wife C. B. [her heirs, executors, administrators and assigns, according to the nature and tenure thereof] absolutely: And I appoint her executrix of this my will.

In witness whereof I have hereunto set my hand this 3rd day of December, 1880.

A. B.

Signed by the said A. B. as his last
   will in the presence of us, who in
   his presence at his request, and in
   the presence of each other, have
   hereunto subscribed our names as
   witnesses.

E. F., of &c.
G. H., of &c.

CXXV.

Will *making various* Devises *and* Bequests, *and giving the* Residue *to Testator's* Children.

This is the last will of me, A. B., of &c. I bequeath to my wife C. B. the sum of £100 to be paid within one calr month

---

[1] Where brevity is an object the words in brackets may be omitted.

after my decease. I devise unto my son Thomas, his heirs and assigns, my farm known as "The Holly Farm," consisting of a messge and outbuildings, and about fifty acres of land, situate at [Nettlebed], in the county of [Oxford], [free from the mortgage of £1000 thereon, in favour of William Jackson, which sum of £1000 and all interest due thereon, I direct shall be paid out of my personal estate after payment of the legacies bequeathed by this my will].[1] I devise unto my son John, his heirs and assigns, all that my freehold messge situate at and being No. [500, St. Paul's Churchyard], in the city of [London]. I bequeath unto my sd wife all my household furniture and chattels of every description. I bequeath unto my friend E. F., of &c., the sum of £100: And I devise and bequeath all the residue of my real and personal estate and effects unto and to the use of my sd sons Thomas and John, their heirs, executors, administrators, and assigns, according to the natures and tenures thof, as tenants in common. I appoint my sd sons Thomas and John, and my friend G. H., of &c., exors of this my will; and I bequeath to the sd G. H. £100 if he shall prove my will.

In witness, &c.

———

CXXVI.

Will *giving* Real and Personal Estate *to Trustees for the benefit of Testator's* Wife *and* Children; *with* Special Provisions.

This is the last Will of me, A. B. of [*insert residence and description*]. I bequeath to my wife C. B. absolutely, my wines, liquors, fuel, and other consumable household stores and provons, linen, china, and glass, wearing apparel, watches, jewels, and personal ornaments. Also a legacy of [£100] to be paid to her within one calr month after my death. I bequeath to my sd wife, so long as she shall

[1] In the absence of this clause, Thomas would have to pay off the mortgage out of his own pocket, or take the farm subject to it.

remain my widow, the use and enjoyment of my plate, plated articles, books, pictures, prints, musical instruments, furniture, and other articles of household use or ornament not hrnbefre bequeathed ['and after her decease or future marriage again (which shall first happen) I BEQUEATH the same to all my children or any my child who shall have attained or shall attain twenty-one years of age, and, if more than one, to be divided between them as nearly as may be in equal shares by my trees, whose determination shall be final, and who shall have power conclusively to direct that any sums of money for equality of partition shall be paid by any one or more to any other of the psons becoming entitled to a share in the same effects]. I DEVISE AND BEQUEATH all the residue of my real and psonal este unto R. S., of &c., T. W., of &c., and X. Y., of &c., their hrs, exors, admors, and assns, upon trust that they or the survors or survor of them, or the exors or admors of such survor, their, her, or his assns (hrnbfre and hrnfter called " my trees ") shall, in such manner in all respects as they shall think fit, convert into money such part thof as shall not consist of money. AND SHALL, out of the proceeds thof and the money of which I shall be possed at my death, pay my funeral and testamentary expenses and debts AND SHALL invest the residue thof in any of the investments hrnftr authorized, and shall pay the income thof and of the sd investments (hrnftr called " my trust fund ") to my sd wife so long as she shall remain my widow. And after her death or future marre,[2] shall hold my trust fund upon trust for all my children or any my child who, either before or after my death shall attain twenty-one years of age, and if more than one in equal shares [subject, never-

---

[1] If this clause were omitted the furniture would fall into the testator's residuary estate and be sold on the death or future marriage of his widow.

[2] If it is desired not to give the widow the whole income of the residue the following clause may be used :—

AND SHALL out of the income [&c., *as above*] pay to my sd wife an anny of [£500] so long as she shall remain my widow by quarterly payments, the first to be made three calr months after my death and a proportionate part of the sd anny to be pd down to the day of the death or future marre of my sd wife, and subject thereto shall hold [*trusts for children as above*].

theless, to the provons of this my will concerning the share
of each daur of mine]. [AND I DECLARE that my trees
shall hold the share of each daur of mine in my trust fund
upon trust to pay the annual income thof to such daur during
her life without power of anticipation, and after her decease
In trust for all or any such one or more of the issue of such
daur born in her lifetime, in such manner in all respects as
she, whether covert or sole, shall by will or codicil appoint,
and in default of such appointment Upon trust for such one
or more of the children of such daur as, being male shall
attain twenty-one years of age, or being female shall attain
that age or marry, and if more than one in equal shares,
but no child who or whose issue shall take any part of
my trust fund under any such apptmt shall participate in the
unappointed portion thof without bringing the benefit of such
apptmt into hotchpot, and if there shall be no child of such
daur who being male shall attain twenty-one years of age,
or being female shall attain that age or marry, In trust for
the others or other of my sd children who shall have attained
or shall attain the age of twenty-one years, and if more than
one in equal shares, but so that the share or shares accruing
to every daur of mine shall be held upon the same trusts (so
far as circes will admit) as her original share.] AND I DE-
CLARE that if any of my children shall die under the age of
twenty-one years, and shall leave any child who being male
shall attain the age of twenty-one years, or being female
attain that age or marry, such child or children shall take
the share in my trust fund to which his, her, or their parent
would have been entitled if he or she had attained twenty-
one. AND I DECLARE that every provou made by this my
will for a female is for her separate use. AND I DECLARE
that my trees may, with the consent of the tenant for life (if
any), and if none at their discretion, apply any part or parts
(not exceeding altogether one-half) of the then expectant,
presumptive, or vested share of any infant in my trust fund,
for or towards the advancement or benefit of such infant.
[AND I DECLARE that my trees may, at their sole discretion,
postpone the conversion of any of my residuary este so long

as they shall judge expedient, but, for the purpose of transmission my residuary real este shall be considered as converted in equity from the time of my decease, and the nett
income from every part of my residuary este, previously to
as well as after the conversion thof, shall be applied as income of my trust fund.   AND I DECLARE that my trees may
apply any part of my trust fund in erecting any buildings,
fixtures, and machinery, upon and making any other additions to and improvements in, and may grant easements over
my residuary real este and chattels real for the time being
remaining unsold, and may generally manage and improve
and lease the same from year to year, or for any term not
exceeding fourteen years, to take effect in posson or within
twelve calr months from the making of the lease at rackrent.]   AND I DECLARE that my trees may invest any trust-
moneys which may come into their hands under this my will
in any of the public stocks or funds of Great Britain, or upon
Government, real, long leasehold, or copyhold securities, or
in or upon the stocks, funds, shares, or securities of any Co
incorporated by royal charter, or by or under any public or
private Act of Parliament, or in or upon the securities of any
municipal corporation, board of guardians, board of health,
local board, burial board, baths and washhouses commissioners,
or other similar public body, and that they may, at their or
his discretion, vary the said stocks, funds, shares, and securities, for any other investments of the nature afsd.   AND I
DECLARE that my trees shall have power to investigate,
arrange, and settle, all accounts and transactions whatsoever
between me and any other pson or psons with whom I am or
shall be concerned in any partnership, or between me and
the repres of any such pson or psons, and to wind up all the
affairs of such partnership, and generally to do and execute
all such acts, matters, and things as shall appear to them to
be necessary or expedient for effecting or facilitating the
final settlement of all matters arising out of any partnership
concerns in which I shall be engaged at my death, or shall
at any former period have been engaged.   I DEVISE all estes
vested in me upon trust or mtge unto the sd R. S., T. W.,

and X. Y., their hrs and assns, upon the trusts and subject to the equities subsisting therein resply, but the money secured on such mtges shall form part of my psnal este. I APPT the sd R. S., T. W., and X. Y., exors of this my will, and I revoke all wills and testamentary dispositions heretofore made by me.

IN WITNESS, &c.

THE END.

INDEX.

N.B.—The numbers in brackets—thus [237]—refer to the Forms.

N.B.—The numbers in brackets—thus [237]—refer to the Forms.

N.B.—*The numbers in brackets—thus* [237]—*refer to the Forms.*

N.B.—The numbers in brackets—thus [237]—*refer to the Forms.*

N.B.—The numbers in brackets—thus [237]—*refer to the Forms.*

N.B —The numbers in brackets—thus [237]—*refer to the Forms.*

N.B.—The numbers in brackets—thus [237]—refer to the Forms.

REQUISITIONS,
copyholds, as to, 108
replies to, 21, 22
stipulations as to, [200], [203], [252], [259], [269], [277], [283], [287]

RESERVATION,
easement of, [384]
minerals of, in lease, [384]
timber and minerals, of (in lease), [375], [377]

RIVERS,
deed of covenant by riparian owners, [356]

REVERSIONARY INTEREST,
assignment of, [333], [335]
mortgage of, 66

SALARY AND COMMISSION,
provisions as to, [218], [224,] [226], [228], [231] [233], [236,] [240]

SALE OF REAL ESTATE,
auction by (*and see* CONDITIONS OF SALE).
advertising, 15
conditions of sale, 16–19
particulars, 15–16
proceedings at sale, 19, 20
completion, 26–30, 57–8
deeds handed over on, 29, 58
insurance, purchaser not entitled to benefit of, 29, 41
interest on purchase-money, 28
keys handed over on, 58
copyholds (*See* COPYHOLDS).
cost of covenant for production, 12
drafting contract, 13
insurance money belongs to vendor in case of fire, 29, 41
married woman, belonging to, 53
open contract for, 10, 33
perusal of draft conveyance, 21
private contract for, 12–14, 33.

SEARCHES,
on purchase of real estate, 49

SEISIN,
recital of, [339], [343]

SETTLED ESTATES,
leases of, 84
sales of, 12

SETTLEMENT,
advancement clause necessary, 112
form of, [125]

N.B.—The numbers in brackets—thus [237]*—refer to the Forms.*

N.B.—The numbers in brackets—thus [237]—*refer to the Forms.*

N.B.—The numbers in brackets—thus [237]—refer to the Forms.

LONDON:
PRINTED BY WILLIAM CLOWES AND SONS, LIMITED,
STANFORD STREET AND CHARING CROSS.

www.ingramcontent.com/pod-product-compliance
Lightning Source LLC
Chambersburg PA
CBHW031820270326
41932CB00008B/478